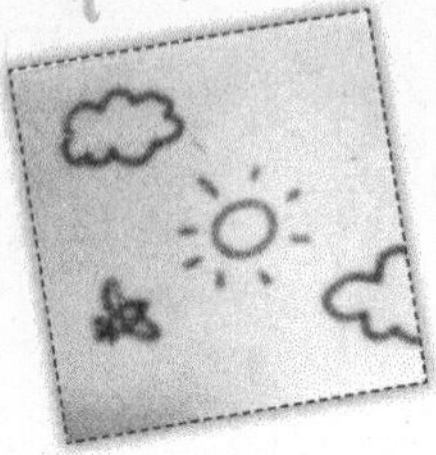

We're all connected by the same sky. It's true!

—Tsugumi Ohba

I try to work hard every day, but I end up spending the whole day working hard to work hard.

—Takeshi Obata

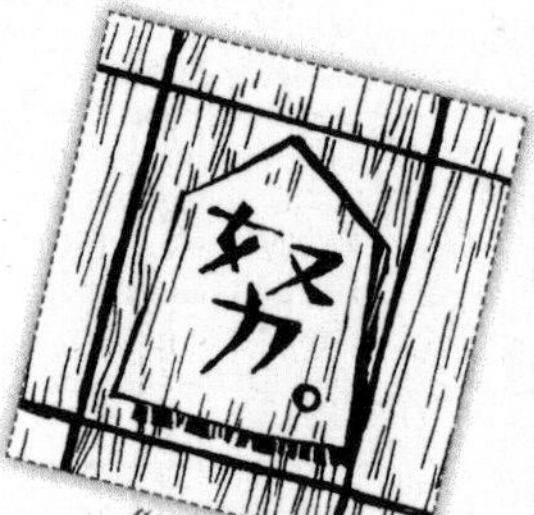

努力

(Hard Work)

Tsugumi Ohba

Born in Tokyo, Tsugumi Ohba is the author of the hit series *Death Note*. His current series *Bakuman。* is serialized in *Weekly Shonen Jump*.

Takeshi Obata

Takeshi Obata was born in 1969 in Niigata, Japan, and is the artist of the wildly popular SHONEN JUMP title *Hikaru no Go*, which won the 2003 Tezuka Osamu Cultural Prize: Shinsei "New Hope" award and the 2000 Shogakukan Manga award. Obata is also the artist of *Arabian Majin Bokentan Lamp Lamp*, *Ayatsuri Sakon*, *Cyborg Jichan G.*, and the smash hit manga *Death Note*. His current series *Bakuman。* is serialized in *Weekly Shonen Jump*.

Volume 10

SHONEN JUMP Manga Edition

Story by **TSUGUMI OHBA**
Art by **TAKESHI OBATA**

Translation | **Tetsuichiro Miyaki**
English Adaptation | **Hope Donovan**
Touch-up Art & Lettering | **James Gaubatz**
Design | **Fawn Lau**
Editor | **Alexis Kirsch**

BAKUMAN。© 2008 by Tsugumi Ohba, Takeshi Obata
All rights reserved.
First published in Japan in 2008 by SHUEISHA Inc., Tokyo.
English translation rights arranged by SHUEISHA Inc.

The rights of the author(s) of the work(s) in this publication to be
so identified have been asserted in accordance with the Copyright,
Designs and Patents Act 1988. A CIP catalogue record for this book
is available from the British Library.

The stories, characters and incidents mentioned in this publication are
entirely fictional.

No portion of this book may be reproduced or transmitted in any
form or by any means without written permission from the copyright
holders.

Printed in the U.S.A.

Published by VIZ Media, LLC
P.O. Box 77010
San Francisco, CA 94107

10 9 8 7 6 5 4 3 2 1
First printing, April 2012

PARENTAL ADVISORY
BAKUMAN。 is rated T for Teen
and is recommended for ages
13 and up. This volume contains
suggestive themes.
ratings.viz.com

RATED
T
FOR
TEEN

VIZ
media
www.viz.com

SHONEN JUMP
www.shonenjump.com

BAKUMAN。

10

VISUALIZATION and IMAGINATION

STORY BY
TSUGUMI OHBA

ART BY
TAKESHI OBATA

SHONENJUMP MANGA

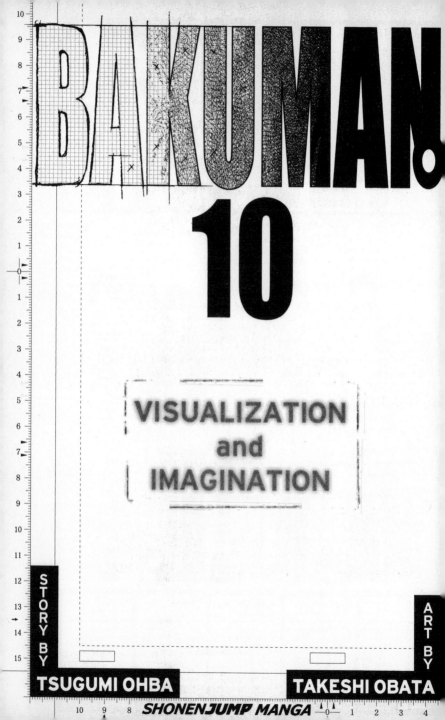

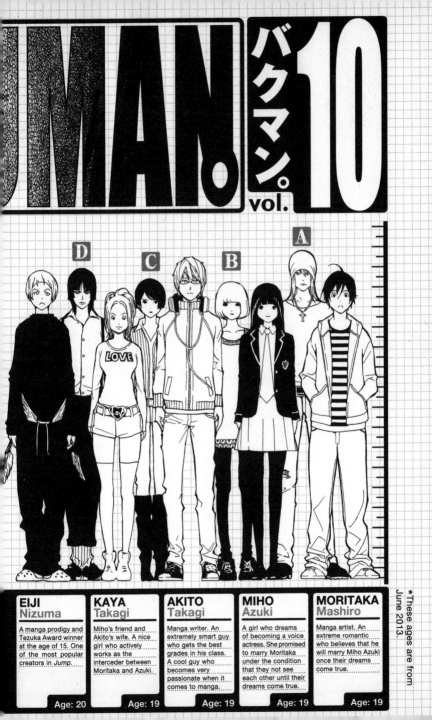

UMAN。 バクマン。 vol. 10

D
C
B
A
LOVE

EIJI
Nizuma

A manga prodigy and Tezuka Award winner at the age of 15. One of the most popular creators in *Jump*.

Age: 20

KAYA
Takagi

Miho's friend and Akito's wife. A nice girl who actively works as the interceder between Moritaka and Azuki.

Age: 19

AKITO
Takagi

Manga writer. An extremely smart guy who gets the best grades in his class. A cool guy who becomes very passionate when it comes to manga.

Age: 19

MIHO
Azuki

A girl who dreams of becoming a voice actress. She promised to marry Moritaka under the condition that they not see each other until their dreams come true.

Age: 19

MORITAKA
Mashiro

Manga artist. An extreme romantic who believes that he will marry Miho Azuki once their dreams come true.

Age: 19

*These ages are from June 2013.

STORY In order to attain the glory that only a handful of people can, two young men decide to walk the rough "path of manga" and become professional manga creators. This is the story of a great artist, Moritaka Mashiro, a talented writer, Akito Takagi, and their quest to become manga legends!

BAKU

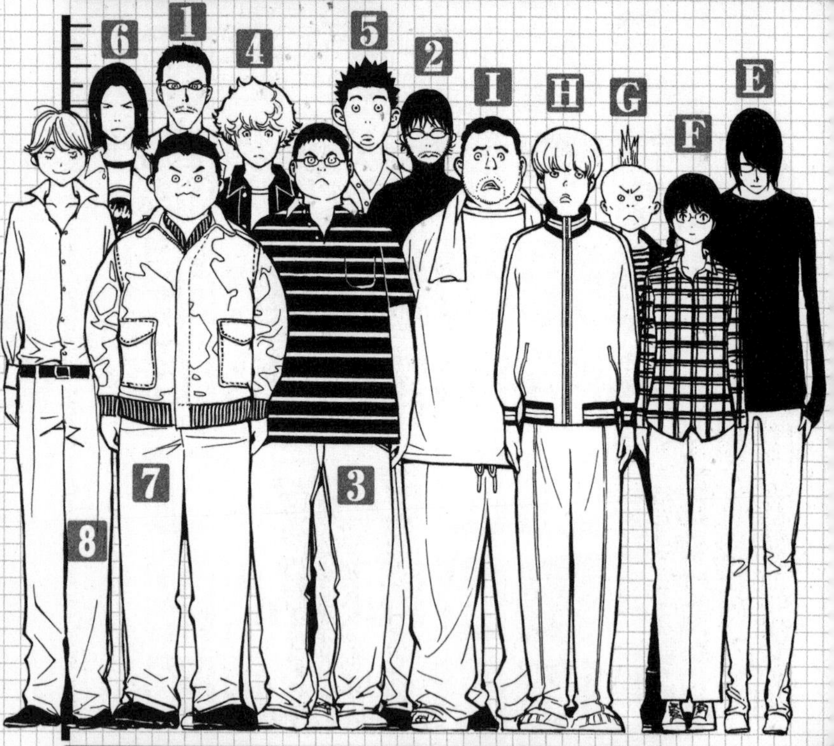

6
1
4
5
2
I
H
G
F
E
7
3
8

WEEKLY SHONEN JUMP Editorial Office

1. Editor in Chief Sasaki
2. Deputy Editor in Chief Heishi
3. Soichi Aida
4. Yujiro Hattori
5. Akira Hattori
6. Koji Yoshida
7. Goro Miura
8. Masakazu Yamahisa

The MANGA ARTISTS and ASSISTANTS

- A SHINTA FUKUDA
- B KO AOKI
- C AIKO IWASE
- D KAZUYA HIRAMARU
- E RYU SHIZUKA
- F NATSUMI KATO
- G YASUOKA
- H SHOYO TAKAHAMA
- I TAKURO NAKAI

BAKUMAN。 vol.10

CONTENTS

(VISUALIZATION AND IMAGINATION)

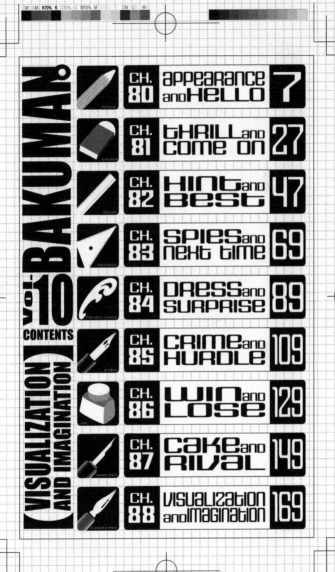

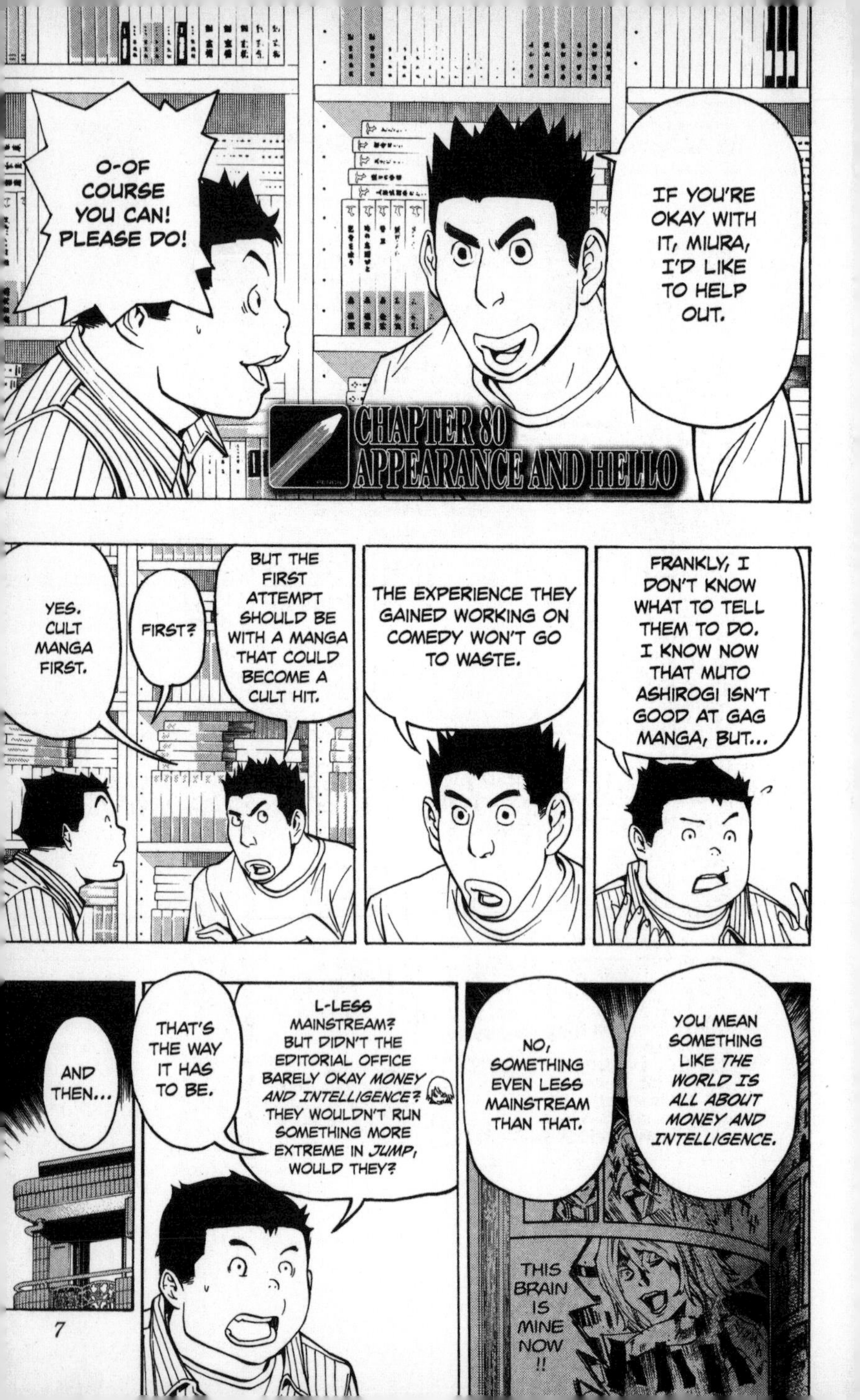
IF YOU'RE OKAY WITH IT, MIURA, I'D LIKE TO HELP OUT.
O-OF COURSE YOU CAN! PLEASE DO!
CHAPTER 80 APPEARANCE AND HELLO
FRANKLY, I DON'T KNOW WHAT TO TELL THEM TO DO. I KNOW NOW THAT MUTO ASHIROGI ISN'T GOOD AT GAG MANGA, BUT...
THE EXPERIENCE THEY GAINED WORKING ON COMEDY WON'T GO TO WASTE.
BUT THE FIRST ATTEMPT SHOULD BE WITH A MANGA THAT COULD BECOME A CULT HIT.
FIRST?
YES. CULT MANGA FIRST.
YOU MEAN SOMETHING LIKE *THE WORLD IS ALL ABOUT MONEY AND INTELLIGENCE*.
NO, SOMETHING EVEN LESS MAINSTREAM THAN THAT.
THIS BRAIN IS MINE NOW!!
L-LESS MAINSTREAM? BUT DIDN'T THE EDITORIAL OFFICE BARELY OKAY *MONEY AND INTELLIGENCE*? THEY WOULDN'T RUN SOMETHING MORE EXTREME IN *JUMP*, WOULD THEY?
THAT'S THE WAY IT HAS TO BE.
AND THEN...

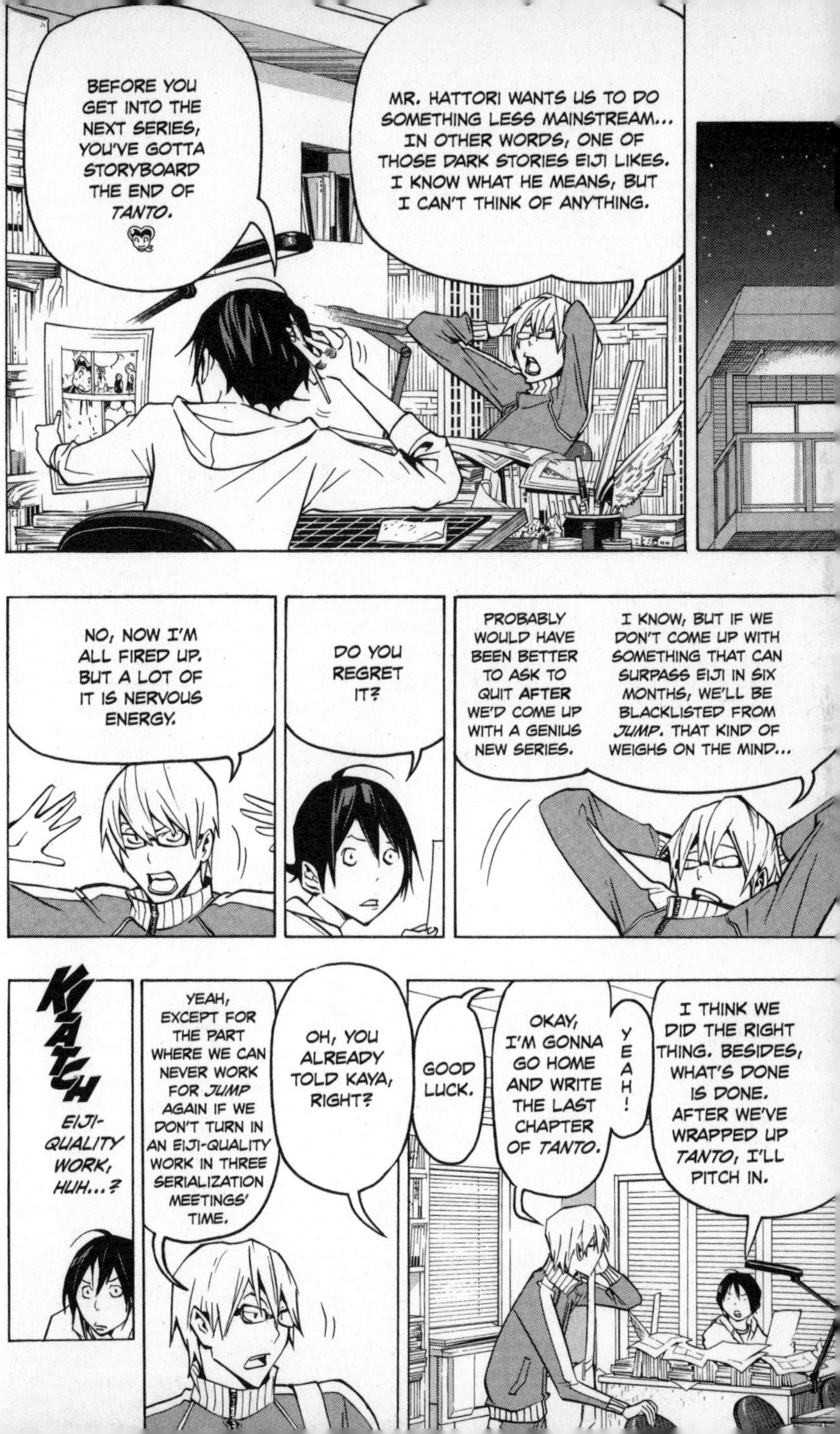
MR. HATTORI WANTS US TO DO SOMETHING LESS MAINSTREAM... IN OTHER WORDS, ONE OF THOSE DARK STORIES EIJI LIKES. I KNOW WHAT HE MEANS, BUT I CAN'T THINK OF ANYTHING.
BEFORE YOU GET INTO THE NEXT SERIES, YOU'VE GOTTA STORYBOARD THE END OF *TANTO*.
I KNOW, BUT IF WE DON'T COME UP WITH SOMETHING THAT CAN SURPASS EIJI IN SIX MONTHS, WE'LL BE BLACKLISTED FROM *JUMP*. THAT KIND OF WEIGHS ON THE MIND...
PROBABLY WOULD HAVE BEEN BETTER TO ASK TO QUIT AFTER WE'D COME UP WITH A GENIUS NEW SERIES.
DO YOU REGRET IT?
NO, NOW I'M ALL FIRED UP. BUT A LOT OF IT IS NERVOUS ENERGY.
I THINK WE DID THE RIGHT THING. BESIDES, WHAT'S DONE IS DONE. AFTER WE'VE WRAPPED UP *TANTO*, I'LL PITCH IN.
YEAH!
OKAY, I'M GONNA GO HOME AND WRITE THE LAST CHAPTER OF *TANTO*.
GOOD LUCK.
OH, YOU ALREADY TOLD KAYA, RIGHT?
YEAH, EXCEPT FOR THE PART WHERE WE CAN NEVER WORK FOR *JUMP* AGAIN IF WE DON'T TURN IN AN EIJI-QUALITY WORK IN THREE SERIALIZATION MEETINGS' TIME.
KLATCH
EIJI-QUALITY WORK, HUH...?

READ THIS WAY

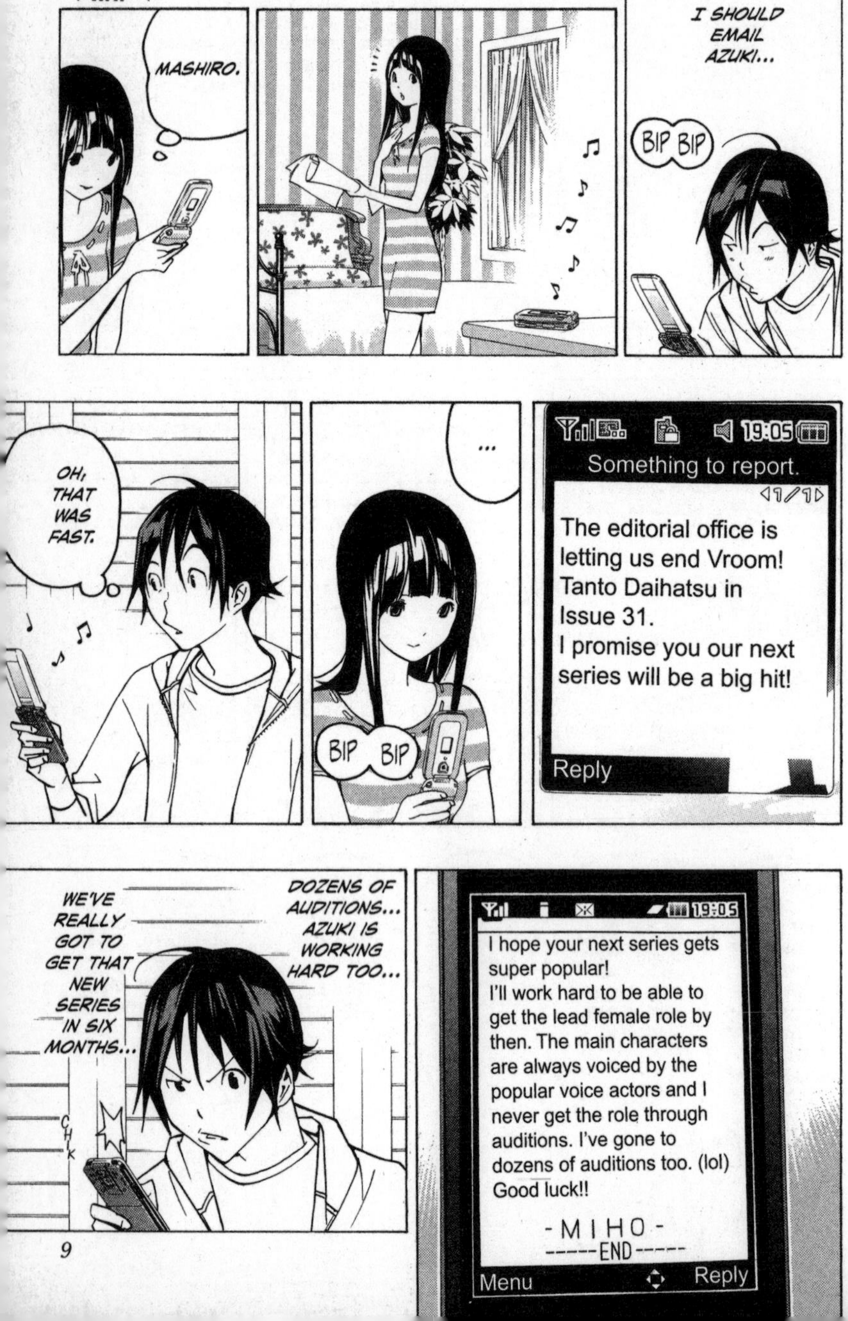
I SHOULD EMAIL AZUKI...
BIP BIP
MASHIRO.
Something to report.
1/1
The editorial office is letting us end Vroom! Tanto Daihatsu in Issue 31.
I promise you our next series will be a big hit!
Reply
...
BIP BIP
OH, THAT WAS FAST.
I hope your next series gets super popular!
I'll work hard to be able to get the lead female role by then. The main characters are always voiced by the popular voice actors and I never get the role through auditions. I've gone to dozens of auditions too. (lol)
Good luck!!
-MIHO-
-----END-----
Menu
Reply
DOZENS OF AUDITIONS... AZUKI IS WORKING HARD TOO...
WE'VE REALLY GOT TO GET THAT NEW SERIES IN SIX MONTHS...
CHIK

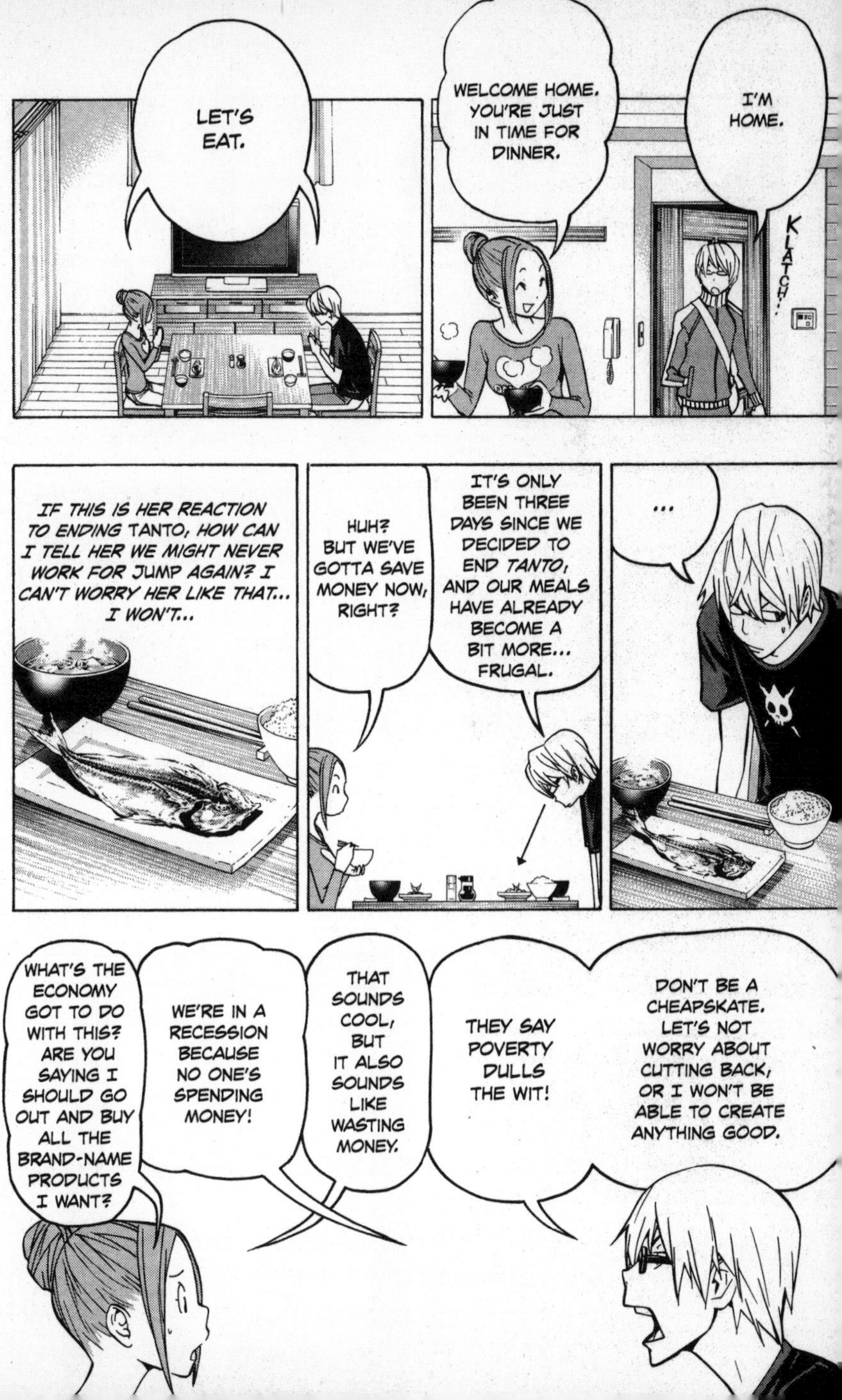
I'M HOME.
KLATCH...
WELCOME HOME. YOU'RE JUST IN TIME FOR DINNER.
LET'S EAT.
...
IT'S ONLY BEEN THREE DAYS SINCE WE DECIDED TO END *TANTO*, AND OUR MEALS HAVE ALREADY BECOME A BIT MORE... FRUGAL.
HUH? BUT WE'VE GOTTA SAVE MONEY NOW, RIGHT?
IF THIS IS HER REACTION TO ENDING TANTO, *HOW CAN I TELL HER WE MIGHT NEVER WORK FOR JUMP AGAIN? I CAN'T WORRY HER LIKE THAT... I WON'T...*
DON'T BE A CHEAPSKATE. LET'S NOT WORRY ABOUT CUTTING BACK, OR I WON'T BE ABLE TO CREATE ANYTHING GOOD.
THEY SAY POVERTY DULLS THE WIT!
THAT SOUNDS COOL, BUT IT ALSO SOUNDS LIKE WASTING MONEY.
WE'RE IN A RECESSION BECAUSE NO ONE'S SPENDING MONEY!
WHAT'S THE ECONOMY GOT TO DO WITH THIS? ARE YOU SAYING I SHOULD GO OUT AND BUY ALL THE BRAND-NAME PRODUCTS I WANT?

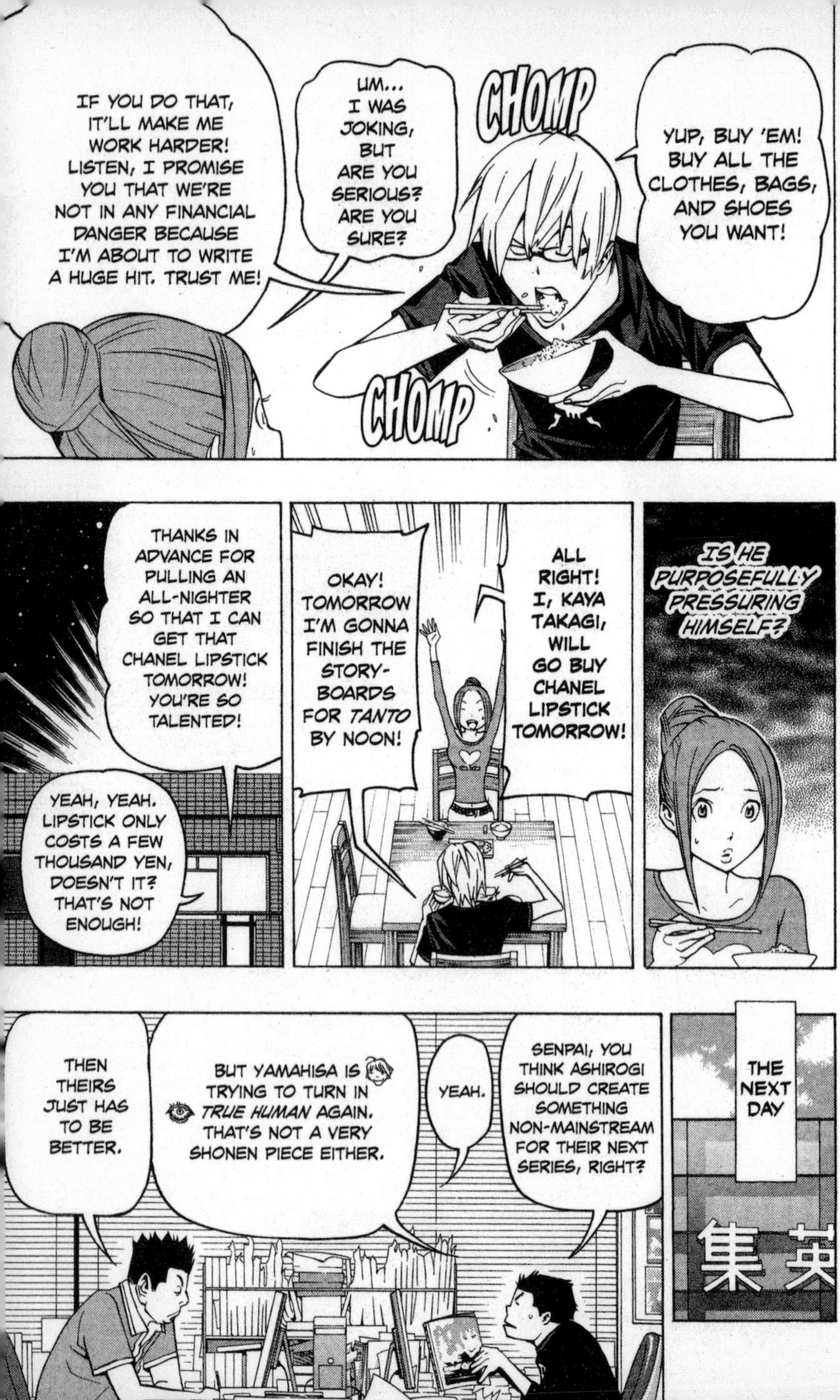
YUP, BUY 'EM! BUY ALL THE CLOTHES, BAGS, AND SHOES YOU WANT!
CHOMP
UM... I WAS JOKING, BUT ARE YOU SERIOUS? ARE YOU SURE?
IF YOU DO THAT, IT'LL MAKE ME WORK HARDER! LISTEN, I PROMISE YOU THAT WE'RE NOT IN ANY FINANCIAL DANGER BECAUSE I'M ABOUT TO WRITE A HUGE HIT. TRUST ME!
CHOMP
IS HE PURPOSEFULLY PRESSURING HIMSELF?
ALL RIGHT! I, KAYA TAKAGI, WILL GO BUY CHANEL LIPSTICK TOMORROW!
OKAY! TOMORROW I'M GONNA FINISH THE STORY-BOARDS FOR *TANTO* BY NOON!
THANKS IN ADVANCE FOR PULLING AN ALL-NIGHTER SO THAT I CAN GET THAT CHANEL LIPSTICK TOMORROW! YOU'RE SO TALENTED!
YEAH, YEAH. LIPSTICK ONLY COSTS A FEW THOUSAND YEN, DOESN'T IT? THAT'S NOT ENOUGH!
THE NEXT DAY
集英
SENPAI, YOU THINK ASHIROGI SHOULD CREATE SOMETHING NON-MAINSTREAM FOR THEIR NEXT SERIES, RIGHT?
YEAH.
BUT YAMAHISA IS TRYING TO TURN IN *TRUE HUMAN* AGAIN. THAT'S NOT A VERY SHONEN PIECE EITHER.
THEN THEIRS JUST HAS TO BE BETTER.

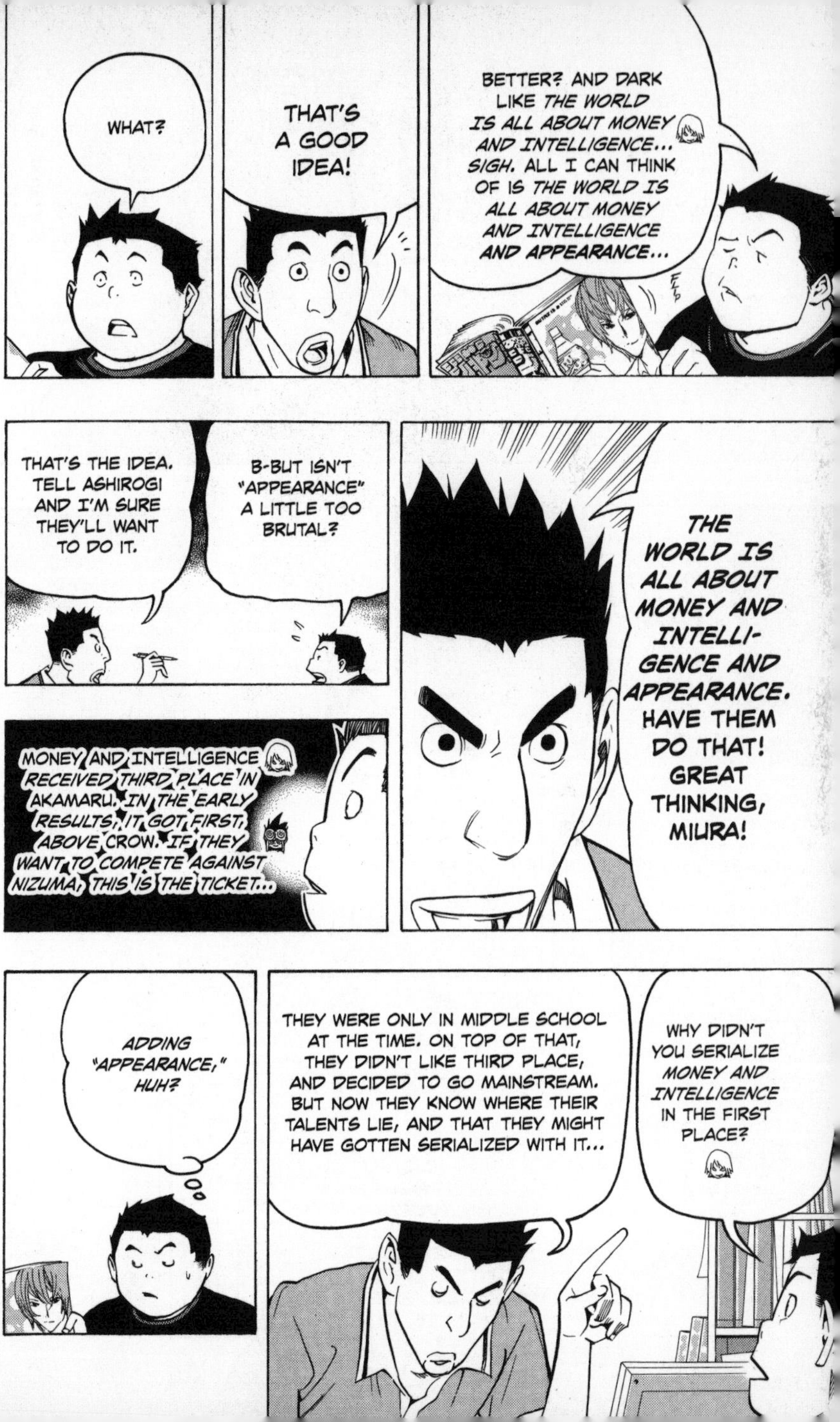

BETTER? AND DARK LIKE THE WORLD IS ALL ABOUT MONEY AND INTELLIGENCE... SIGH. ALL I CAN THINK OF IS THE WORLD IS ALL ABOUT MONEY AND INTELLIGENCE AND APPEARANCE...
THAT'S A GOOD IDEA!
WHAT?
THE WORLD IS ALL ABOUT MONEY AND INTELLI-GENCE AND APPEARANCE. HAVE THEM DO THAT! GREAT THINKING, MIURA!
B-BUT ISN'T "APPEARANCE" A LITTLE TOO BRUTAL?
THAT'S THE IDEA. TELL ASHIROGI AND I'M SURE THEY'LL WANT TO DO IT.
MONEY AND INTELLIGENCE RECEIVED THIRD PLACE IN AKAMARU. IN THE EARLY RESULTS, IT GOT FIRST, ABOVE CROW. IF THEY WANT TO COMPETE AGAINST NIZUMA, THIS IS THE TICKET...
WHY DIDN'T YOU SERIALIZE MONEY AND INTELLIGENCE IN THE FIRST PLACE?
THEY WERE ONLY IN MIDDLE SCHOOL AT THE TIME. ON TOP OF THAT, THEY DIDN'T LIKE THIRD PLACE, AND DECIDED TO GO MAINSTREAM. BUT NOW THEY KNOW WHERE THEIR TALENTS LIE, AND THAT THEY MIGHT HAVE GOTTEN SERIALIZED WITH IT...
ADDING "APPEARANCE," HUH?

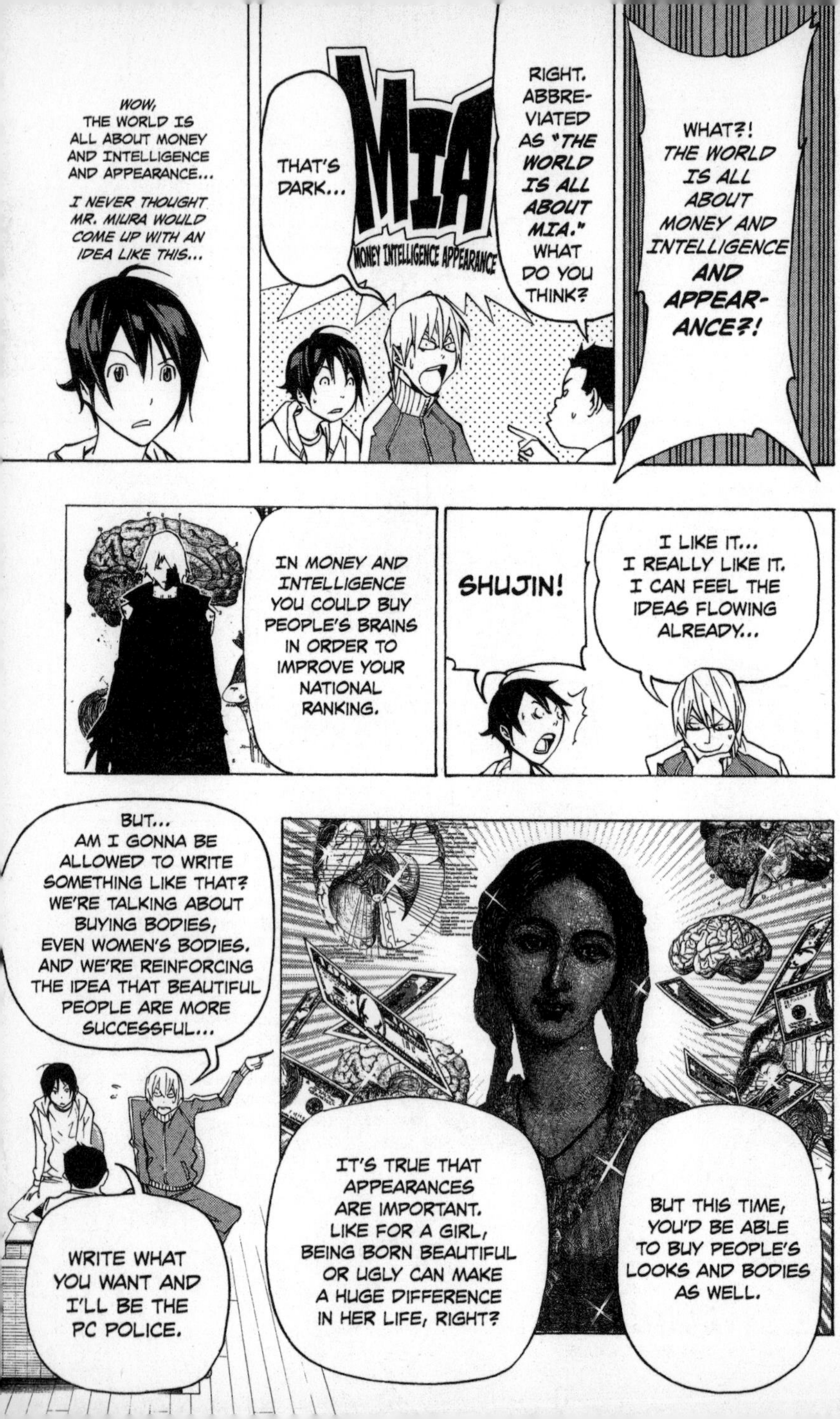
WHAT?! THE WORLD IS ALL ABOUT MONEY AND INTELLIGENCE AND APPEARANCE?!
RIGHT. ABBREVIATED AS "THE WORLD IS ALL ABOUT MIA." WHAT DO YOU THINK?
MIA
MONEY INTELLIGENCE APPEARANCE
THAT'S DARK...
WOW, THE WORLD IS ALL ABOUT MONEY AND INTELLIGENCE AND APPEARANCE...
I NEVER THOUGHT MR. MIURA WOULD COME UP WITH AN IDEA LIKE THIS...
I LIKE IT... I REALLY LIKE IT. I CAN FEEL THE IDEAS FLOWING ALREADY...
SHUJIN!
IN MONEY AND INTELLIGENCE YOU COULD BUY PEOPLE'S BRAINS IN ORDER TO IMPROVE YOUR NATIONAL RANKING.
BUT THIS TIME, YOU'D BE ABLE TO BUY PEOPLE'S LOOKS AND BODIES AS WELL.
IT'S TRUE THAT APPEARANCES ARE IMPORTANT. LIKE FOR A GIRL, BEING BORN BEAUTIFUL OR UGLY CAN MAKE A HUGE DIFFERENCE IN HER LIFE, RIGHT?
BUT... AM I GONNA BE ALLOWED TO WRITE SOMETHING LIKE THAT? WE'RE TALKING ABOUT BUYING BODIES, EVEN WOMEN'S BODIES. AND WE'RE REINFORCING THE IDEA THAT BEAUTIFUL PEOPLE ARE MORE SUCCESSFUL...
WRITE WHAT YOU WANT AND I'LL BE THE PC POLICE.

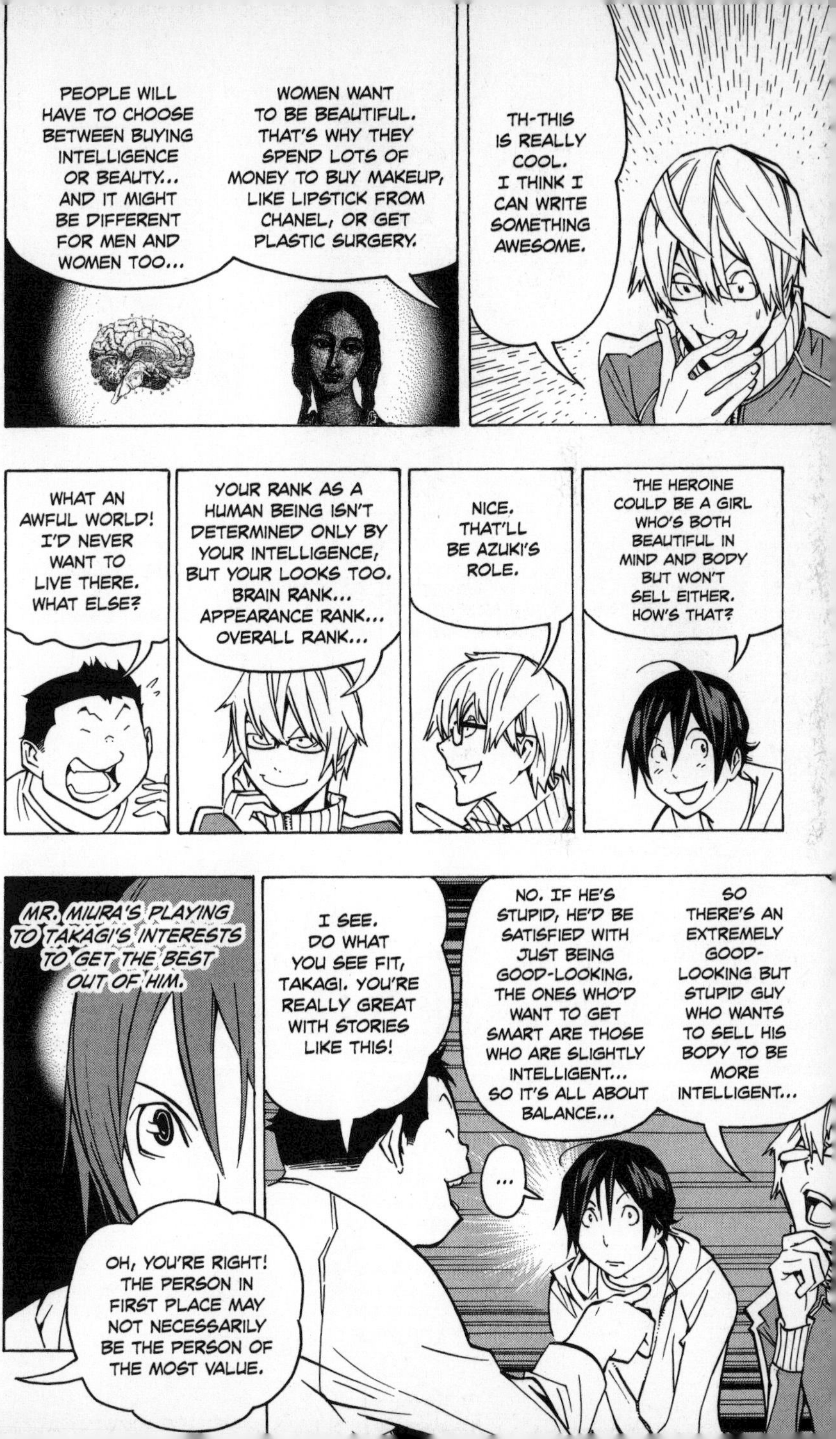
TH-THIS IS REALLY COOL. I THINK I CAN WRITE SOMETHING AWESOME.
WOMEN WANT TO BE BEAUTIFUL. THAT'S WHY THEY SPEND LOTS OF MONEY TO BUY MAKEUP, LIKE LIPSTICK FROM CHANEL, OR GET PLASTIC SURGERY.
PEOPLE WILL HAVE TO CHOOSE BETWEEN BUYING INTELLIGENCE OR BEAUTY... AND IT MIGHT BE DIFFERENT FOR MEN AND WOMEN TOO...
THE HEROINE COULD BE A GIRL WHO'S BOTH BEAUTIFUL IN MIND AND BODY BUT WON'T SELL EITHER. HOW'S THAT?
NICE. THAT'LL BE AZUKI'S ROLE.
YOUR RANK AS A HUMAN BEING ISN'T DETERMINED ONLY BY YOUR INTELLIGENCE, BUT YOUR LOOKS TOO. BRAIN RANK... APPEARANCE RANK... OVERALL RANK...
WHAT AN AWFUL WORLD! I'D NEVER WANT TO LIVE THERE. WHAT ELSE?
SO THERE'S AN EXTREMELY GOOD-LOOKING BUT STUPID GUY WHO WANTS TO SELL HIS BODY TO BE MORE INTELLIGENT...
NO. IF HE'S STUPID, HE'D BE SATISFIED WITH JUST BEING GOOD-LOOKING. THE ONES WHO'D WANT TO GET SMART ARE THOSE WHO ARE SLIGHTLY INTELLIGENT... SO IT'S ALL ABOUT BALANCE...
I SEE. DO WHAT YOU SEE FIT, TAKAGI. YOU'RE REALLY GREAT WITH STORIES LIKE THIS!
...
MR. MIURA'S PLAYING TO TAKAGI'S INTERESTS TO GET THE BEST OUT OF HIM.
OH, YOU'RE RIGHT! THE PERSON IN FIRST PLACE MAY NOT NECESSARILY BE THE PERSON OF THE MOST VALUE.

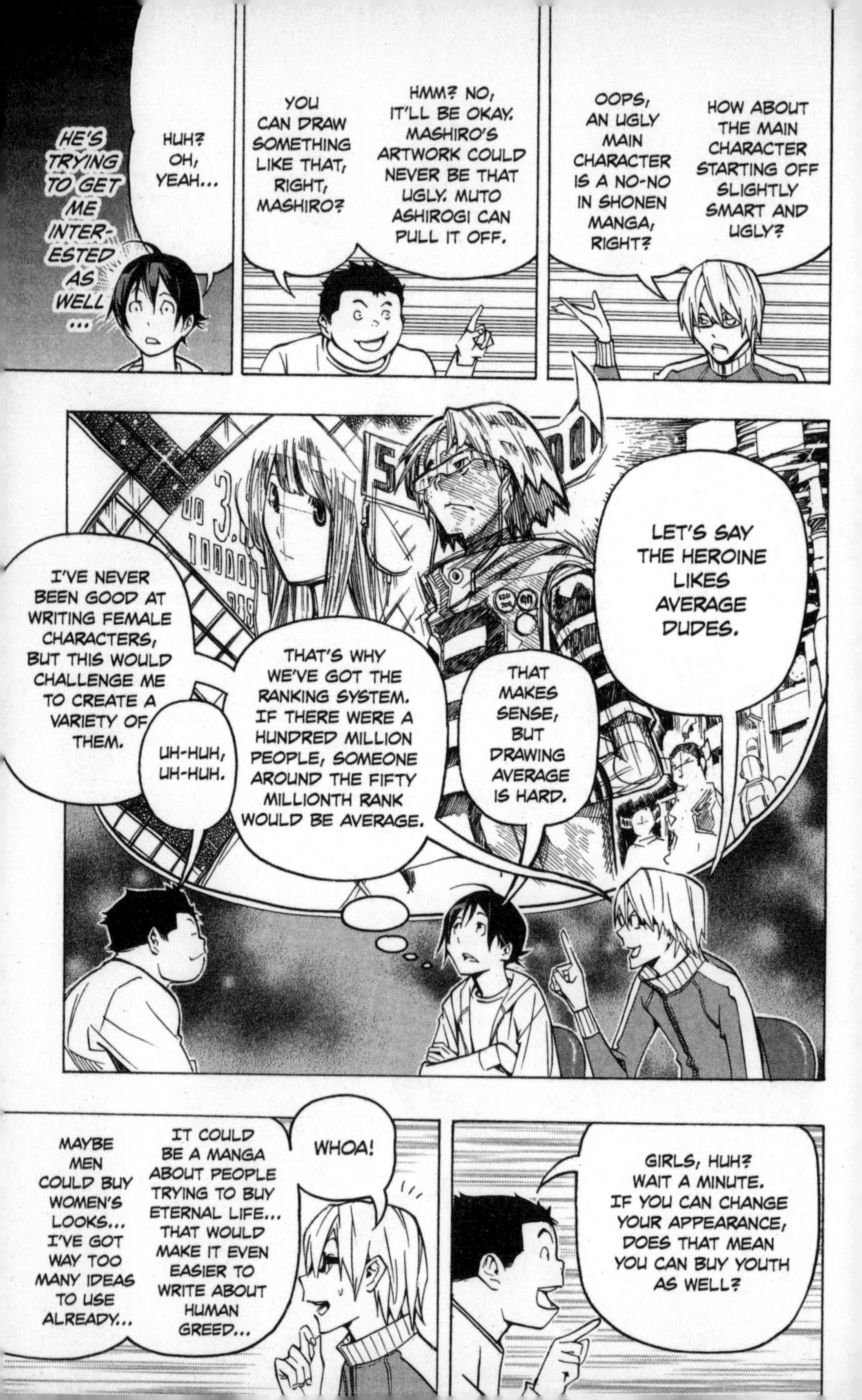
HOW ABOUT THE MAIN CHARACTER STARTING OFF SLIGHTLY SMART AND UGLY?
OOPS, AN UGLY MAIN CHARACTER IS A NO-NO IN SHONEN MANGA, RIGHT?
HMM? NO, IT'LL BE OKAY. MASHIRO'S ARTWORK COULD NEVER BE THAT UGLY. MUTO ASHIROGI CAN PULL IT OFF.
YOU CAN DRAW SOMETHING LIKE THAT, RIGHT, MASHIRO?
HUH? OH, YEAH...
HE'S TRYING TO GET ME INTER-ESTED AS WELL...
LET'S SAY THE HEROINE LIKES AVERAGE DUDES.
THAT MAKES SENSE, BUT DRAWING AVERAGE IS HARD.
THAT'S WHY WE'VE GOT THE RANKING SYSTEM. IF THERE WERE A HUNDRED MILLION PEOPLE, SOMEONE AROUND THE FIFTY MILLIONTH RANK WOULD BE AVERAGE.
UH-HUH, UH-HUH.
I'VE NEVER BEEN GOOD AT WRITING FEMALE CHARACTERS, BUT THIS WOULD CHALLENGE ME TO CREATE A VARIETY OF THEM.
GIRLS, HUH? WAIT A MINUTE. IF YOU CAN CHANGE YOUR APPEARANCE, DOES THAT MEAN YOU CAN BUY YOUTH AS WELL?
WHOA!
IT COULD BE A MANGA ABOUT PEOPLE TRYING TO BUY ETERNAL LIFE... THAT WOULD MAKE IT EVEN EASIER TO WRITE ABOUT HUMAN GREED...
MAYBE MEN COULD BUY WOMEN'S LOOKS... I'VE GOT WAY TOO MANY IDEAS TO USE ALREADY...

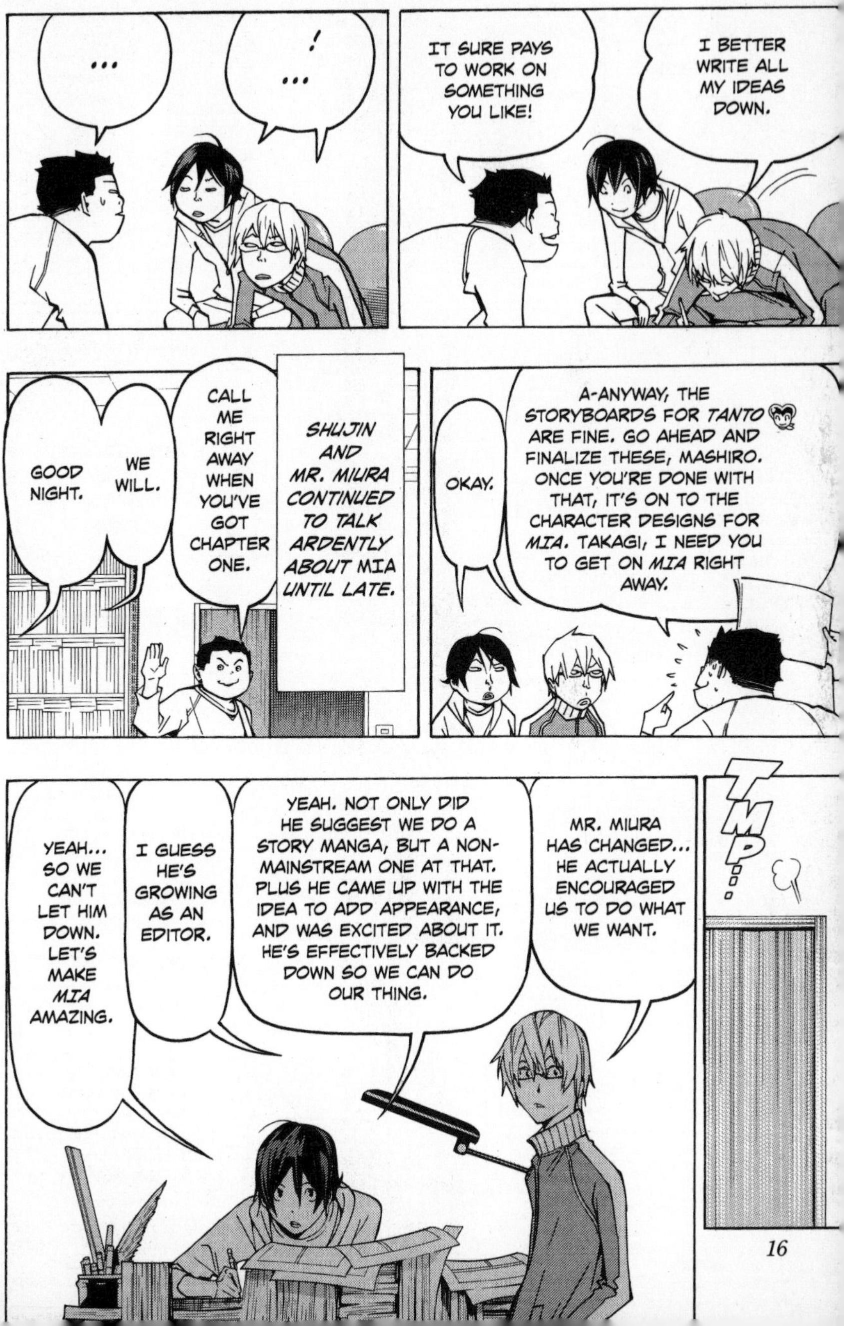
I BETTER WRITE ALL MY IDEAS DOWN.
IT SURE PAYS TO WORK ON SOMETHING YOU LIKE!
! ...
...
A-ANYWAY, THE STORYBOARDS FOR *TANTO* ARE FINE. GO AHEAD AND FINALIZE THESE, MASHIRO. ONCE YOU'RE DONE WITH THAT, IT'S ON TO THE CHARACTER DESIGNS FOR *MIA*. TAKAGI, I NEED YOU TO GET ON *MIA* RIGHT AWAY.
OKAY.
SHUJIN AND MR. MIURA CONTINUED TO TALK ARDENTLY ABOUT MIA *UNTIL LATE.*
CALL ME RIGHT AWAY WHEN YOU'VE GOT CHAPTER ONE.
WE WILL.
GOOD NIGHT.
TMP...
MR. MIURA HAS CHANGED... HE ACTUALLY ENCOURAGED US TO DO WHAT WE WANT.
YEAH. NOT ONLY DID HE SUGGEST WE DO A STORY MANGA, BUT A NON-MAINSTREAM ONE AT THAT. PLUS HE CAME UP WITH THE IDEA TO ADD APPEARANCE, AND WAS EXCITED ABOUT IT. HE'S EFFECTIVELY BACKED DOWN SO WE CAN DO OUR THING.
I GUESS HE'S GROWING AS AN EDITOR.
YEAH... SO WE CAN'T LET HIM DOWN. LET'S MAKE *MIA* AMAZING.

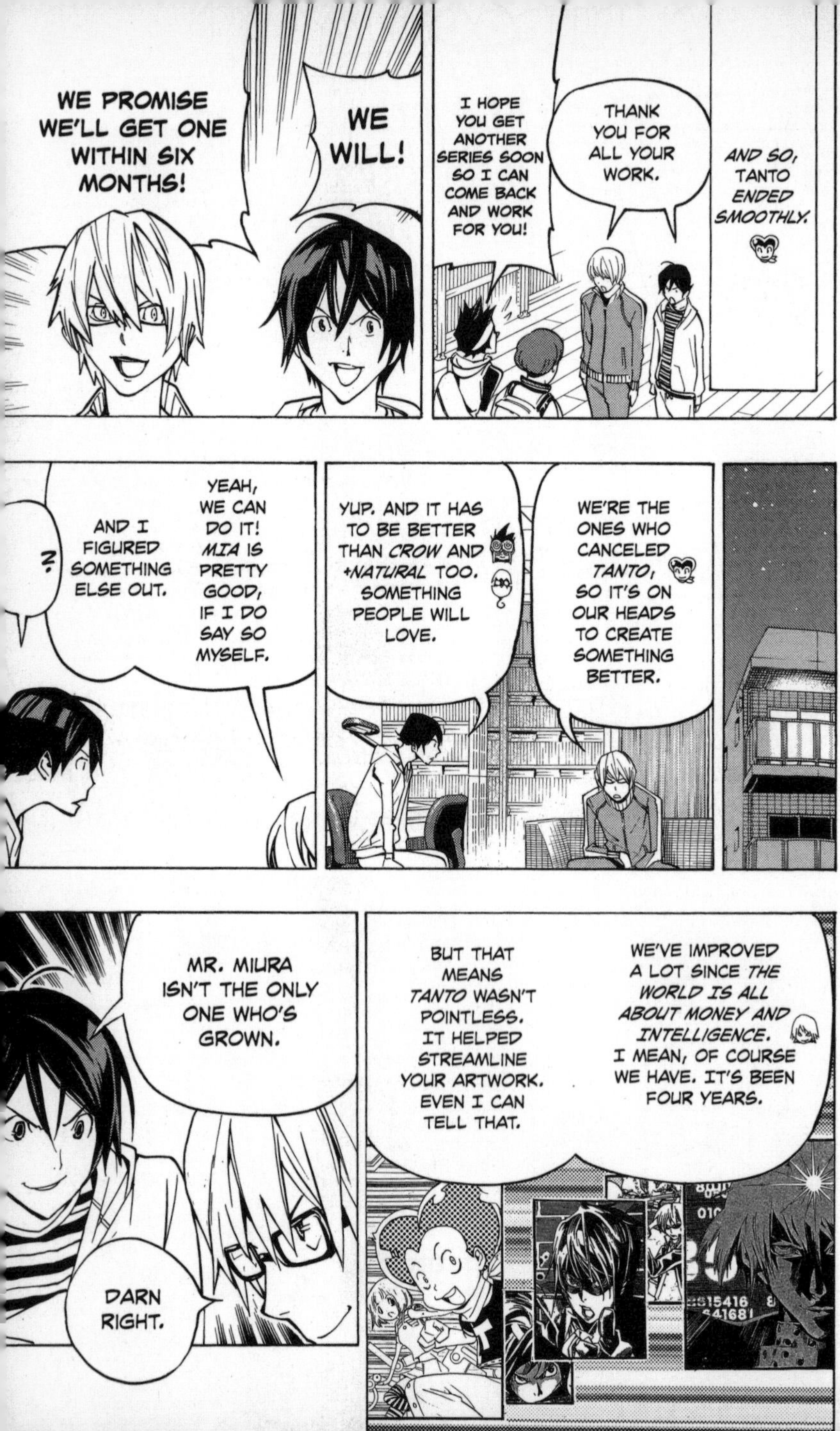
AND SO, TANTO ENDED SMOOTHLY.
THANK YOU FOR ALL YOUR WORK.
I HOPE YOU GET ANOTHER SERIES SOON SO I CAN COME BACK AND WORK FOR YOU!
WE WILL!
WE PROMISE WE'LL GET ONE WITHIN SIX MONTHS!
WE'RE THE ONES WHO CANCELED TANTO, SO IT'S ON OUR HEADS TO CREATE SOMETHING BETTER.
YUP. AND IT HAS TO BE BETTER THAN CROW AND +NATURAL TOO. SOMETHING PEOPLE WILL LOVE.
YEAH, WE CAN DO IT! MIA IS PRETTY GOOD, IF I DO SAY SO MYSELF.
AND I FIGURED SOMETHING ELSE OUT.
?
WE'VE IMPROVED A LOT SINCE THE WORLD IS ALL ABOUT MONEY AND INTELLIGENCE. I MEAN, OF COURSE WE HAVE. IT'S BEEN FOUR YEARS.
BUT THAT MEANS TANTO WASN'T POINTLESS. IT HELPED STREAMLINE YOUR ARTWORK. EVEN I CAN TELL THAT.
MR. MIURA ISN'T THE ONLY ONE WHO'S GROWN.
DARN RIGHT.

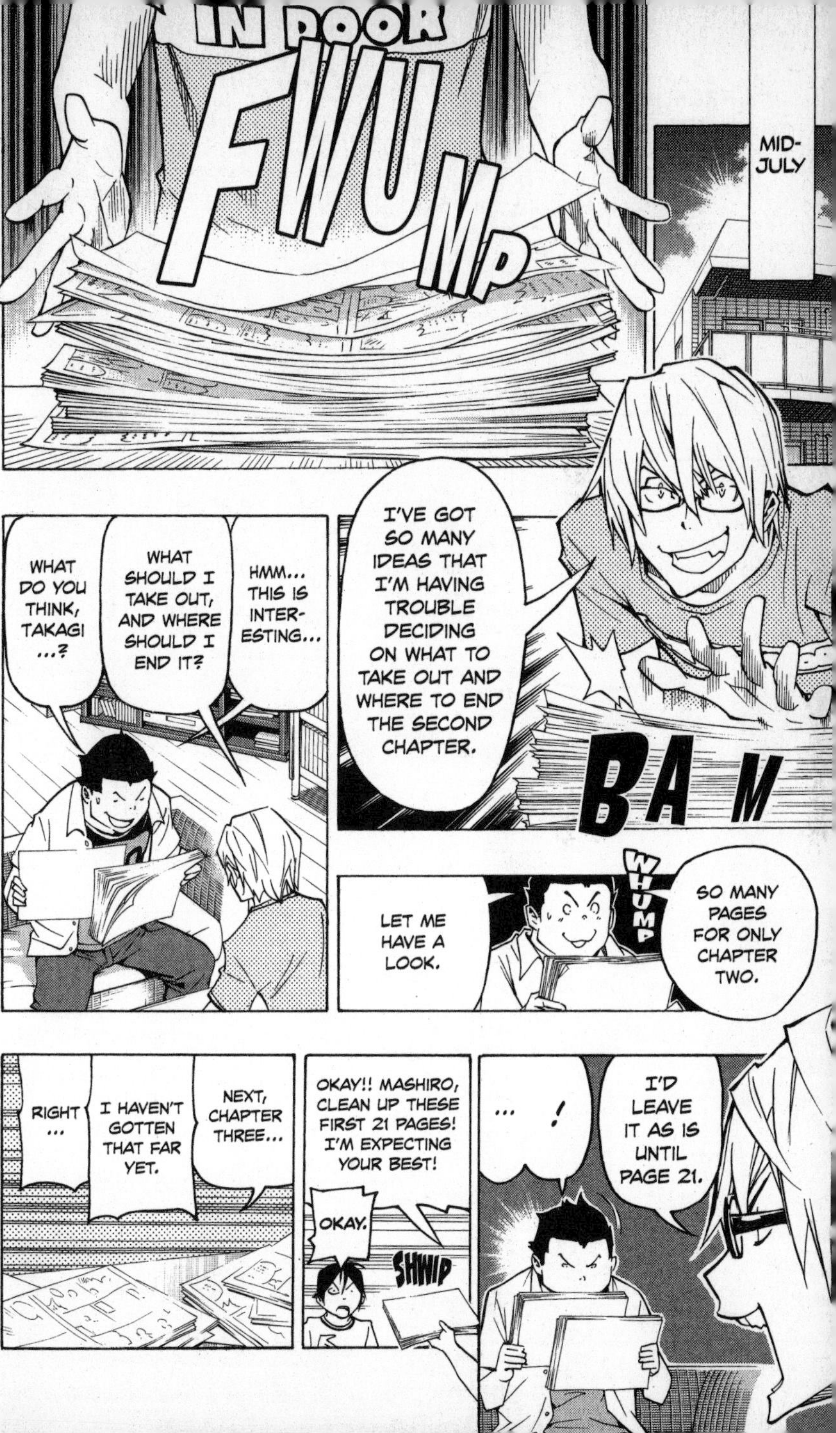
MID-JULY
IN DOOR
FWUMP
I'VE GOT SO MANY IDEAS THAT I'M HAVING TROUBLE DECIDING ON WHAT TO TAKE OUT AND WHERE TO END THE SECOND CHAPTER.
BAM
HMM... THIS IS INTERESTING...
WHAT SHOULD I TAKE OUT, AND WHERE SHOULD I END IT?
WHAT DO YOU THINK, TAKAGI ...?
SO MANY PAGES FOR ONLY CHAPTER TWO.
WHUMP
LET ME HAVE A LOOK.
I'D LEAVE IT AS IS UNTIL PAGE 21.
... !
OKAY!! MASHIRO, CLEAN UP THESE FIRST 21 PAGES! I'M EXPECTING YOUR BEST!
OKAY.
SHWIP
NEXT, CHAPTER THREE...
I HAVEN'T GOTTEN THAT FAR YET.
RIGHT ...

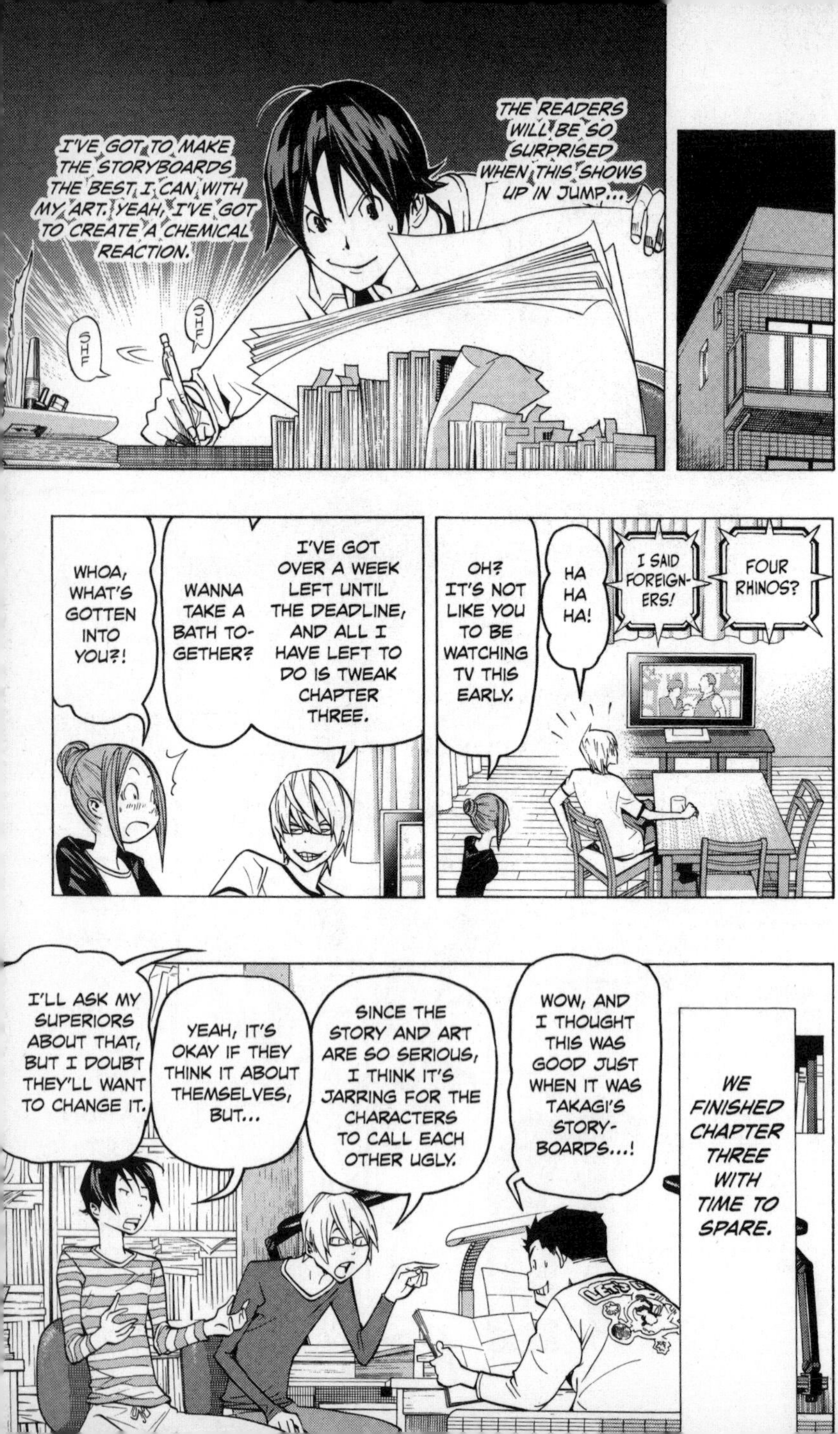
THE READERS WILL BE SO SURPRISED WHEN THIS SHOWS UP IN JUMP...
I'VE GOT TO MAKE THE STORYBOARDS THE BEST I CAN WITH MY ART. YEAH, I'VE GOT TO CREATE A CHEMICAL REACTION.
SHF
SHF
FOUR RHINOS?
I SAID FOREIGNERS!
HA HA HA!
OH? IT'S NOT LIKE YOU TO BE WATCHING TV THIS EARLY.
I'VE GOT OVER A WEEK LEFT UNTIL THE DEADLINE, AND ALL I HAVE LEFT TO DO IS TWEAK CHAPTER THREE.
WANNA TAKE A BATH TOGETHER?
WHOA, WHAT'S GOTTEN INTO YOU?!
WE FINISHED CHAPTER THREE WITH TIME TO SPARE.
WOW, AND I THOUGHT THIS WAS GOOD JUST WHEN IT WAS TAKAGI'S STORYBOARDS...!
SINCE THE STORY AND ART ARE SO SERIOUS, I THINK IT'S JARRING FOR THE CHARACTERS TO CALL EACH OTHER UGLY.
YEAH, IT'S OKAY IF THEY THINK IT ABOUT THEMSELVES, BUT...
I'LL ASK MY SUPERIORS ABOUT THAT, BUT I DOUBT THEY'LL WANT TO CHANGE IT.

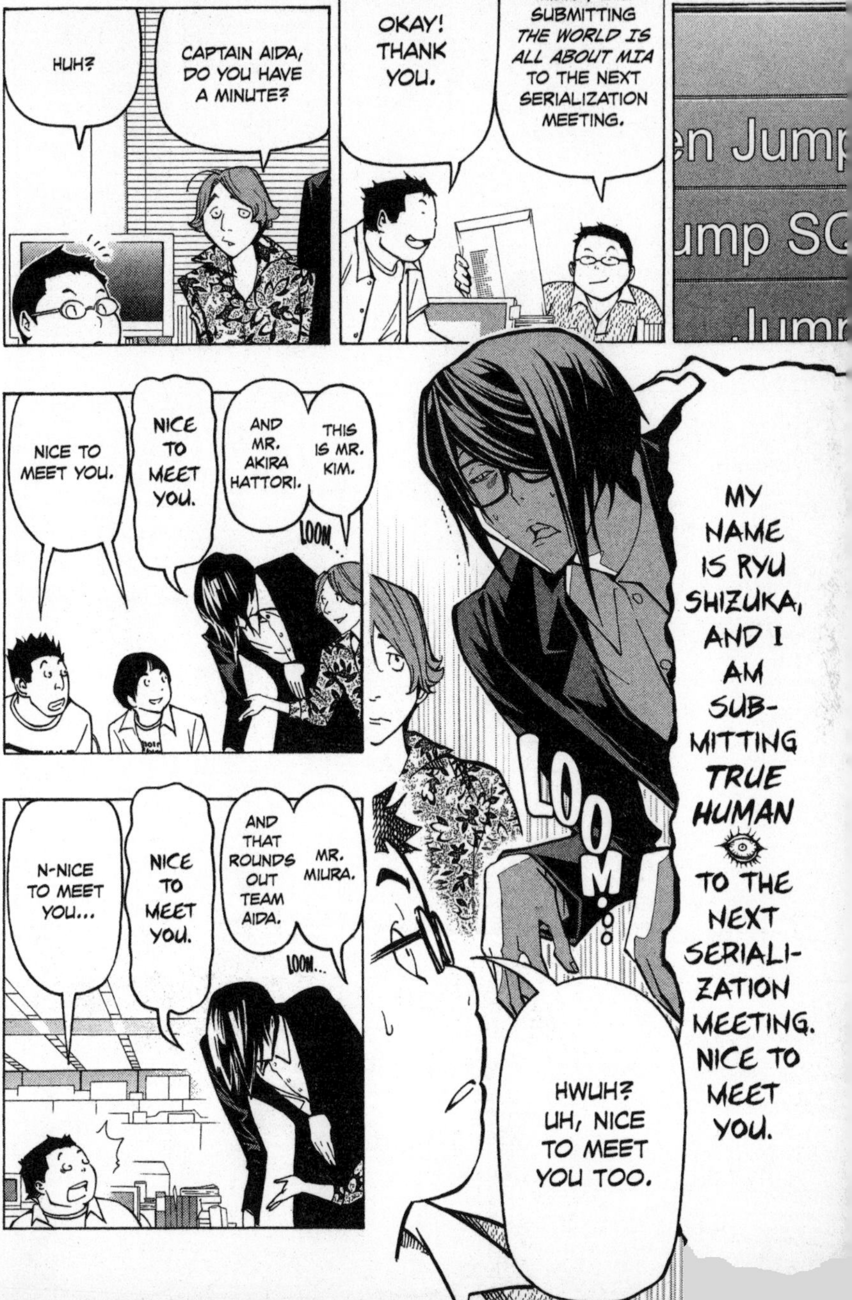
MIURA, I'M SUBMITTING *THE WORLD IS ALL ABOUT MIA* TO THE NEXT SERIALIZATION MEETING.
OKAY! THANK YOU.
CAPTAIN AIDA, DO YOU HAVE A MINUTE?
HUH?
MY NAME IS RYU SHIZUKA, AND I AM SUBMITTING *TRUE HUMAN* TO THE NEXT SERIALIZATION MEETING. NICE TO MEET YOU.
LOOOM...
HWUH? UH, NICE TO MEET YOU TOO.
THIS IS MR. KIM.
AND MR. AKIRA HATTORI.
LOOM...
NICE TO MEET YOU.
NICE TO MEET YOU.
MR. MIURA.
AND THAT ROUNDS OUT TEAM AIDA.
LOOM...
NICE TO MEET YOU.
N-NICE TO MEET YOU...

READ THIS WAY

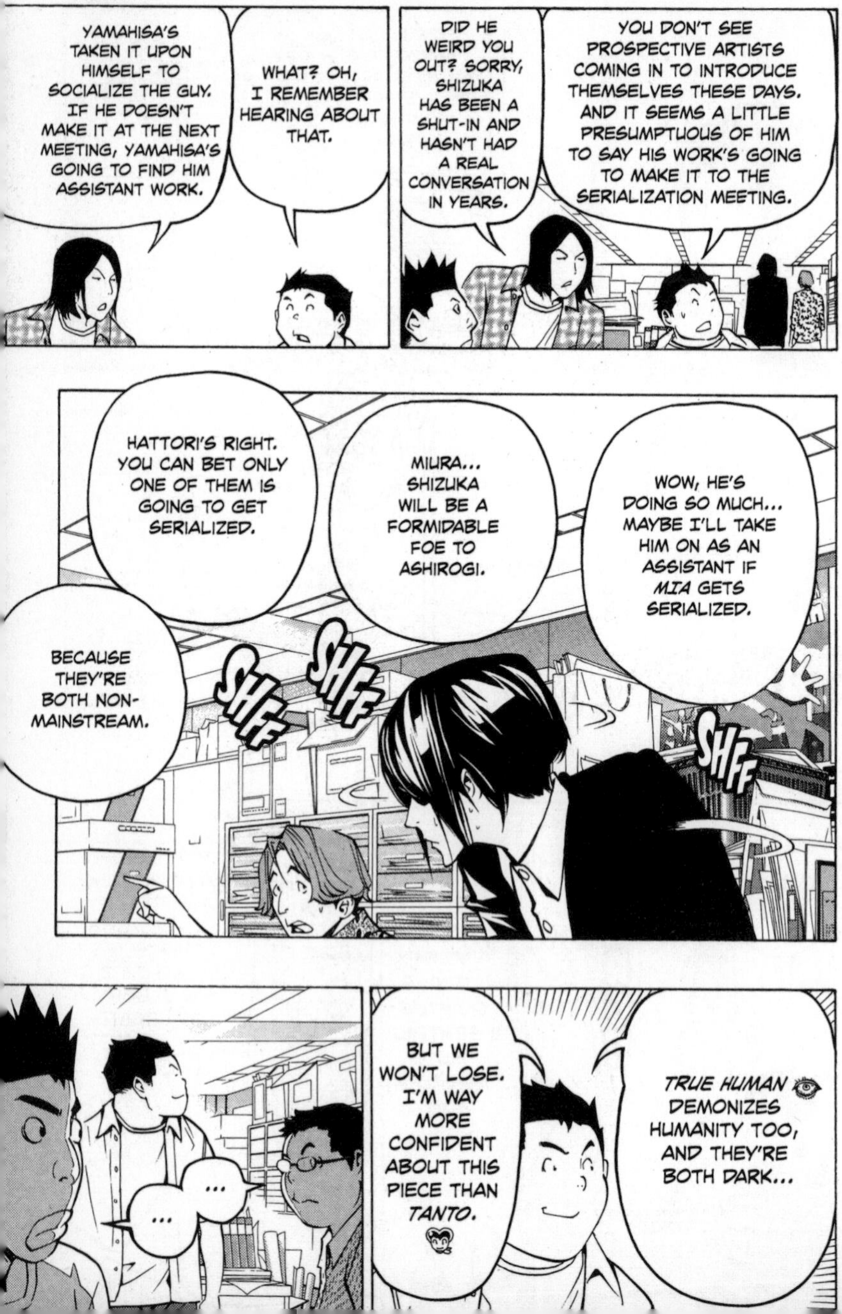

YOU DON'T SEE PROSPECTIVE ARTISTS COMING IN TO INTRODUCE THEMSELVES THESE DAYS. AND IT SEEMS A LITTLE PRESUMPTUOUS OF HIM TO SAY HIS WORK'S GOING TO MAKE IT TO THE SERIALIZATION MEETING.
DID HE WEIRD YOU OUT? SORRY, SHIZUKA HAS BEEN A SHUT-IN AND HASN'T HAD A REAL CONVERSATION IN YEARS.
WHAT? OH, I REMEMBER HEARING ABOUT THAT.
YAMAHISA'S TAKEN IT UPON HIMSELF TO SOCIALIZE THE GUY. IF HE DOESN'T MAKE IT AT THE NEXT MEETING, YAMAHISA'S GOING TO FIND HIM ASSISTANT WORK.
WOW, HE'S DOING SO MUCH... MAYBE I'LL TAKE HIM ON AS AN ASSISTANT IF *MIA* GETS SERIALIZED.
SHFF
MIURA... SHIZUKA WILL BE A FORMIDABLE FOE TO ASHIROGI.
SHFF
HATTORI'S RIGHT. YOU CAN BET ONLY ONE OF THEM IS GOING TO GET SERIALIZED.
SHFF
BECAUSE THEY'RE BOTH NON-MAINSTREAM.
TRUE HUMAN DEMONIZES HUMANITY TOO, AND THEY'RE BOTH DARK...
BUT WE WON'T LOSE. I'M WAY MORE CONFIDENT ABOUT THIS PIECE THAN *TANTO*.
...
...

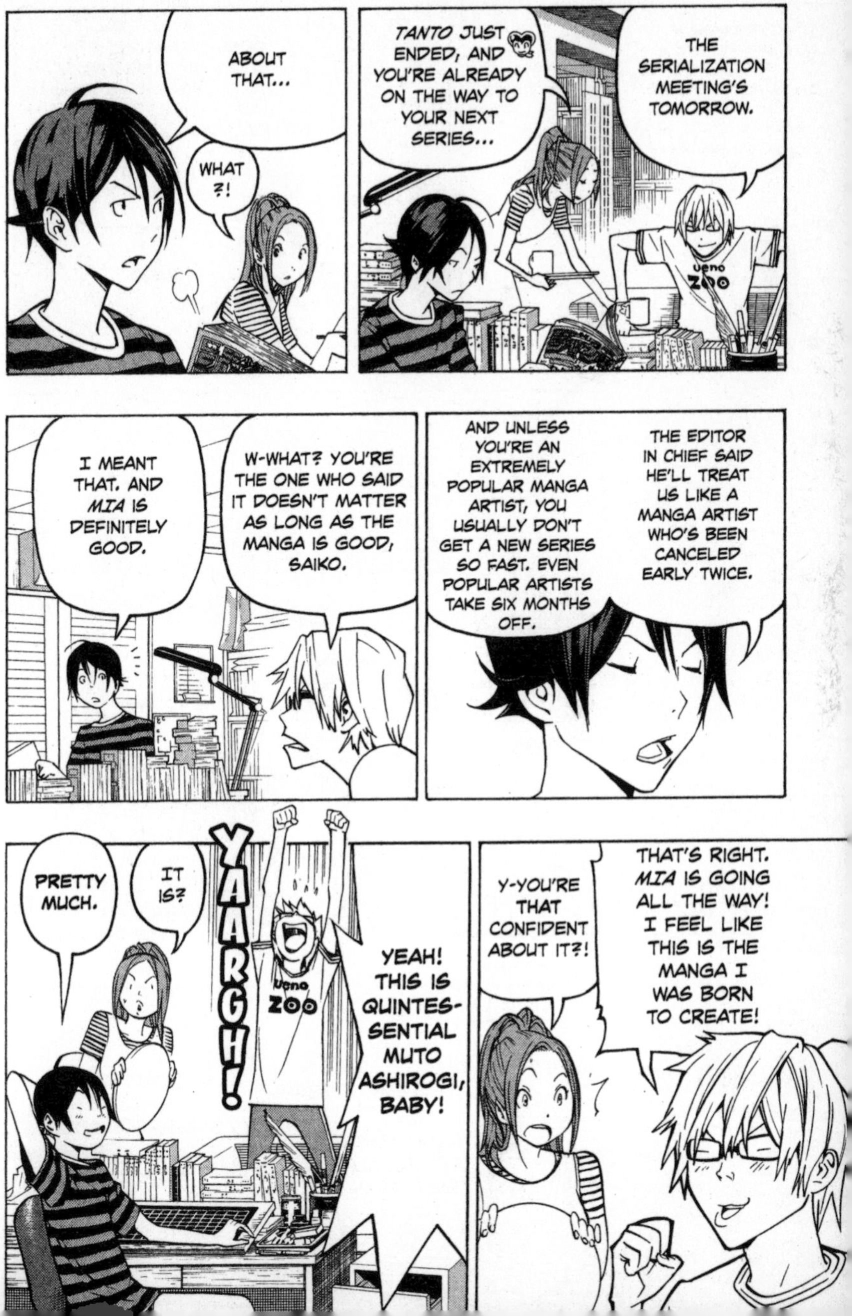
THE SERIALIZATION MEETING'S TOMORROW.
TANTO JUST ENDED, AND YOU'RE ALREADY ON THE WAY TO YOUR NEXT SERIES...
ABOUT THAT...
WHAT?!
THE EDITOR IN CHIEF SAID HE'LL TREAT US LIKE A MANGA ARTIST WHO'S BEEN CANCELED EARLY TWICE.
AND UNLESS YOU'RE AN EXTREMELY POPULAR MANGA ARTIST, YOU USUALLY DON'T GET A NEW SERIES SO FAST. EVEN POPULAR ARTISTS TAKE SIX MONTHS OFF.
W-WHAT? YOU'RE THE ONE WHO SAID IT DOESN'T MATTER AS LONG AS THE MANGA IS GOOD, SAIKO.
I MEANT THAT. AND MIA IS DEFINITELY GOOD.
THAT'S RIGHT. MIA IS GOING ALL THE WAY! I FEEL LIKE THIS IS THE MANGA I WAS BORN TO CREATE!
Y-YOU'RE THAT CONFIDENT ABOUT IT?!
YAARGH!
IT IS?
PRETTY MUCH.
YEAH! THIS IS QUINTES-SENTIAL MUTO ASHIROGI, BABY!

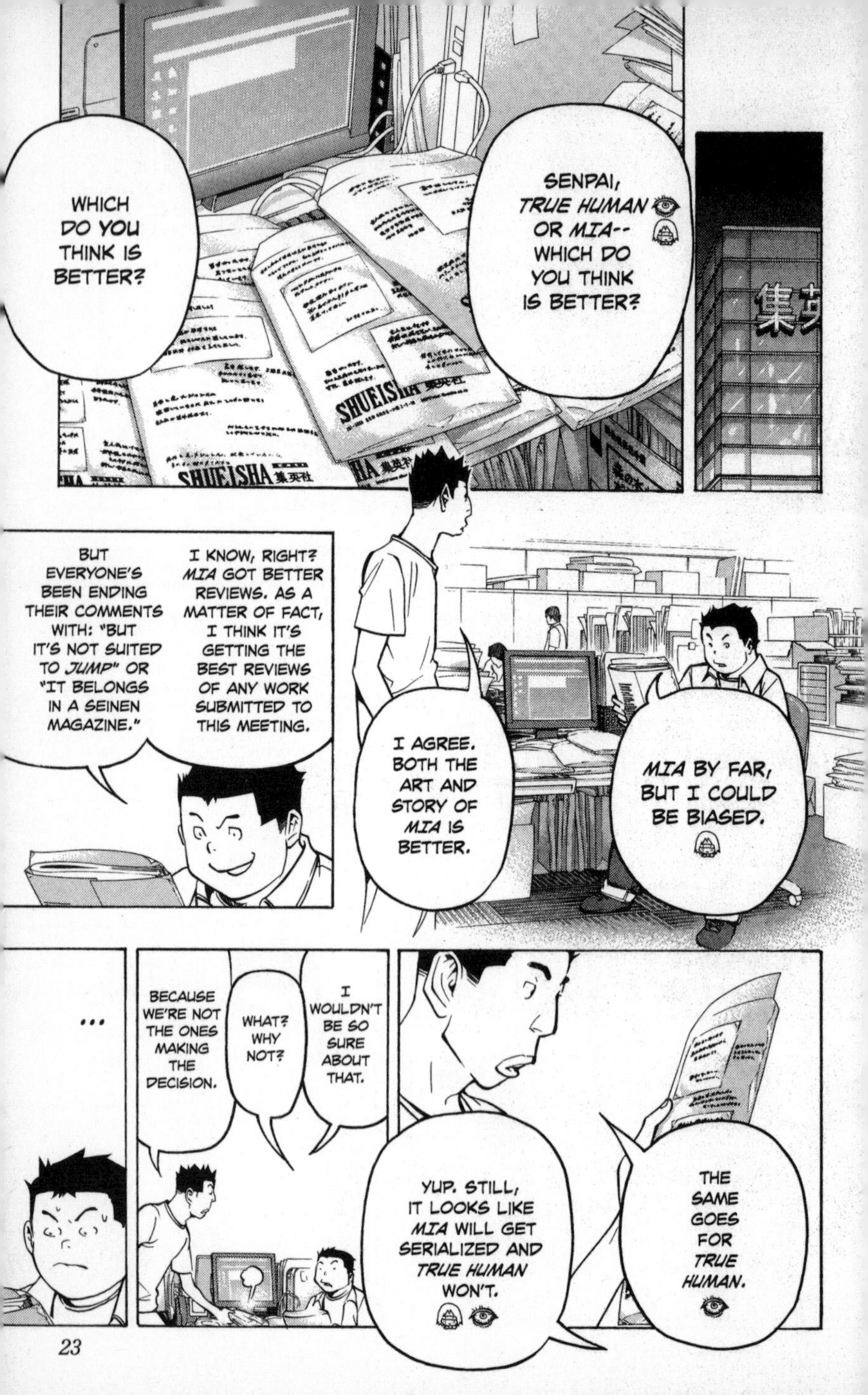
SENPAI, TRUE HUMAN OR MIA-- WHICH DO YOU THINK IS BETTER?
WHICH DO YOU THINK IS BETTER?
SHUEISHA 集英社
MIA BY FAR, BUT I COULD BE BIASED.
I AGREE. BOTH THE ART AND STORY OF MIA IS BETTER.
I KNOW, RIGHT? MIA GOT BETTER REVIEWS. AS A MATTER OF FACT, I THINK IT'S GETTING THE BEST REVIEWS OF ANY WORK SUBMITTED TO THIS MEETING.
BUT EVERYONE'S BEEN ENDING THEIR COMMENTS WITH: "BUT IT'S NOT SUITED TO JUMP" OR "IT BELONGS IN A SEINEN MAGAZINE."
THE SAME GOES FOR TRUE HUMAN.
YUP. STILL, IT LOOKS LIKE MIA WILL GET SERIALIZED AND TRUE HUMAN WON'T.
I WOULDN'T BE SO SURE ABOUT THAT.
WHAT? WHY NOT?
BECAUSE WE'RE NOT THE ONES MAKING THE DECISION.
...

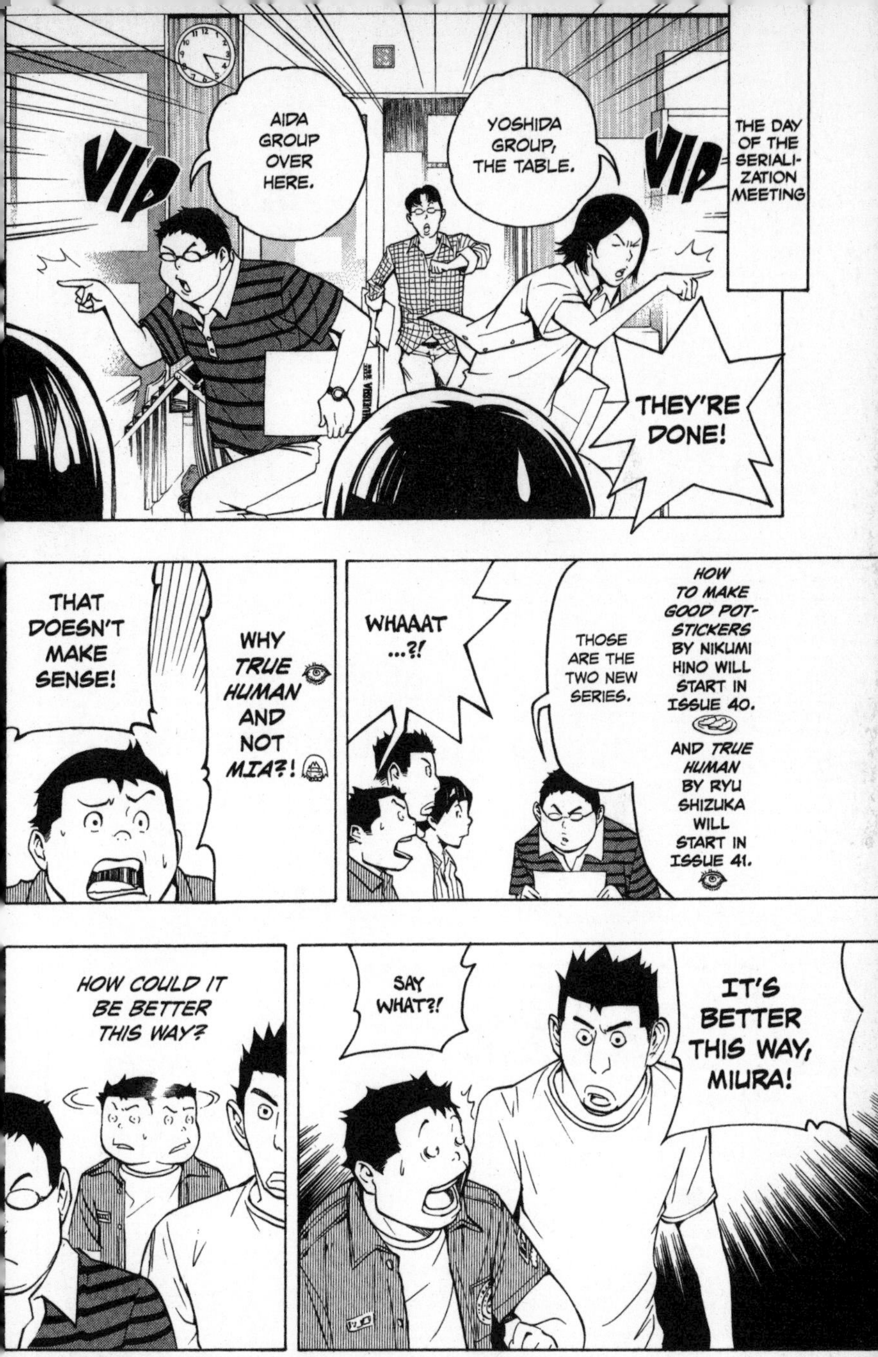
THE DAY OF THE SERIALIZATION MEETING
VIP
YOSHIDA GROUP, THE TABLE.
AIDA GROUP OVER HERE.
VIP
THEY'RE DONE!
HOW TO MAKE GOOD POT-STICKERS BY NIKUMI HINO WILL START IN ISSUE 40.
AND TRUE HUMAN BY RYU SHIZUKA WILL START IN ISSUE 41.
THOSE ARE THE TWO NEW SERIES.
WHAAAT...?!
WHY TRUE HUMAN AND NOT MIA?!
THAT DOESN'T MAKE SENSE!
IT'S BETTER THIS WAY, MIURA!
SAY WHAT?!
HOW COULD IT BE BETTER THIS WAY?

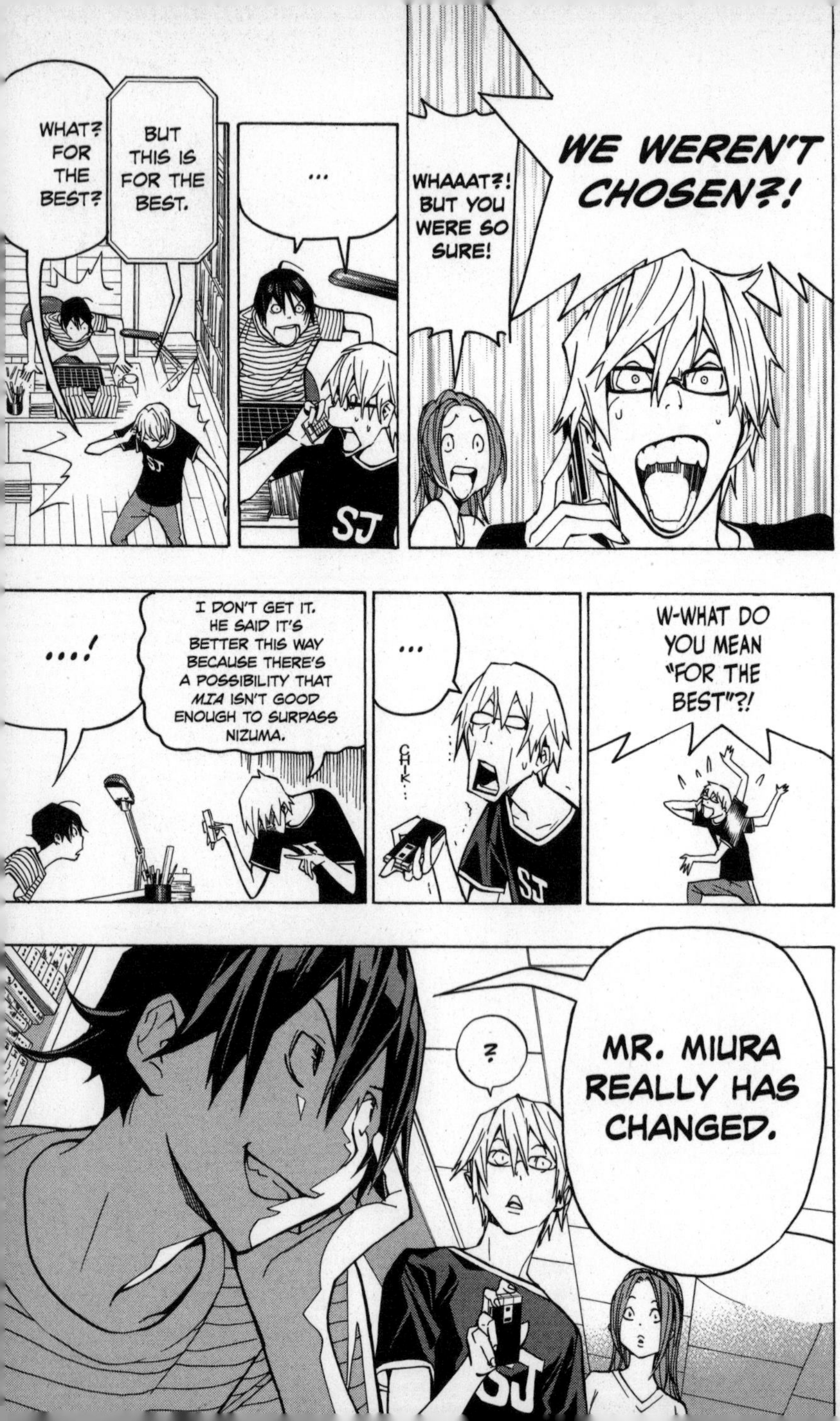
WE WEREN'T CHOSEN?!
WHAAAT?! BUT YOU WERE SO SURE!
...
BUT THIS IS FOR THE BEST.
WHAT? FOR THE BEST?
W-WHAT DO YOU MEAN "FOR THE BEST"?!
...
CHIK...
I DON'T GET IT. HE SAID IT'S BETTER THIS WAY BECAUSE THERE'S A POSSIBILITY THAT *MIA* ISN'T GOOD ENOUGH TO SURPASS NIZUMA.
...!
MR. MIURA REALLY HAS CHANGED.
?

OHBA'S STORYBOARD

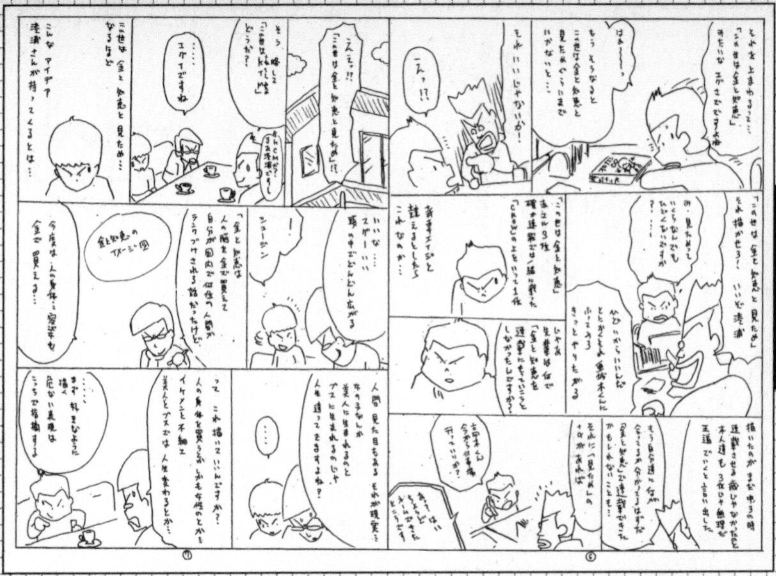

OBATA'S STORYBOARD

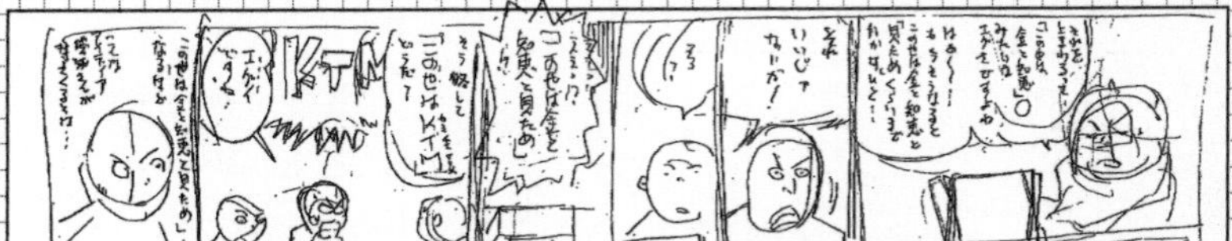

COMPLETE!

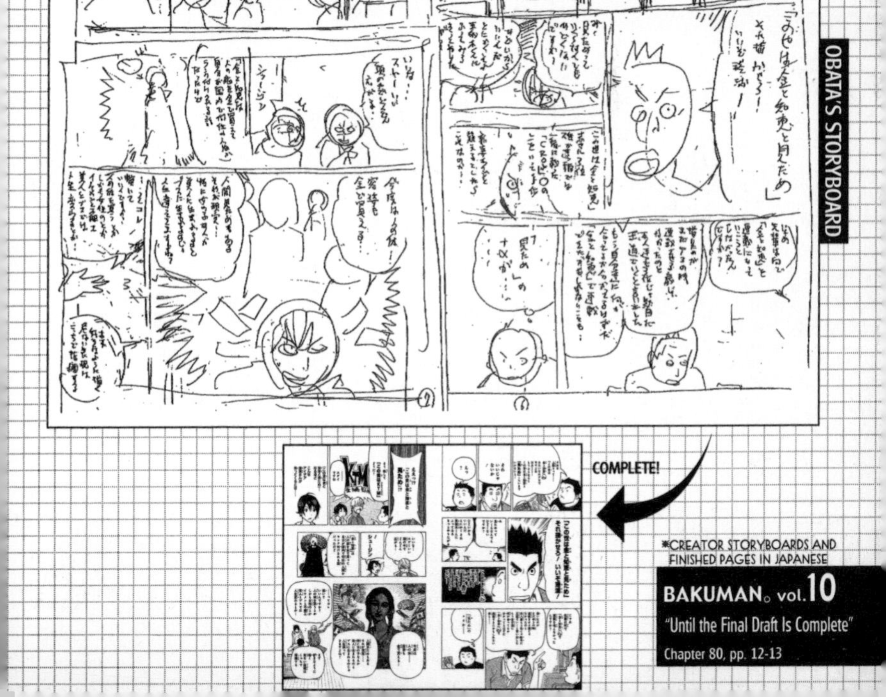

*CREATOR STORYBOARDS AND FINISHED PAGES IN JAPANESE

BAKUMAN。 vol.10

"Until the Final Draft Is Complete"

Chapter 80, pp. 12-13

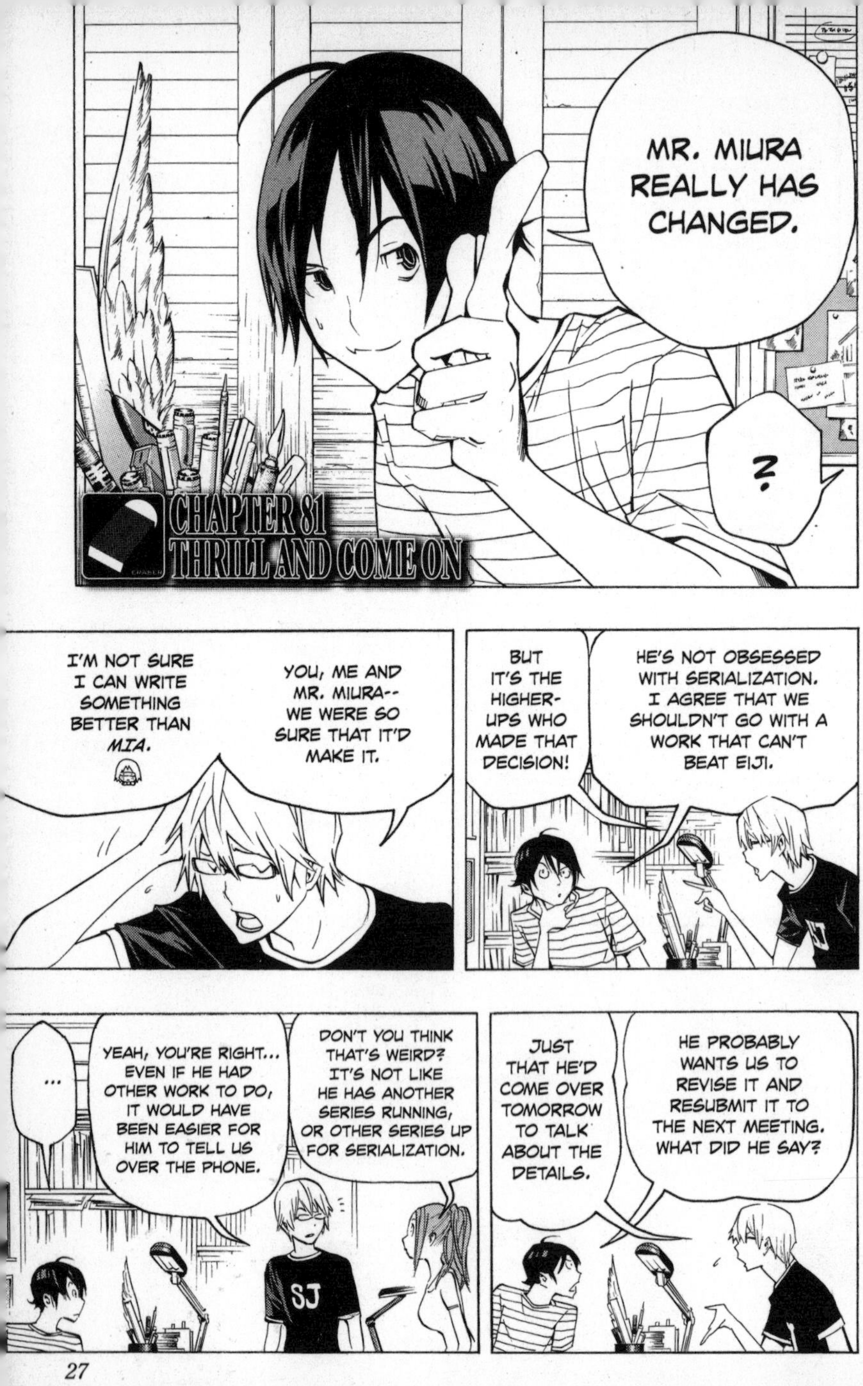
MR. MIURA REALLY HAS CHANGED.
?
CHAPTER 81 THRILL AND COME ON
HE'S NOT OBSESSED WITH SERIALIZATION. I AGREE THAT WE SHOULDN'T GO WITH A WORK THAT CAN'T BEAT EIJI.
BUT IT'S THE HIGHER-UPS WHO MADE THAT DECISION!
YOU, ME AND MR. MIURA-- WE WERE SO SURE THAT IT'D MAKE IT.
I'M NOT SURE I CAN WRITE SOMETHING BETTER THAN *MIA*.
HE PROBABLY WANTS US TO REVISE IT AND RESUBMIT IT TO THE NEXT MEETING. WHAT DID HE SAY?
JUST THAT HE'D COME OVER TOMORROW TO TALK ABOUT THE DETAILS.
DON'T YOU THINK THAT'S WEIRD? IT'S NOT LIKE HE HAS ANOTHER SERIES RUNNING, OR OTHER SERIES UP FOR SERIALIZATION.
YEAH, YOU'RE RIGHT... EVEN IF HE HAD OTHER WORK TO DO, IT WOULD HAVE BEEN EASIER FOR HIM TO TELL US OVER THE PHONE.
...

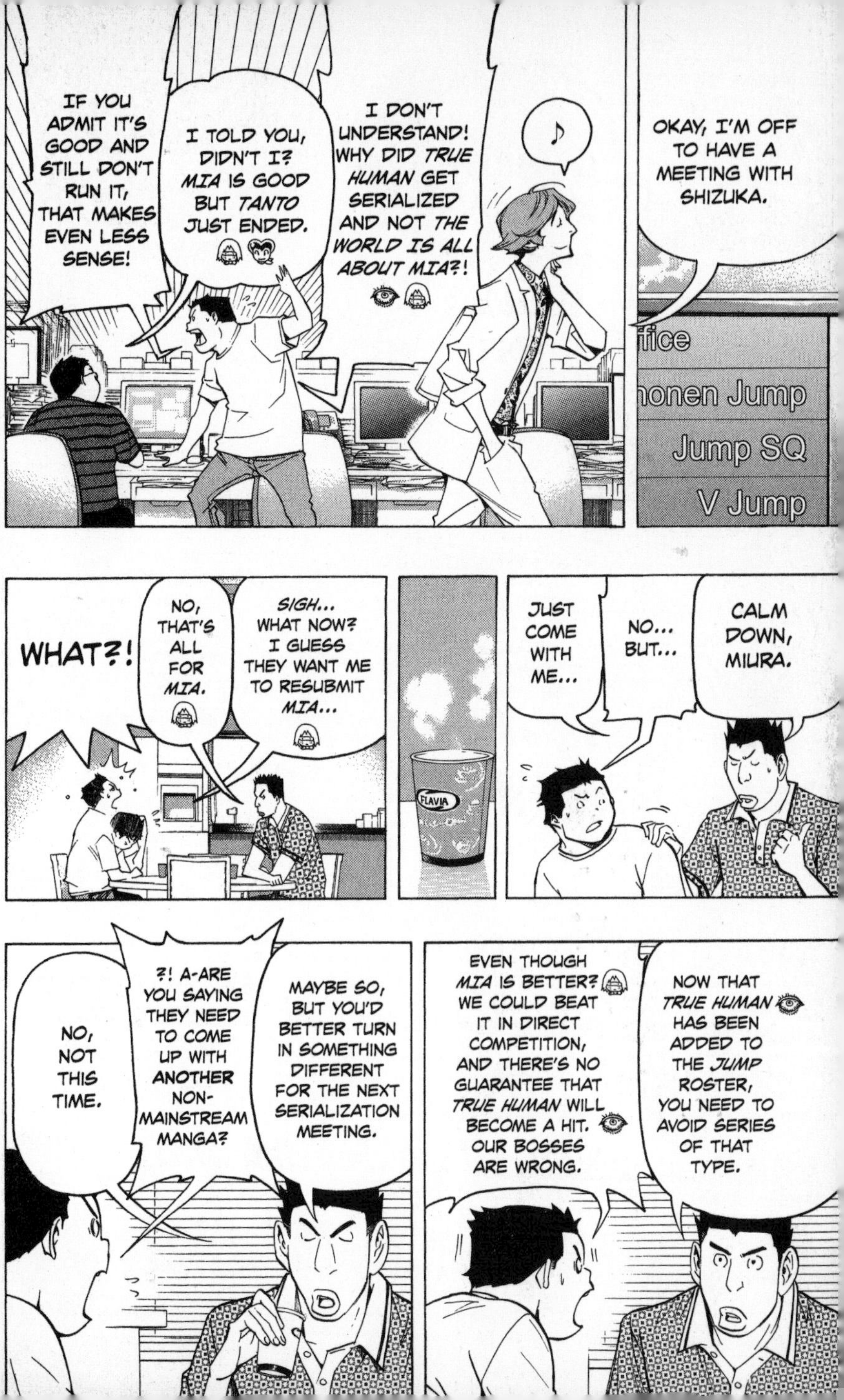
OKAY, I'M OFF TO HAVE A MEETING WITH SHIZUKA.
Jump SQ
V Jump
♪
I DON'T UNDERSTAND! WHY DID *TRUE HUMAN* GET SERIALIZED AND NOT *THE WORLD IS ALL ABOUT MIA*?!
I TOLD YOU, DIDN'T I? *MIA* IS GOOD BUT *TANTO* JUST ENDED.
IF YOU ADMIT IT'S GOOD AND STILL DON'T RUN IT, THAT MAKES EVEN LESS SENSE!
CALM DOWN, MIURA.
NO... BUT...
JUST COME WITH ME...
FLAVIA
SIGH... WHAT NOW? I GUESS THEY WANT ME TO RESUBMIT *MIA*...
NO, THAT'S ALL FOR *MIA*.
WHAT?!
NOW THAT *TRUE HUMAN* HAS BEEN ADDED TO THE *JUMP* ROSTER, YOU NEED TO AVOID SERIES OF THAT TYPE.
EVEN THOUGH *MIA* IS BETTER? WE COULD BEAT IT IN DIRECT COMPETITION, AND THERE'S NO GUARANTEE THAT *TRUE HUMAN* WILL BECOME A HIT. OUR BOSSES ARE WRONG.
MAYBE SO, BUT YOU'D BETTER TURN IN SOMETHING DIFFERENT FOR THE NEXT SERIALIZATION MEETING.
?! A-ARE YOU SAYING THEY NEED TO COME UP WITH **ANOTHER** NON-MAINSTREAM MANGA?
NO, NOT THIS TIME.

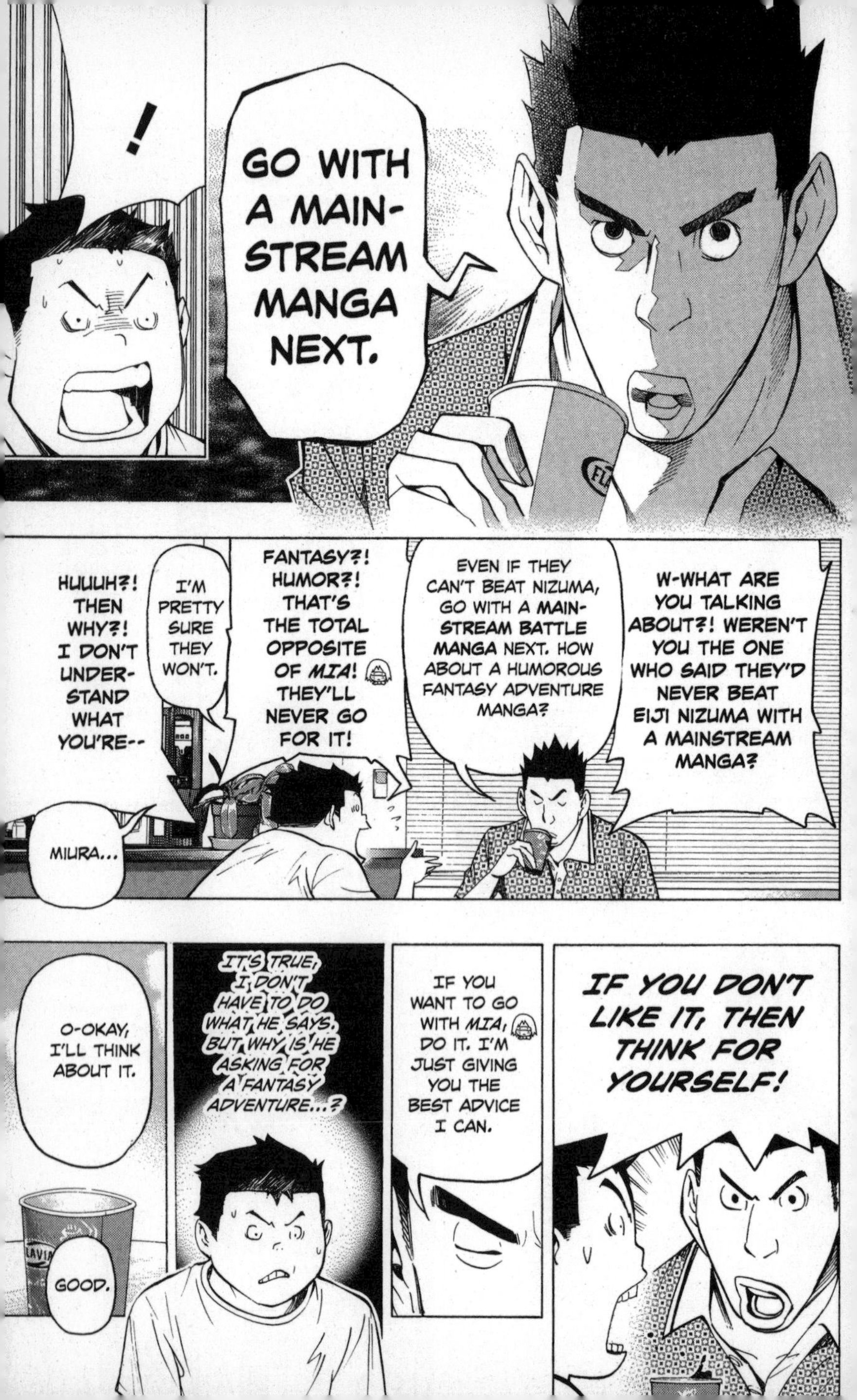
GO WITH A MAIN-STREAM MANGA NEXT.
!
W-WHAT ARE YOU TALKING ABOUT?! WEREN'T YOU THE ONE WHO SAID THEY'D NEVER BEAT EIJI NIZUMA WITH A MAINSTREAM MANGA?
EVEN IF THEY CAN'T BEAT NIZUMA, GO WITH A MAIN-STREAM BATTLE MANGA NEXT. HOW ABOUT A HUMOROUS FANTASY ADVENTURE MANGA?
FANTASY?! HUMOR?! THAT'S THE TOTAL OPPOSITE OF MIA! THEY'LL NEVER GO FOR IT!
I'M PRETTY SURE THEY WON'T.
HUUUH?! THEN WHY?! I DON'T UNDER-STAND WHAT YOU'RE--
MIURA...
IF YOU DON'T LIKE IT, THEN THINK FOR YOURSELF!
IF YOU WANT TO GO WITH MIA, DO IT. I'M JUST GIVING YOU THE BEST ADVICE I CAN.
IT'S TRUE, I DON'T HAVE TO DO WHAT HE SAYS. BUT WHY IS HE ASKING FOR A FANTASY ADVENTURE...?
O-OKAY, I'LL THINK ABOUT IT.
GOOD.

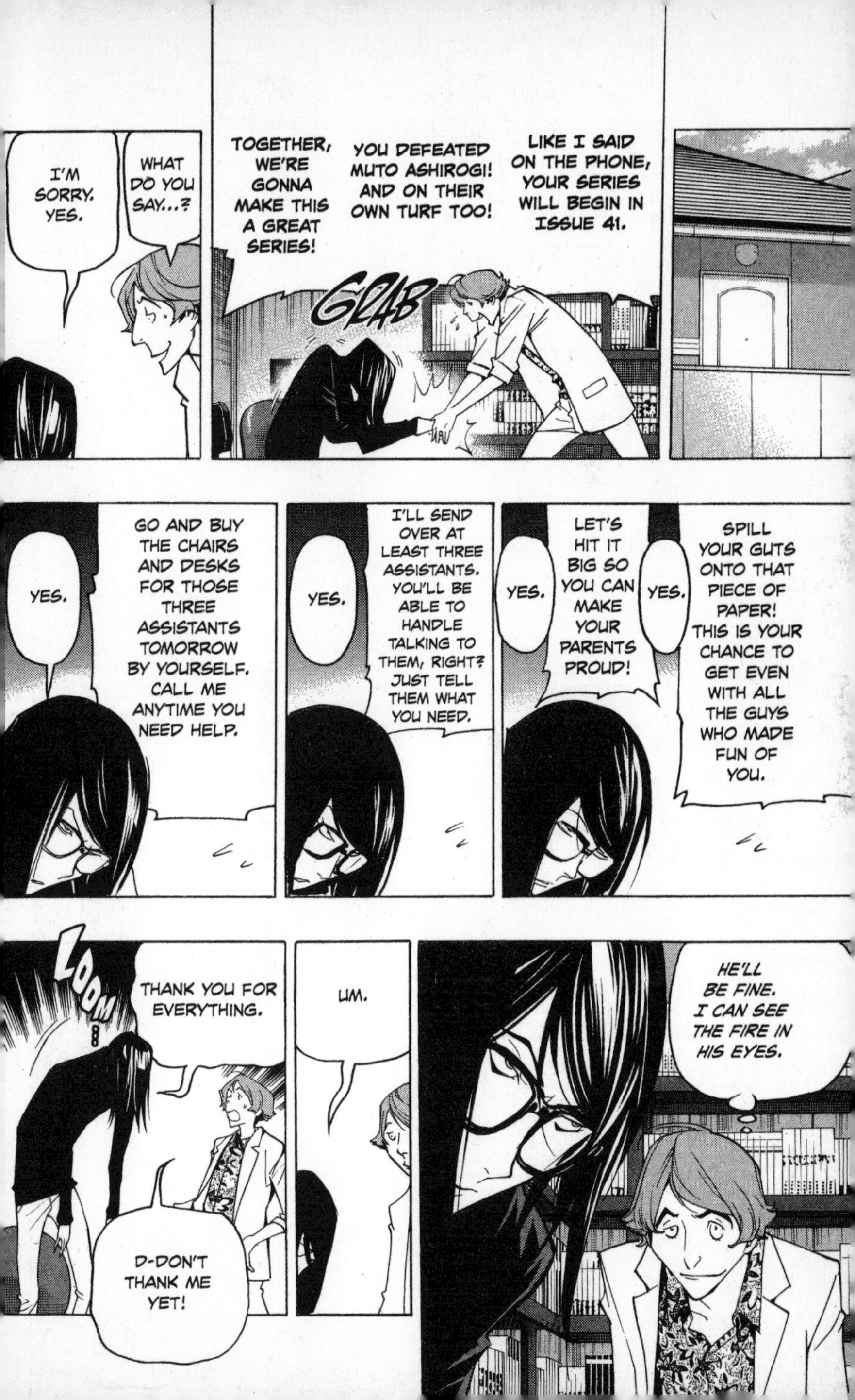
LIKE I SAID ON THE PHONE, YOUR SERIES WILL BEGIN IN ISSUE 41.
YOU DEFEATED MUTO ASHIROGI! AND ON THEIR OWN TURF TOO!
TOGETHER, WE'RE GONNA MAKE THIS A GREAT SERIES!
GRAB
WHAT DO YOU SAY...?
I'M SORRY. YES.
SPILL YOUR GUTS ONTO THAT PIECE OF PAPER! THIS IS YOUR CHANCE TO GET EVEN WITH ALL THE GUYS WHO MADE FUN OF YOU.
YES.
LET'S HIT IT BIG SO YOU CAN MAKE YOUR PARENTS PROUD!
YES.
I'LL SEND OVER AT LEAST THREE ASSISTANTS. YOU'LL BE ABLE TO HANDLE TALKING TO THEM, RIGHT? JUST TELL THEM WHAT YOU NEED.
YES.
GO AND BUY THE CHAIRS AND DESKS FOR THOSE THREE ASSISTANTS TOMORROW BY YOURSELF. CALL ME ANYTIME YOU NEED HELP.
YES.
HE'LL BE FINE. I CAN SEE THE FIRE IN HIS EYES.
UM.
LOOM
THANK YOU FOR EVERYTHING.
D-DON'T THANK ME YET!

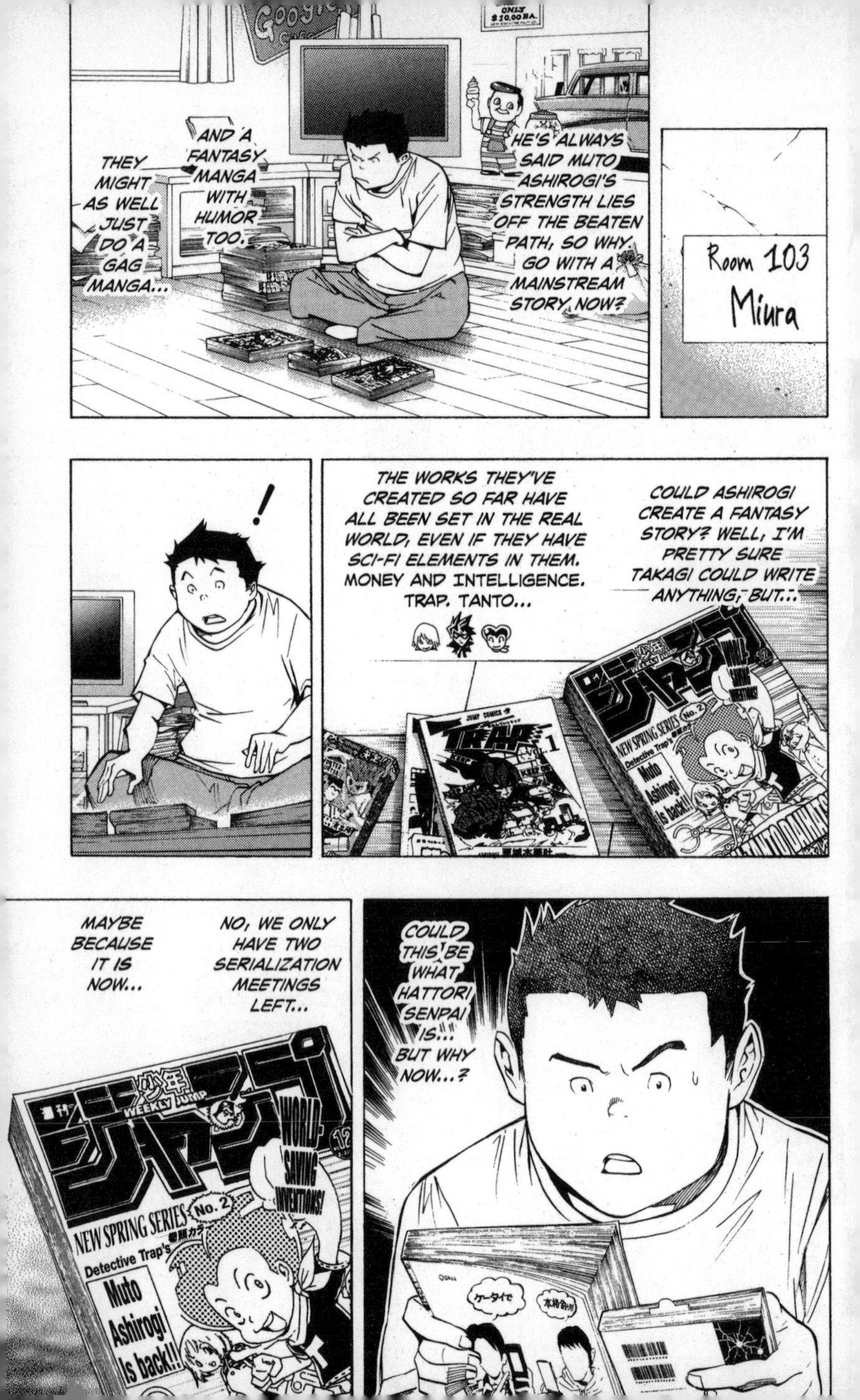
Room 103
Miura
ONLY $10.00 EA.
HE'S ALWAYS SAID MUTO ASHIROGI'S STRENGTH LIES OFF THE BEATEN PATH, SO WHY GO WITH A MAINSTREAM STORY NOW?
AND A FANTASY MANGA WITH HUMOR TOO.
THEY MIGHT AS WELL JUST DO A GAG MANGA...
COULD ASHIROGI CREATE A FANTASY STORY? WELL, I'M PRETTY SURE TAKAGI COULD WRITE ANYTHING, BUT...
THE WORKS THEY'VE CREATED SO FAR HAVE ALL BEEN SET IN THE REAL WORLD, EVEN IF THEY HAVE SCI-FI ELEMENTS IN THEM. MONEY AND INTELLIGENCE. TRAP. TANTO...
WEEKLY JUMP
NEW SPRING SERIES No. 2
Detective Trap's
Muto Ashirogi Is back!!
TRAP
!
COULD THIS BE WHAT HATTORI SENPAI IS...!! BUT WHY NOW...?
NO, WE ONLY HAVE TWO SERIALIZATION MEETINGS LEFT...
MAYBE BECAUSE IT IS NOW...
WEEKLY JUMP
WORLD-SAVING INVENTIONS!
NEW SPRING SERIES No. 2
Detective Trap's
Muto Ashirogi Is back!!

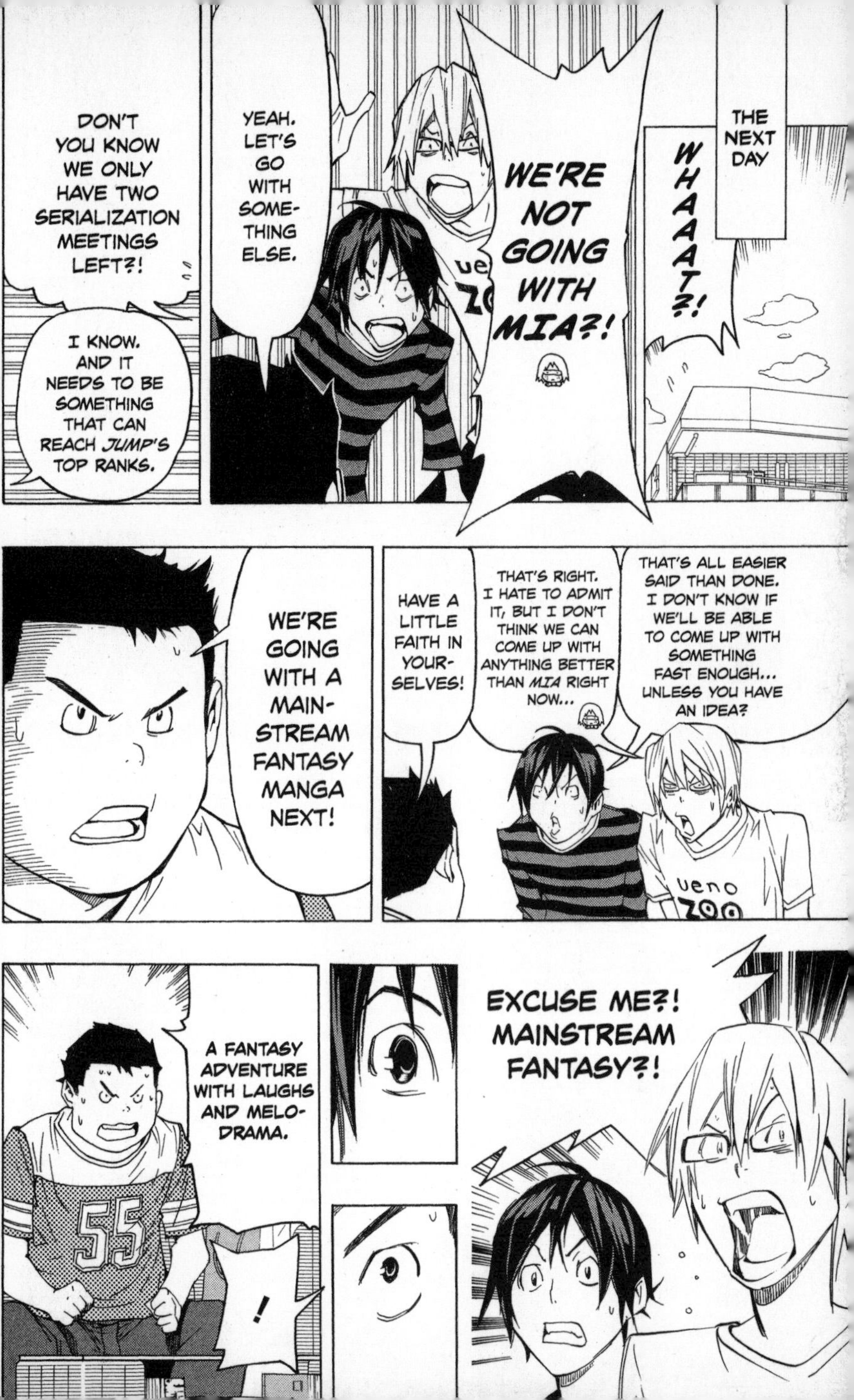
THE NEXT DAY
WHAAAAT?!
WE'RE NOT GOING WITH MIA?!
YEAH. LET'S GO WITH SOMETHING ELSE.
DON'T YOU KNOW WE ONLY HAVE TWO SERIALIZATION MEETINGS LEFT?!
I KNOW. AND IT NEEDS TO BE SOMETHING THAT CAN REACH *JUMP*'S TOP RANKS.
THAT'S ALL EASIER SAID THAN DONE. I DON'T KNOW IF WE'LL BE ABLE TO COME UP WITH SOMETHING FAST ENOUGH... UNLESS YOU HAVE AN IDEA?
THAT'S RIGHT. I HATE TO ADMIT IT, BUT I DON'T THINK WE CAN COME UP WITH ANYTHING BETTER THAN *MIA* RIGHT NOW...
HAVE A LITTLE FAITH IN YOURSELVES!
WE'RE GOING WITH A MAINSTREAM FANTASY MANGA NEXT!
EXCUSE ME?! MAINSTREAM FANTASY?!
!
A FANTASY ADVENTURE WITH LAUGHS AND MELODRAMA.

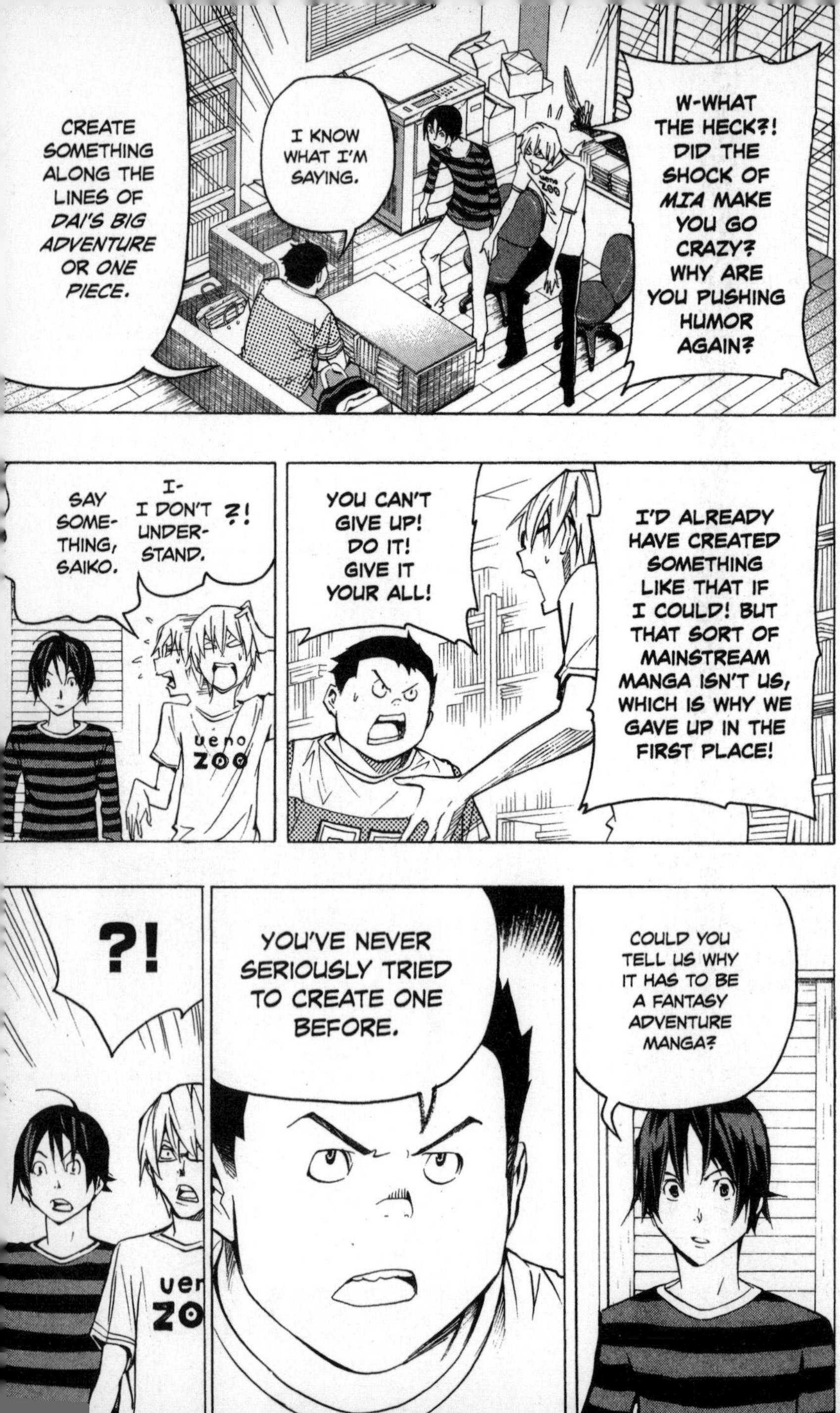
W-WHAT THE HECK?! DID THE SHOCK OF *MIA* MAKE YOU GO CRAZY? WHY ARE YOU PUSHING HUMOR AGAIN?
I KNOW WHAT I'M SAYING.
CREATE SOMETHING ALONG THE LINES OF *DAI'S BIG ADVENTURE* OR *ONE PIECE*.
ueno ZOO
I'D ALREADY HAVE CREATED SOMETHING LIKE THAT IF I COULD! BUT THAT SORT OF MAINSTREAM MANGA ISN'T US, WHICH IS WHY WE GAVE UP IN THE FIRST PLACE!
YOU CAN'T GIVE UP! DO IT! GIVE IT YOUR ALL!
?!
I- I DON'T UNDERSTAND.
SAY SOME-THING, SAIKO.
ueno ZOO
COULD YOU TELL US WHY IT HAS TO BE A FANTASY ADVENTURE MANGA?
YOU'VE NEVER SERIOUSLY TRIED TO CREATE ONE BEFORE.
?!

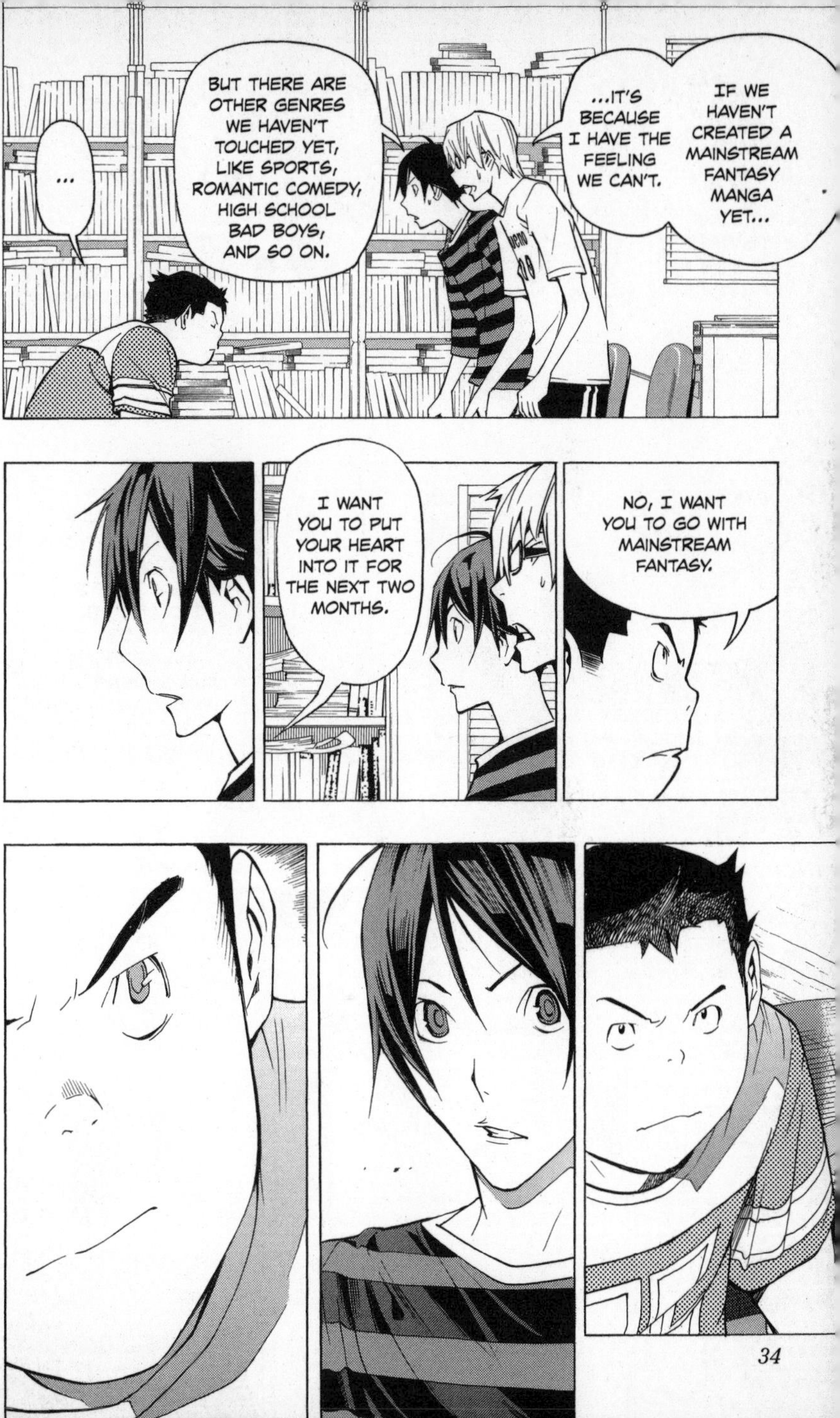
IF WE HAVEN'T CREATED A MAINSTREAM FANTASY MANGA YET...
...IT'S BECAUSE I HAVE THE FEELING WE CAN'T.
BUT THERE ARE OTHER GENRES WE HAVEN'T TOUCHED YET, LIKE SPORTS, ROMANTIC COMEDY, HIGH SCHOOL BAD BOYS, AND SO ON.
...
NO, I WANT YOU TO GO WITH MAINSTREAM FANTASY.
I WANT YOU TO PUT YOUR HEART INTO IT FOR THE NEXT TWO MONTHS.

READ THIS WAY

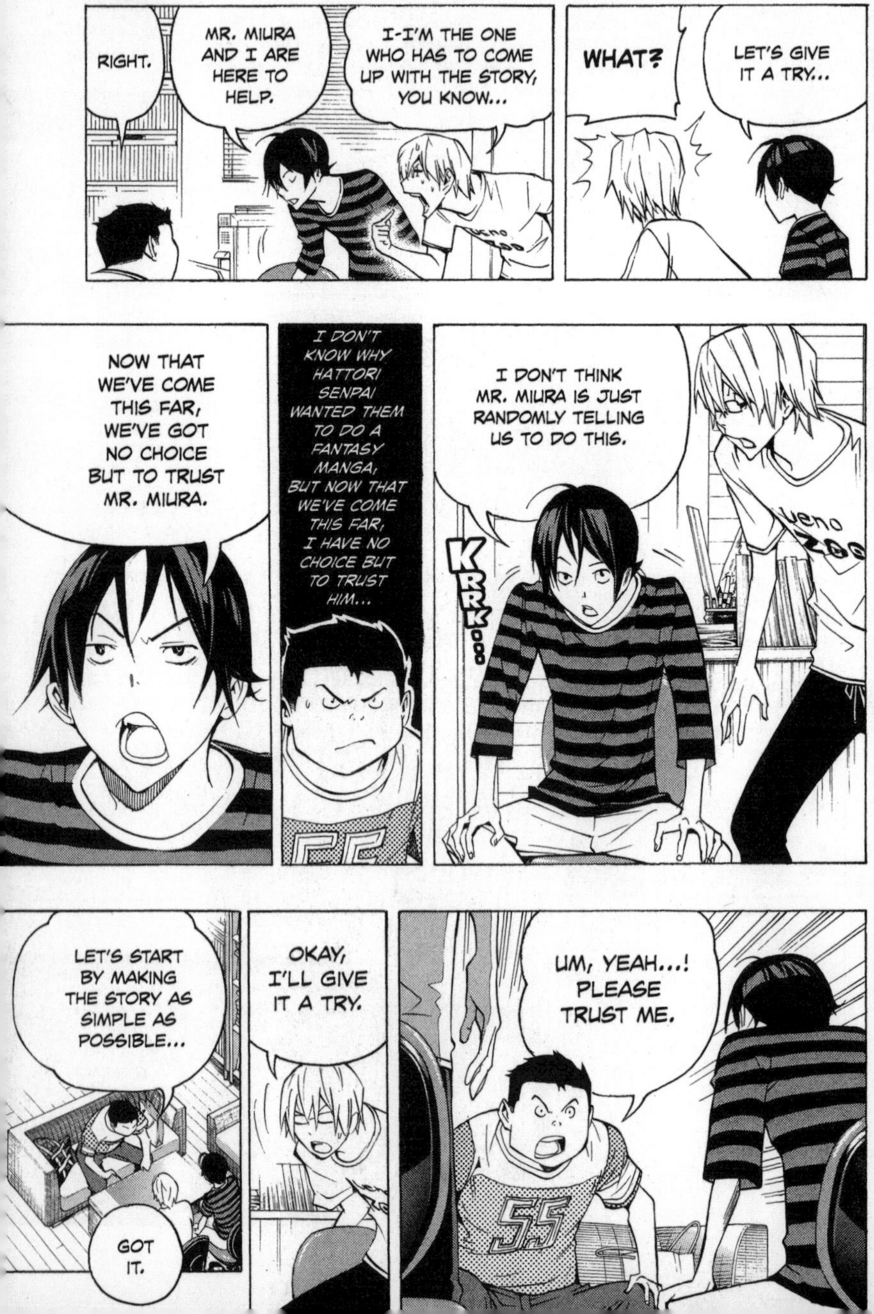
LET'S GIVE IT A TRY...
WHAT?
I-I'M THE ONE WHO HAS TO COME UP WITH THE STORY, YOU KNOW...
MR. MIURA AND I ARE HERE TO HELP.
RIGHT.
I DON'T THINK MR. MIURA IS JUST RANDOMLY TELLING US TO DO THIS.
KRRK
I DON'T KNOW WHY HATTORI SENPAI WANTED THEM TO DO A FANTASY MANGA, BUT NOW THAT WE'VE COME THIS FAR, I HAVE NO CHOICE BUT TO TRUST HIM...
NOW THAT WE'VE COME THIS FAR, WE'VE GOT NO CHOICE BUT TO TRUST MR. MIURA.
UM, YEAH...! PLEASE TRUST ME.
OKAY, I'LL GIVE IT A TRY.
LET'S START BY MAKING THE STORY AS SIMPLE AS POSSIBLE...
GOT IT.

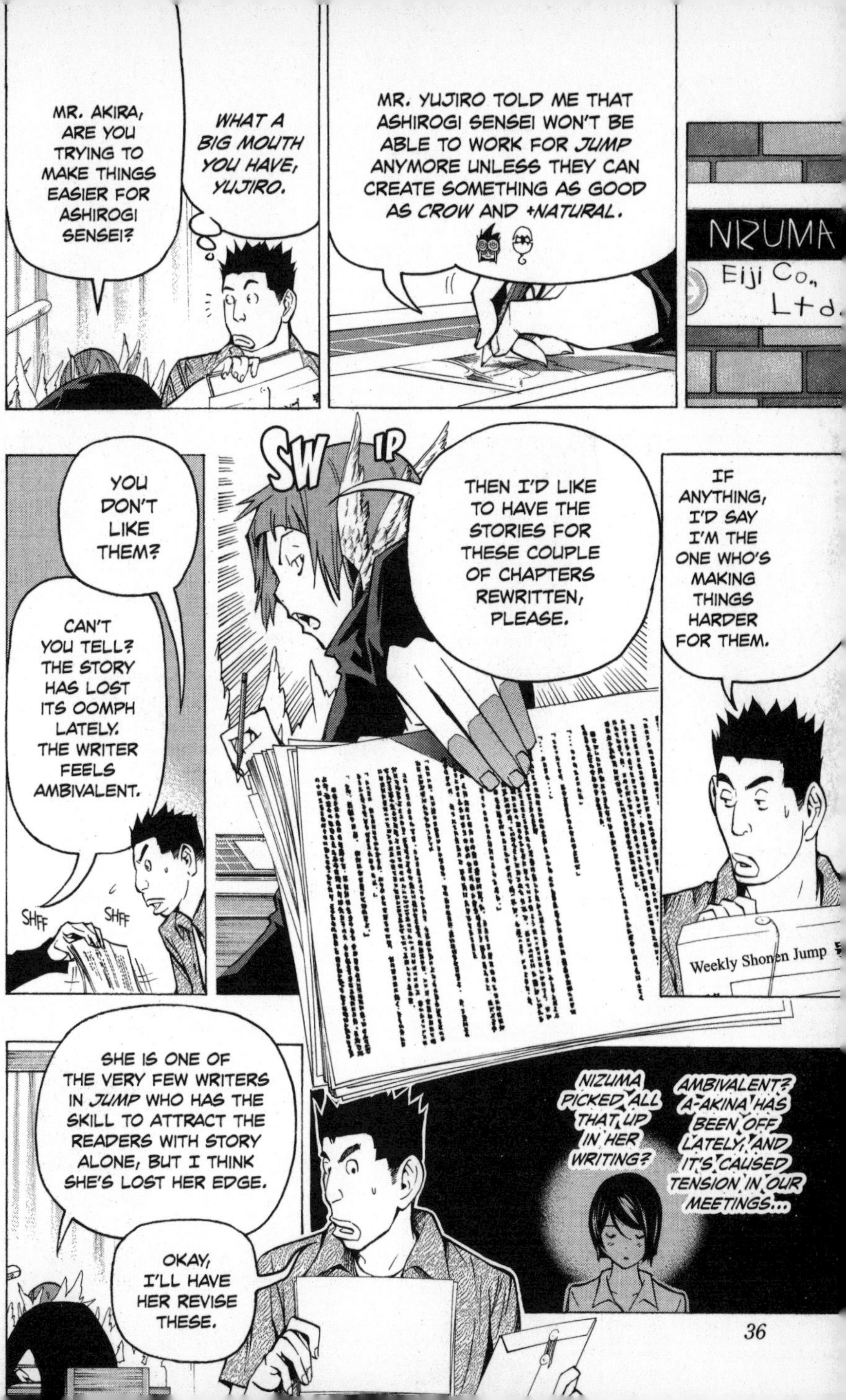
NIZUMA
Eiji Co., Ltd.
MR. YUJIRO TOLD ME THAT ASHIROGI SENSEI WON'T BE ABLE TO WORK FOR *JUMP* ANYMORE UNLESS THEY CAN CREATE SOMETHING AS GOOD AS *CROW* AND *+NATURAL*.
MR. AKIRA, ARE YOU TRYING TO MAKE THINGS EASIER FOR ASHIROGI SENSEI?
WHAT A BIG MOUTH YOU HAVE, YUJIRO.
IF ANYTHING, I'D SAY I'M THE ONE WHO'S MAKING THINGS HARDER FOR THEM.
Weekly Shonen Jump
SWIP
THEN I'D LIKE TO HAVE THE STORIES FOR THESE COUPLE OF CHAPTERS REWRITTEN, PLEASE.
YOU DON'T LIKE THEM?
CAN'T YOU TELL? THE STORY HAS LOST ITS OOMPH LATELY. THE WRITER FEELS AMBIVALENT.
SHFF
SHFF
AMBIVALENT? A-AKINA HAS BEEN OFF LATELY, AND IT'S CAUSED TENSION IN OUR MEETINGS...
NIZUMA PICKED ALL THAT UP IN HER WRITING?
SHE IS ONE OF THE VERY FEW WRITERS IN *JUMP* WHO HAS THE SKILL TO ATTRACT THE READERS WITH STORY ALONE, BUT I THINK SHE'S LOST HER EDGE.
OKAY, I'LL HAVE HER REVISE THESE.

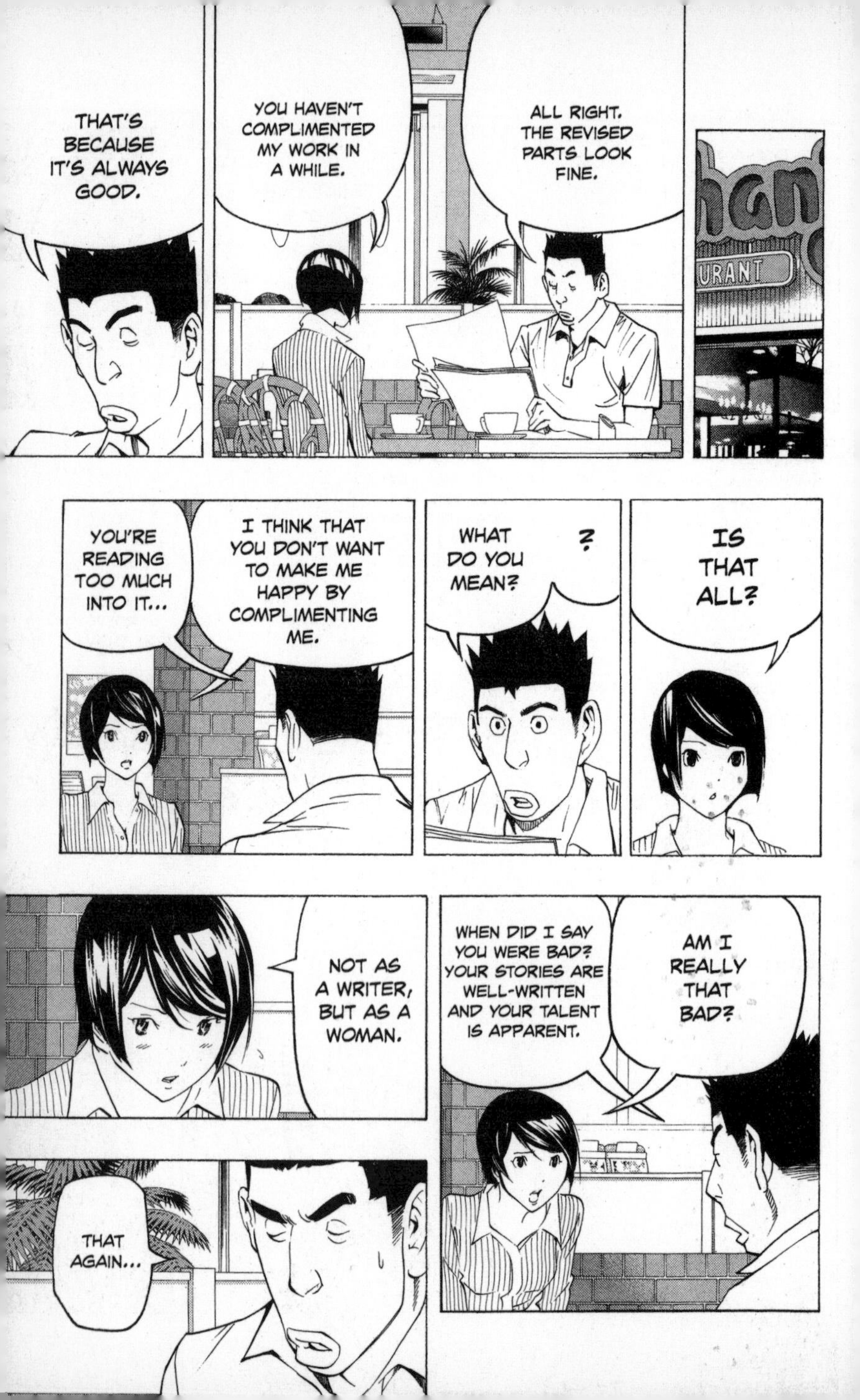
URANT
ALL RIGHT. THE REVISED PARTS LOOK FINE.
YOU HAVEN'T COMPLIMENTED MY WORK IN A WHILE.
THAT'S BECAUSE IT'S ALWAYS GOOD.
IS THAT ALL?
WHAT DO YOU MEAN?
?
I THINK THAT YOU DON'T WANT TO MAKE ME HAPPY BY COMPLIMENTING ME.
YOU'RE READING TOO MUCH INTO IT...
AM I REALLY THAT BAD?
WHEN DID I SAY YOU WERE BAD? YOUR STORIES ARE WELL-WRITTEN AND YOUR TALENT IS APPARENT.
NOT AS A WRITER, BUT AS A WOMAN.
THAT AGAIN...

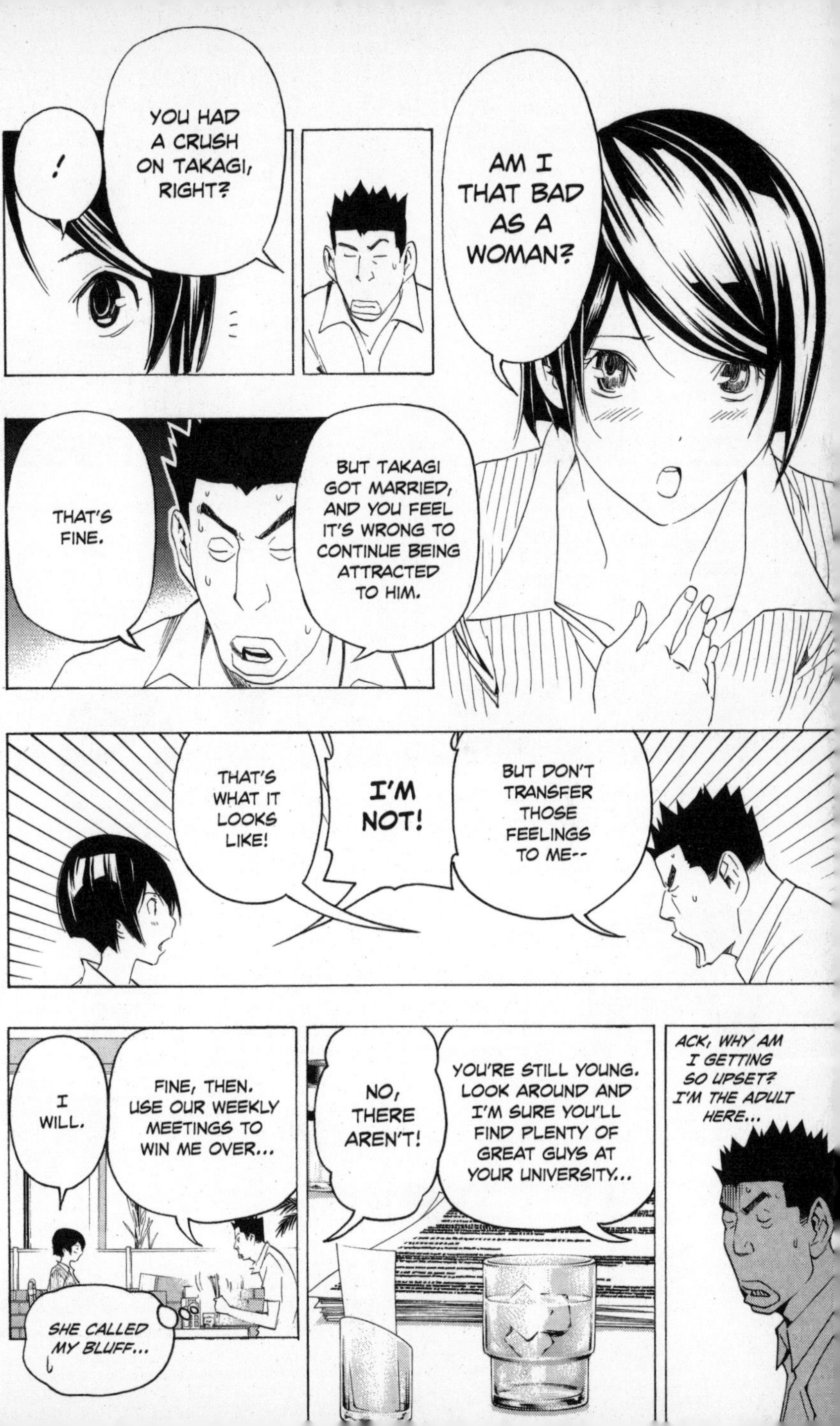
AM I THAT BAD AS A WOMAN?
YOU HAD A CRUSH ON TAKAGI, RIGHT?
!
BUT TAKAGI GOT MARRIED, AND YOU FEEL IT'S WRONG TO CONTINUE BEING ATTRACTED TO HIM.
THAT'S FINE.
BUT DON'T TRANSFER THOSE FEELINGS TO ME--
I'M NOT!
THAT'S WHAT IT LOOKS LIKE!
ACK, WHY AM I GETTING SO UPSET? I'M THE ADULT HERE...
YOU'RE STILL YOUNG. LOOK AROUND AND I'M SURE YOU'LL FIND PLENTY OF GREAT GUYS AT YOUR UNIVERSITY...
NO, THERE AREN'T!
FINE, THEN. USE OUR WEEKLY MEETINGS TO WIN ME OVER...
I WILL.
SHE CALLED MY BLUFF...

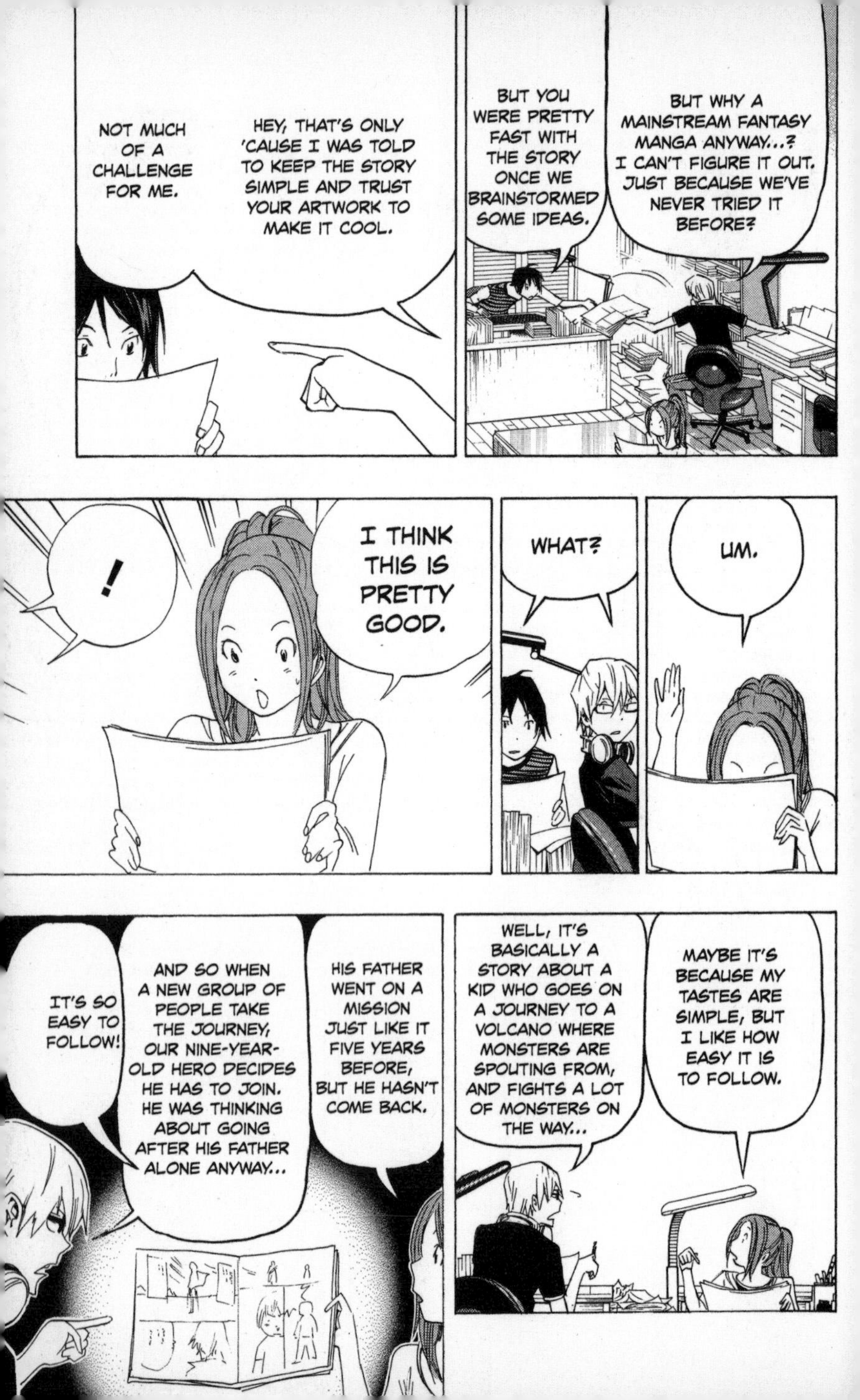
BUT WHY A MAINSTREAM FANTASY MANGA ANYWAY...? I CAN'T FIGURE IT OUT. JUST BECAUSE WE'VE NEVER TRIED IT BEFORE?
BUT YOU WERE PRETTY FAST WITH THE STORY ONCE WE BRAINSTORMED SOME IDEAS.
HEY, THAT'S ONLY 'CAUSE I WAS TOLD TO KEEP THE STORY SIMPLE AND TRUST YOUR ARTWORK TO MAKE IT COOL.
NOT MUCH OF A CHALLENGE FOR ME.
UM.
WHAT?
I THINK THIS IS PRETTY GOOD.
!
MAYBE IT'S BECAUSE MY TASTES ARE SIMPLE, BUT I LIKE HOW EASY IT IS TO FOLLOW.
WELL, IT'S BASICALLY A STORY ABOUT A KID WHO GOES ON A JOURNEY TO A VOLCANO WHERE MONSTERS ARE SPOUTING FROM, AND FIGHTS A LOT OF MONSTERS ON THE WAY...
HIS FATHER WENT ON A MISSION JUST LIKE IT FIVE YEARS BEFORE, BUT HE HASN'T COME BACK.
AND SO WHEN A NEW GROUP OF PEOPLE TAKE THE JOURNEY, OUR NINE-YEAR-OLD HERO DECIDES HE HAS TO JOIN. HE WAS THINKING ABOUT GOING AFTER HIS FATHER ALONE ANYWAY...
IT'S SO EASY TO FOLLOW!

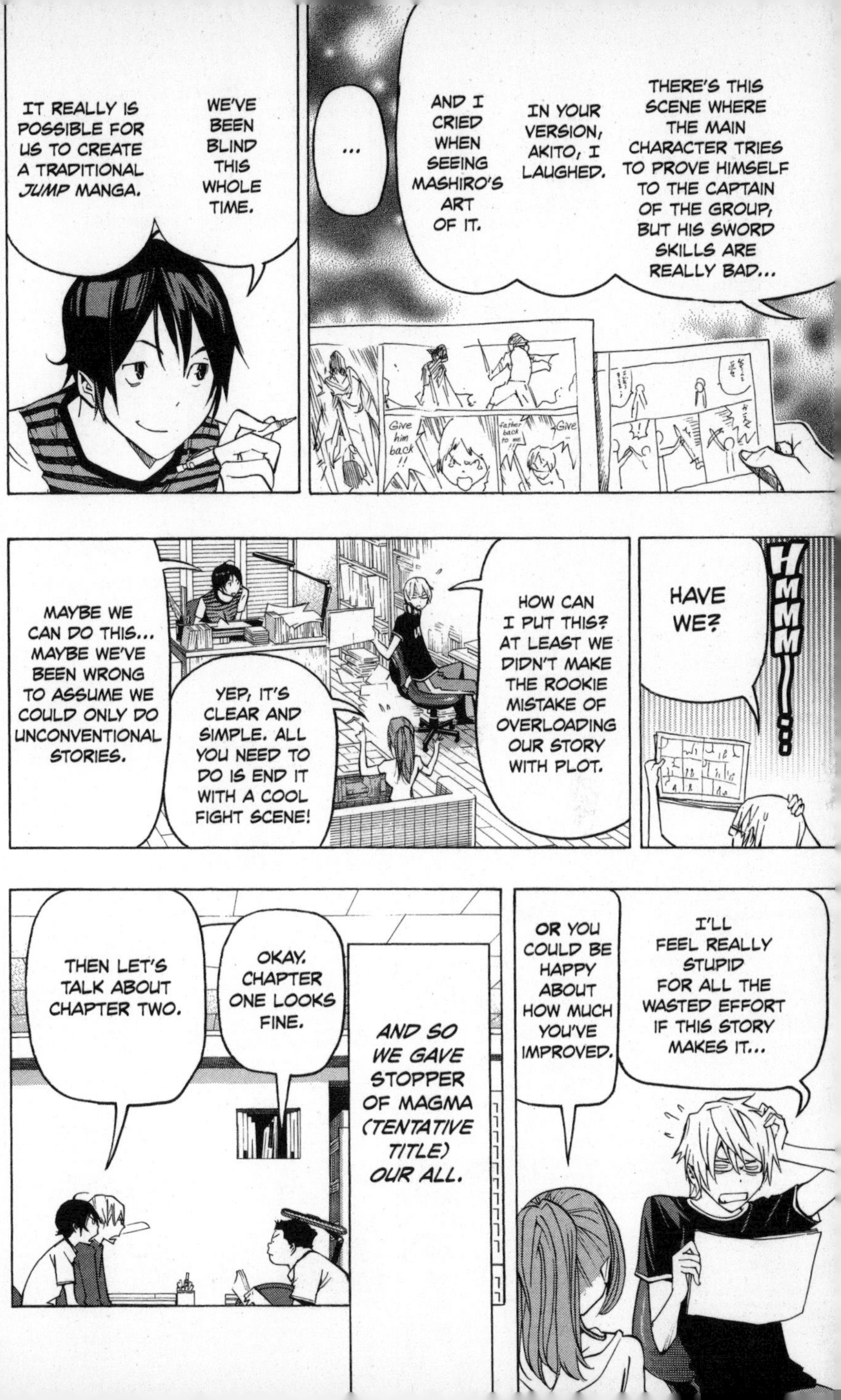
THERE'S THIS SCENE WHERE THE MAIN CHARACTER TRIES TO PROVE HIMSELF TO THE CAPTAIN OF THE GROUP, BUT HIS SWORD SKILLS ARE REALLY BAD...
IN YOUR VERSION, AKITO, I LAUGHED.
AND I CRIED WHEN SEEING MASHIRO'S ART OF IT.
...
Give him back!!
father back to me!!
Give
WE'VE BEEN BLIND THIS WHOLE TIME.
IT REALLY IS POSSIBLE FOR US TO CREATE A TRADITIONAL *JUMP* MANGA.
HMMM...
HAVE WE?
HOW CAN I PUT THIS? AT LEAST WE DIDN'T MAKE THE ROOKIE MISTAKE OF OVERLOADING OUR STORY WITH PLOT.
YEP, IT'S CLEAR AND SIMPLE. ALL YOU NEED TO DO IS END IT WITH A COOL FIGHT SCENE!
MAYBE WE CAN DO THIS... MAYBE WE'VE BEEN WRONG TO ASSUME WE COULD ONLY DO UNCONVENTIONAL STORIES.
I'LL FEEL REALLY STUPID FOR ALL THE WASTED EFFORT IF THIS STORY MAKES IT...
OR YOU COULD BE HAPPY ABOUT HOW MUCH YOU'VE IMPROVED.
AND SO WE GAVE STOPPER OF MAGMA (TENTATIVE TITLE) OUR ALL.
OKAY. CHAPTER ONE LOOKS FINE.
THEN LET'S TALK ABOUT CHAPTER TWO.

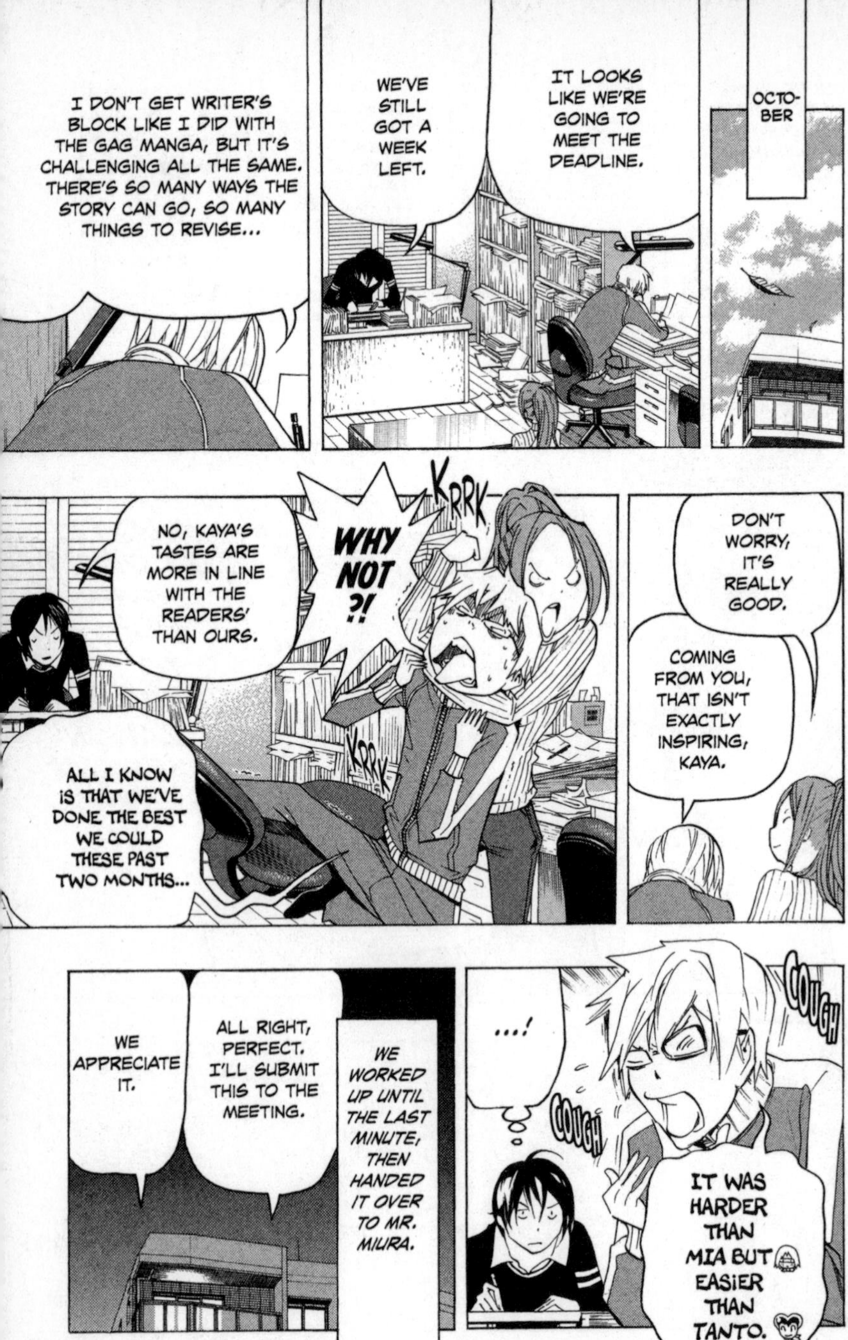
OCTOBER
IT LOOKS LIKE WE'RE GOING TO MEET THE DEADLINE.
WE'VE STILL GOT A WEEK LEFT.
I DON'T GET WRITER'S BLOCK LIKE I DID WITH THE GAG MANGA, BUT IT'S CHALLENGING ALL THE SAME. THERE'S SO MANY WAYS THE STORY CAN GO, SO MANY THINGS TO REVISE...
DON'T WORRY, IT'S REALLY GOOD.
COMING FROM YOU, THAT ISN'T EXACTLY INSPIRING, KAYA.
NO, KAYA'S TASTES ARE MORE IN LINE WITH THE READERS' THAN OURS.
WHY NOT?!
KRRK
KRRK
ALL I KNOW IS THAT WE'VE DONE THE BEST WE COULD THESE PAST TWO MONTHS...
COUGH
...!
COUGH
IT WAS HARDER THAN MIA BUT EASIER THAN TANTO.
WE WORKED UP UNTIL THE LAST MINUTE, THEN HANDED IT OVER TO MR. MIURA.
ALL RIGHT, PERFECT. I'LL SUBMIT THIS TO THE MEETING.
WE APPRECIATE IT.

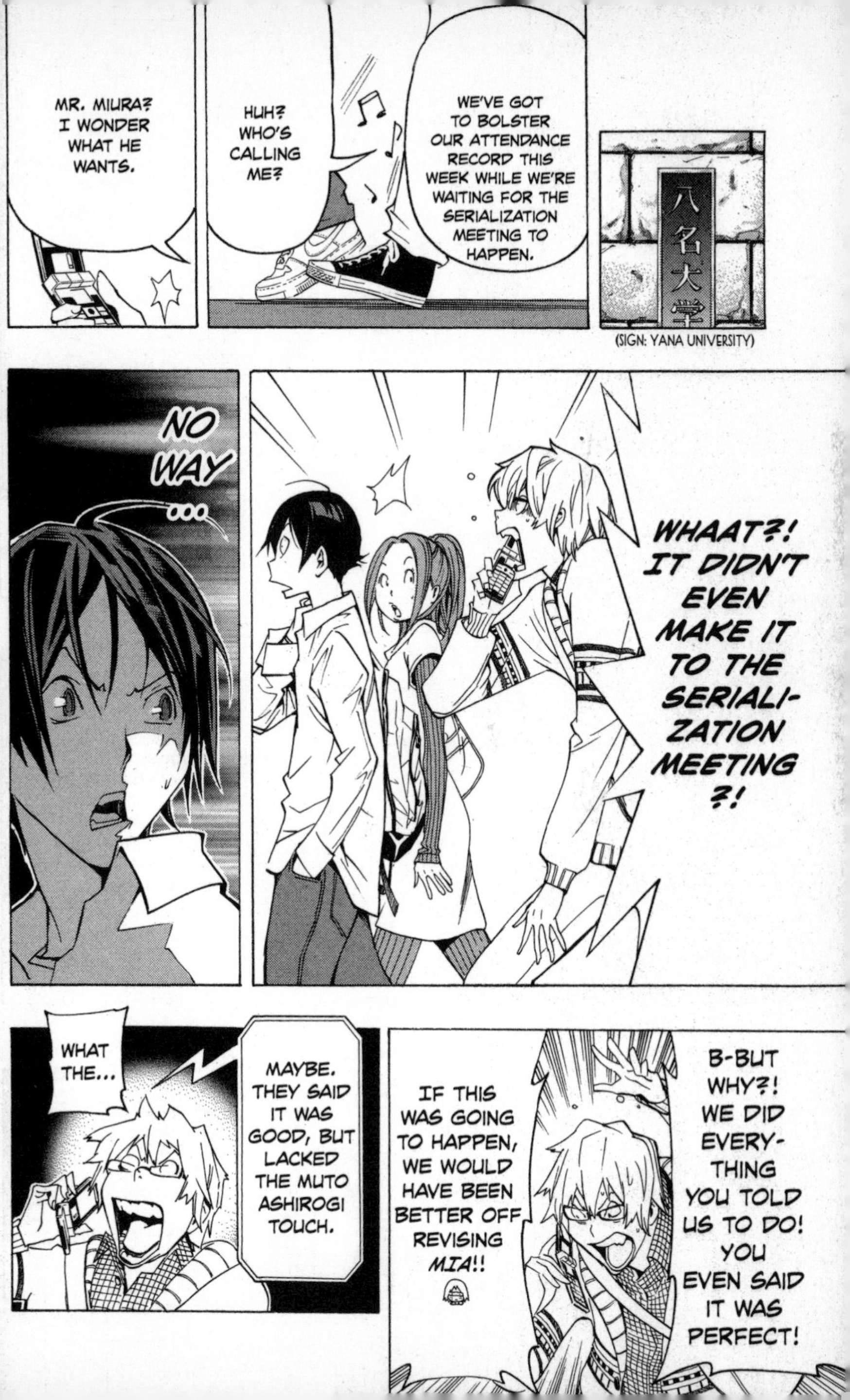
八名大学
(SIGN: YANA UNIVERSITY)
WE'VE GOT TO BOLSTER OUR ATTENDANCE RECORD THIS WEEK WHILE WE'RE WAITING FOR THE SERIALIZATION MEETING TO HAPPEN.
HUH? WHO'S CALLING ME?
MR. MIURA? I WONDER WHAT HE WANTS.
WHAAT?! IT DIDN'T EVEN MAKE IT TO THE SERIALI-ZATION MEETING?!
NO WAY...
B-BUT WHY?! WE DID EVERY-THING YOU TOLD US TO DO! YOU EVEN SAID IT WAS PERFECT!
IF THIS WAS GOING TO HAPPEN, WE WOULD HAVE BEEN BETTER OFF REVISING *MIA*!!
MAYBE. THEY SAID IT WAS GOOD, BUT LACKED THE MUTO ASHIROGI TOUCH.
WHAT THE...

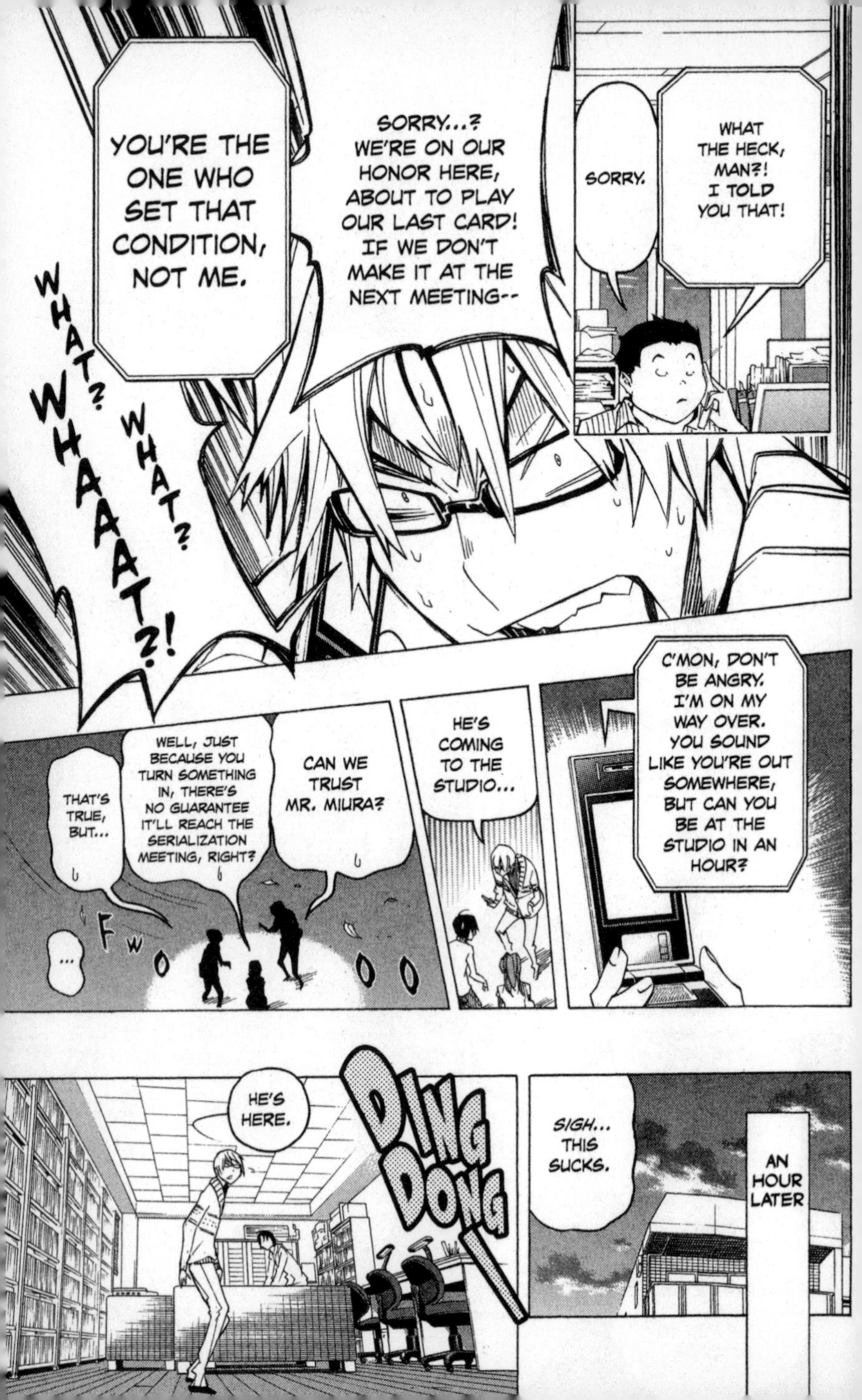
WHAT THE HECK, MAN?! I TOLD YOU THAT!
SORRY.
SORRY...? WE'RE ON OUR HONOR HERE, ABOUT TO PLAY OUR LAST CARD! IF WE DON'T MAKE IT AT THE NEXT MEETING--
YOU'RE THE ONE WHO SET THAT CONDITION, NOT ME.
WHAT? WHAT? WHAAAAT?!
C'MON, DON'T BE ANGRY. I'M ON MY WAY OVER. YOU SOUND LIKE YOU'RE OUT SOMEWHERE, BUT CAN YOU BE AT THE STUDIO IN AN HOUR?
HE'S COMING TO THE STUDIO...
CAN WE TRUST MR. MIURA?
WELL, JUST BECAUSE YOU TURN SOMETHING IN, THERE'S NO GUARANTEE IT'LL REACH THE SERIALIZATION MEETING, RIGHT?
THAT'S TRUE, BUT...
...
FWOOOO
AN HOUR LATER
SIGH... THIS SUCKS.
DING DONG
HE'S HERE.

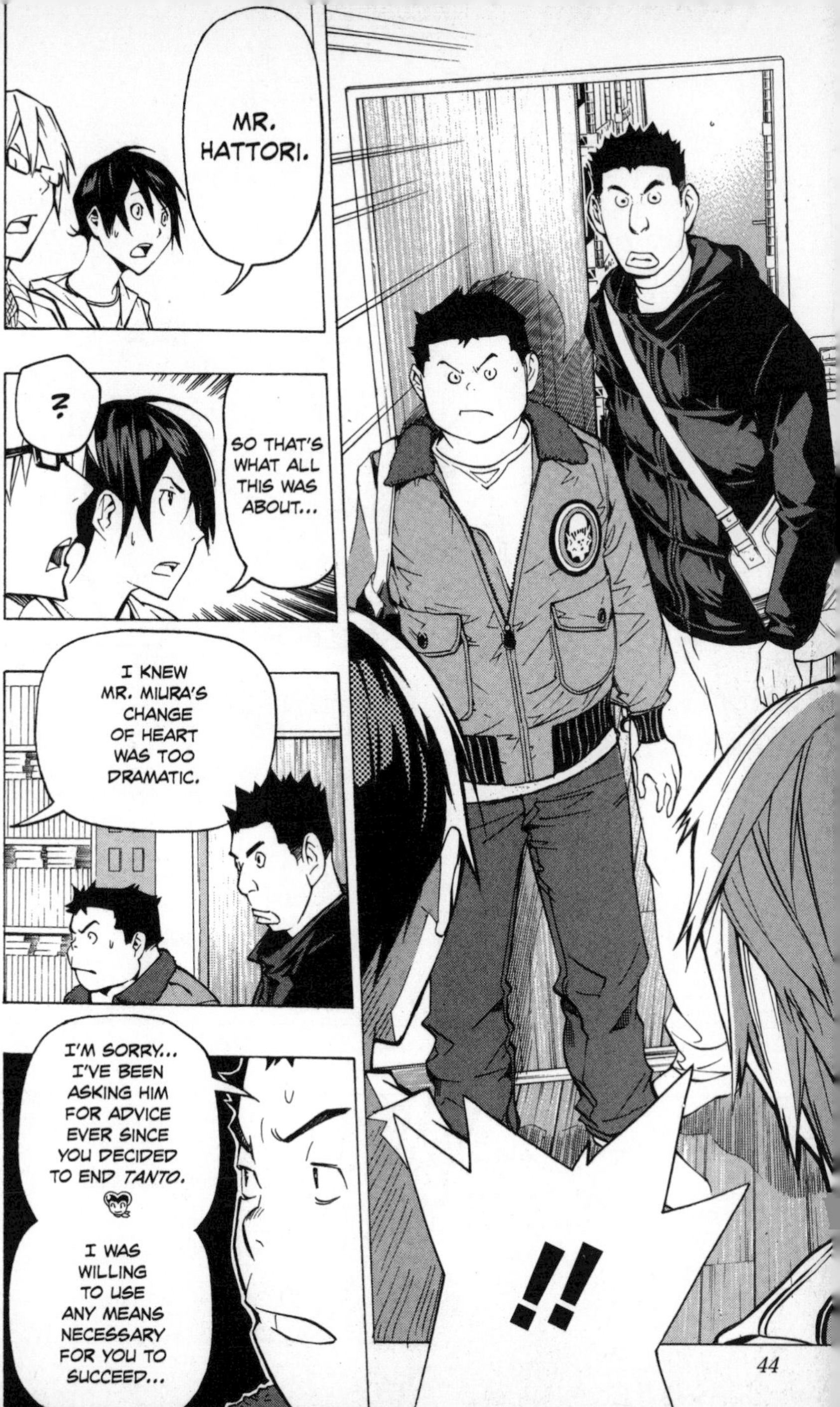
!!
MR. HATTORI.
?
SO THAT'S WHAT ALL THIS WAS ABOUT...
I KNEW MR. MIURA'S CHANGE OF HEART WAS TOO DRAMATIC.
I'M SORRY... I'VE BEEN ASKING HIM FOR ADVICE EVER SINCE YOU DECIDED TO END *TANTO*.
I WAS WILLING TO USE ANY MEANS NECESSARY FOR YOU TO SUCCEED...

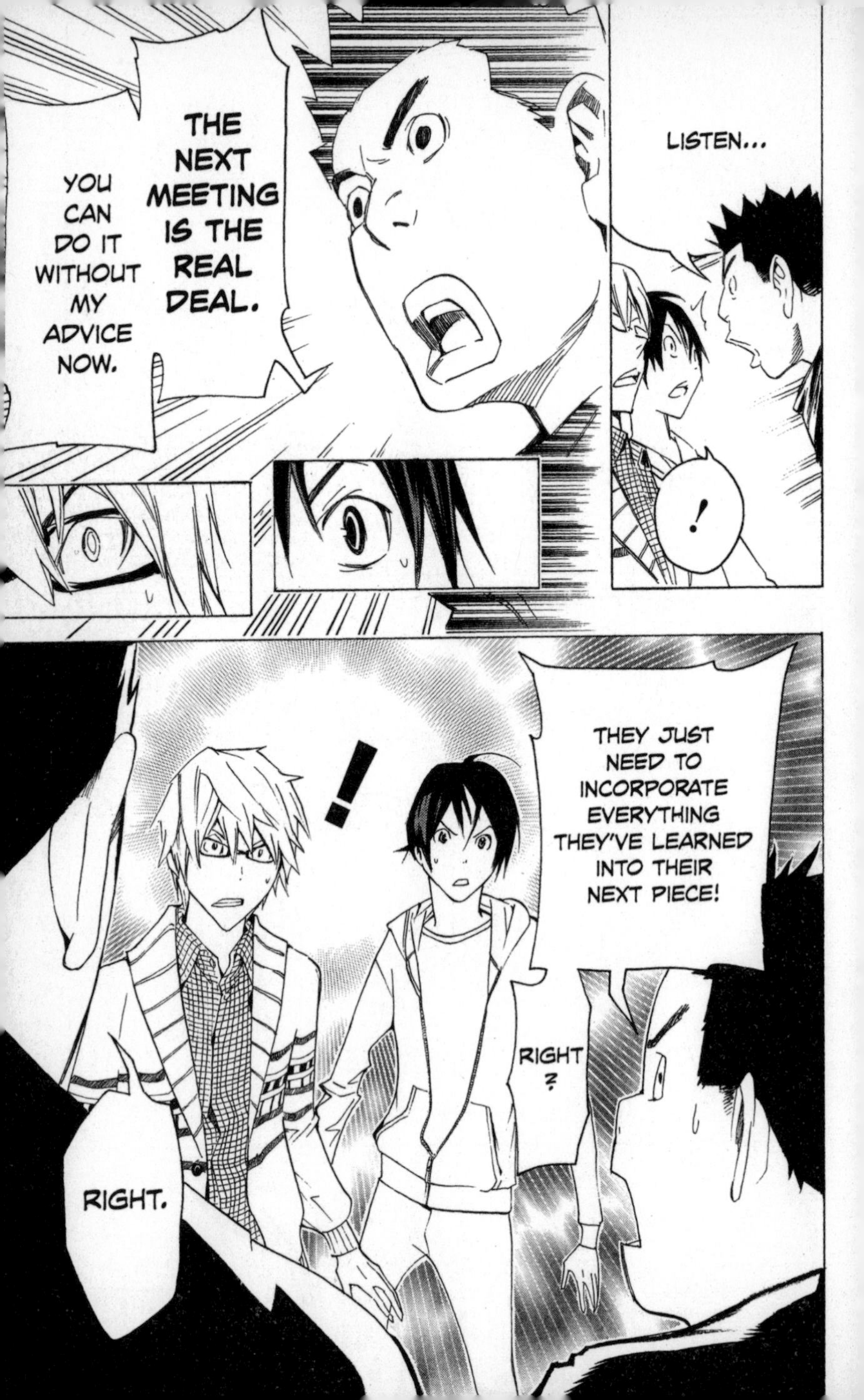
LISTEN...
!
THE NEXT MEETING IS THE REAL DEAL.
YOU CAN DO IT WITHOUT MY ADVICE NOW.
THEY JUST NEED TO INCORPORATE EVERYTHING THEY'VE LEARNED INTO THEIR NEXT PIECE!
!
RIGHT?
RIGHT.

OHBA'S STORYBOARD

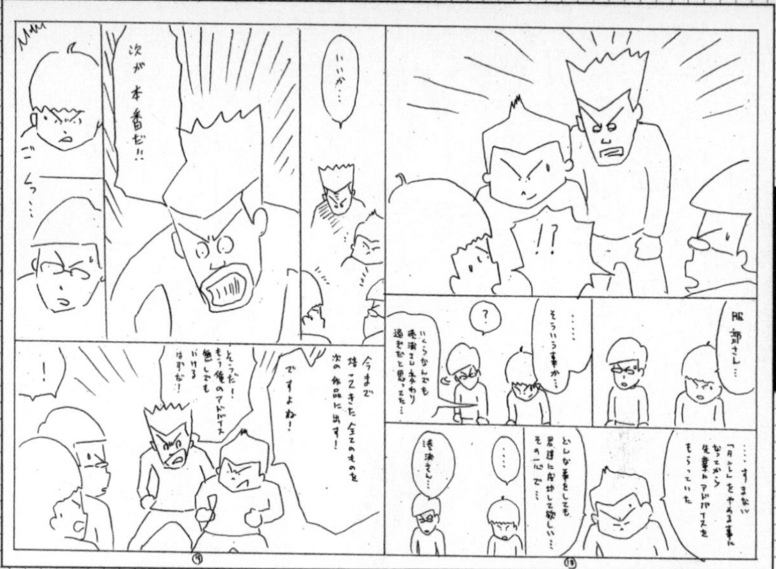
!?
服部さん…
そういう事か…
……
？
いくらなんでも港浦さん来すぎだと思ってた…
…すまない 「月ツル」をやめる事になってから先輩にアドバイスをもらっていた
どんな事をしても君達に成功して欲しい… その一心で…
……
港浦さん…
いいか…
次が本番だ!!
ごくっ…
今まで培ってきた全てのものを次の作品に出す!
ですよね!
そうだ! もう俺のアドバイス無しでもいけるはずだ!
!

OBATA'S STORYBOARD

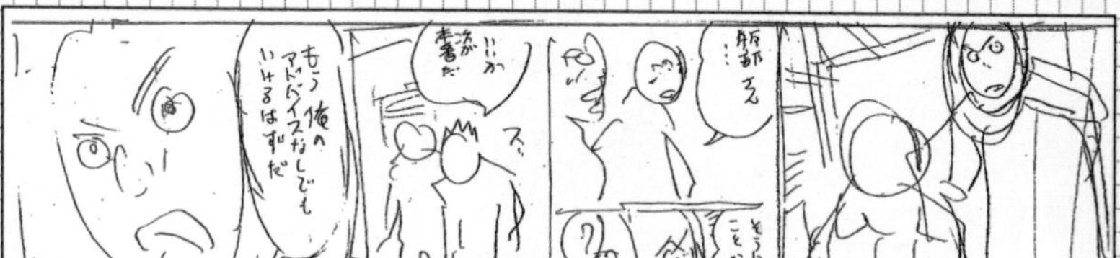
服部さん…
そういうことか…
？
いくらなんでも港浦さん来すぎだと思ってた
…すまない 「月ツル」をやめる事になってから先輩にアドバイスをもらっていた
どんな事をしても君達に成功して欲しい… その一心で…!
いいか 次が本番だ
!
今まで培ってきた全てのものを次の作品に出す!!
ですね
そうだ!
もう俺のアドバイスなしでもいけるはずだ

COMPLETE!

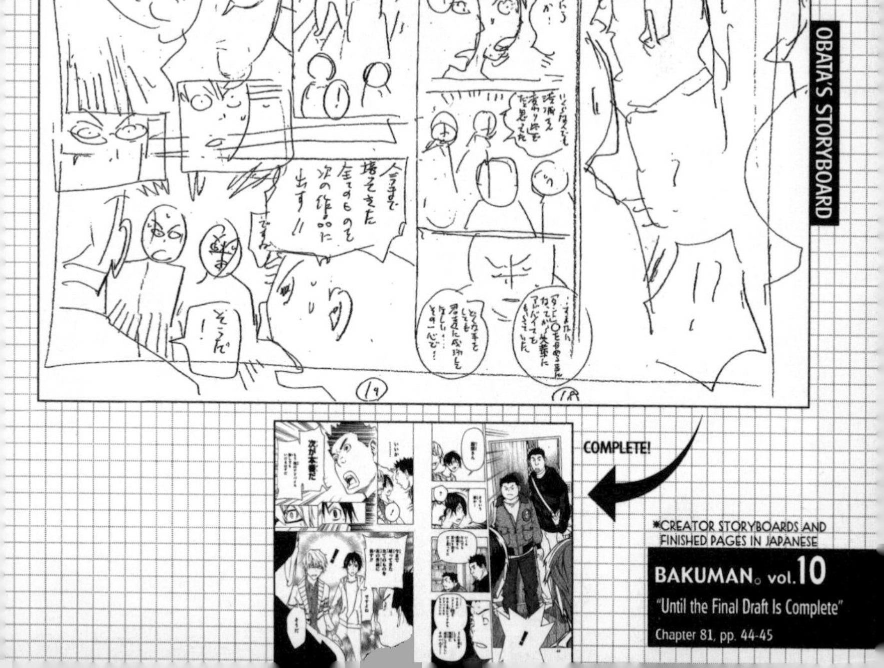

*CREATOR STORYBOARDS AND FINISHED PAGES IN JAPANESE

BAKUMAN。 vol.10

"Until the Final Draft Is Complete"

Chapter 81, pp. 44-45

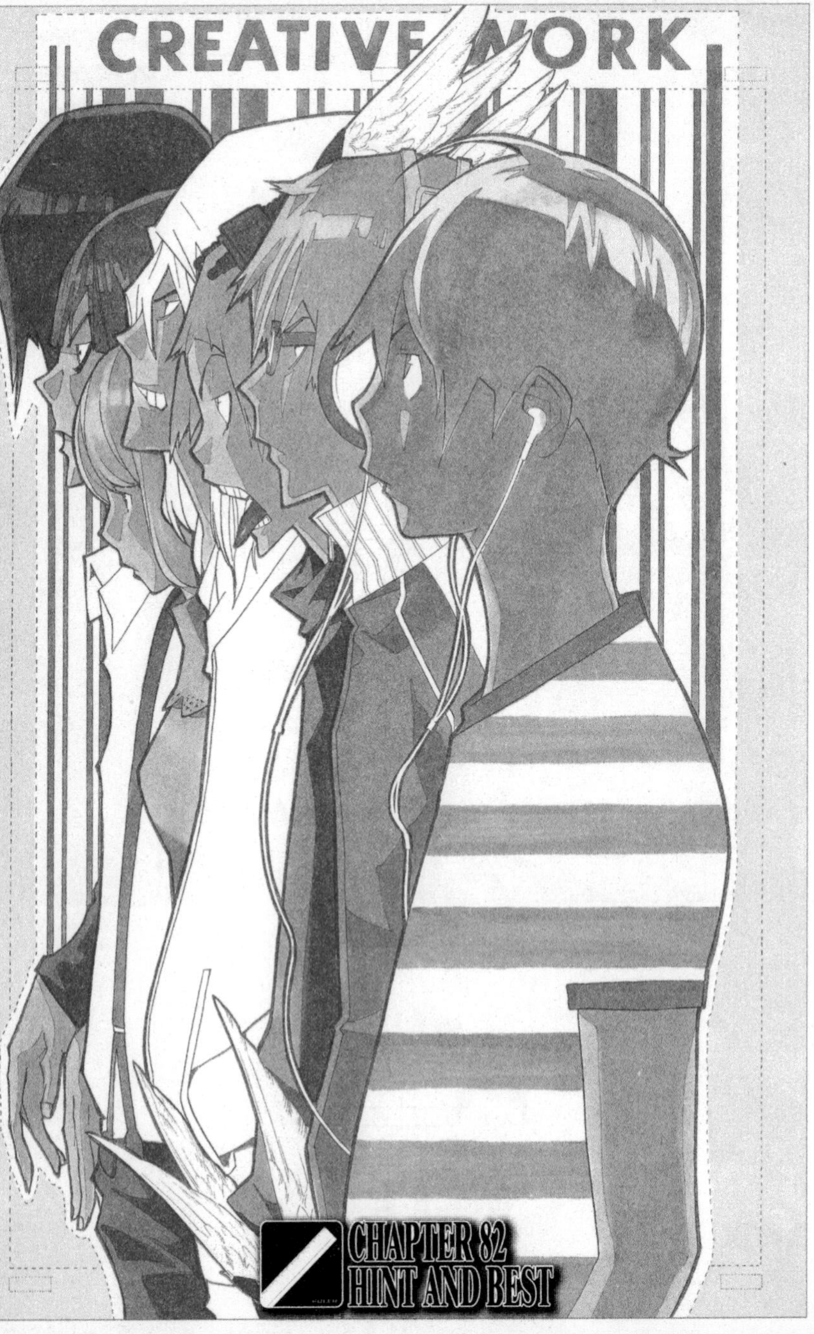
CREATIVE WORK

CHAPTER 82
HINT AND BEST

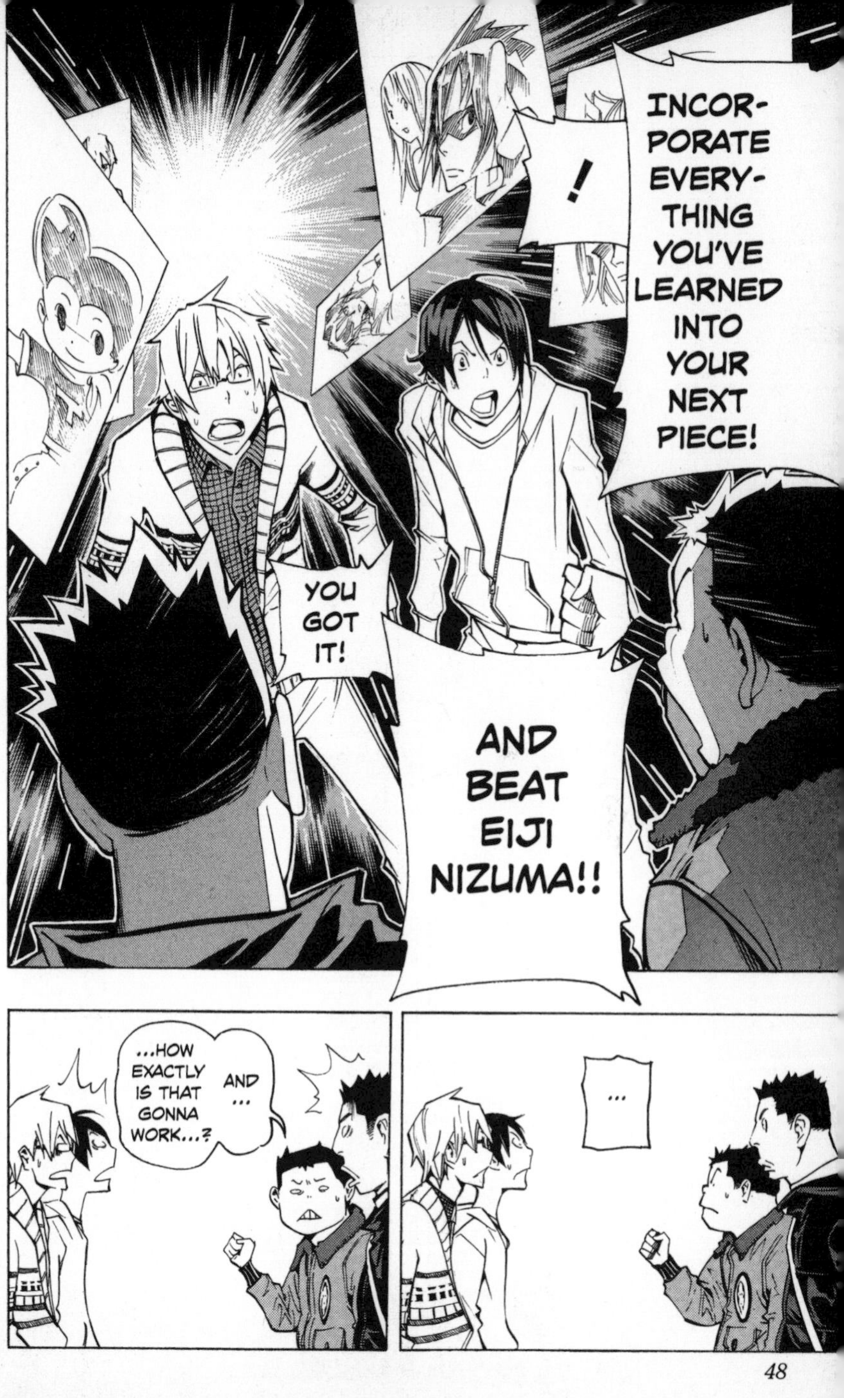
INCORPORATE EVERYTHING YOU'VE LEARNED INTO YOUR NEXT PIECE!
!
AND BEAT EIJI NIZUMA!!
YOU GOT IT!
...
AND ...
...HOW EXACTLY IS THAT GONNA WORK...?

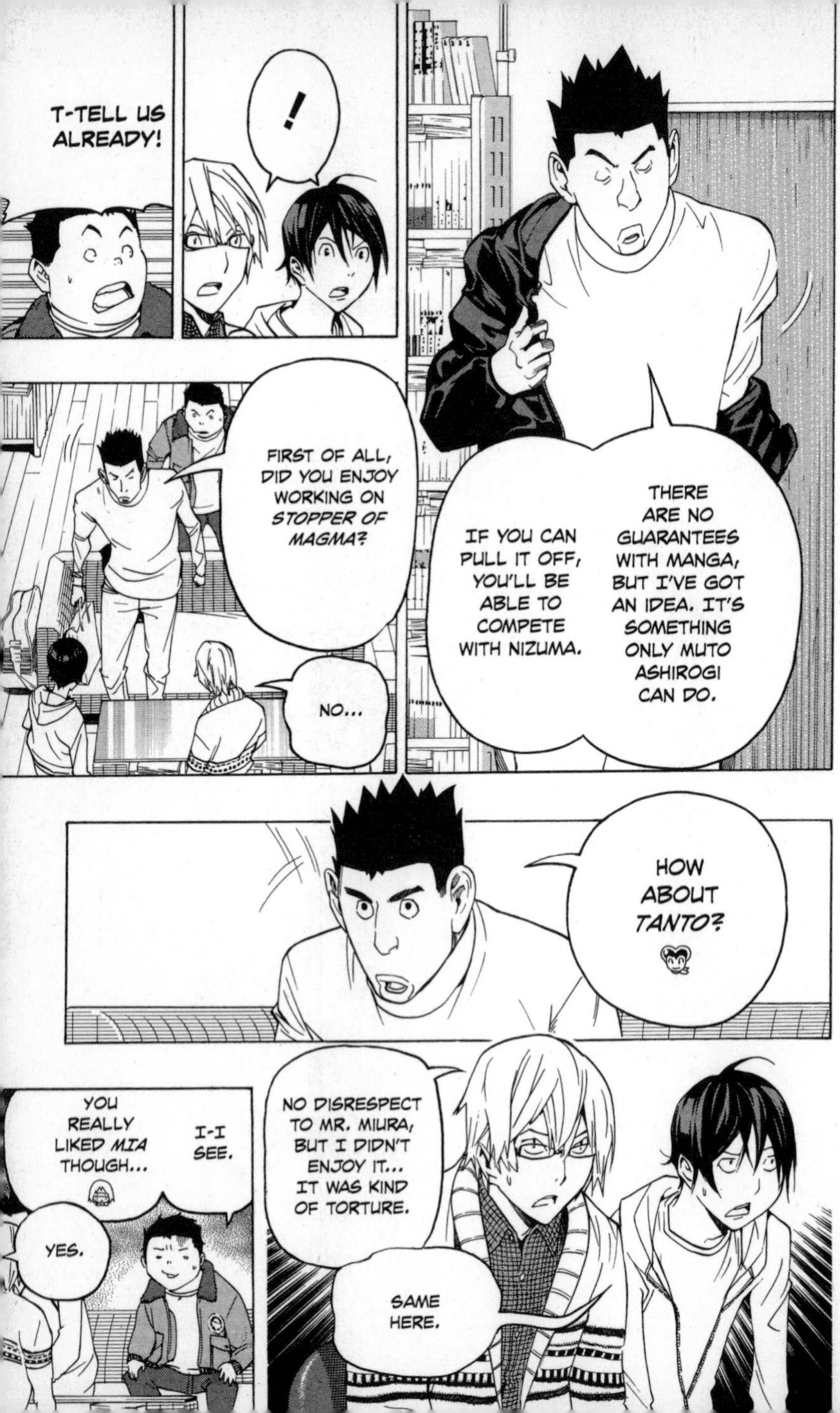
THERE ARE NO GUARANTEES WITH MANGA, BUT I'VE GOT AN IDEA. IT'S SOMETHING ONLY MUTO ASHIROGI CAN DO. IF YOU CAN PULL IT OFF, YOU'LL BE ABLE TO COMPETE WITH NIZUMA.
!
T-TELL US ALREADY!
FIRST OF ALL, DID YOU ENJOY WORKING ON *STOPPER OF MAGMA*?
NO...
HOW ABOUT *TANTO*?
NO DISRESPECT TO MR. MIURA, BUT I DIDN'T ENJOY IT... IT WAS KIND OF TORTURE.
SAME HERE.
I-I SEE.
YOU REALLY LIKED *MIA* THOUGH...
YES.

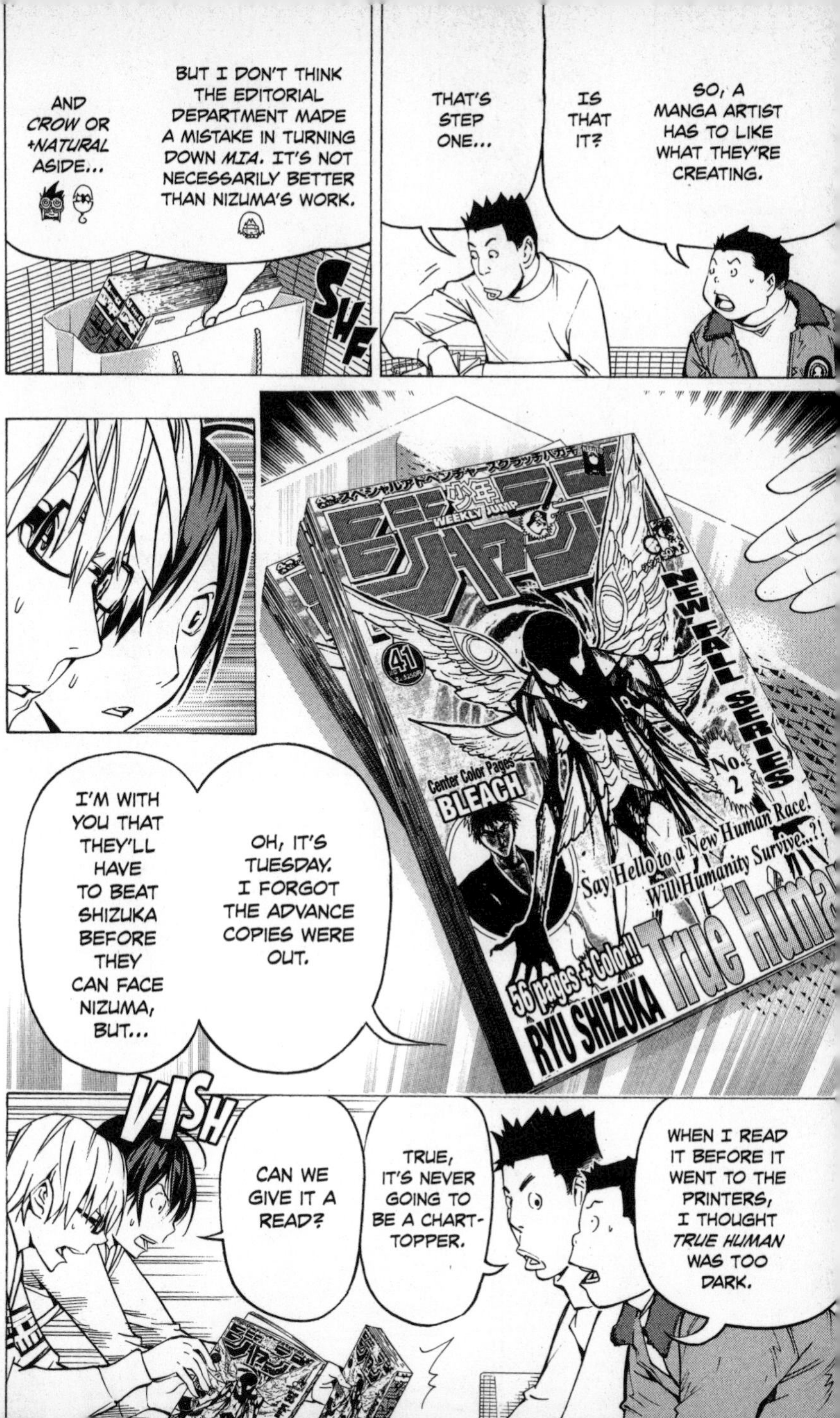

SO, A MANGA ARTIST HAS TO LIKE WHAT THEY'RE CREATING.
IS THAT IT?
THAT'S STEP ONE...
BUT I DON'T THINK THE EDITORIAL DEPARTMENT MADE A MISTAKE IN TURNING DOWN *MIA*. IT'S NOT NECESSARILY BETTER THAN NIZUMA'S WORK.
AND *CROW* OR *+NATURAL* ASIDE...
SHF
WEEKLY JUMP
41
NEW FALL SERIES
No. 2
Center Color Pages
BLEACH
Say Hello to a New Human Race!
Will Humanity Survive...?!
56 pages + Color!!
RYU SHIZUKA
I'M WITH YOU THAT THEY'LL HAVE TO BEAT SHIZUKA BEFORE THEY CAN FACE NIZUMA, BUT...
OH, IT'S TUESDAY. I FORGOT THE ADVANCE COPIES WERE OUT.
WHEN I READ IT BEFORE IT WENT TO THE PRINTERS, I THOUGHT *TRUE HUMAN* WAS TOO DARK.
TRUE, IT'S NEVER GOING TO BE A CHART-TOPPER.
CAN WE GIVE IT A READ?
VISH

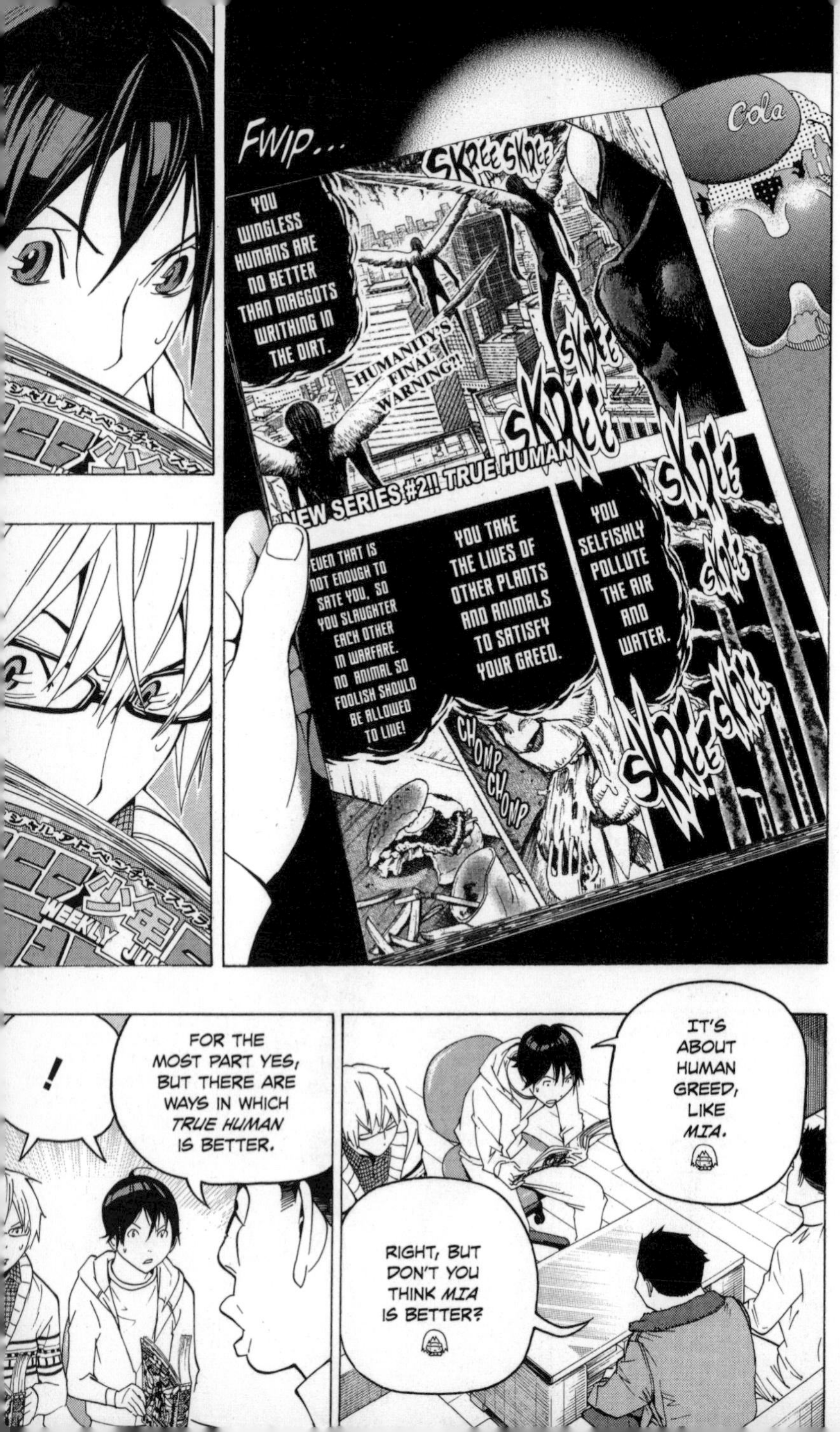
FWIP...
YOU WINGLESS HUMANS ARE NO BETTER THAN MAGGOTS WRITHING IN THE DIRT.
HUMANITY'S FINAL WARNING?!
SKREE SKREE
SKREE
SKREE
NEW SERIES #2!! TRUE HUMAN
SKREE
YOU SELFISHLY POLLUTE THE AIR AND WATER.
YOU TAKE THE LIVES OF OTHER PLANTS AND ANIMALS TO SATISFY YOUR GREED.
EVEN THAT IS NOT ENOUGH TO SATE YOU, SO YOU SLAUGHTER EACH OTHER IN WARFARE. NO ANIMAL SO FOOLISH SHOULD BE ALLOWED TO LIVE!
SKREE
SKREE SKREE
CHOMP CHOMP
IT'S ABOUT HUMAN GREED, LIKE MIA.
RIGHT, BUT DON'T YOU THINK MIA IS BETTER?
FOR THE MOST PART YES, BUT THERE ARE WAYS IN WHICH TRUE HUMAN IS BETTER.
!

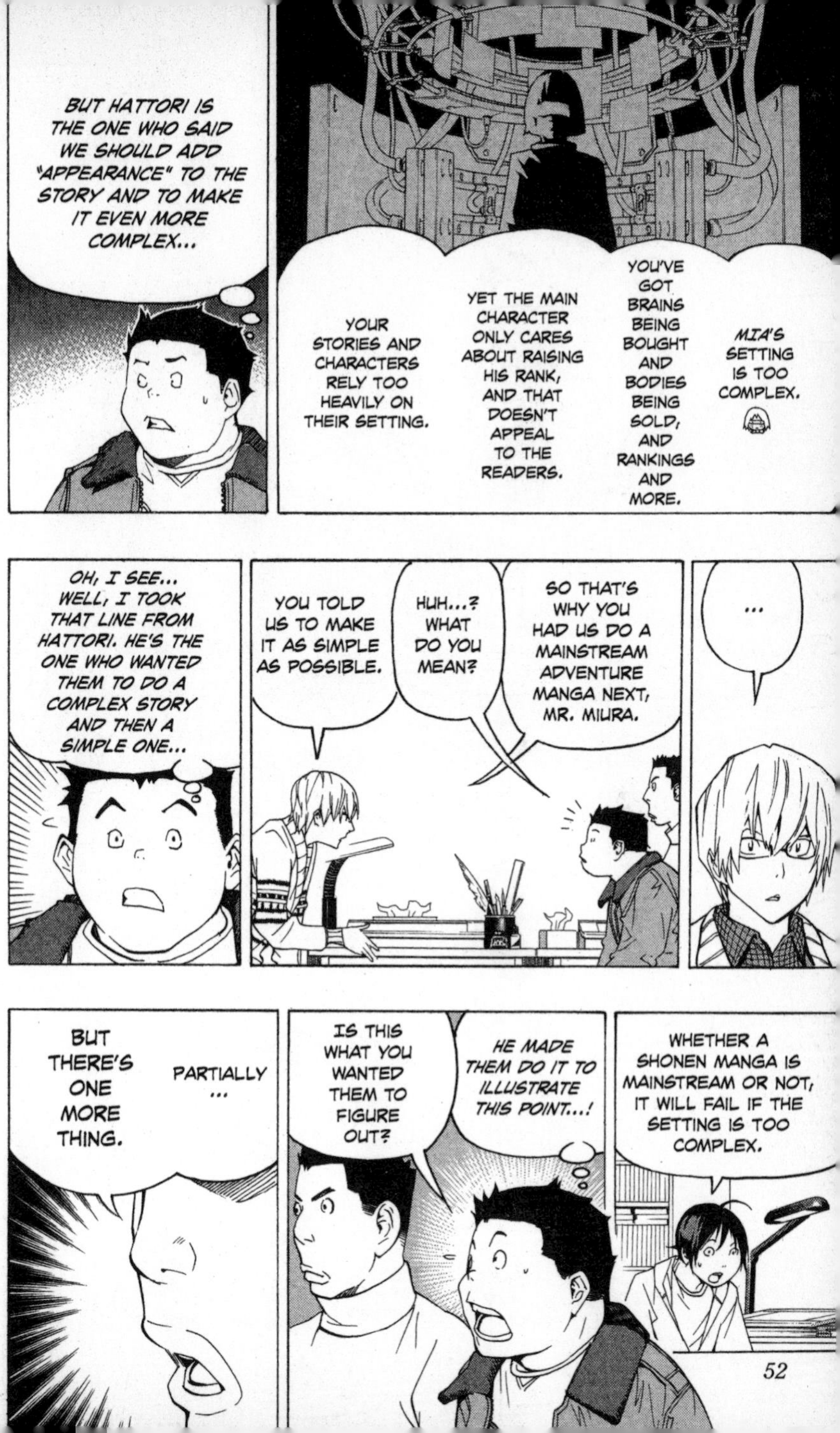
MIA'S SETTING IS TOO COMPLEX.
YOU'VE GOT BRAINS BEING BOUGHT AND BODIES BEING SOLD, AND RANKINGS AND MORE.
YET THE MAIN CHARACTER ONLY CARES ABOUT RAISING HIS RANK, AND THAT DOESN'T APPEAL TO THE READERS.
YOUR STORIES AND CHARACTERS RELY TOO HEAVILY ON THEIR SETTING.
BUT HATTORI IS THE ONE WHO SAID WE SHOULD ADD "APPEARANCE" TO THE STORY AND TO MAKE IT EVEN MORE COMPLEX...
...
SO THAT'S WHY YOU HAD US DO A MAINSTREAM ADVENTURE MANGA NEXT, MR. MIURA.
HUH...? WHAT DO YOU MEAN?
YOU TOLD US TO MAKE IT AS SIMPLE AS POSSIBLE.
OH, I SEE... WELL, I TOOK THAT LINE FROM HATTORI. HE'S THE ONE WHO WANTED THEM TO DO A COMPLEX STORY AND THEN A SIMPLE ONE...
WHETHER A SHONEN MANGA IS MAINSTREAM OR NOT, IT WILL FAIL IF THE SETTING IS TOO COMPLEX.
HE MADE THEM DO IT TO ILLUSTRATE THIS POINT...!
IS THIS WHAT YOU WANTED THEM TO FIGURE OUT?
PARTIALLY...
BUT THERE'S ONE MORE THING.

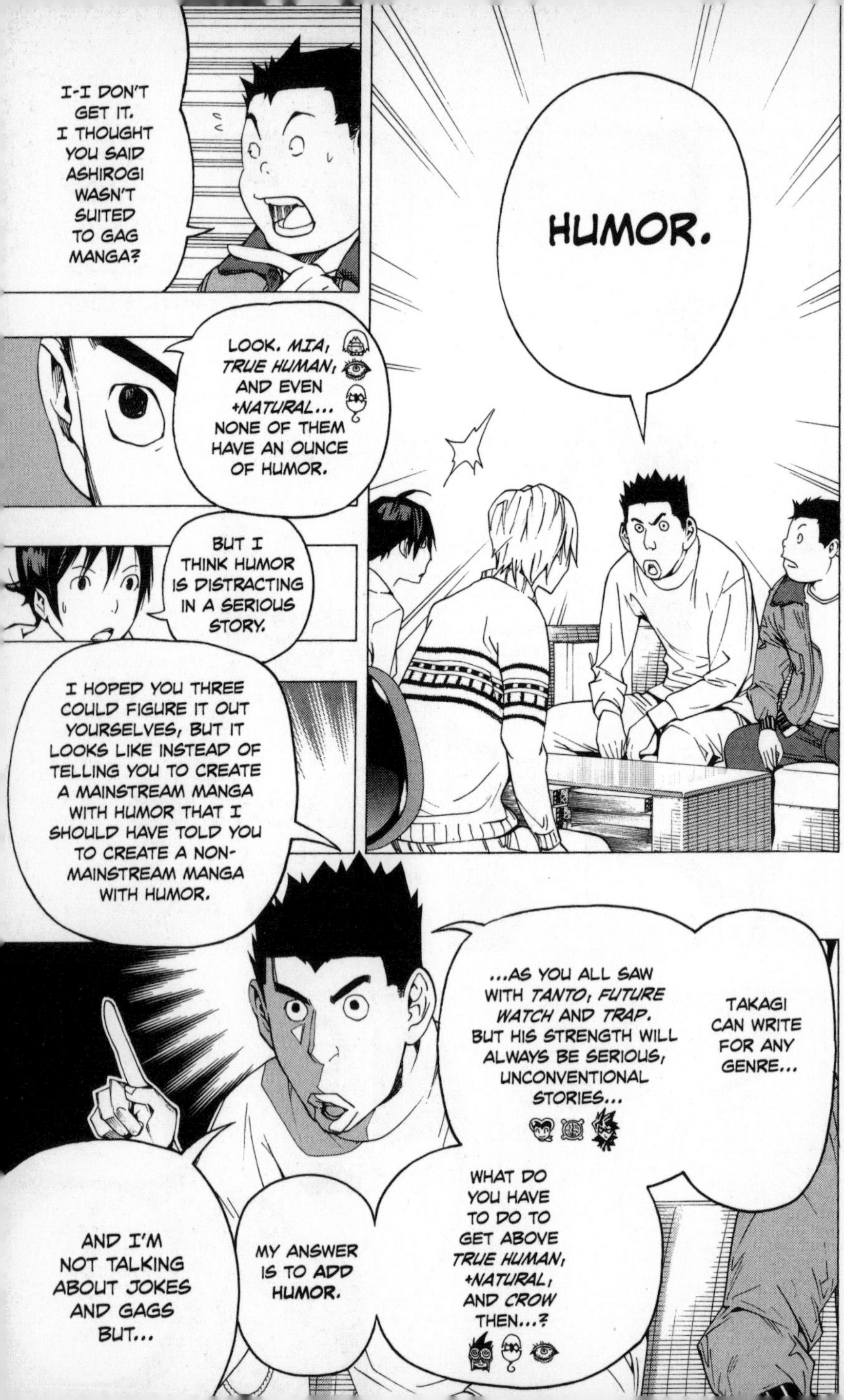
HUMOR.
I-I DON'T GET IT. I THOUGHT YOU SAID ASHIROGI WASN'T SUITED TO GAG MANGA?
LOOK. *MIA*, *TRUE HUMAN*, AND EVEN *+NATURAL*... NONE OF THEM HAVE AN OUNCE OF HUMOR.
BUT I THINK HUMOR IS DISTRACTING IN A SERIOUS STORY.
I HOPED YOU THREE COULD FIGURE IT OUT YOURSELVES, BUT IT LOOKS LIKE INSTEAD OF TELLING YOU TO CREATE A MAINSTREAM MANGA WITH HUMOR THAT I SHOULD HAVE TOLD YOU TO CREATE A NON-MAINSTREAM MANGA WITH HUMOR.
TAKAGI CAN WRITE FOR ANY GENRE...
...AS YOU ALL SAW WITH *TANTO*, *FUTURE WATCH* AND *TRAP*. BUT HIS STRENGTH WILL ALWAYS BE SERIOUS, UNCONVENTIONAL STORIES...
WHAT DO YOU HAVE TO DO TO GET ABOVE *TRUE HUMAN*, *+NATURAL*, AND *CROW* THEN...?
MY ANSWER IS TO ADD HUMOR.
AND I'M NOT TALKING ABOUT JOKES AND GAGS BUT...

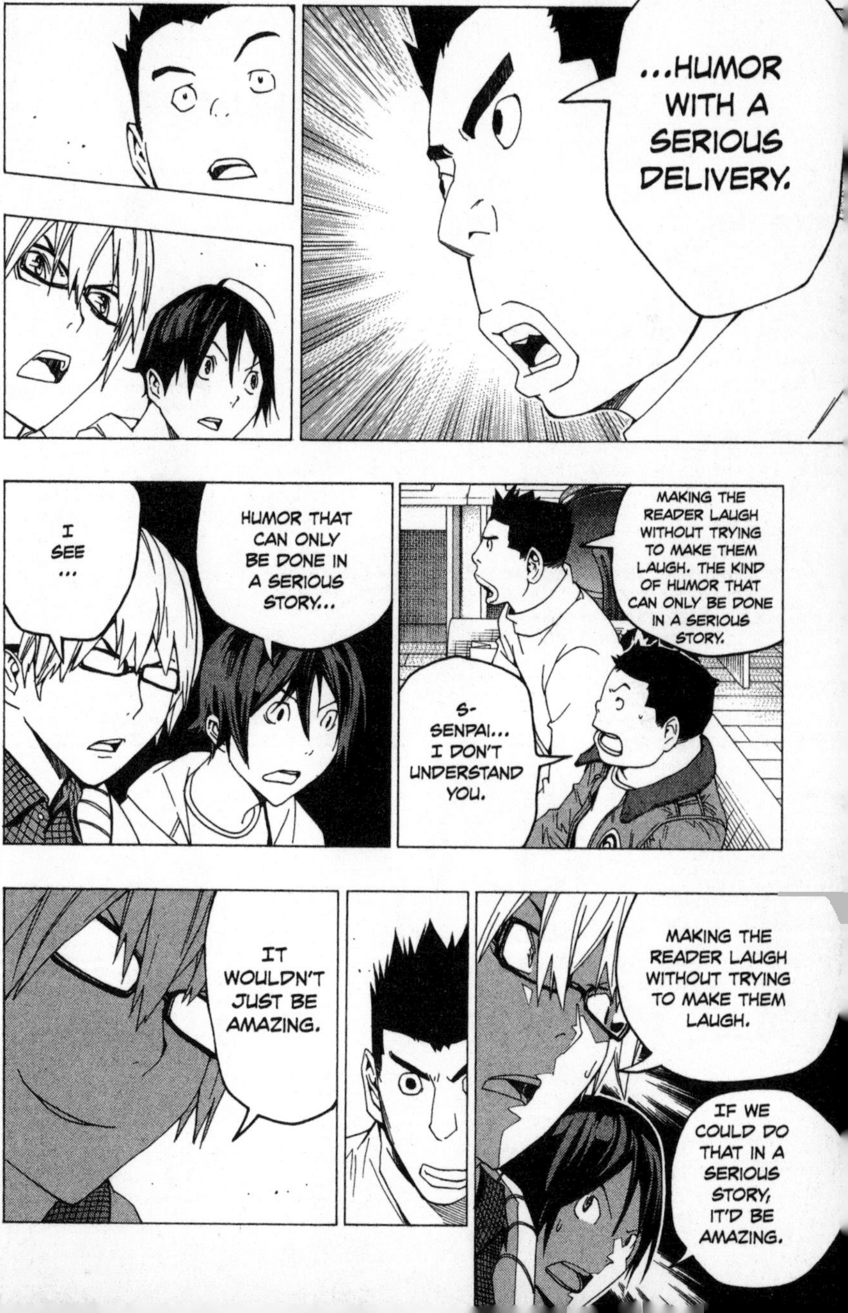
...HUMOR WITH A SERIOUS DELIVERY.
MAKING THE READER LAUGH WITHOUT TRYING TO MAKE THEM LAUGH. THE KIND OF HUMOR THAT CAN ONLY BE DONE IN A SERIOUS STORY.
S-SENPAI... I DON'T UNDERSTAND YOU.
HUMOR THAT CAN ONLY BE DONE IN A SERIOUS STORY...
I SEE...
MAKING THE READER LAUGH WITHOUT TRYING TO MAKE THEM LAUGH.
IF WE COULD DO THAT IN A SERIOUS STORY, IT'D BE AMAZING.
IT WOULDN'T JUST BE AMAZING.

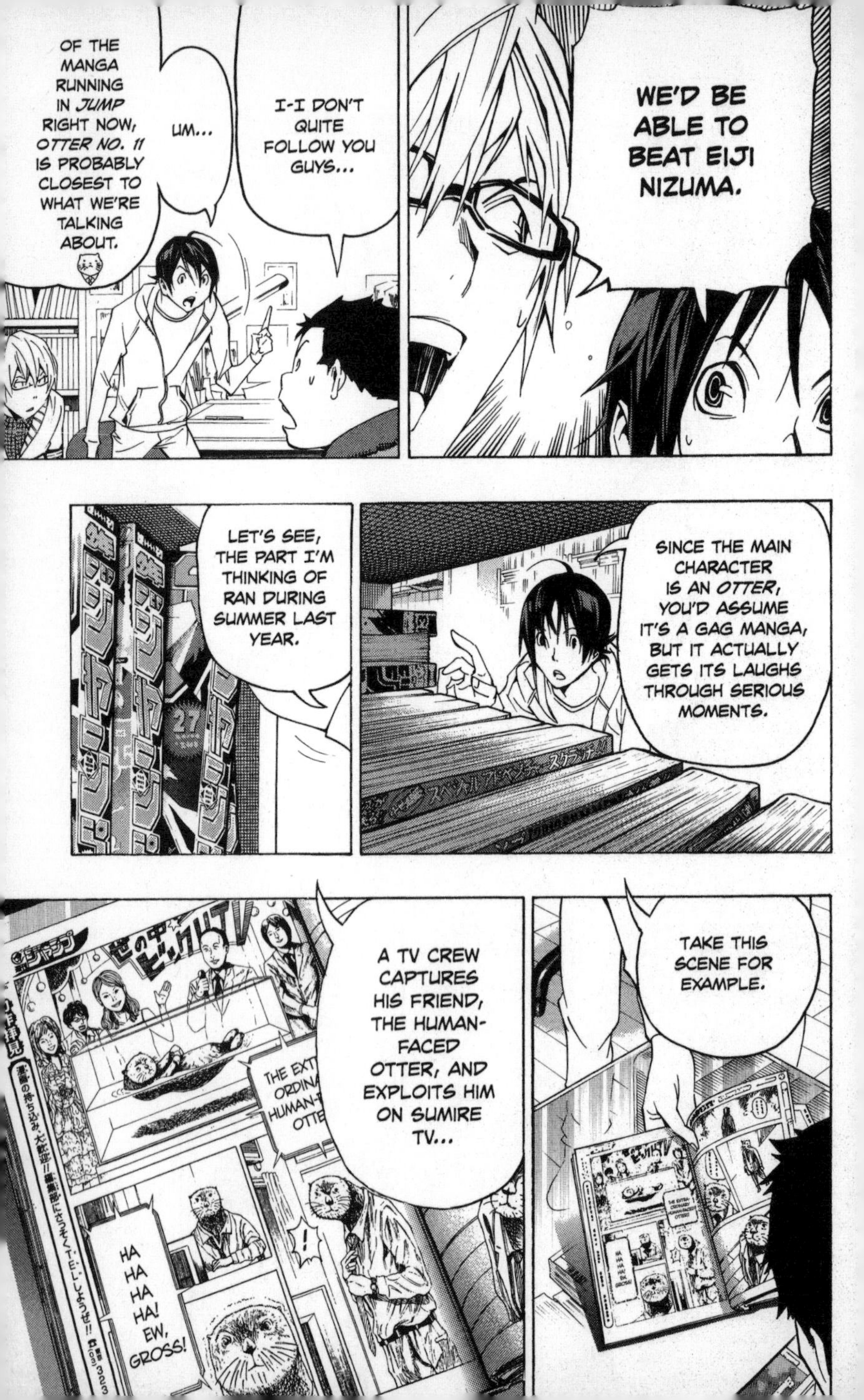
WE'D BE ABLE TO BEAT EIJI NIZUMA.
I-I DON'T QUITE FOLLOW YOU GUYS...
UM...
OF THE MANGA RUNNING IN *JUMP* RIGHT NOW, *OTTER NO. 11* IS PROBABLY CLOSEST TO WHAT WE'RE TALKING ABOUT.
SINCE THE MAIN CHARACTER IS AN *OTTER*, YOU'D ASSUME IT'S A GAG MANGA, BUT IT ACTUALLY GETS ITS LAUGHS THROUGH SERIOUS MOMENTS.
LET'S SEE, THE PART I'M THINKING OF RAN DURING SUMMER LAST YEAR.
TAKE THIS SCENE FOR EXAMPLE.
A TV CREW CAPTURES HIS FRIEND, THE HUMAN-FACED OTTER, AND EXPLOITS HIM ON SUMIRE TV...
!
HA HA HA HA! EW, GROSS!

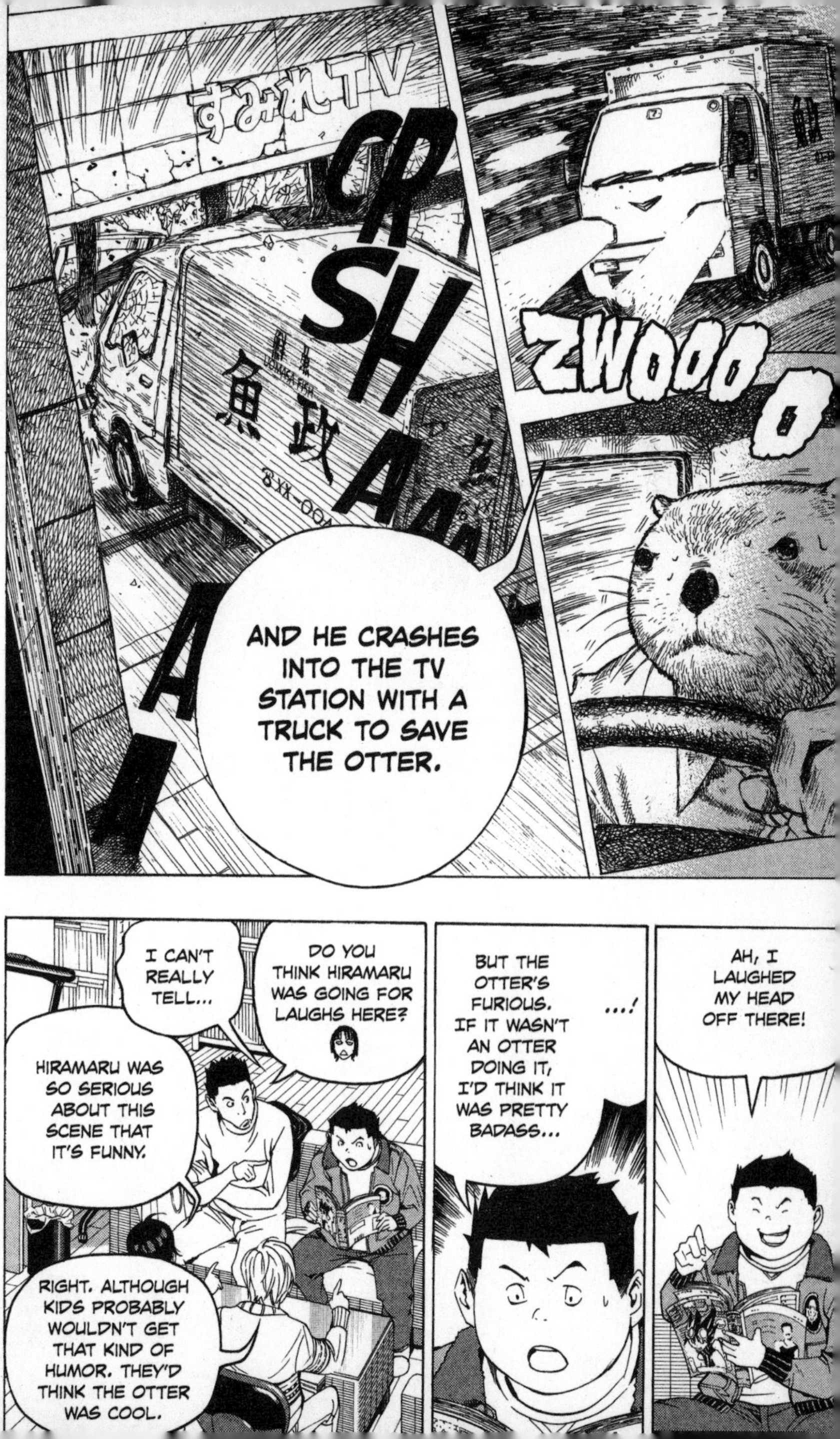
ZWOOOO
すみれTV
魚政
CRSHAAAA
AND HE CRASHES INTO THE TV STATION WITH A TRUCK TO SAVE THE OTTER.
AH, I LAUGHED MY HEAD OFF THERE!
...!
BUT THE OTTER'S FURIOUS. IF IT WASN'T AN OTTER DOING IT, I'D THINK IT WAS PRETTY BADASS...
DO YOU THINK HIRAMARU WAS GOING FOR LAUGHS HERE?
I CAN'T REALLY TELL...
HIRAMARU WAS SO SERIOUS ABOUT THIS SCENE THAT IT'S FUNNY.
RIGHT. ALTHOUGH KIDS PROBABLY WOULDN'T GET THAT KIND OF HUMOR. THEY'D THINK THE OTTER WAS COOL.

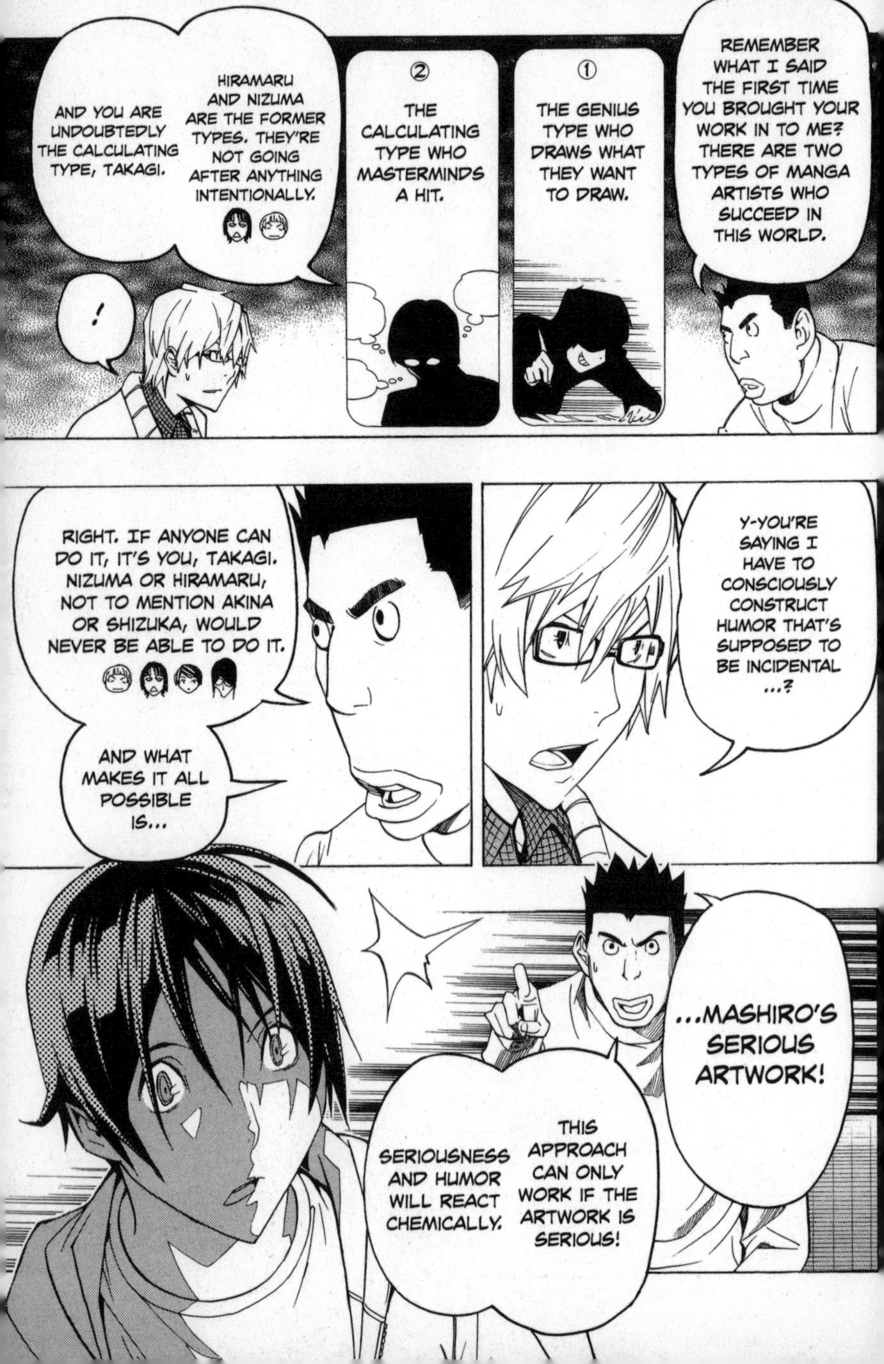
REMEMBER WHAT I SAID THE FIRST TIME YOU BROUGHT YOUR WORK IN TO ME? THERE ARE TWO TYPES OF MANGA ARTISTS WHO SUCCEED IN THIS WORLD.
① THE GENIUS TYPE WHO DRAWS WHAT THEY WANT TO DRAW.
② THE CALCULATING TYPE WHO MASTERMINDS A HIT.
HIRAMARU AND NIZUMA ARE THE FORMER TYPES. THEY'RE NOT GOING AFTER ANYTHING INTENTIONALLY.
AND YOU ARE UNDOUBTEDLY THE CALCULATING TYPE, TAKAGI.
!
Y-YOU'RE SAYING I HAVE TO CONSCIOUSLY CONSTRUCT HUMOR THAT'S SUPPOSED TO BE INCIDENTAL ...?
RIGHT. IF ANYONE CAN DO IT, IT'S YOU, TAKAGI. NIZUMA OR HIRAMARU, NOT TO MENTION AKINA OR SHIZUKA, WOULD NEVER BE ABLE TO DO IT.
AND WHAT MAKES IT ALL POSSIBLE IS...
...MASHIRO'S SERIOUS ARTWORK!
THIS APPROACH CAN ONLY WORK IF THE ARTWORK IS SERIOUS!
SERIOUSNESS AND HUMOR WILL REACT CHEMICALLY.

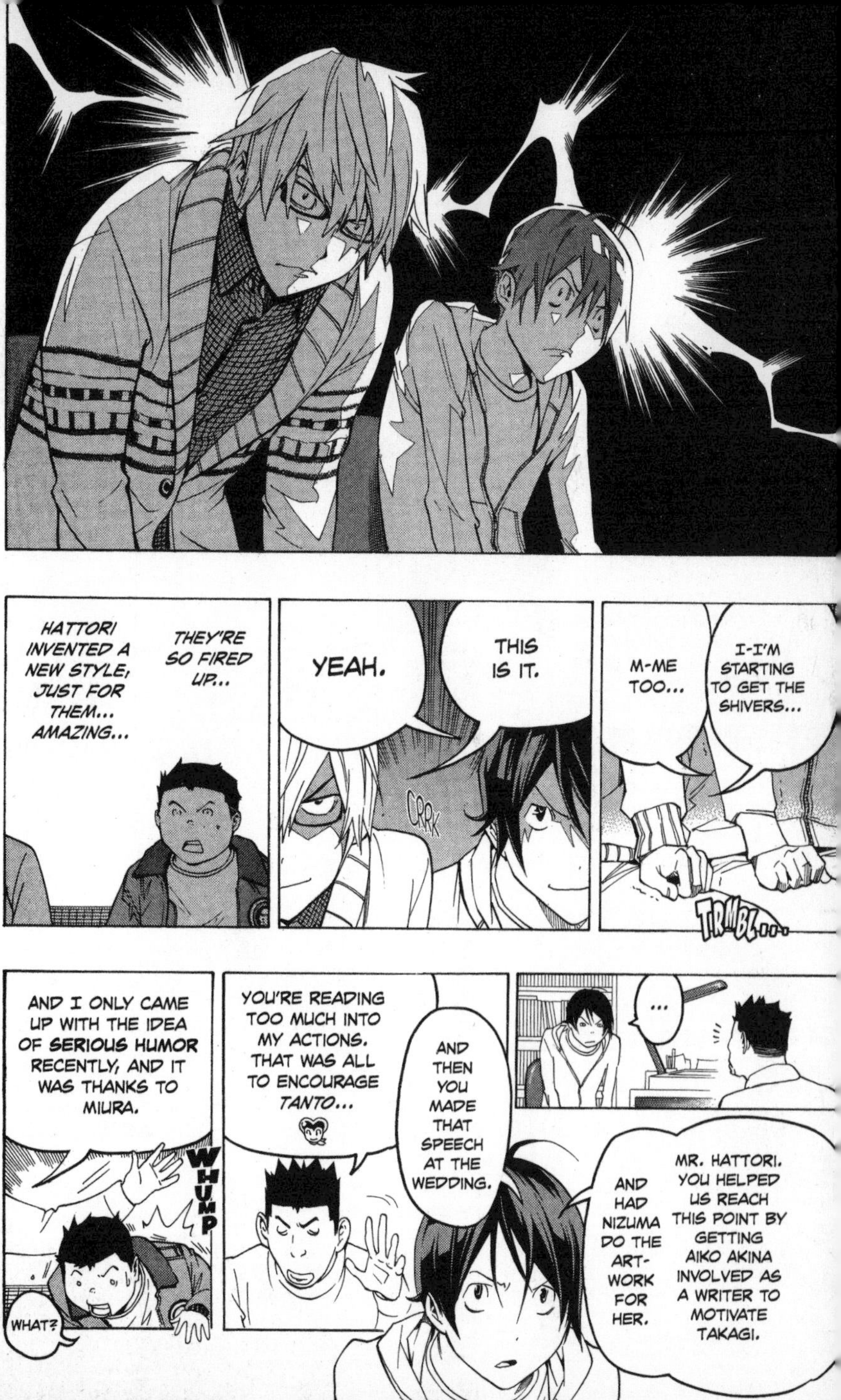
I-I'M STARTING TO GET THE SHIVERS...
M-ME TOO...
TRMBL...
THIS IS IT.
YEAH.
CRRK
THEY'RE SO FIRED UP...
HATTORI INVENTED A NEW STYLE, JUST FOR THEM... AMAZING...
...
MR. HATTORI. YOU HELPED US REACH THIS POINT BY GETTING AIKO AKINA INVOLVED AS A WRITER TO MOTIVATE TAKAGI.
AND HAD NIZUMA DO THE ART-WORK FOR HER.
AND THEN YOU MADE THAT SPEECH AT THE WEDDING.
YOU'RE READING TOO MUCH INTO MY ACTIONS. THAT WAS ALL TO ENCOURAGE TANTO...
AND I ONLY CAME UP WITH THE IDEA OF SERIOUS HUMOR RECENTLY, AND IT WAS THANKS TO MIURA.
WHUMP
WHAT?

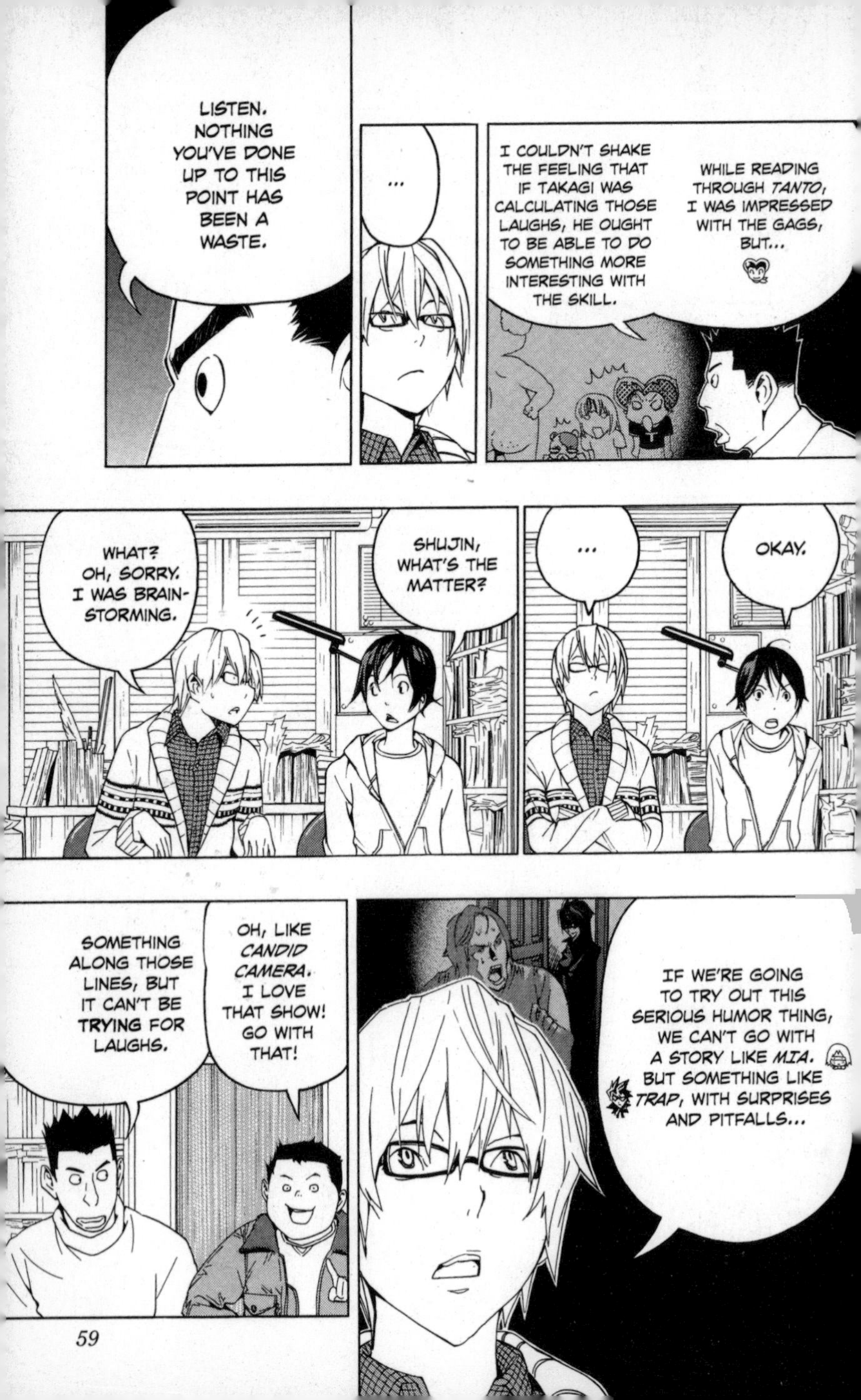
WHILE READING THROUGH *TANTO*, I WAS IMPRESSED WITH THE GAGS, BUT...
I COULDN'T SHAKE THE FEELING THAT IF TAKAGI WAS CALCULATING THOSE LAUGHS, HE OUGHT TO BE ABLE TO DO SOMETHING MORE INTERESTING WITH THE SKILL.
...
LISTEN. NOTHING YOU'VE DONE UP TO THIS POINT HAS BEEN A WASTE.
OKAY.
...
SHUJIN, WHAT'S THE MATTER?
WHAT? OH, SORRY. I WAS BRAIN-STORMING.
IF WE'RE GOING TO TRY OUT THIS SERIOUS HUMOR THING, WE CAN'T GO WITH A STORY LIKE *MIA*. BUT SOMETHING LIKE *TRAP*, WITH SURPRISES AND PITFALLS...
OH, LIKE *CANDID CAMERA*. I LOVE THAT SHOW! GO WITH THAT!
SOMETHING ALONG THOSE LINES, BUT IT CAN'T BE **TRYING** FOR LAUGHS.

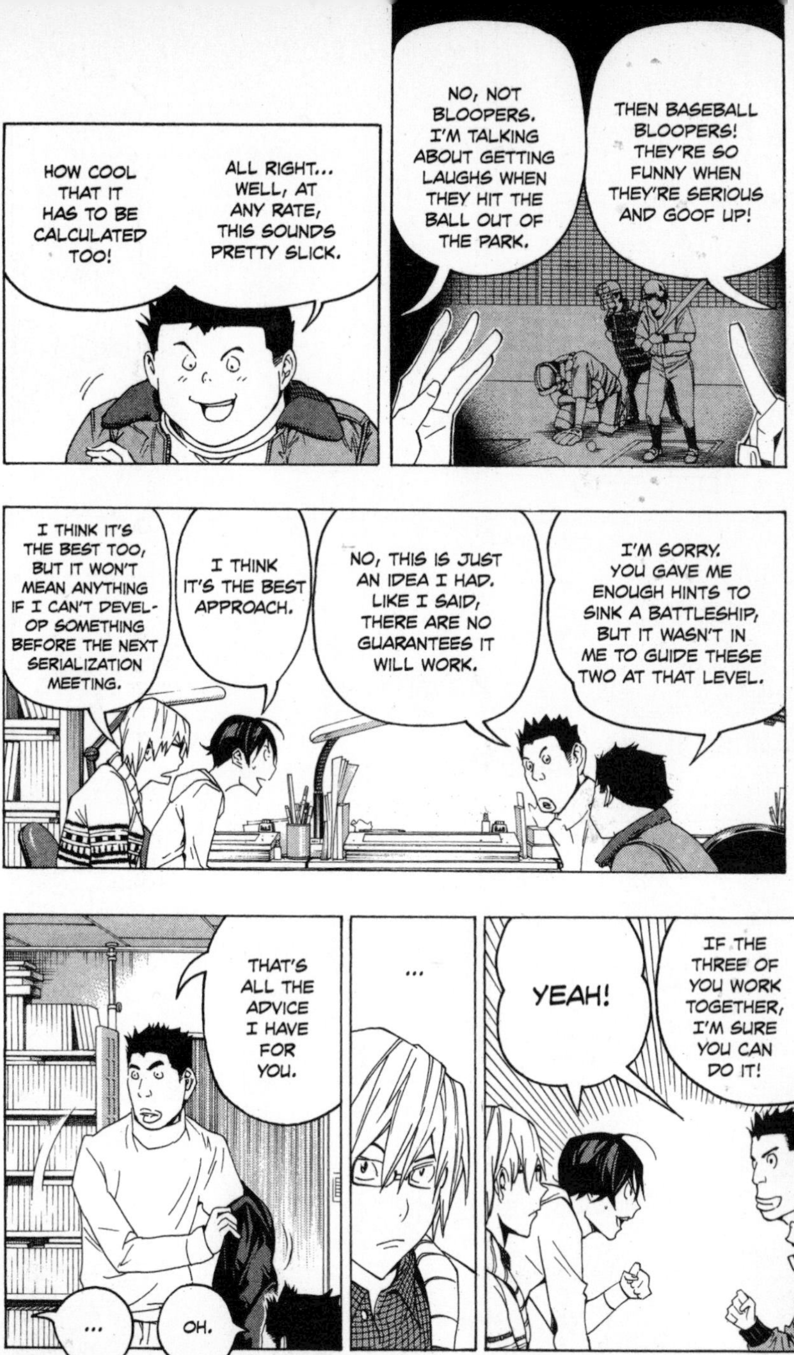
THEN BASEBALL BLOOPERS! THEY'RE SO FUNNY WHEN THEY'RE SERIOUS AND GOOF UP!
NO, NOT BLOOPERS. I'M TALKING ABOUT GETTING LAUGHS WHEN THEY HIT THE BALL OUT OF THE PARK.
ALL RIGHT... WELL, AT ANY RATE, THIS SOUNDS PRETTY SLICK.
HOW COOL THAT IT HAS TO BE CALCULATED TOO!
I'M SORRY. YOU GAVE ME ENOUGH HINTS TO SINK A BATTLESHIP, BUT IT WASN'T IN ME TO GUIDE THESE TWO AT THAT LEVEL.
NO, THIS IS JUST AN IDEA I HAD. LIKE I SAID, THERE ARE NO GUARANTEES IT WILL WORK.
I THINK IT'S THE BEST APPROACH.
I THINK IT'S THE BEST TOO, BUT IT WON'T MEAN ANYTHING IF I CAN'T DEVELOP SOMETHING BEFORE THE NEXT SERIALIZATION MEETING.
IF THE THREE OF YOU WORK TOGETHER, I'M SURE YOU CAN DO IT!
YEAH!
...
THAT'S ALL THE ADVICE I HAVE FOR YOU.
OH.
...

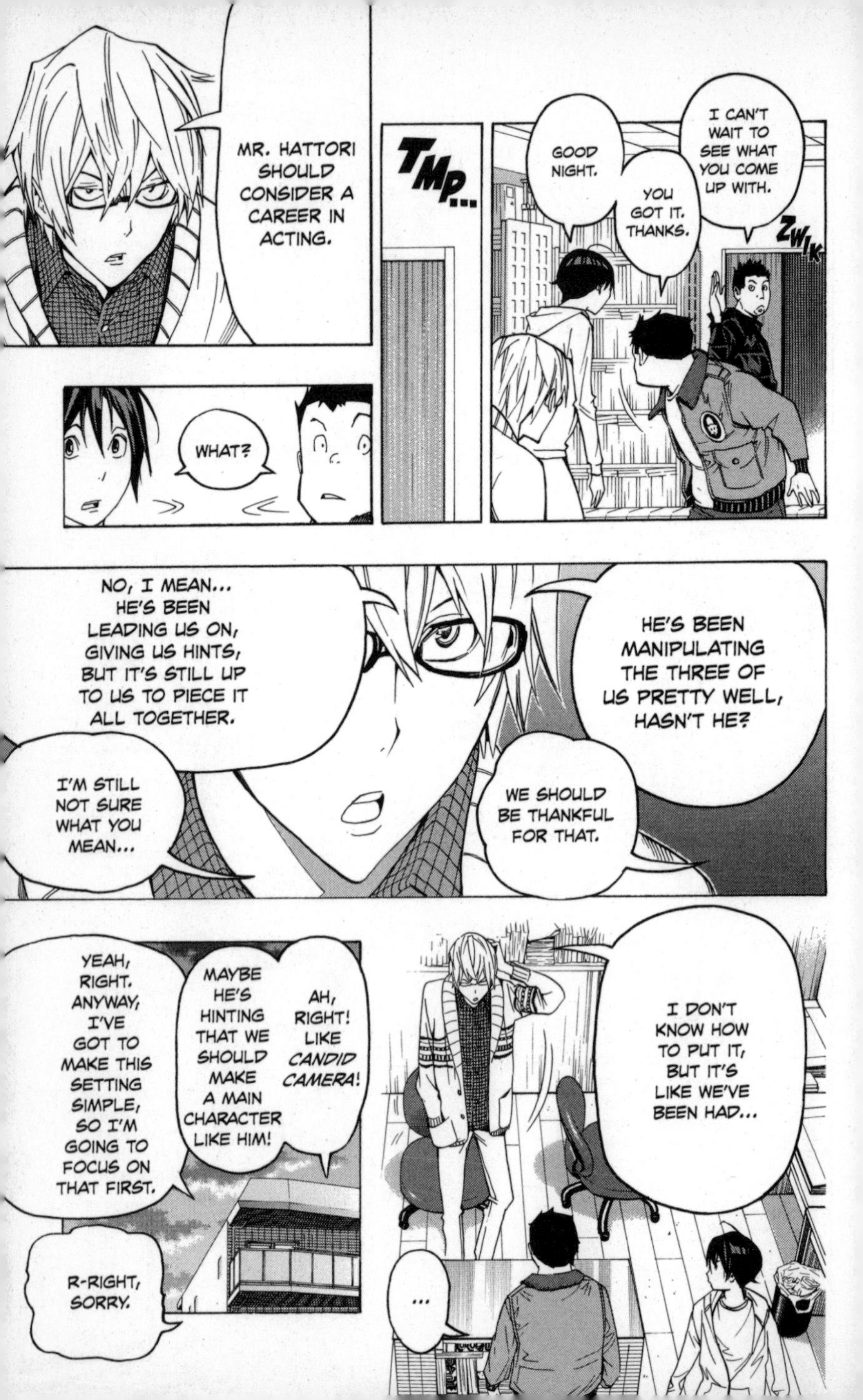
I CAN'T WAIT TO SEE WHAT YOU COME UP WITH.
YOU GOT IT. THANKS.
GOOD NIGHT.
ZWIK
TMP...
MR. HATTORI SHOULD CONSIDER A CAREER IN ACTING.
WHAT?
HE'S BEEN MANIPULATING THE THREE OF US PRETTY WELL, HASN'T HE?
WE SHOULD BE THANKFUL FOR THAT.
NO, I MEAN... HE'S BEEN LEADING US ON, GIVING US HINTS, BUT IT'S STILL UP TO US TO PIECE IT ALL TOGETHER.
I'M STILL NOT SURE WHAT YOU MEAN...
I DON'T KNOW HOW TO PUT IT, BUT IT'S LIKE WE'VE BEEN HAD...
...
AH, RIGHT! LIKE *CANDID CAMERA*!
MAYBE HE'S HINTING THAT WE SHOULD MAKE A MAIN CHARACTER LIKE HIM!
YEAH, RIGHT. ANYWAY, I'VE GOT TO MAKE THIS SETTING SIMPLE, SO I'M GOING TO FOCUS ON THAT FIRST.
R-RIGHT, SORRY.

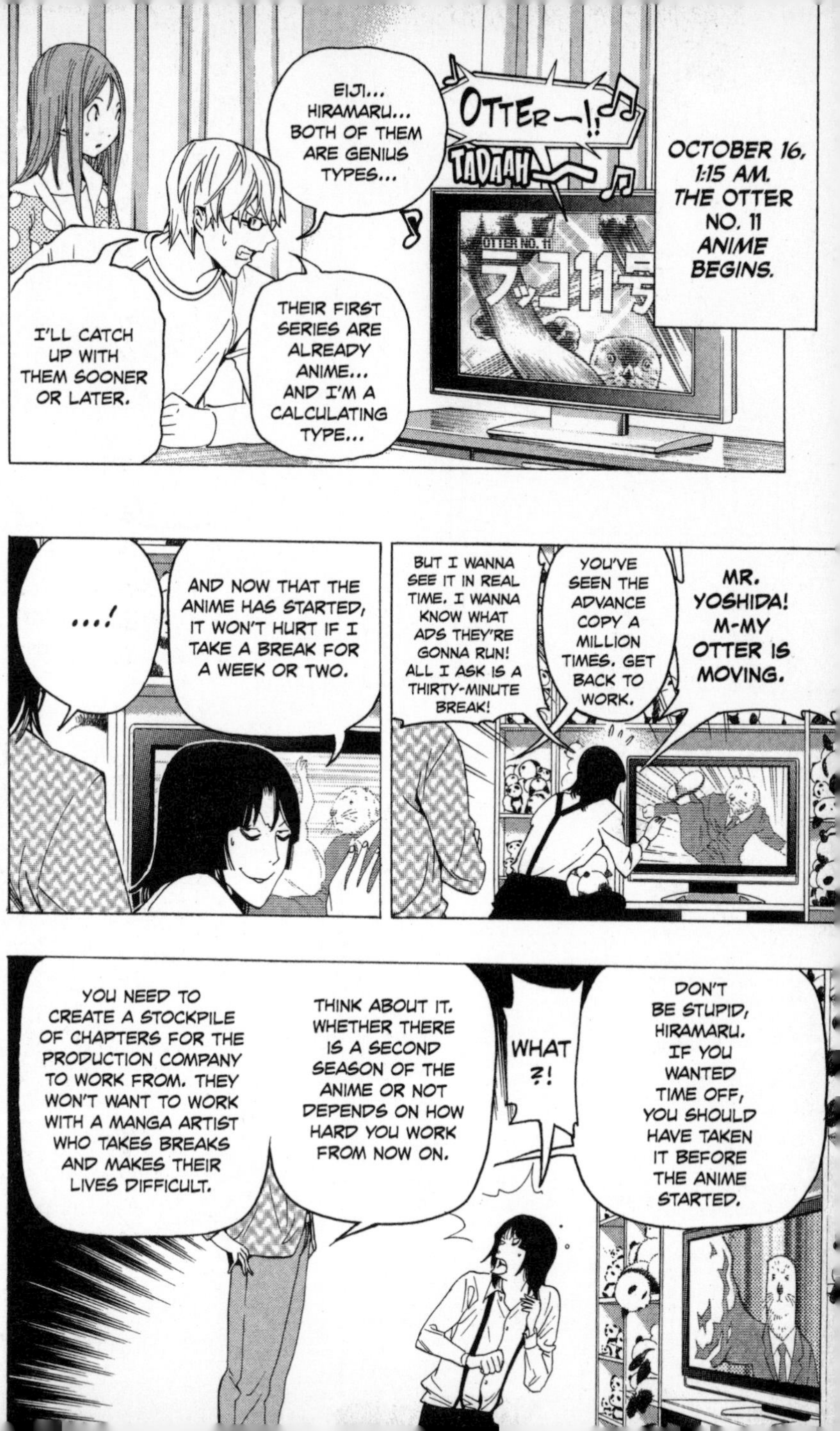
OCTOBER 16, 1:15 AM. THE OTTER NO. 11 ANIME BEGINS.
OTTER NO. 11
ラッコ11号
OTTER—!!
TADAAH
EIJI... HIRAMARU... BOTH OF THEM ARE GENIUS TYPES...
THEIR FIRST SERIES ARE ALREADY ANIME... AND I'M A CALCULATING TYPE...
I'LL CATCH UP WITH THEM SOONER OR LATER.
MR. YOSHIDA! M-MY OTTER IS MOVING.
YOU'VE SEEN THE ADVANCE COPY A MILLION TIMES. GET BACK TO WORK.
BUT I WANNA SEE IT IN REAL TIME. I WANNA KNOW WHAT ADS THEY'RE GONNA RUN! ALL I ASK IS A THIRTY-MINUTE BREAK!
AND NOW THAT THE ANIME HAS STARTED, IT WON'T HURT IF I TAKE A BREAK FOR A WEEK OR TWO.
...!
DON'T BE STUPID, HIRAMARU. IF YOU WANTED TIME OFF, YOU SHOULD HAVE TAKEN IT BEFORE THE ANIME STARTED.
WHAT?!
THINK ABOUT IT. WHETHER THERE IS A SECOND SEASON OF THE ANIME OR NOT DEPENDS ON HOW HARD YOU WORK FROM NOW ON.
YOU NEED TO CREATE A STOCKPILE OF CHAPTERS FOR THE PRODUCTION COMPANY TO WORK FROM. THEY WON'T WANT TO WORK WITH A MANGA ARTIST WHO TAKES BREAKS AND MAKES THEIR LIVES DIFFICULT.

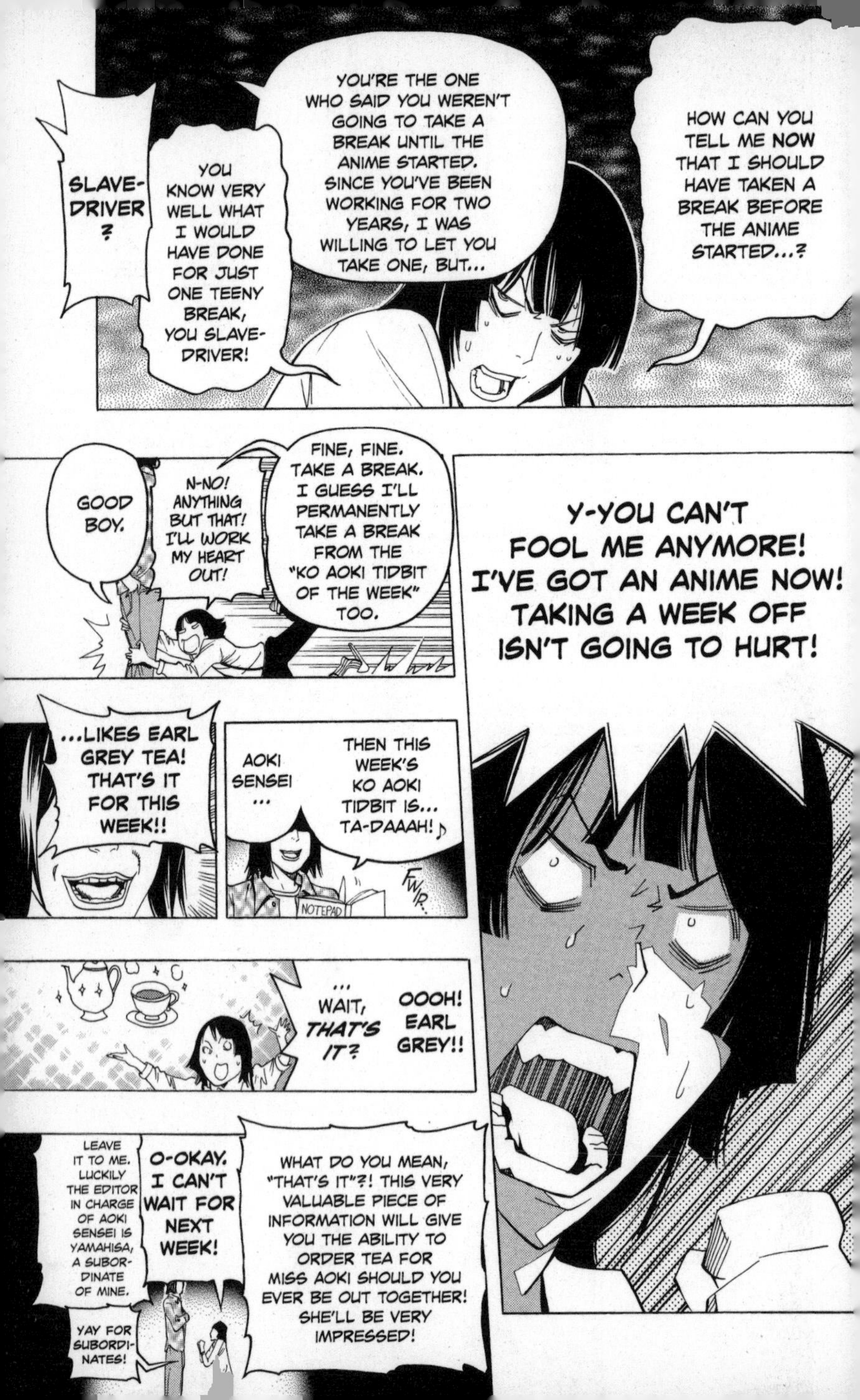
HOW CAN YOU TELL ME NOW THAT I SHOULD HAVE TAKEN A BREAK BEFORE THE ANIME STARTED...?
YOU'RE THE ONE WHO SAID YOU WEREN'T GOING TO TAKE A BREAK UNTIL THE ANIME STARTED. SINCE YOU'VE BEEN WORKING FOR TWO YEARS, I WAS WILLING TO LET YOU TAKE ONE, BUT...
YOU KNOW VERY WELL WHAT I WOULD HAVE DONE FOR JUST ONE TEENY BREAK, YOU SLAVE-DRIVER!
SLAVE-DRIVER?
Y-YOU CAN'T FOOL ME ANYMORE! I'VE GOT AN ANIME NOW! TAKING A WEEK OFF ISN'T GOING TO HURT!
FINE, FINE. TAKE A BREAK. I GUESS I'LL PERMANENTLY TAKE A BREAK FROM THE "KO AOKI TIDBIT OF THE WEEK" TOO.
N-NO! ANYTHING BUT THAT! I'LL WORK MY HEART OUT!
GOOD BOY.
THEN THIS WEEK'S KO AOKI TIDBIT IS... TA-DAAAH!♪
AOKI SENSEI...
FWIP
NOTEPAD
...LIKES EARL GREY TEA! THAT'S IT FOR THIS WEEK!!
OOOH! EARL GREY!!
... WAIT, THAT'S IT?
WHAT DO YOU MEAN, "THAT'S IT"?! THIS VERY VALUABLE PIECE OF INFORMATION WILL GIVE YOU THE ABILITY TO ORDER TEA FOR MISS AOKI SHOULD YOU EVER BE OUT TOGETHER! SHE'LL BE VERY IMPRESSED!
O-OKAY. I CAN'T WAIT FOR NEXT WEEK!
LEAVE IT TO ME. LUCKILY THE EDITOR IN CHARGE OF AOKI SENSEI IS YAMAHISA, A SUBORDINATE OF MINE.
YAY FOR SUBORDINATES!

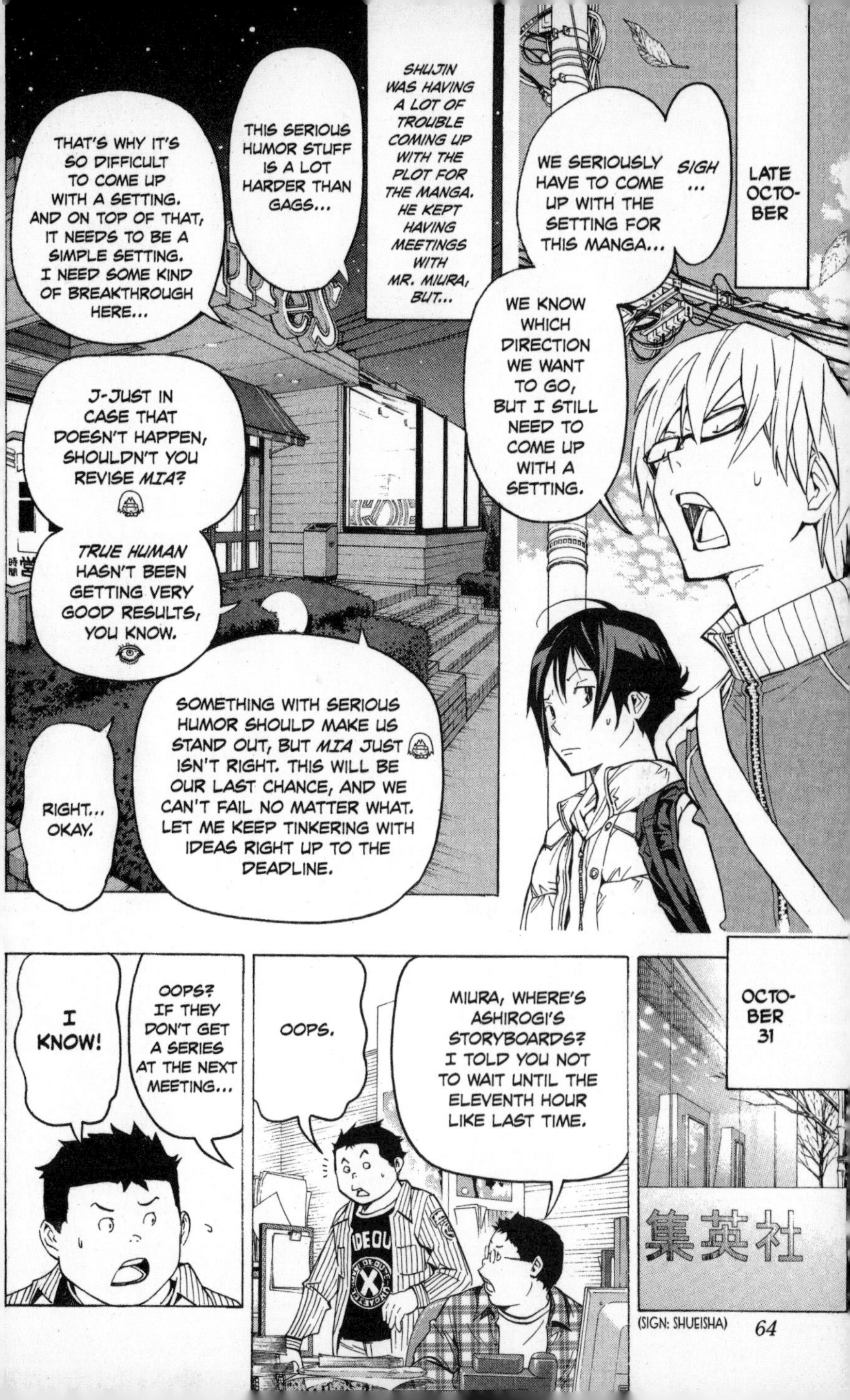
LATE OCTOBER
SIGH...
WE SERIOUSLY HAVE TO COME UP WITH THE SETTING FOR THIS MANGA...
WE KNOW WHICH DIRECTION WE WANT TO GO, BUT I STILL NEED TO COME UP WITH A SETTING.
SHUJIN WAS HAVING A LOT OF TROUBLE COMING UP WITH THE PLOT FOR THE MANGA. HE KEPT HAVING MEETINGS WITH MR. MIURA, BUT...
THIS SERIOUS HUMOR STUFF IS A LOT HARDER THAN GAGS...
THAT'S WHY IT'S SO DIFFICULT TO COME UP WITH A SETTING. AND ON TOP OF THAT, IT NEEDS TO BE A SIMPLE SETTING. I NEED SOME KIND OF BREAKTHROUGH HERE...
J-JUST IN CASE THAT DOESN'T HAPPEN, SHOULDN'T YOU REVISE *MIA*?
TRUE HUMAN HASN'T BEEN GETTING VERY GOOD RESULTS, YOU KNOW.
SOMETHING WITH SERIOUS HUMOR SHOULD MAKE US STAND OUT, BUT *MIA* JUST ISN'T RIGHT. THIS WILL BE OUR LAST CHANCE, AND WE CAN'T FAIL NO MATTER WHAT. LET ME KEEP TINKERING WITH IDEAS RIGHT UP TO THE DEADLINE.
RIGHT... OKAY.
OCTOBER 31
集英社
MIURA, WHERE'S ASHIROGI'S STORYBOARDS? I TOLD YOU NOT TO WAIT UNTIL THE ELEVENTH HOUR LIKE LAST TIME.
OOPS.
OOPS? IF THEY DON'T GET A SERIES AT THE NEXT MEETING...
I KNOW!
(SIGN: SHUEISHA)

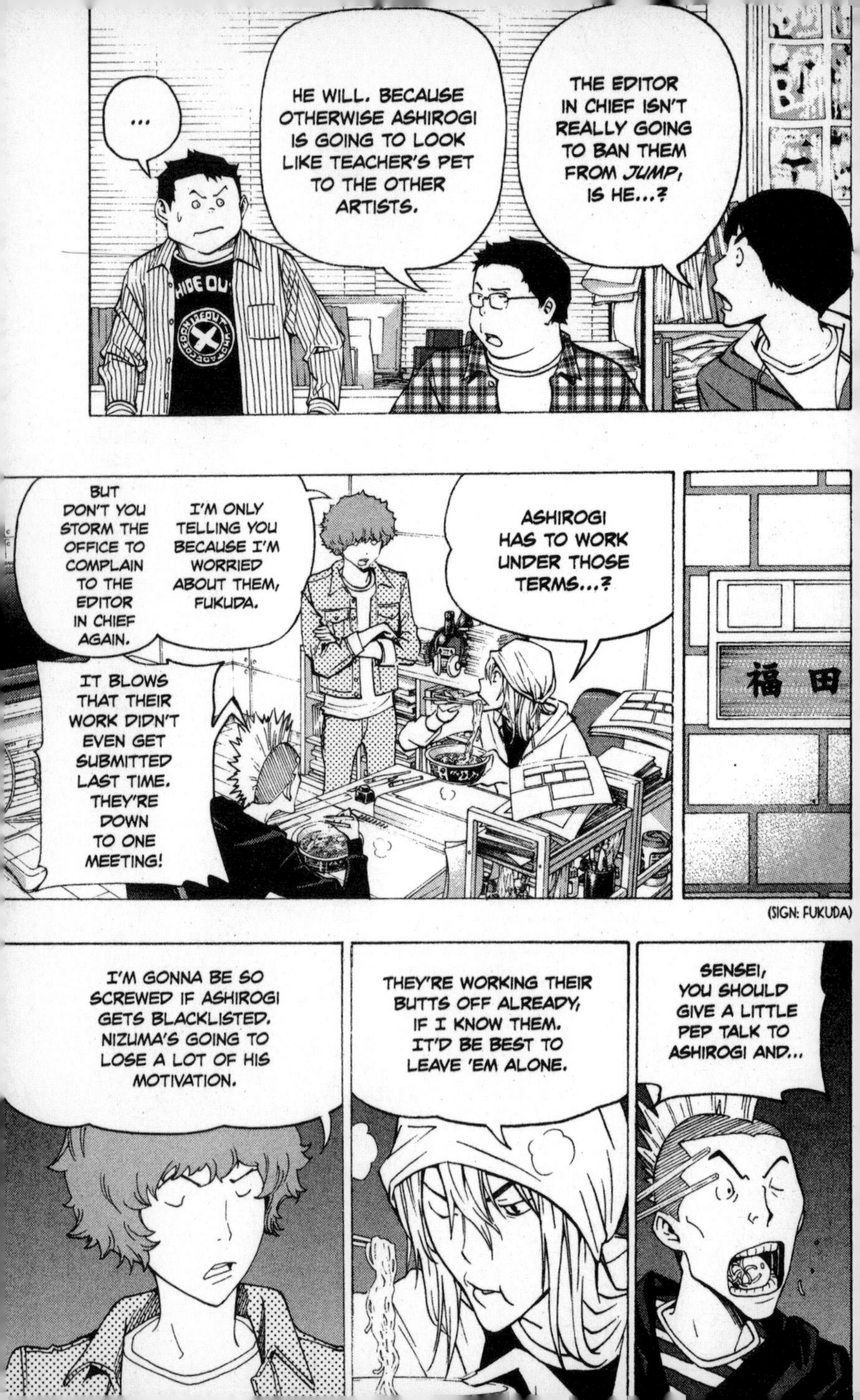
THE EDITOR IN CHIEF ISN'T REALLY GOING TO BAN THEM FROM *JUMP*, IS HE...?
HE WILL. BECAUSE OTHERWISE ASHIROGI IS GOING TO LOOK LIKE TEACHER'S PET TO THE OTHER ARTISTS.
...
福田
(SIGN: FUKUDA)
ASHIROGI HAS TO WORK UNDER THOSE TERMS...?
I'M ONLY TELLING YOU BECAUSE I'M WORRIED ABOUT THEM, FUKUDA.
BUT DON'T YOU STORM THE OFFICE TO COMPLAIN TO THE EDITOR IN CHIEF AGAIN.
IT BLOWS THAT THEIR WORK DIDN'T EVEN GET SUBMITTED LAST TIME. THEY'RE DOWN TO ONE MEETING!
SENSEI, YOU SHOULD GIVE A LITTLE PEP TALK TO ASHIROGI AND...
THEY'RE WORKING THEIR BUTTS OFF ALREADY, IF I KNOW THEM. IT'D BE BEST TO LEAVE 'EM ALONE.
I'M GONNA BE SO SCREWED IF ASHIROGI GETS BLACKLISTED. NIZUMA'S GOING TO LOSE A LOT OF HIS MOTIVATION.

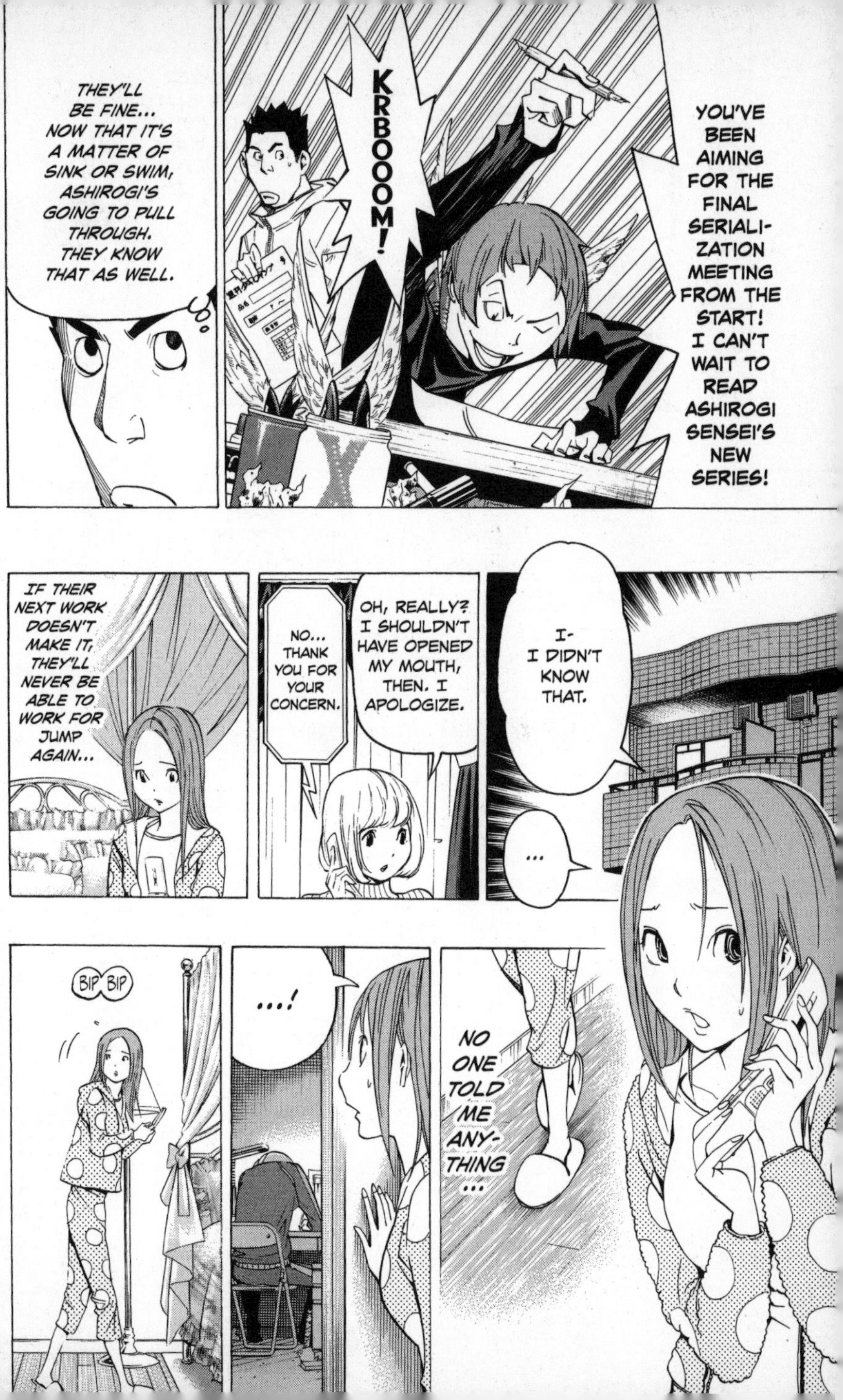
YOU'VE BEEN AIMING FOR THE FINAL SERIALI-ZATION MEETING FROM THE START! I CAN'T WAIT TO READ ASHIROGI SENSEI'S NEW SERIES!
KRBOOOM!
THEY'LL BE FINE... NOW THAT IT'S A MATTER OF SINK OR SWIM, ASHIROGI'S GOING TO PULL THROUGH. THEY KNOW THAT AS WELL.
I- I DIDN'T KNOW THAT.
...
OH, REALLY? I SHOULDN'T HAVE OPENED MY MOUTH, THEN. I APOLOGIZE.
NO... THANK YOU FOR YOUR CONCERN.
IF THEIR NEXT WORK DOESN'T MAKE IT, THEY'LL NEVER BE ABLE TO WORK FOR JUMP AGAIN...
NO ONE TOLD ME ANY-THING...
...!
BIP BIP

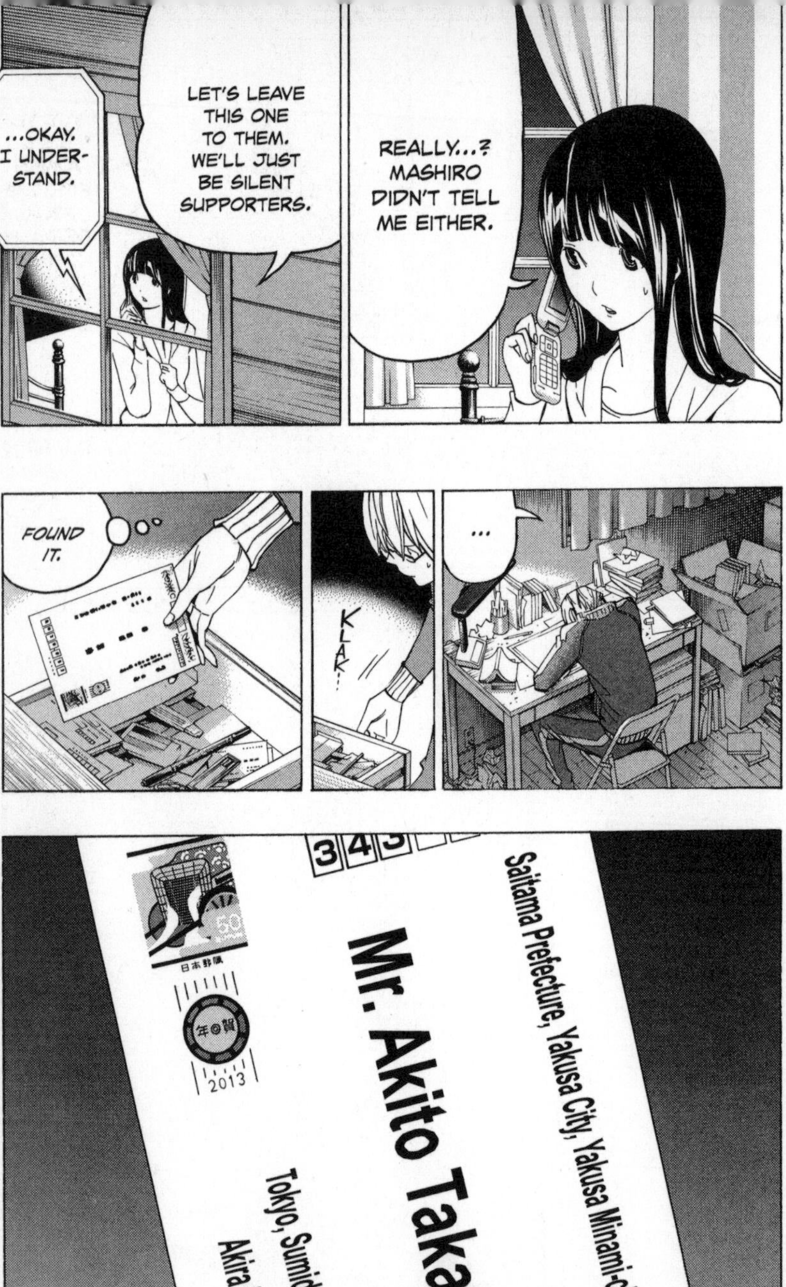
REALLY...? MASHIRO DIDN'T TELL ME EITHER.
LET'S LEAVE THIS ONE TO THEM. WE'LL JUST BE SILENT SUPPORTERS.
...OKAY. I UNDER-STAND.
...
KLAK
FOUND IT.
343
Saitama Prefecture, Yakusa City, Yakusa Minami-cho, 1-4
Mr. Akito Takagi
Tokyo, Sumida-ku, K
Akira Hattori
日本郵便
年賀
2013

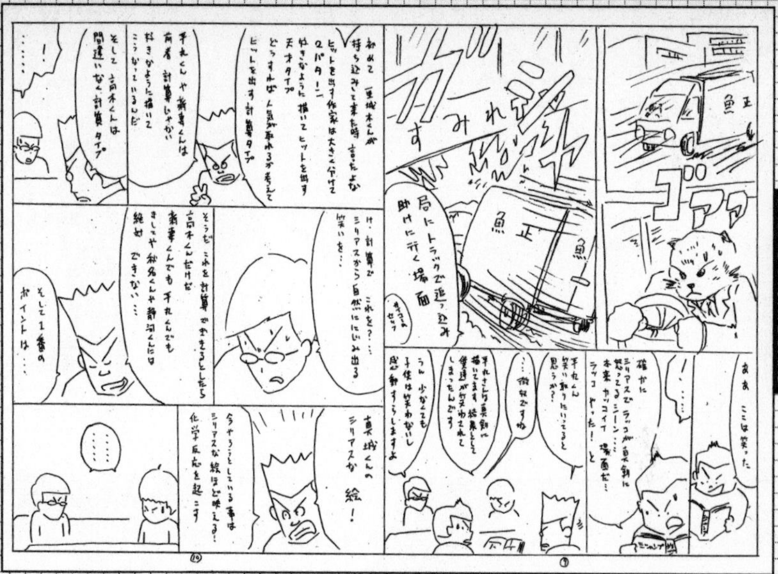
魚正
ゴゴアア
すみれ
局にトラックで追い込み助けに行く場面
ああ ここは笑った
……!
確かにシリアスでラッコが真剣に怒ってるシーン…本来カッコイイ場面だ…ラッコやった!と
平丸くん笑い取りにいってると思うか?
…微妙ですね
平丸さんは真剣に描いてます 結果として僕達が笑わされてしまったんです
うん 少なくても子供は笑わないし感動すらしますよ
初めて亜城木くんが持ち込みに来た時言ったよな ヒットを出す作家は大きく分けて2パターン 好きなように描いてヒットを出す天才タイプ どうすれば人気が取れるか考えてヒットを出す計算タイプ
平丸くんや新妻くんは前者 計算じゃなく好きなように描いてこうなっているんだ
そして高木くんは間違いなく計算タイプ
……!
け…計算でこれを?…シリアスから自然ににじみ出る笑いを…
そうだ これを計算でできるとしたら高木くんだけだ 新妻くんでも平丸くんでもましてや秋名くんや静河くんには絶対できない…
そして1番のポイントは…
真城くんのシリアスな絵!
今やろうとしている事はシリアスな絵ほど映える! 化学反応を起こす
……

OHBA'S STORYBOARD

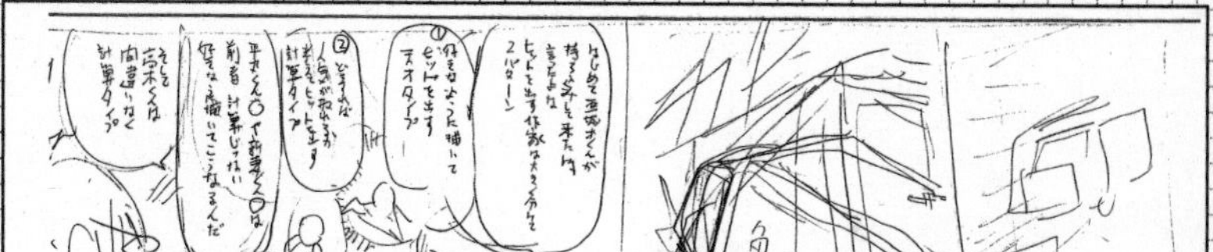
局にトラックで突っ込み助けに行く場面
真城くんのシリアスな絵

OBATA'S STORYBOARD

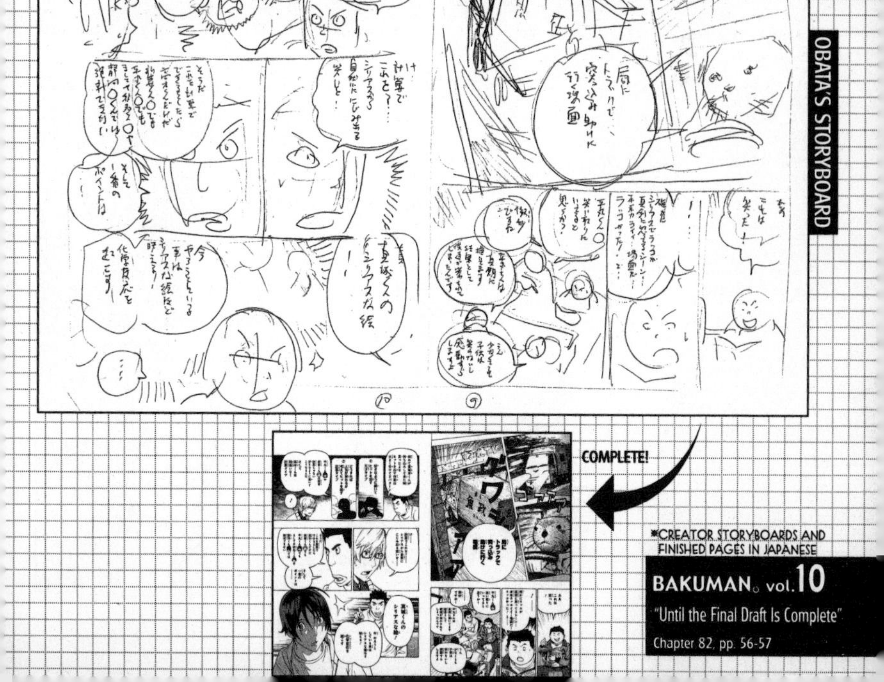

COMPLETE!

*CREATOR STORYBOARDS AND FINISHED PAGES IN JAPANESE

BAKUMAN。 vol.10

"Until the Final Draft Is Complete"

Chapter 82, pp. 56-57

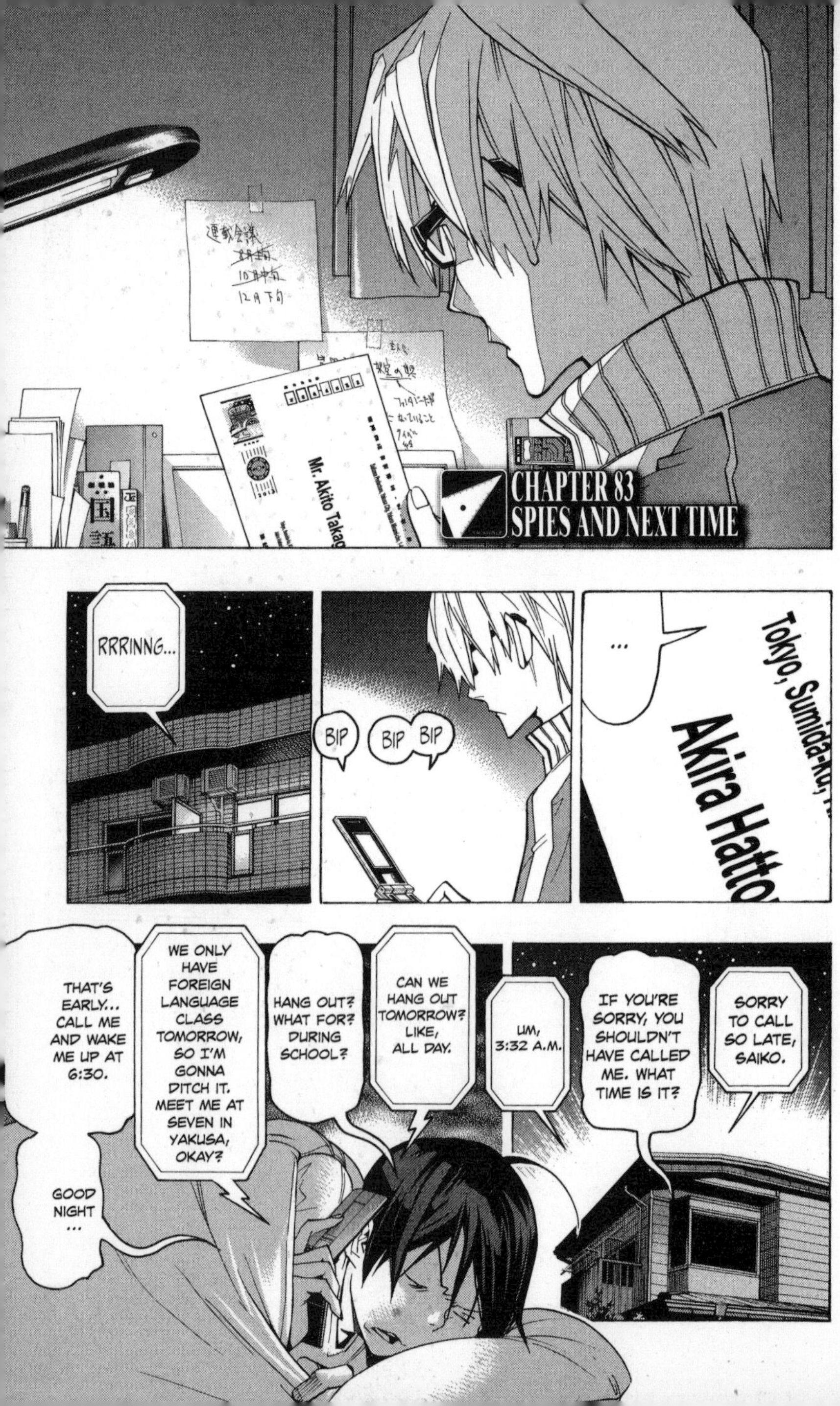
CHAPTER 83
SPIES AND NEXT TIME
...
BIP BIP BIP
RRRINNG...
SORRY TO CALL SO LATE, SAIKO.
IF YOU'RE SORRY, YOU SHOULDN'T HAVE CALLED ME. WHAT TIME IS IT?
UM, 3:32 A.M.
CAN WE HANG OUT TOMORROW? LIKE, ALL DAY.
HANG OUT? WHAT FOR? DURING SCHOOL?
WE ONLY HAVE FOREIGN LANGUAGE CLASS TOMORROW, SO I'M GONNA DITCH IT. MEET ME AT SEVEN IN YAKUSA, OKAY?
THAT'S EARLY... CALL ME AND WAKE ME UP AT 6:30.
GOOD NIGHT ...

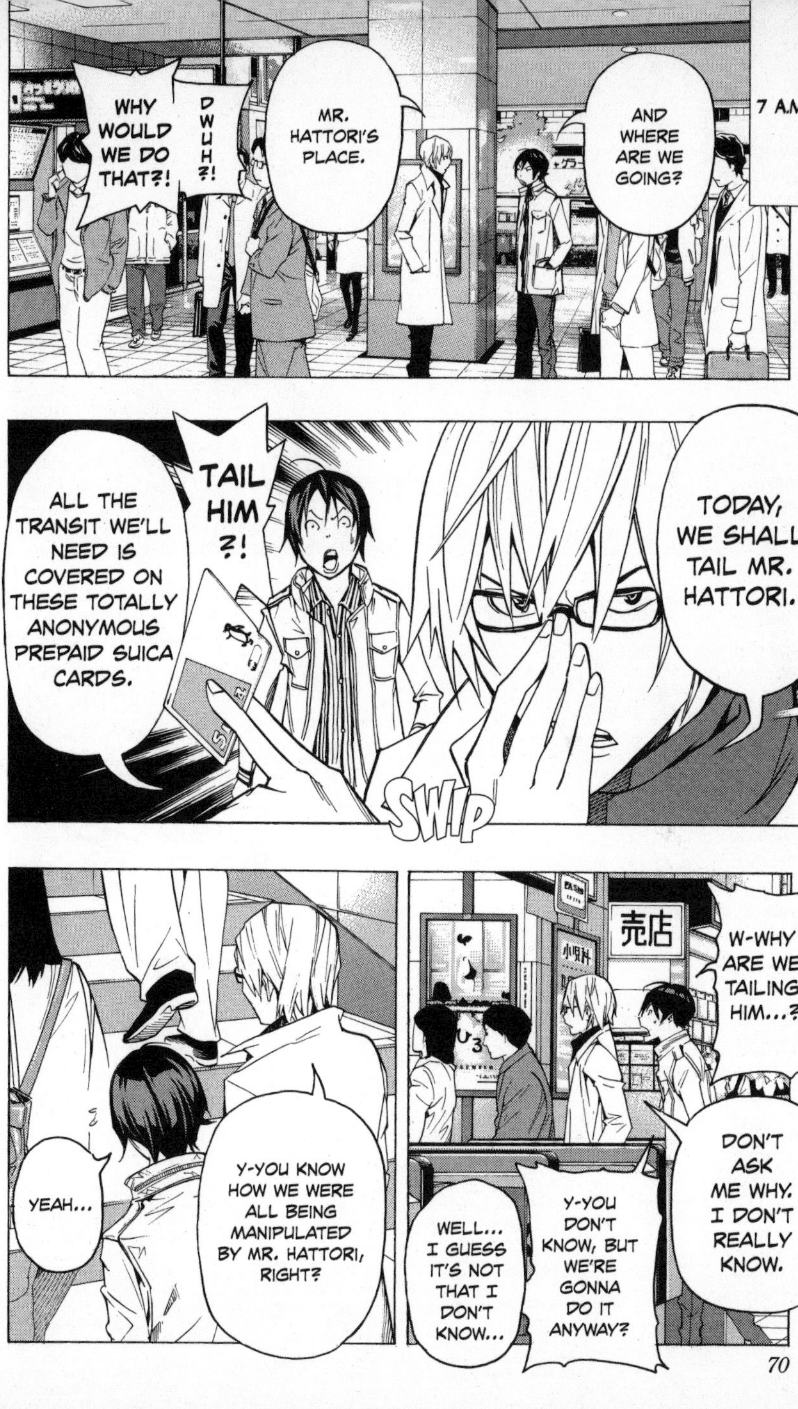
7 A.M.
AND WHERE ARE WE GOING?
MR. HATTORI'S PLACE.
DWUH?!
WHY WOULD WE DO THAT?!
TODAY, WE SHALL TAIL MR. HATTORI.
TAIL HIM?!
ALL THE TRANSIT WE'LL NEED IS COVERED ON THESE TOTALLY ANONYMOUS PREPAID SUICA CARDS.
SWIP
売店
W-WHY ARE WE TAILING HIM...?
DON'T ASK ME WHY. I DON'T REALLY KNOW.
Y-YOU DON'T KNOW, BUT WE'RE GONNA DO IT ANYWAY?
WELL... I GUESS IT'S NOT THAT I DON'T KNOW...
Y-YOU KNOW HOW WE WERE ALL BEING MANIPULATED BY MR. HATTORI, RIGHT?
YEAH...

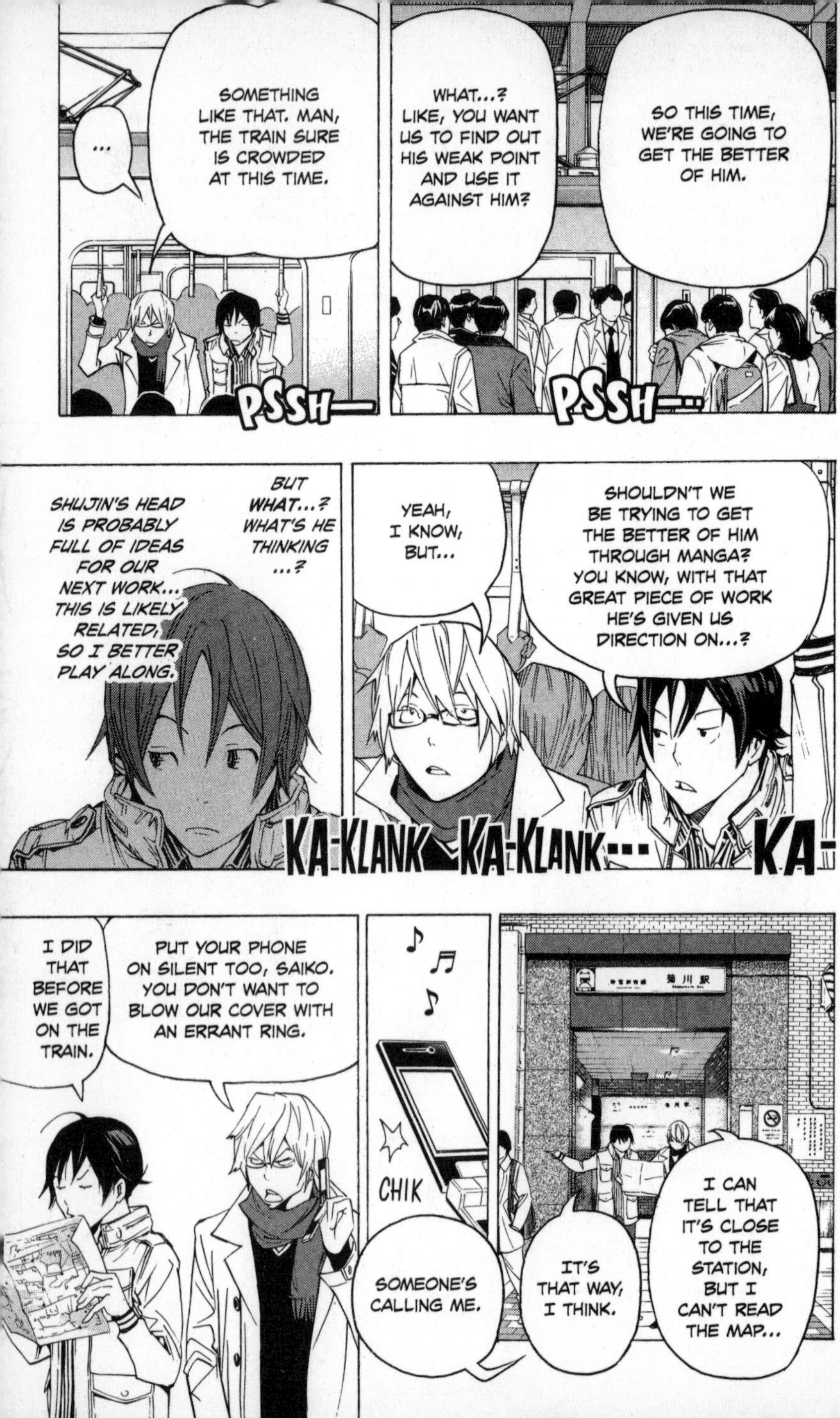
SO THIS TIME, WE'RE GOING TO GET THE BETTER OF HIM.
WHAT...? LIKE, YOU WANT US TO FIND OUT HIS WEAK POINT AND USE IT AGAINST HIM?
PSSH—...
SOMETHING LIKE THAT. MAN, THE TRAIN SURE IS CROWDED AT THIS TIME.
...
PSSH—
SHOULDN'T WE BE TRYING TO GET THE BETTER OF HIM THROUGH MANGA? YOU KNOW, WITH THAT GREAT PIECE OF WORK HE'S GIVEN US DIRECTION ON...?
YEAH, I KNOW, BUT...
KA-KLANK KA-KLANK... KA-
BUT WHAT...? WHAT'S HE THINKING...?
SHUJIN'S HEAD IS PROBABLY FULL OF IDEAS FOR OUR NEXT WORK... THIS IS LIKELY RELATED, SO I BETTER PLAY ALONG.
I CAN TELL THAT IT'S CLOSE TO THE STATION, BUT I CAN'T READ THE MAP...
IT'S THAT WAY, I THINK.
CHIK
SOMEONE'S CALLING ME.
PUT YOUR PHONE ON SILENT TOO, SAIKO. YOU DON'T WANT TO BLOW OUR COVER WITH AN ERRANT RING.
I DID THAT BEFORE WE GOT ON THE TRAIN.

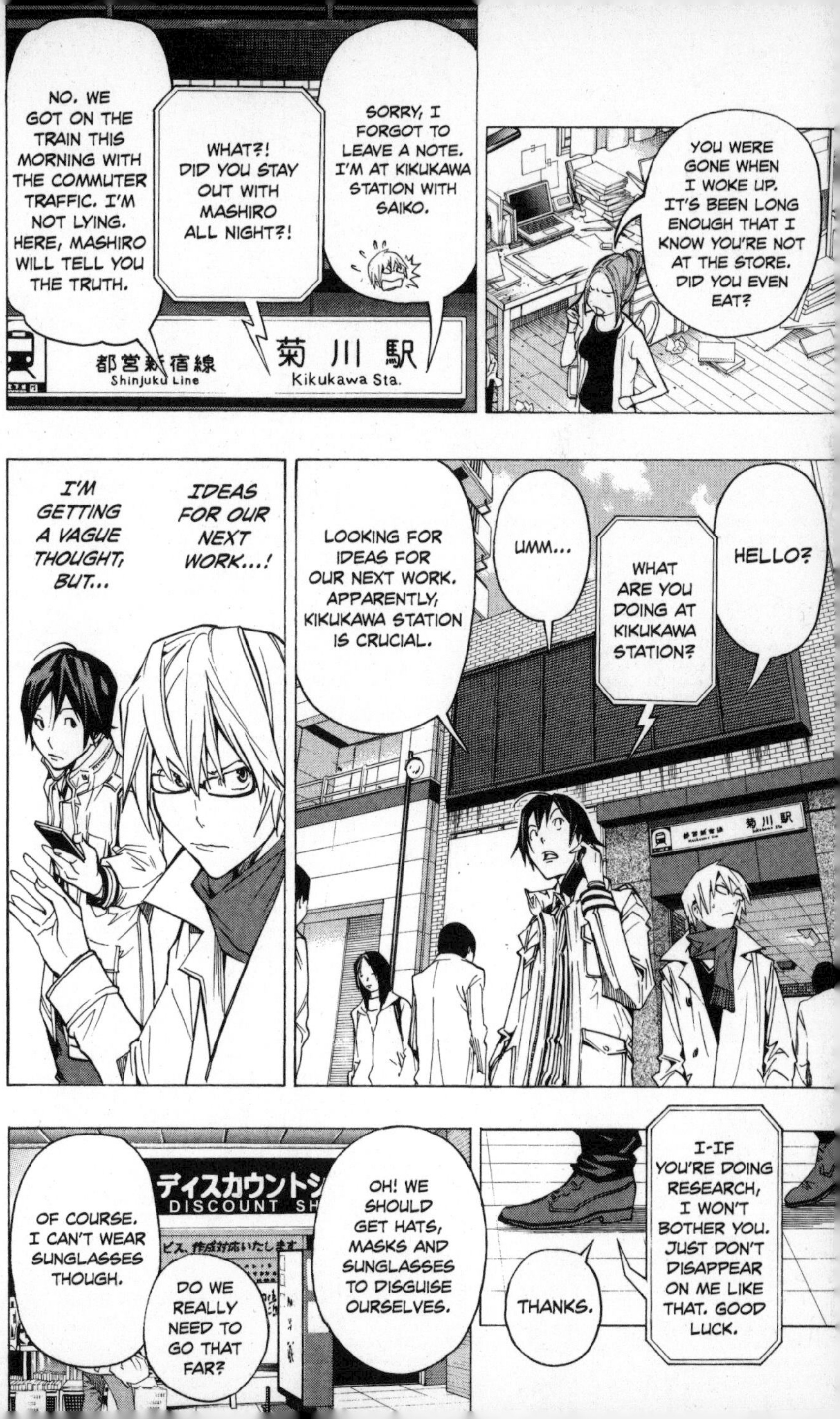
YOU WERE GONE WHEN I WOKE UP. IT'S BEEN LONG ENOUGH THAT I KNOW YOU'RE NOT AT THE STORE. DID YOU EVEN EAT?
SORRY, I FORGOT TO LEAVE A NOTE. I'M AT KIKUKAWA STATION WITH SAIKO.
WHAT?! DID YOU STAY OUT WITH MASHIRO ALL NIGHT?!
NO. WE GOT ON THE TRAIN THIS MORNING WITH THE COMMUTER TRAFFIC. I'M NOT LYING. HERE, MASHIRO WILL TELL YOU THE TRUTH.
菊川駅
Kikukawa Sta.
都営新宿線
Shinjuku Line
HELLO?
WHAT ARE YOU DOING AT KIKUKAWA STATION?
UMM...
LOOKING FOR IDEAS FOR OUR NEXT WORK. APPARENTLY, KIKUKAWA STATION IS CRUCIAL.
IDEAS FOR OUR NEXT WORK...!
I'M GETTING A VAGUE THOUGHT, BUT...
I-IF YOU'RE DOING RESEARCH, I WON'T BOTHER YOU. JUST DON'T DISAPPEAR ON ME LIKE THAT. GOOD LUCK.
THANKS.
OH! WE SHOULD GET HATS, MASKS AND SUNGLASSES TO DISGUISE OURSELVES.
DO WE REALLY NEED TO GO THAT FAR?
OF COURSE. I CAN'T WEAR SUNGLASSES THOUGH.
ディスカウントシ
DISCOUNT SH

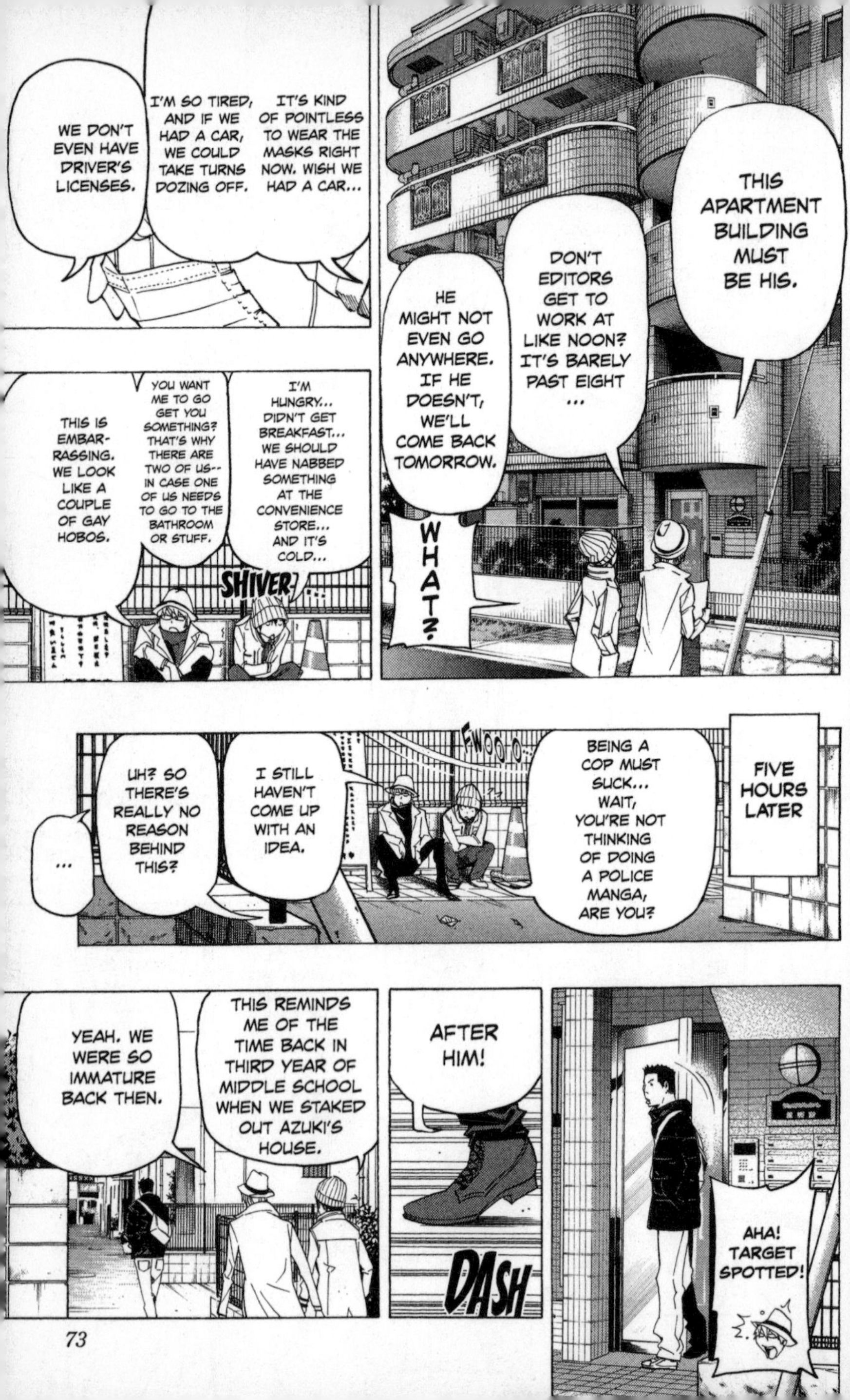
THIS APARTMENT BUILDING MUST BE HIS.
DON'T EDITORS GET TO WORK AT LIKE NOON? IT'S BARELY PAST EIGHT...
HE MIGHT NOT EVEN GO ANYWHERE. IF HE DOESN'T, WE'LL COME BACK TOMORROW.
WHAT?
IT'S KIND OF POINTLESS TO WEAR THE MASKS RIGHT NOW. WISH WE HAD A CAR...
I'M SO TIRED, AND IF WE HAD A CAR, WE COULD TAKE TURNS DOZING OFF.
WE DON'T EVEN HAVE DRIVER'S LICENSES.
I'M HUNGRY... DIDN'T GET BREAKFAST... WE SHOULD HAVE NABBED SOMETHING AT THE CONVENIENCE STORE... AND IT'S COLD...
YOU WANT ME TO GO GET YOU SOMETHING? THAT'S WHY THERE ARE TWO OF US-- IN CASE ONE OF US NEEDS TO GO TO THE BATHROOM OR STUFF.
THIS IS EMBARRASSING. WE LOOK LIKE A COUPLE OF GAY HOBOS.
SHIVER...
FIVE HOURS LATER
BEING A COP MUST SUCK... WAIT, YOU'RE NOT THINKING OF DOING A POLICE MANGA, ARE YOU?
FWOOO...
I STILL HAVEN'T COME UP WITH AN IDEA.
UH? SO THERE'S REALLY NO REASON BEHIND THIS?
...
AHA! TARGET SPOTTED!
AFTER HIM!
DASH
THIS REMINDS ME OF THE TIME BACK IN THIRD YEAR OF MIDDLE SCHOOL WHEN WE STAKED OUT AZUKI'S HOUSE.
YEAH. WE WERE SO IMMATURE BACK THEN.

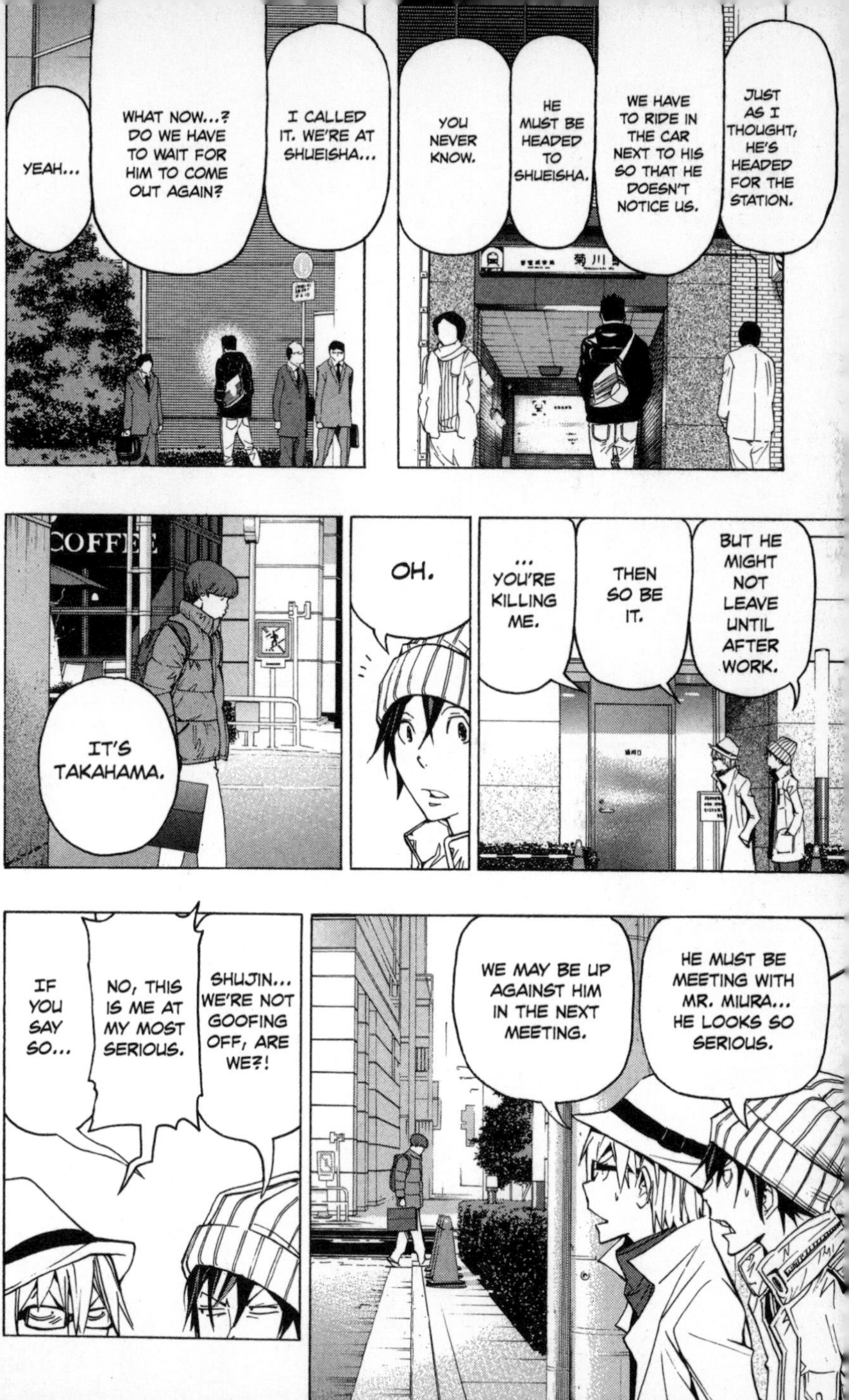
JUST AS I THOUGHT, HE'S HEADED FOR THE STATION.
WE HAVE TO RIDE IN THE CAR NEXT TO HIS SO THAT HE DOESN'T NOTICE US.
HE MUST BE HEADED TO SHUEISHA.
YOU NEVER KNOW.
I CALLED IT. WE'RE AT SHUEISHA...
WHAT NOW...? DO WE HAVE TO WAIT FOR HIM TO COME OUT AGAIN?
YEAH...
BUT HE MIGHT NOT LEAVE UNTIL AFTER WORK.
THEN SO BE IT.
... YOU'RE KILLING ME.
OH.
IT'S TAKAHAMA.
HE MUST BE MEETING WITH MR. MIURA... HE LOOKS SO SERIOUS.
WE MAY BE UP AGAINST HIM IN THE NEXT MEETING.
SHUJIN... WE'RE NOT GOOFING OFF, ARE WE?!
NO, THIS IS ME AT MY MOST SERIOUS.
IF YOU SAY SO...

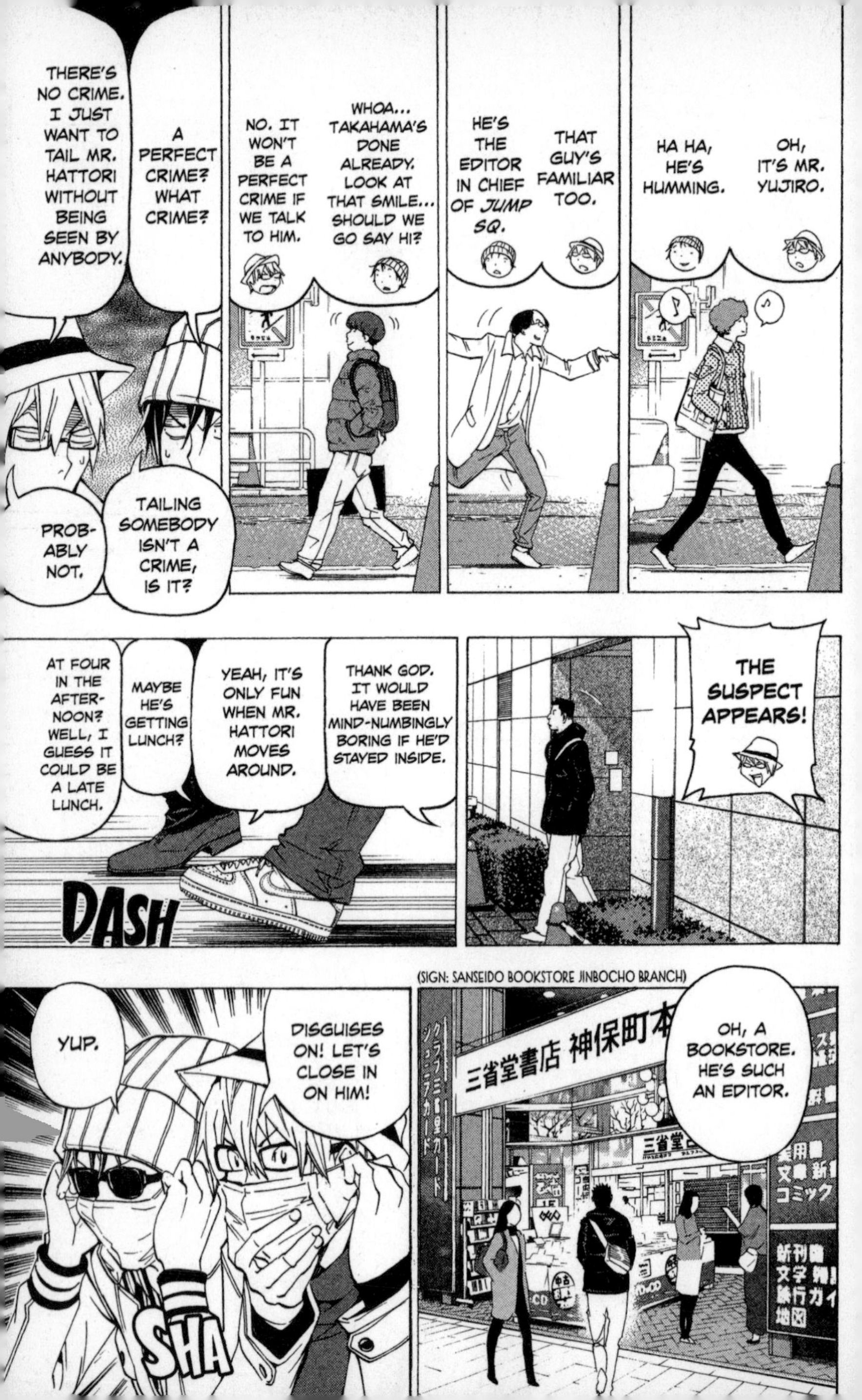
OH, IT'S MR. YUJIRO.
HA HA, HE'S HUMMING.
THAT GUY'S FAMILIAR TOO.
HE'S THE EDITOR IN CHIEF OF *JUMP SQ*.
WHOA... TAKAHAMA'S DONE ALREADY. LOOK AT THAT SMILE... SHOULD WE GO SAY HI?
NO. IT WON'T BE A PERFECT CRIME IF WE TALK TO HIM.
A PERFECT CRIME? WHAT CRIME?
THERE'S NO CRIME. I JUST WANT TO TAIL MR. HATTORI WITHOUT BEING SEEN BY ANYBODY.
TAILING SOMEBODY ISN'T A CRIME, IS IT?
PROB-ABLY NOT.
THE SUSPECT APPEARS!
THANK GOD. IT WOULD HAVE BEEN MIND-NUMBINGLY BORING IF HE'D STAYED INSIDE.
YEAH, IT'S ONLY FUN WHEN MR. HATTORI MOVES AROUND.
MAYBE HE'S GETTING LUNCH?
AT FOUR IN THE AFTER-NOON? WELL, I GUESS IT COULD BE A LATE LUNCH.
DASH
(SIGN: SANSEIDO BOOKSTORE JINBOCHO BRANCH)
三省堂書店
OH, A BOOKSTORE. HE'S SUCH AN EDITOR.
DISGUISES ON! LET'S CLOSE IN ON HIM!
YUP.
SHA

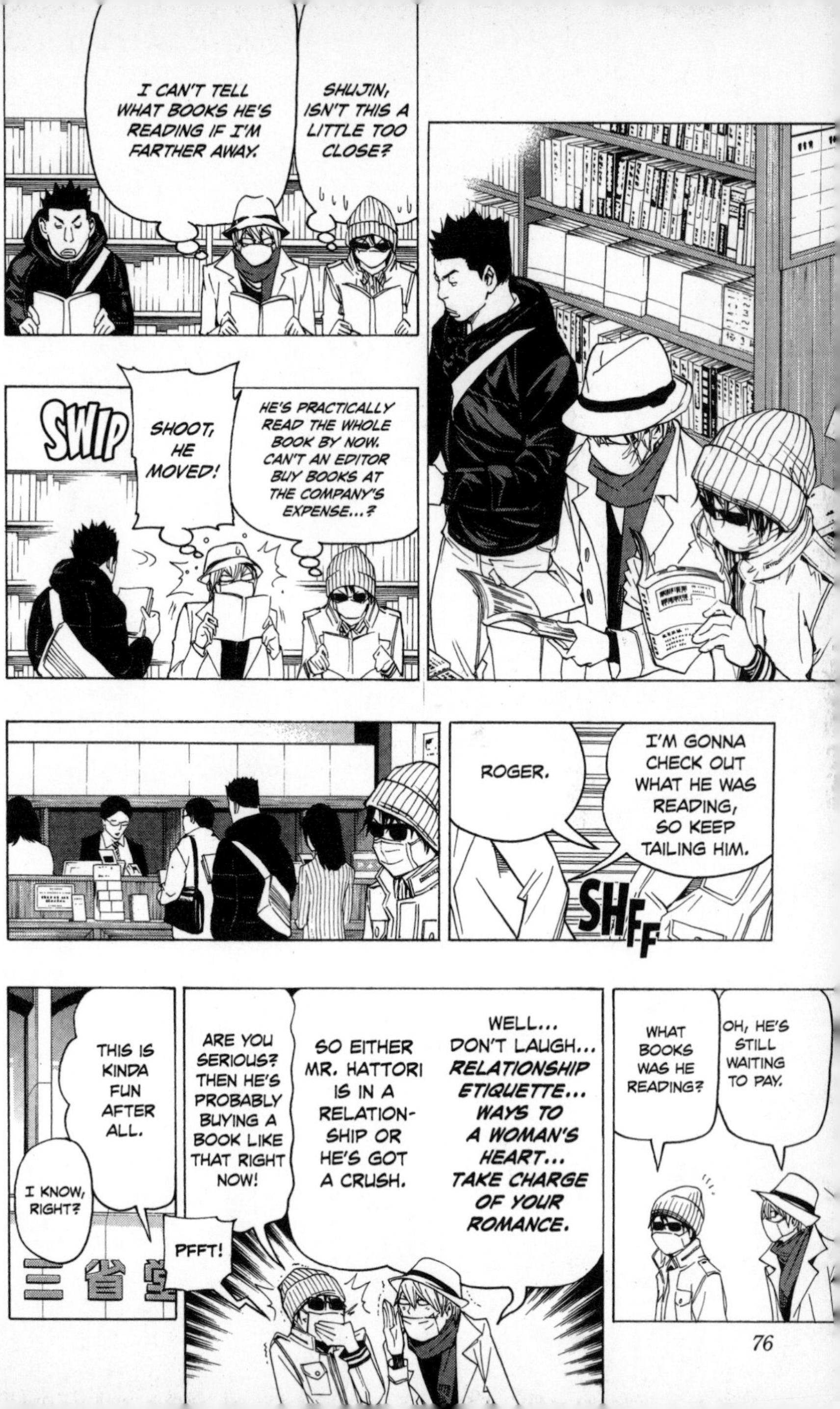
SHUJIN, ISN'T THIS A LITTLE TOO CLOSE?
I CAN'T TELL WHAT BOOKS HE'S READING IF I'M FARTHER AWAY.
HE'S PRACTICALLY READ THE WHOLE BOOK BY NOW. CAN'T AN EDITOR BUY BOOKS AT THE COMPANY'S EXPENSE...?
SHOOT, HE MOVED!
SWIP
I'M GONNA CHECK OUT WHAT HE WAS READING, SO KEEP TAILING HIM.
ROGER.
SHFF
OH, HE'S STILL WAITING TO PAY.
WHAT BOOKS WAS HE READING?
WELL... DON'T LAUGH... *RELATIONSHIP ETIQUETTE... WAYS TO A WOMAN'S HEART... TAKE CHARGE OF YOUR ROMANCE.*
SO EITHER MR. HATTORI IS IN A RELATION-SHIP OR HE'S GOT A CRUSH.
ARE YOU SERIOUS? THEN HE'S PROBABLY BUYING A BOOK LIKE THAT RIGHT NOW!
PFFT!
THIS IS KINDA FUN AFTER ALL.
I KNOW, RIGHT?

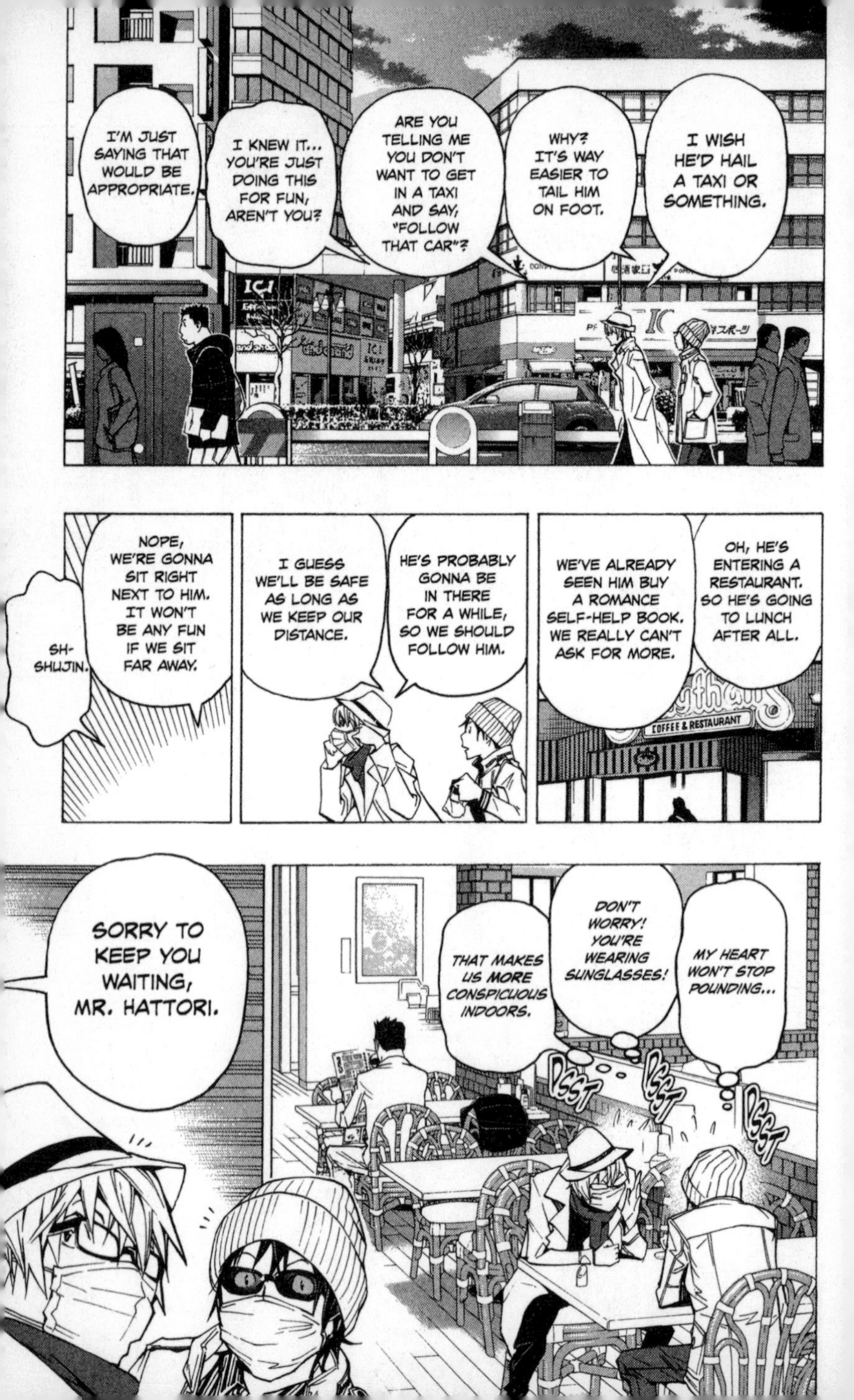
I WISH HE'D HAIL A TAXI OR SOMETHING.
WHY? IT'S WAY EASIER TO TAIL HIM ON FOOT.
ARE YOU TELLING ME YOU DON'T WANT TO GET IN A TAXI AND SAY, "FOLLOW THAT CAR"?
I KNEW IT... YOU'RE JUST DOING THIS FOR FUN, AREN'T YOU?
I'M JUST SAYING THAT WOULD BE APPROPRIATE.
OH, HE'S ENTERING A RESTAURANT. SO HE'S GOING TO LUNCH AFTER ALL.
WE'VE ALREADY SEEN HIM BUY A ROMANCE SELF-HELP BOOK. WE REALLY CAN'T ASK FOR MORE.
COFFEE & RESTAURANT
HE'S PROBABLY GONNA BE IN THERE FOR A WHILE, SO WE SHOULD FOLLOW HIM.
I GUESS WE'LL BE SAFE AS LONG AS WE KEEP OUR DISTANCE.
NOPE, WE'RE GONNA SIT RIGHT NEXT TO HIM. IT WON'T BE ANY FUN IF WE SIT FAR AWAY.
SH-SHUJIN.
MY HEART WON'T STOP POUNDING...
DON'T WORRY! YOU'RE WEARING SUNGLASSES!
THAT MAKES US MORE CONSPICUOUS INDOORS.
PSST
PSST
PSST
SORRY TO KEEP YOU WAITING, MR. HATTORI.

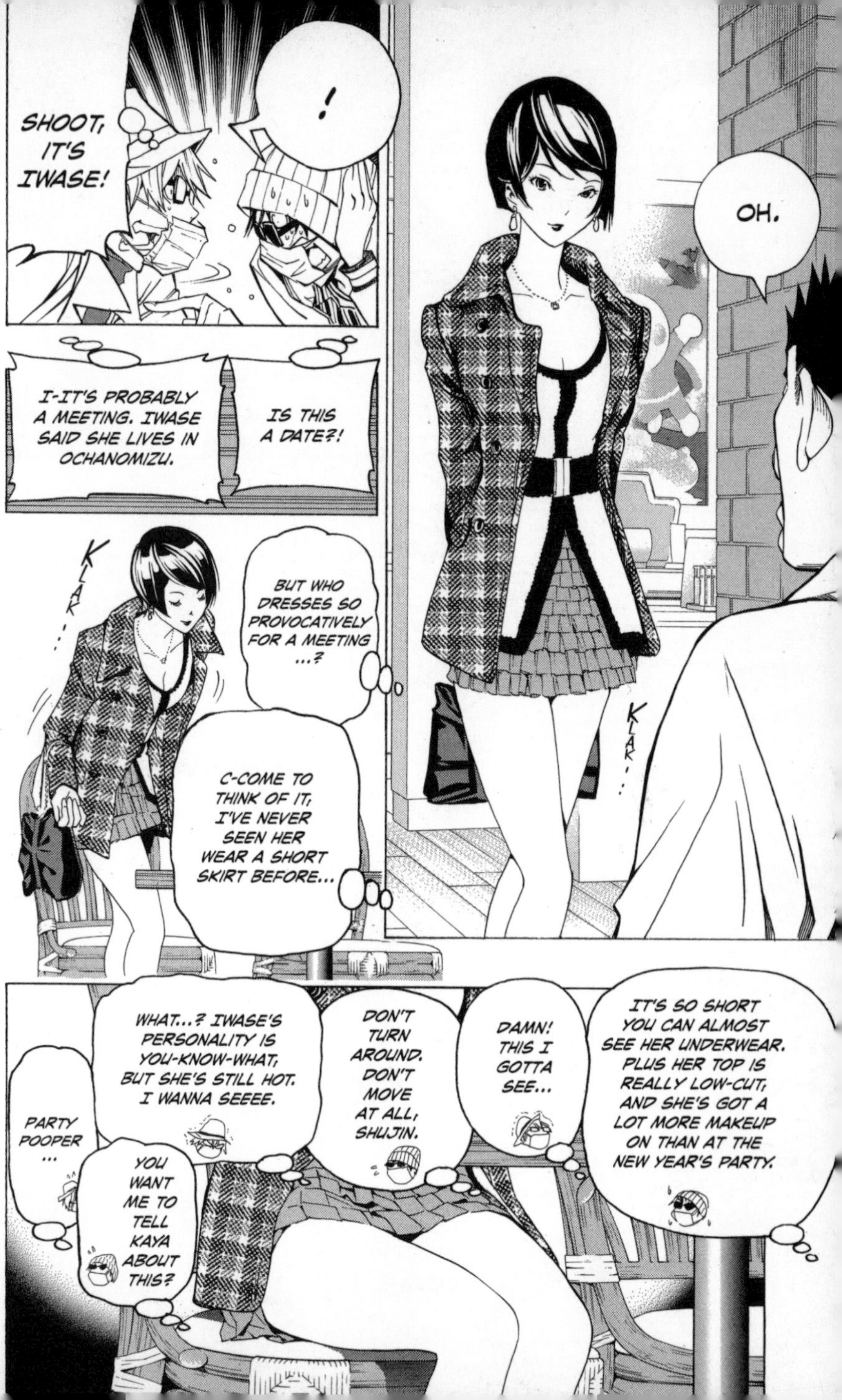
OH.
KLAK...
!
SHOOT, IT'S IWASE!
IS THIS A DATE?!
I-IT'S PROBABLY A MEETING. IWASE SAID SHE LIVES IN OCHANOMIZU.
BUT WHO DRESSES SO PROVOCATIVELY FOR A MEETING ...?
C-COME TO THINK OF IT, I'VE NEVER SEEN HER WEAR A SHORT SKIRT BEFORE...
KLAK...
IT'S SO SHORT YOU CAN ALMOST SEE HER UNDERWEAR. PLUS HER TOP IS REALLY LOW-CUT, AND SHE'S GOT A LOT MORE MAKEUP ON THAN AT THE NEW YEAR'S PARTY.
DAMN! THIS I GOTTA SEE...
DON'T TURN AROUND. DON'T MOVE AT ALL, SHUJIN.
WHAT...? IWASE'S PERSONALITY IS YOU-KNOW-WHAT, BUT SHE'S STILL HOT. I WANNA SEEEE.
YOU WANT ME TO TELL KAYA ABOUT THIS?
PARTY POOPER ...

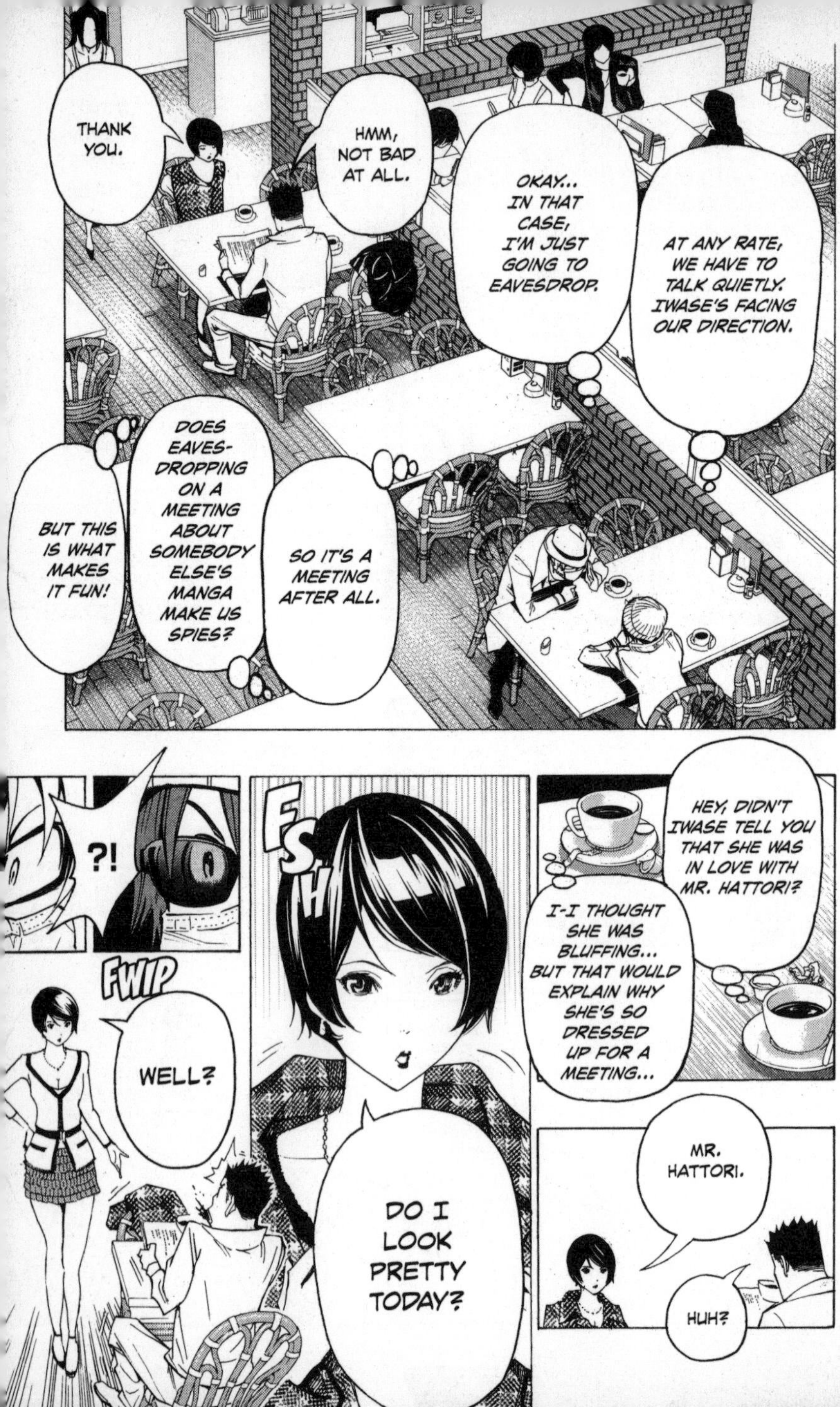
AT ANY RATE, WE HAVE TO TALK QUIETLY. IWASE'S FACING OUR DIRECTION.
OKAY... IN THAT CASE, I'M JUST GOING TO EAVESDROP.
HMM, NOT BAD AT ALL.
THANK YOU.
SO IT'S A MEETING AFTER ALL.
DOES EAVES-DROPPING ON A MEETING ABOUT SOMEBODY ELSE'S MANGA MAKE US SPIES?
BUT THIS IS WHAT MAKES IT FUN!
HEY, DIDN'T IWASE TELL YOU THAT SHE WAS IN LOVE WITH MR. HATTORI?
I-I THOUGHT SHE WAS BLUFFING... BUT THAT WOULD EXPLAIN WHY SHE'S SO DRESSED UP FOR A MEETING...
MR. HATTORI.
HUH?
FSH
DO I LOOK PRETTY TODAY?
?!
FWIP
WELL?

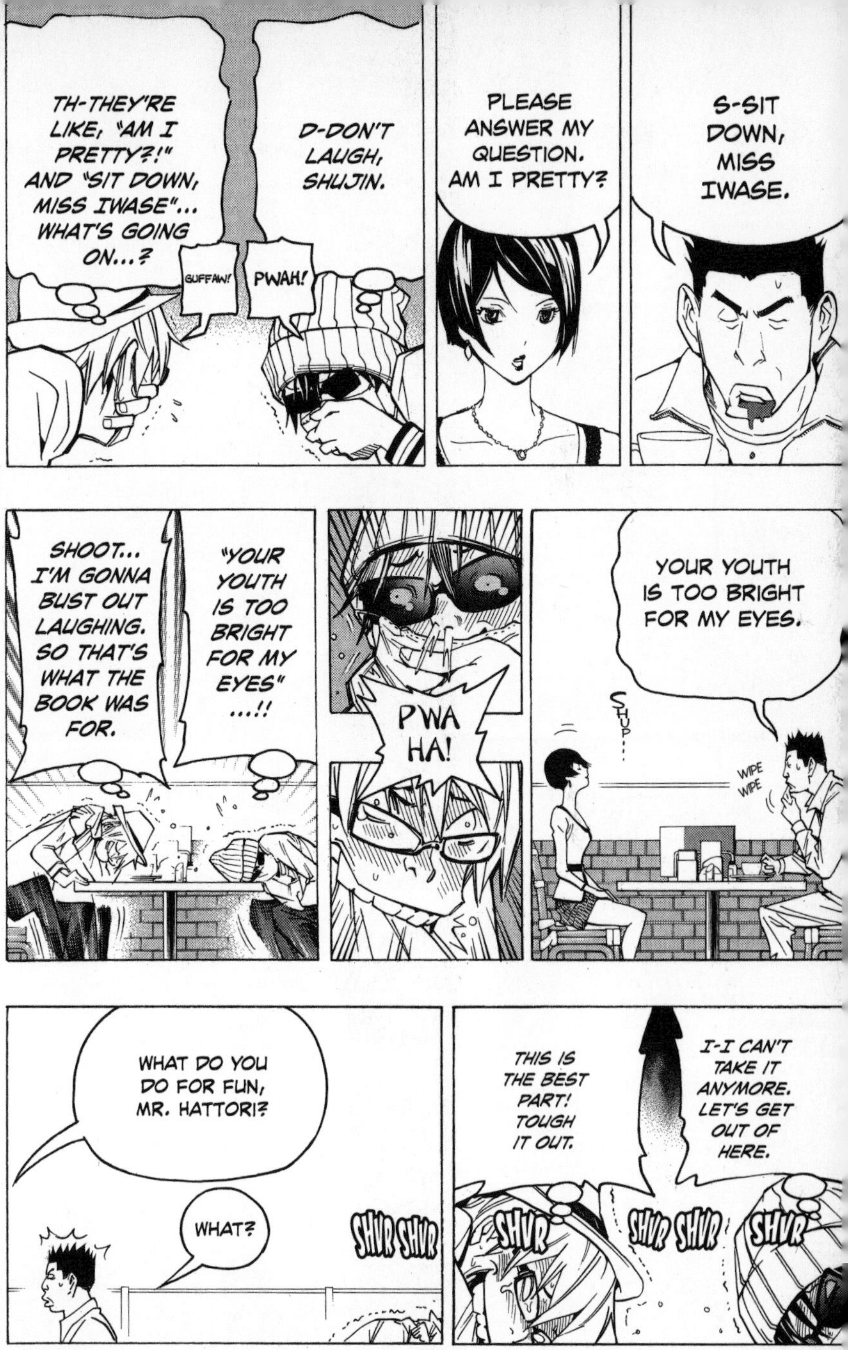
S-SIT DOWN, MISS IWASE.
PLEASE ANSWER MY QUESTION. AM I PRETTY?
D-DON'T LAUGH, SHUJIN.
TH-THEY'RE LIKE, "AM I PRETTY?!" AND "SIT DOWN, MISS IWASE"... WHAT'S GOING ON...?
PWAH!
GUFFAW!
YOUR YOUTH IS TOO BRIGHT FOR MY EYES.
SHUP...
WIPE WIPE
PWA HA!
"YOUR YOUTH IS TOO BRIGHT FOR MY EYES" ...!!
SHOOT... I'M GONNA BUST OUT LAUGHING. SO THAT'S WHAT THE BOOK WAS FOR.
I-I CAN'T TAKE IT ANYMORE. LET'S GET OUT OF HERE.
THIS IS THE BEST PART! TOUGH IT OUT.
SHVR
SHVR SHVR
SHVR
WHAT DO YOU DO FOR FUN, MR. HATTORI?
WHAT?
SHVR SHVR

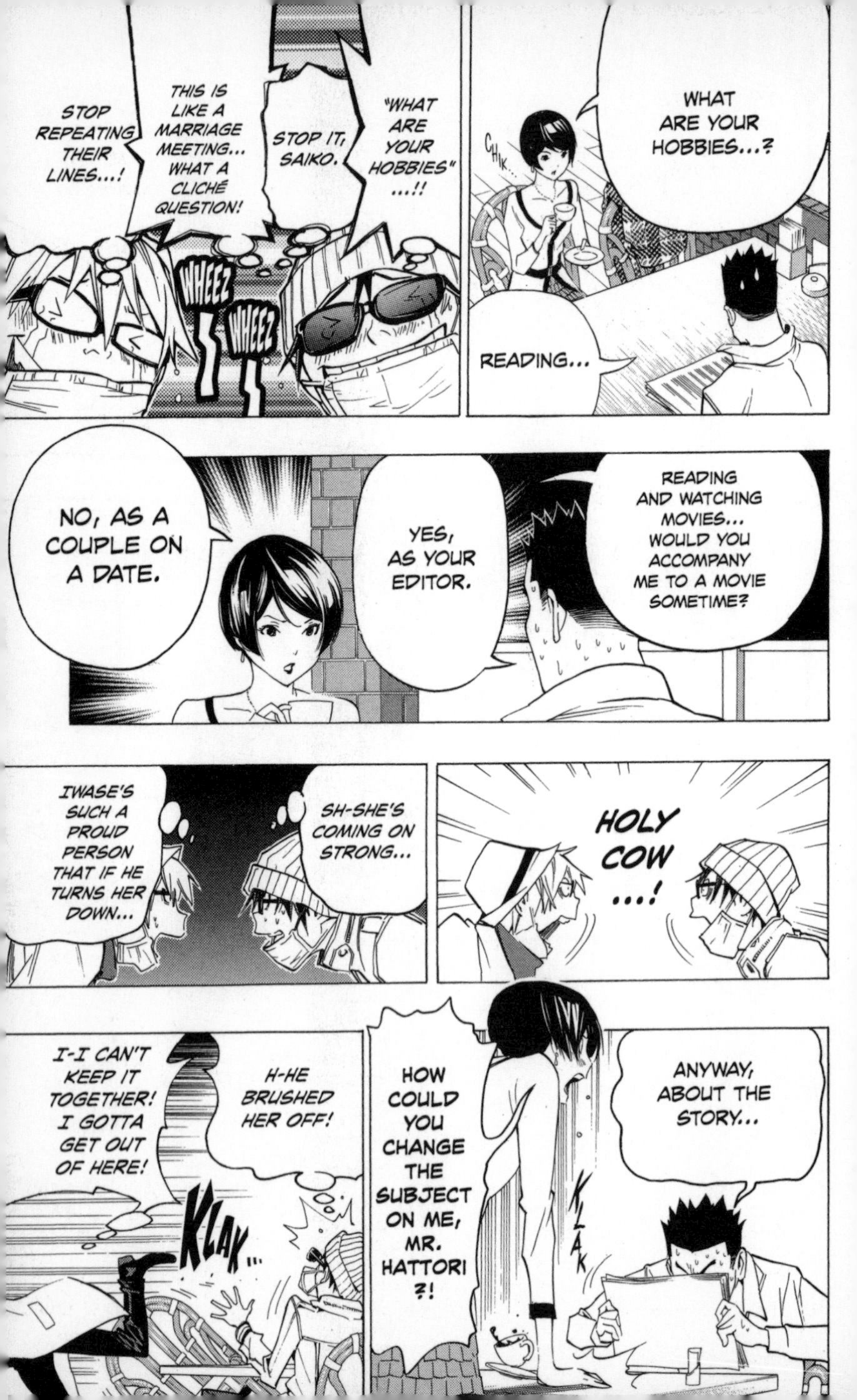
WHAT ARE YOUR HOBBIES...?
CHIK...
READING...
"WHAT ARE YOUR HOBBIES" ...!!
STOP IT, SAIKO.
THIS IS LIKE A MARRIAGE MEETING... WHAT A CLICHÉ QUESTION!
STOP REPEATING THEIR LINES...!
WHEEZ
WHEEZ
READING AND WATCHING MOVIES... WOULD YOU ACCOMPANY ME TO A MOVIE SOMETIME?
YES, AS YOUR EDITOR.
NO, AS A COUPLE ON A DATE.
HOLY COW ...!
SH-SHE'S COMING ON STRONG...
IWASE'S SUCH A PROUD PERSON THAT IF HE TURNS HER DOWN...
ANYWAY, ABOUT THE STORY...
KLAK
HOW COULD YOU CHANGE THE SUBJECT ON ME, MR. HATTORI ?!
H-HE BRUSHED HER OFF!
I-I CAN'T KEEP IT TOGETHER! I GOTTA GET OUT OF HERE!
KLAK...

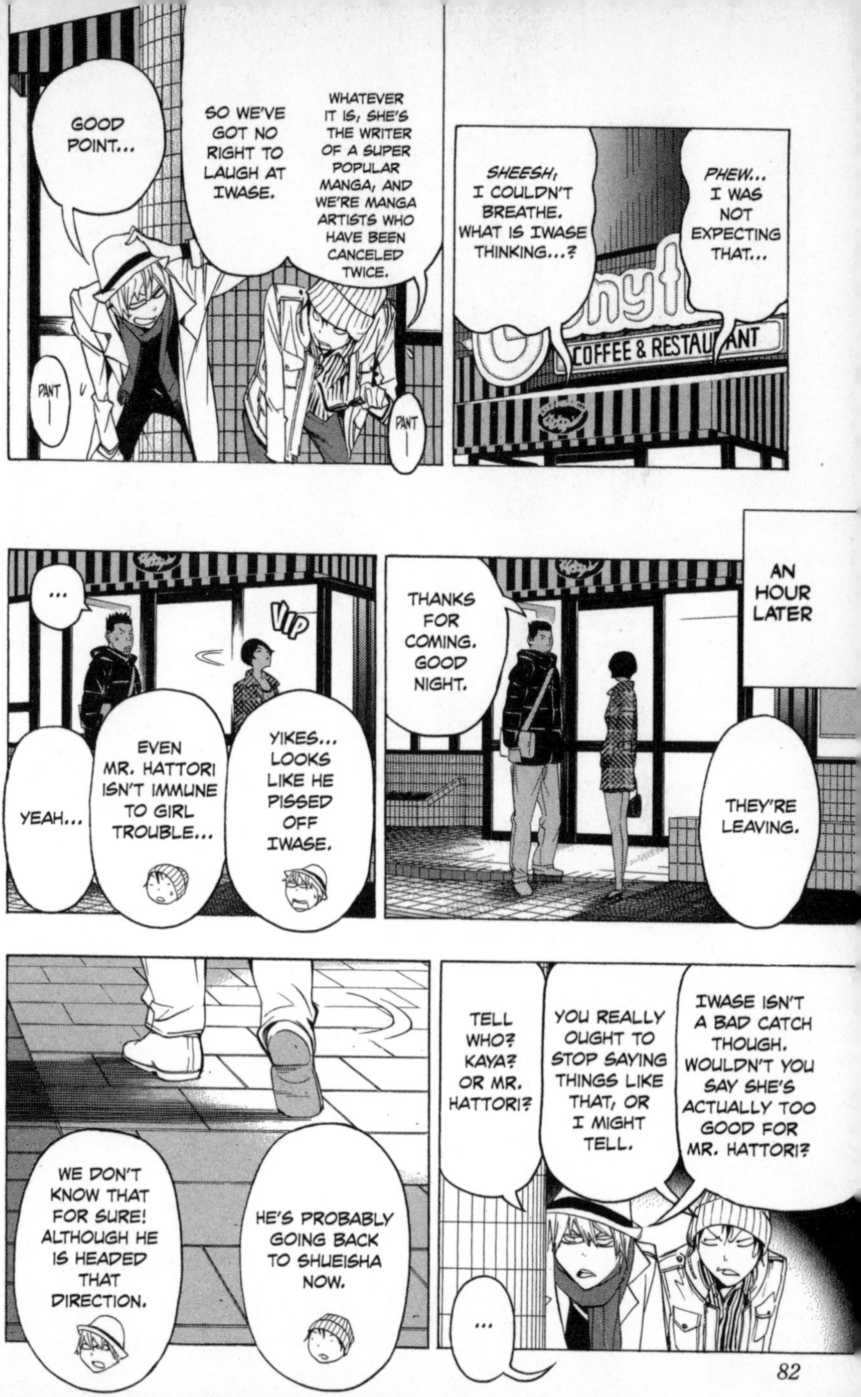
PHEW... I WAS NOT EXPECTING THAT...
SHEESH, I COULDN'T BREATHE. WHAT IS IWASE THINKING...?
COFFEE & RESTAU ANT
WHATEVER IT IS, SHE'S THE WRITER OF A SUPER POPULAR MANGA, AND WE'RE MANGA ARTISTS WHO HAVE BEEN CANCELED TWICE.
SO WE'VE GOT NO RIGHT TO LAUGH AT IWASE.
GOOD POINT...
PANT
PANT
AN HOUR LATER
THEY'RE LEAVING.
THANKS FOR COMING. GOOD NIGHT.
VIP
...
YIKES... LOOKS LIKE HE PISSED OFF IWASE.
EVEN MR. HATTORI ISN'T IMMUNE TO GIRL TROUBLE...
YEAH...
IWASE ISN'T A BAD CATCH THOUGH. WOULDN'T YOU SAY SHE'S ACTUALLY TOO GOOD FOR MR. HATTORI?
YOU REALLY OUGHT TO STOP SAYING THINGS LIKE THAT, OR I MIGHT TELL.
TELL WHO? KAYA? OR MR. HATTORI?
...
HE'S PROBABLY GOING BACK TO SHUEISHA NOW.
WE DON'T KNOW THAT FOR SURE! ALTHOUGH HE IS HEADED THAT DIRECTION.

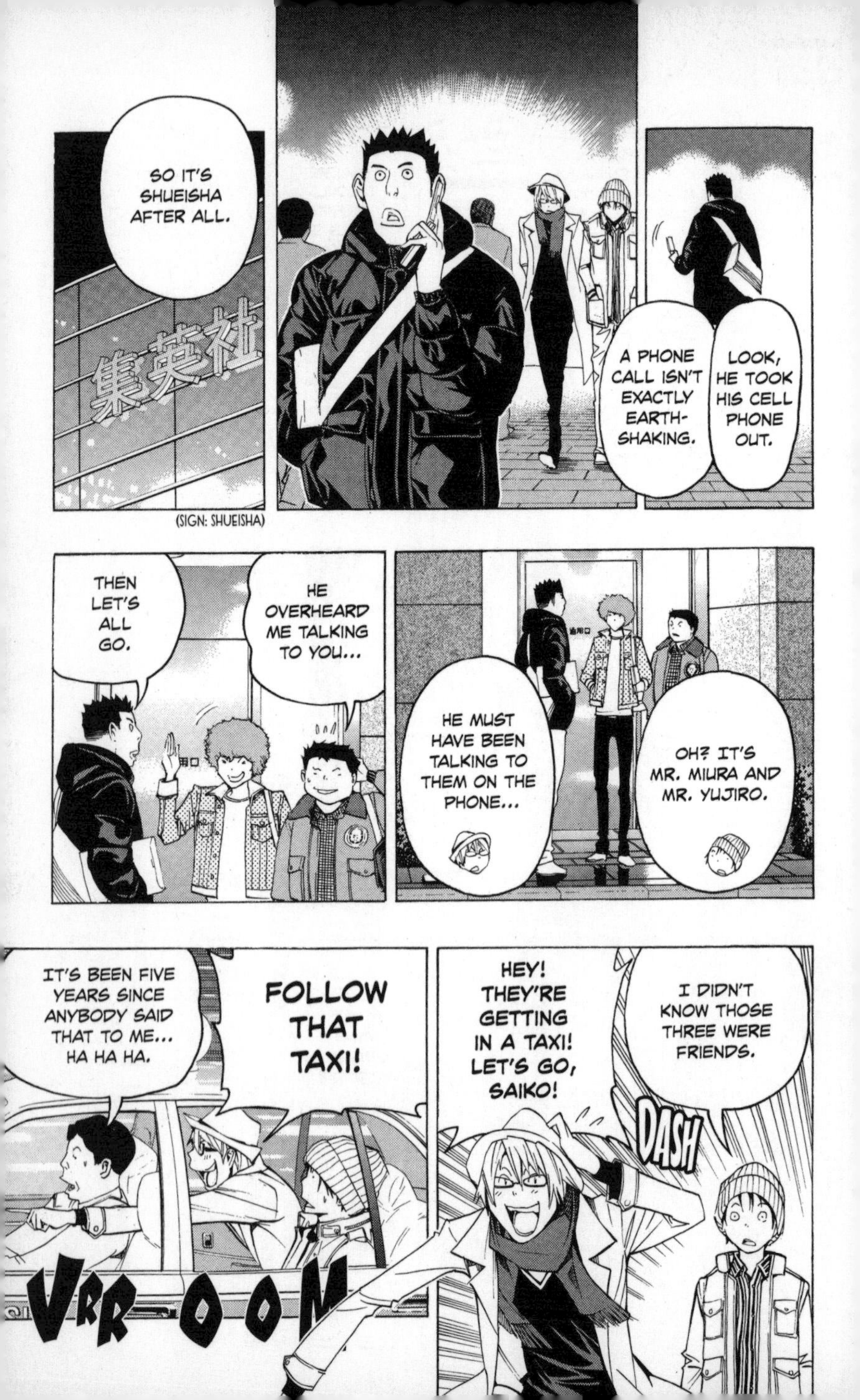
LOOK, HE TOOK HIS CELL PHONE OUT.
A PHONE CALL ISN'T EXACTLY EARTH-SHAKING.
SO IT'S SHUEISHA AFTER ALL.
集英社
(SIGN: SHUEISHA)
OH? IT'S MR. MIURA AND MR. YUJIRO.
HE MUST HAVE BEEN TALKING TO THEM ON THE PHONE...
HE OVERHEARD ME TALKING TO YOU...
THEN LET'S ALL GO.
I DIDN'T KNOW THOSE THREE WERE FRIENDS.
DASH
HEY! THEY'RE GETTING IN A TAXI! LET'S GO, SAIKO!
FOLLOW THAT TAXI!
IT'S BEEN FIVE YEARS SINCE ANYBODY SAID THAT TO ME... HA HA HA.
VRR-O-O-M

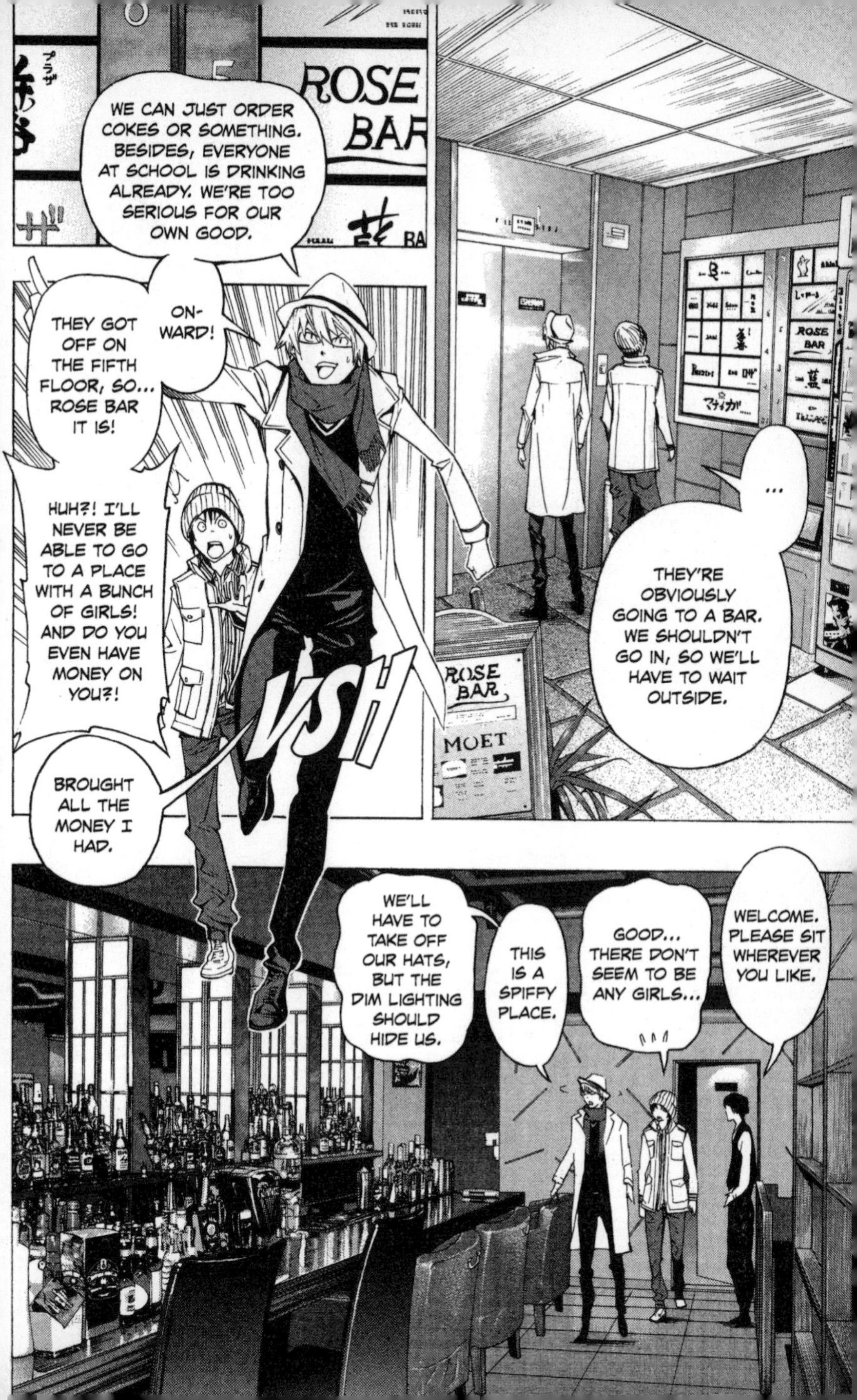
...
THEY'RE OBVIOUSLY GOING TO A BAR. WE SHOULDN'T GO IN, SO WE'LL HAVE TO WAIT OUTSIDE.
ROSE BAR
MOET
WE CAN JUST ORDER COKES OR SOMETHING. BESIDES, EVERYONE AT SCHOOL IS DRINKING ALREADY. WE'RE TOO SERIOUS FOR OUR OWN GOOD.
ROSE BAR
ON-WARD!
THEY GOT OFF ON THE FIFTH FLOOR, SO... ROSE BAR IT IS!
HUH?! I'LL NEVER BE ABLE TO GO TO A PLACE WITH A BUNCH OF GIRLS! AND DO YOU EVEN HAVE MONEY ON YOU?!
VSH
BROUGHT ALL THE MONEY I HAD.
WELCOME. PLEASE SIT WHEREVER YOU LIKE.
GOOD... THERE DON'T SEEM TO BE ANY GIRLS...
THIS IS A SPIFFY PLACE.
WE'LL HAVE TO TAKE OFF OUR HATS, BUT THE DIM LIGHTING SHOULD HIDE US.

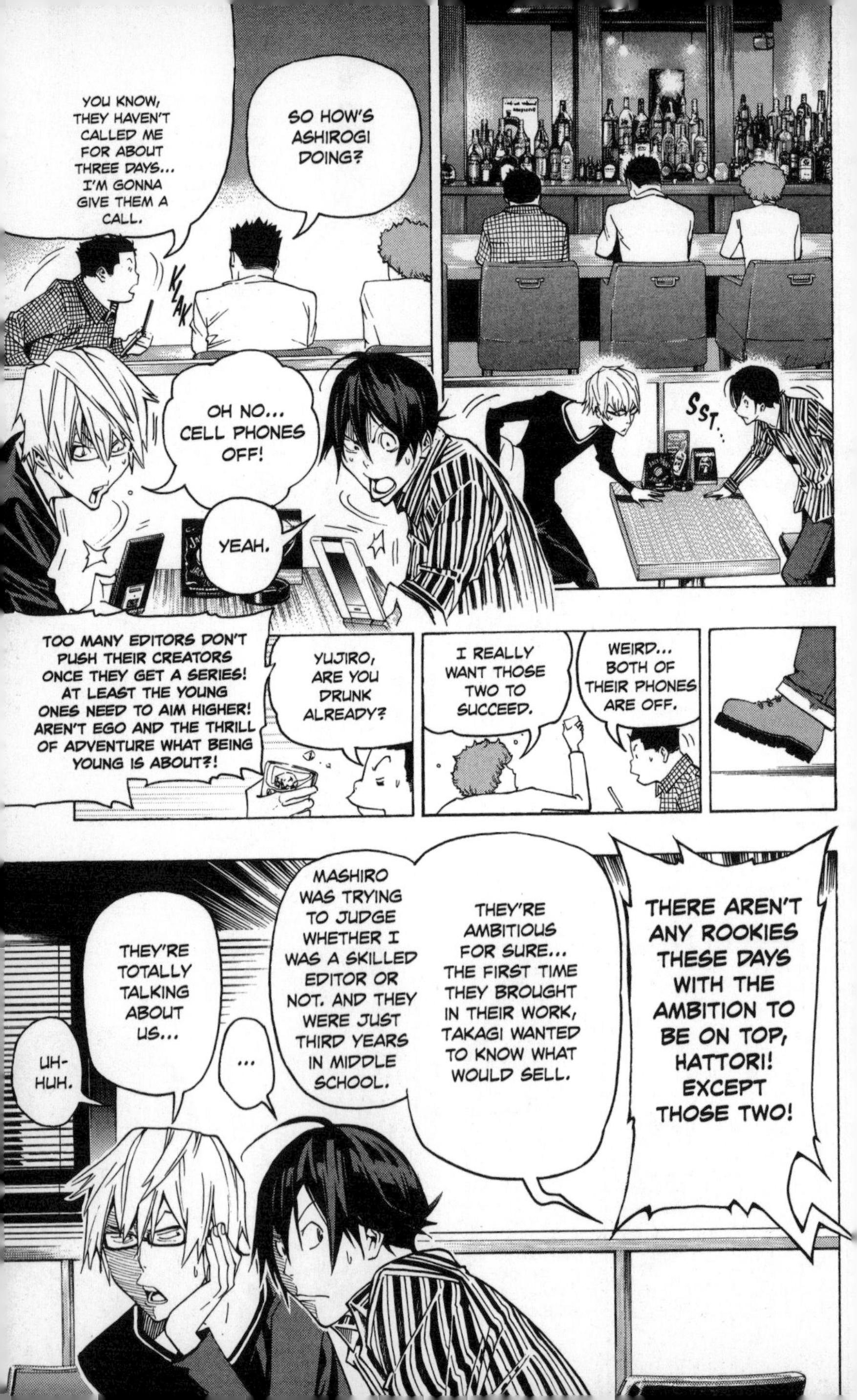
SO HOW'S ASHIROGI DOING?
YOU KNOW, THEY HAVEN'T CALLED ME FOR ABOUT THREE DAYS... I'M GONNA GIVE THEM A CALL.
KLAK
SST...
OH NO... CELL PHONES OFF!
YEAH.
WEIRD... BOTH OF THEIR PHONES ARE OFF.
I REALLY WANT THOSE TWO TO SUCCEED.
YUJIRO, ARE YOU DRUNK ALREADY?
TOO MANY EDITORS DON'T PUSH THEIR CREATORS ONCE THEY GET A SERIES! AT LEAST THE YOUNG ONES NEED TO AIM HIGHER! AREN'T EGO AND THE THRILL OF ADVENTURE WHAT BEING YOUNG IS ABOUT?!
THERE AREN'T ANY ROOKIES THESE DAYS WITH THE AMBITION TO BE ON TOP, HATTORI! EXCEPT THOSE TWO!
THEY'RE AMBITIOUS FOR SURE... THE FIRST TIME THEY BROUGHT IN THEIR WORK, TAKAGI WANTED TO KNOW WHAT WOULD SELL.
MASHIRO WAS TRYING TO JUDGE WHETHER I WAS A SKILLED EDITOR OR NOT. AND THEY WERE JUST THIRD YEARS IN MIDDLE SCHOOL.
...
THEY'RE TOTALLY TALKING ABOUT US...
UH-HUH.

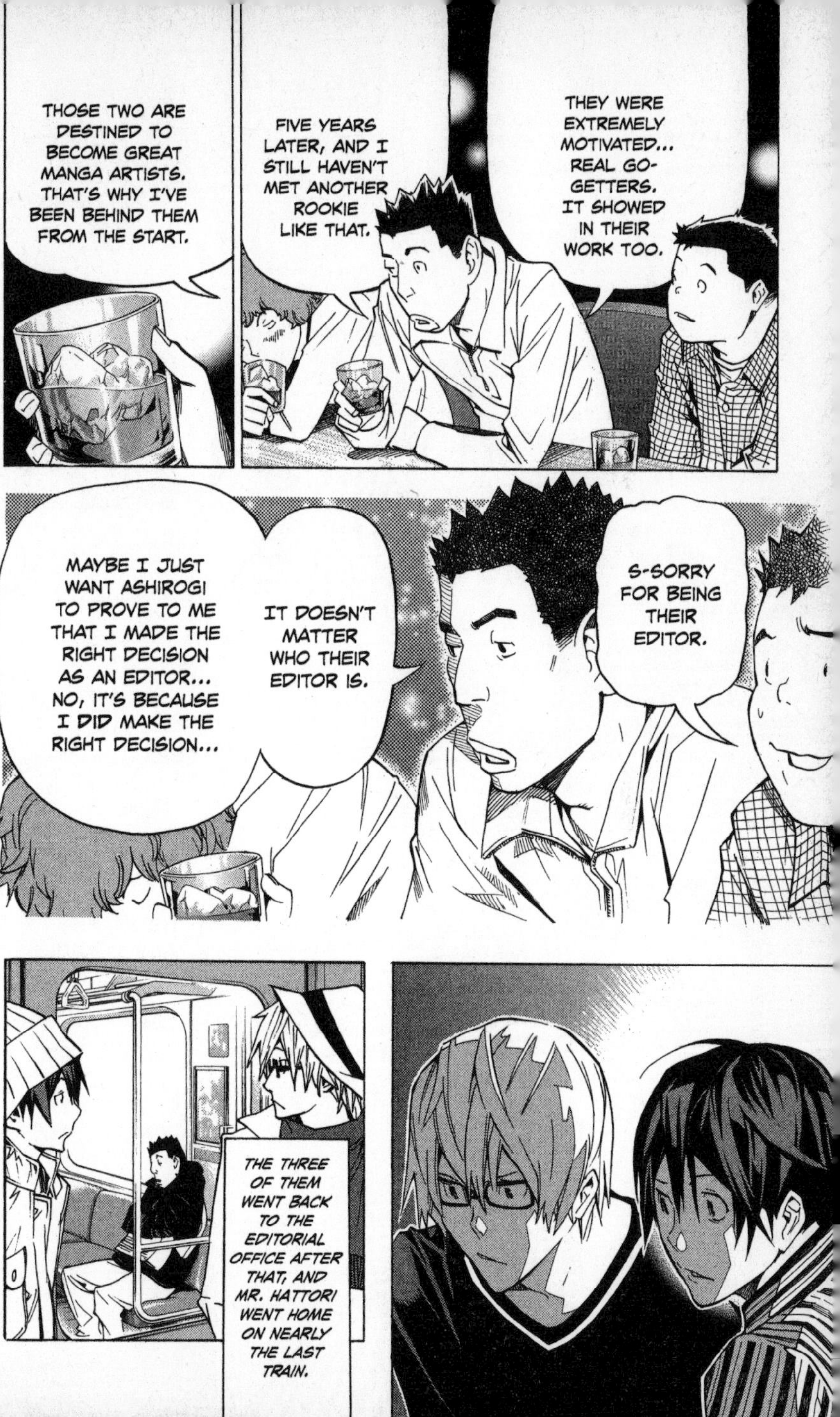
THEY WERE EXTREMELY MOTIVATED... REAL GO-GETTERS. IT SHOWED IN THEIR WORK TOO.
FIVE YEARS LATER, AND I STILL HAVEN'T MET ANOTHER ROOKIE LIKE THAT.
THOSE TWO ARE DESTINED TO BECOME GREAT MANGA ARTISTS. THAT'S WHY I'VE BEEN BEHIND THEM FROM THE START.
S-SORRY FOR BEING THEIR EDITOR.
IT DOESN'T MATTER WHO THEIR EDITOR IS.
MAYBE I JUST WANT ASHIROGI TO PROVE TO ME THAT I MADE THE RIGHT DECISION AS AN EDITOR... NO, IT'S BECAUSE I DID MAKE THE RIGHT DECISION...
THE THREE OF THEM WENT BACK TO THE EDITORIAL OFFICE AFTER THAT, AND MR. HATTORI WENT HOME ON NEARLY THE LAST TRAIN.

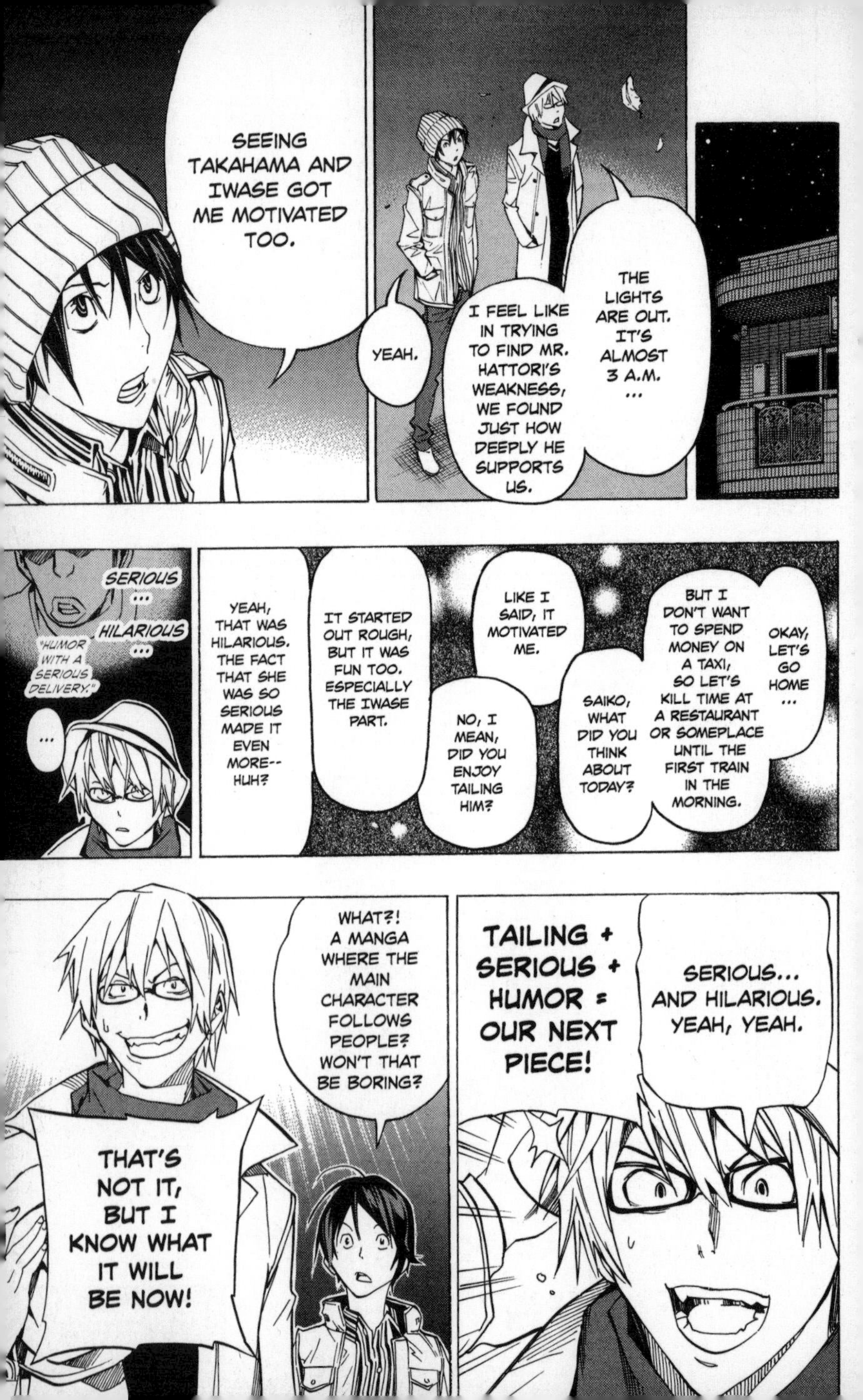
THE LIGHTS ARE OUT. IT'S ALMOST 3 A.M. ...
I FEEL LIKE IN TRYING TO FIND MR. HATTORI'S WEAKNESS, WE FOUND JUST HOW DEEPLY HE SUPPORTS US.
YEAH.
SEEING TAKAHAMA AND IWASE GOT ME MOTIVATED TOO.
OKAY, LET'S GO HOME ...
BUT I DON'T WANT TO SPEND MONEY ON A TAXI, SO LET'S KILL TIME AT A RESTAURANT OR SOMEPLACE UNTIL THE FIRST TRAIN IN THE MORNING.
SAIKO, WHAT DID YOU THINK ABOUT TODAY?
LIKE I SAID, IT MOTIVATED ME.
NO, I MEAN, DID YOU ENJOY TAILING HIM?
IT STARTED OUT ROUGH, BUT IT WAS FUN TOO. ESPECIALLY THE IWASE PART.
YEAH, THAT WAS HILARIOUS. THE FACT THAT SHE WAS SO SERIOUS MADE IT EVEN MORE-- HUH?
SERIOUS ...
HILARIOUS ...
"HUMOR WITH A SERIOUS DELIVERY."
...
SERIOUS... AND HILARIOUS. YEAH, YEAH.
TAILING + SERIOUS + HUMOR = OUR NEXT PIECE!
WHAT?! A MANGA WHERE THE MAIN CHARACTER FOLLOWS PEOPLE? WON'T THAT BE BORING?
THAT'S NOT IT, BUT I KNOW WHAT IT WILL BE NOW!

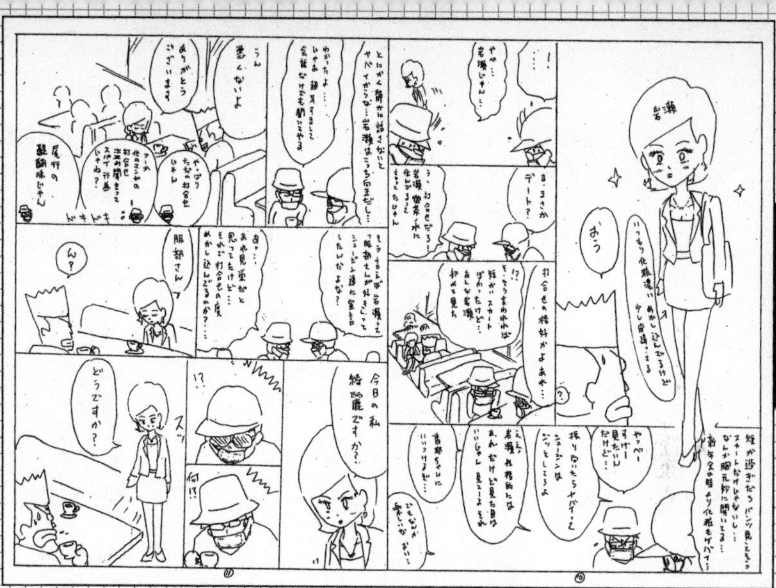
岩瀬
おう
……
!
やべ…岩瀬じゃん…
ま、まさか デート？
打合せの格好かよ あれ…
とにかく静かに話さないとヤバイからな…岩瀬はこっち向きだし…
うん 悪くないよ
ありがとうございます
やっぱりただの打合せじゃん
尾行の醍醐味じゃん
ドキドキ
服部さん
ん？
今日の私 綺麗ですか？
!?
何!?
どうですか？
スッ

OHBA'S STORYBOARD

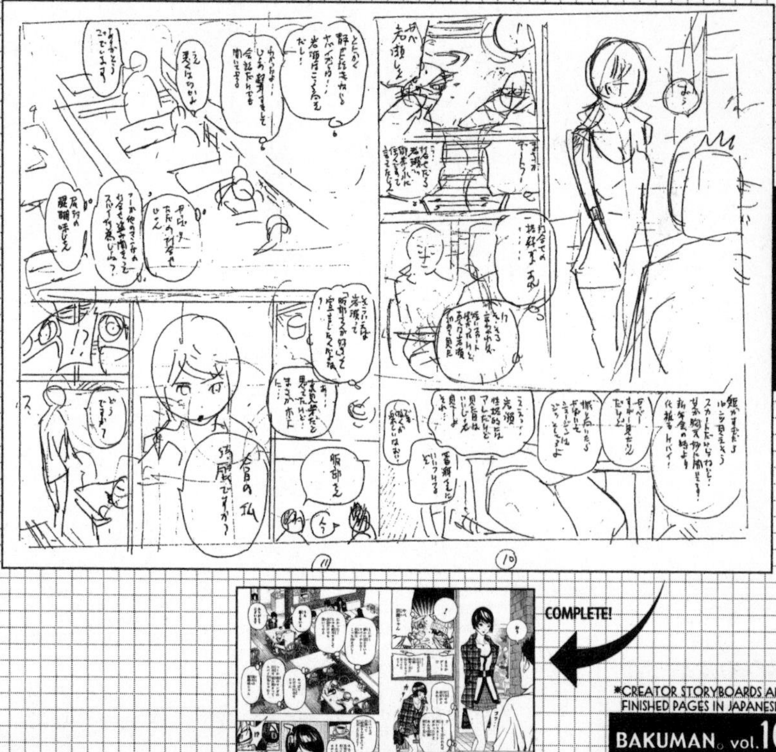

OBATA'S STORYBOARD

COMPLETE!

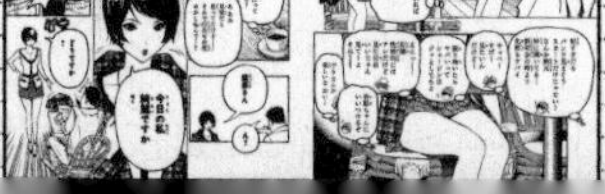

*CREATOR STORYBOARDS AND FINISHED PAGES IN JAPANESE

BAKUMAN。 vol.10

"Until the Final Draft Is Complete"

Chapter 83, pp. 78-79

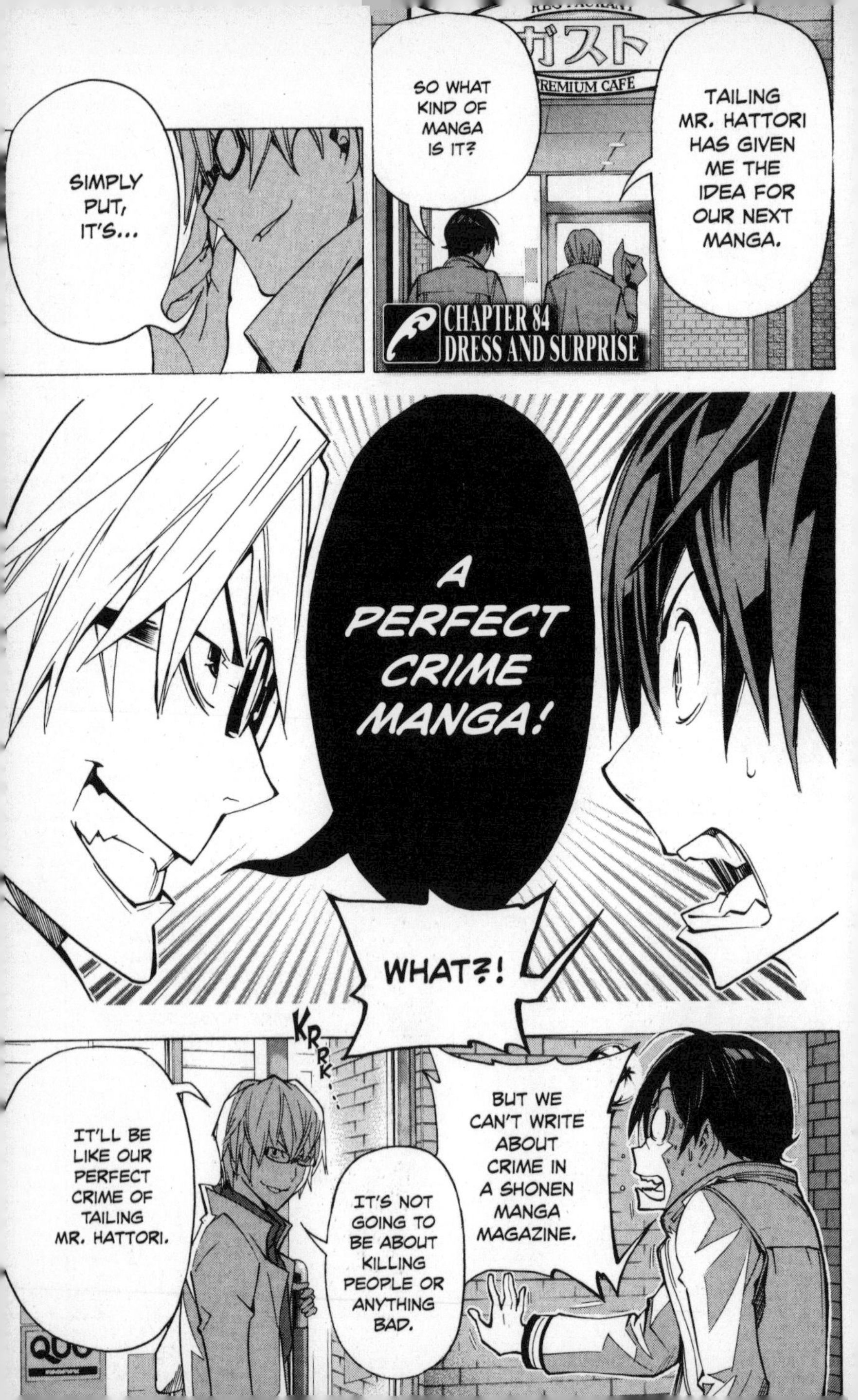
ガスト
TAILING MR. HATTORI HAS GIVEN ME THE IDEA FOR OUR NEXT MANGA.
SO WHAT KIND OF MANGA IS IT?
CHAPTER 84
DRESS AND SURPRISE
SIMPLY PUT, IT'S...
A PERFECT CRIME MANGA!
WHAT?!
KRRK...
BUT WE CAN'T WRITE ABOUT CRIME IN A SHONEN MANGA MAGAZINE.
IT'S NOT GOING TO BE ABOUT KILLING PEOPLE OR ANYTHING BAD.
IT'LL BE LIKE OUR PERFECT CRIME OF TAILING MR. HATTORI.

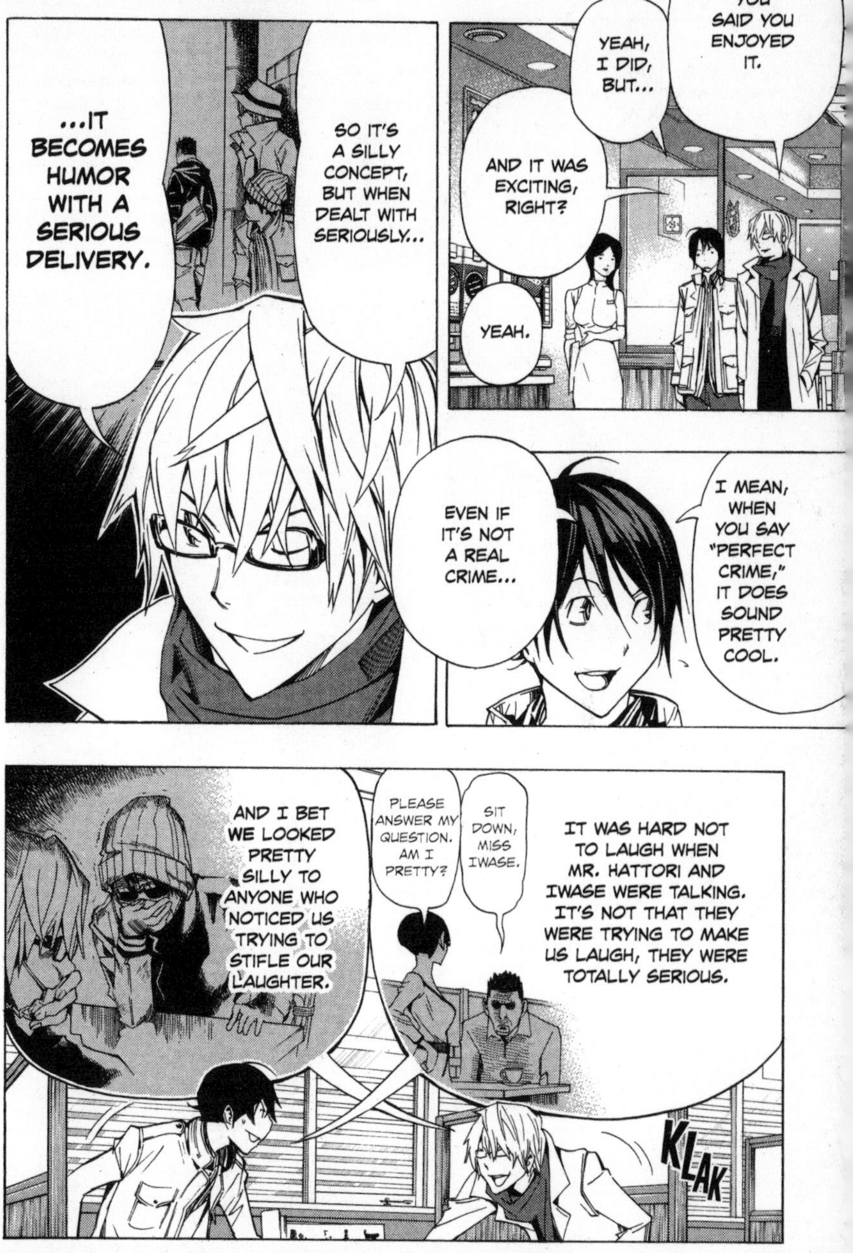
YOU SAID YOU ENJOYED IT.
YEAH, I DID, BUT...
AND IT WAS EXCITING, RIGHT?
YEAH.
I MEAN, WHEN YOU SAY "PERFECT CRIME," IT DOES SOUND PRETTY COOL.
EVEN IF IT'S NOT A REAL CRIME...
SO IT'S A SILLY CONCEPT, BUT WHEN DEALT WITH SERIOUSLY...
...IT BECOMES HUMOR WITH A SERIOUS DELIVERY.
IT WAS HARD NOT TO LAUGH WHEN MR. HATTORI AND IWASE WERE TALKING. IT'S NOT THAT THEY WERE TRYING TO MAKE US LAUGH, THEY WERE TOTALLY SERIOUS.
KLAK
SIT DOWN, MISS IWASE.
PLEASE ANSWER MY QUESTION. AM I PRETTY?
AND I BET WE LOOKED PRETTY SILLY TO ANYONE WHO NOTICED US TRYING TO STIFLE OUR LAUGHTER.

READ THIS WAY

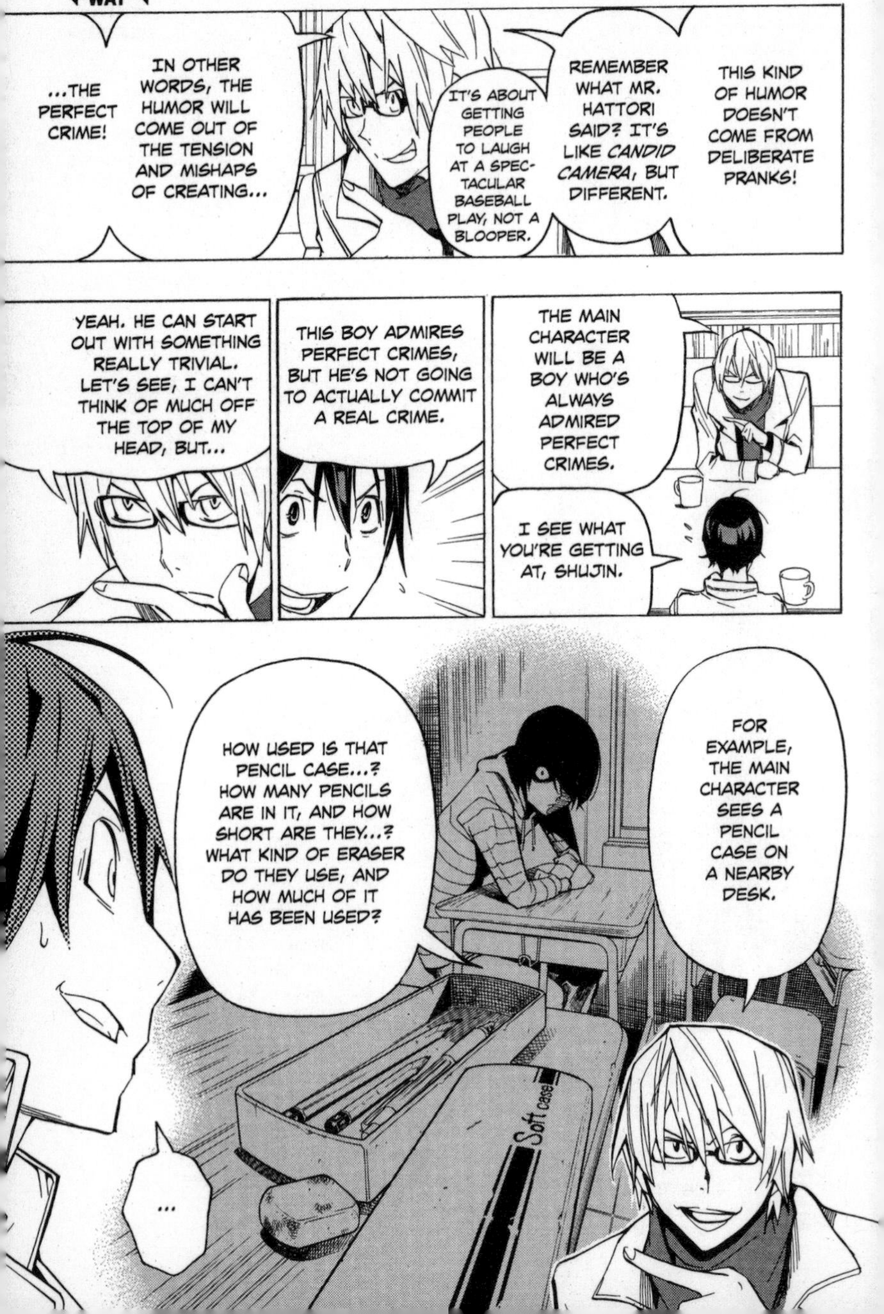
THIS KIND OF HUMOR DOESN'T COME FROM DELIBERATE PRANKS!
REMEMBER WHAT MR. HATTORI SAID? IT'S LIKE *CANDID CAMERA*, BUT DIFFERENT.
IT'S ABOUT GETTING PEOPLE TO LAUGH AT A SPECTACULAR BASEBALL PLAY, NOT A BLOOPER.
IN OTHER WORDS, THE HUMOR WILL COME OUT OF THE TENSION AND MISHAPS OF CREATING...
...THE PERFECT CRIME!
THE MAIN CHARACTER WILL BE A BOY WHO'S ALWAYS ADMIRED PERFECT CRIMES.
I SEE WHAT YOU'RE GETTING AT, SHUJIN.
THIS BOY ADMIRES PERFECT CRIMES, BUT HE'S NOT GOING TO ACTUALLY COMMIT A REAL CRIME.
YEAH. HE CAN START OUT WITH SOMETHING REALLY TRIVIAL. LET'S SEE, I CAN'T THINK OF MUCH OFF THE TOP OF MY HEAD, BUT...
FOR EXAMPLE, THE MAIN CHARACTER SEES A PENCIL CASE ON A NEARBY DESK.
HOW USED IS THAT PENCIL CASE...? HOW MANY PENCILS ARE IN IT, AND HOW SHORT ARE THEY...? WHAT KIND OF ERASER DO THEY USE, AND HOW MUCH OF IT HAS BEEN USED?
Soft case
...

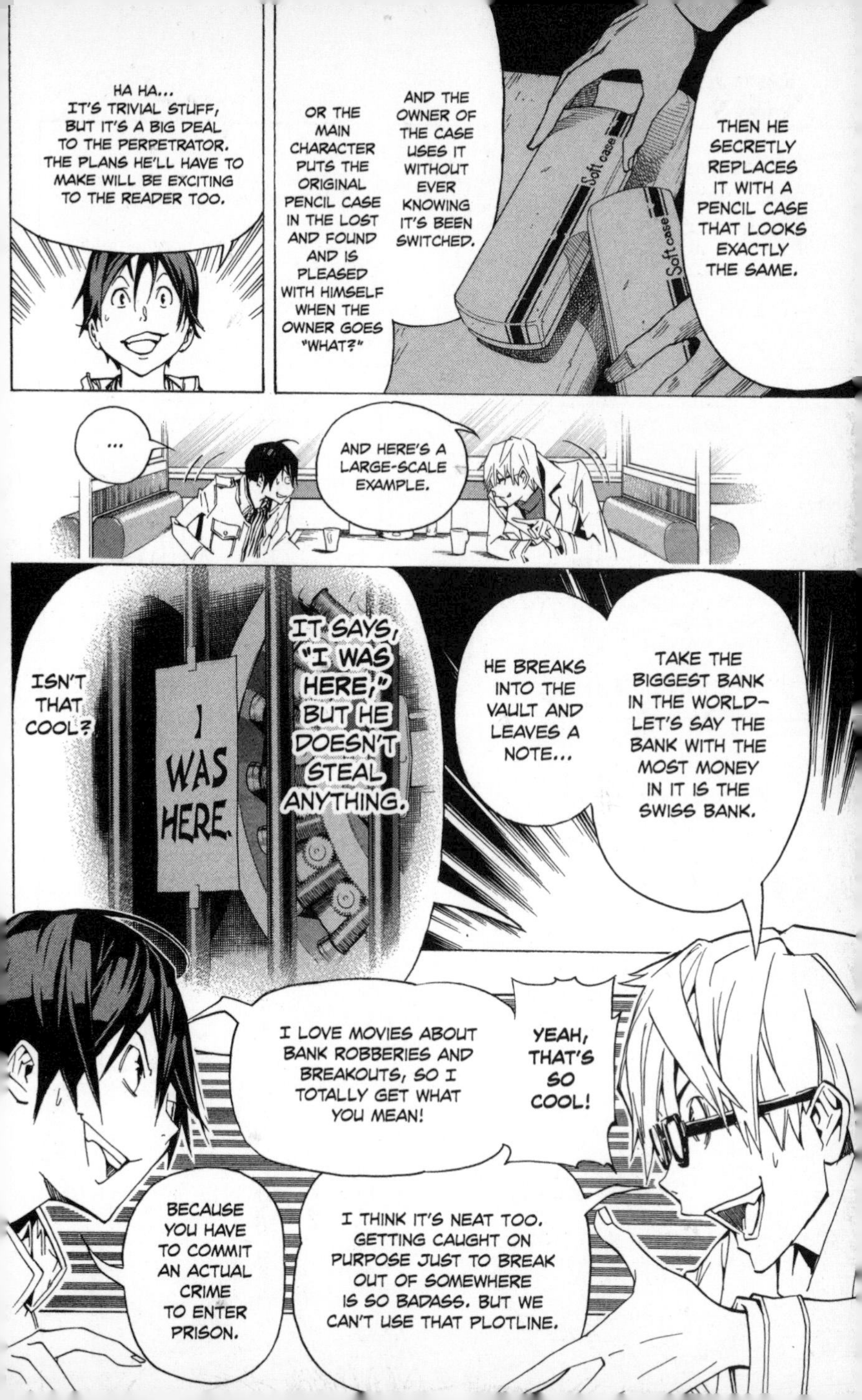
THEN HE SECRETLY REPLACES IT WITH A PENCIL CASE THAT LOOKS EXACTLY THE SAME.
Soft case
Soft case
AND THE OWNER OF THE CASE USES IT WITHOUT EVER KNOWING IT'S BEEN SWITCHED.
OR THE MAIN CHARACTER PUTS THE ORIGINAL PENCIL CASE IN THE LOST AND FOUND AND IS PLEASED WITH HIMSELF WHEN THE OWNER GOES "WHAT?"
HA HA... IT'S TRIVIAL STUFF, BUT IT'S A BIG DEAL TO THE PERPETRATOR. THE PLANS HE'LL HAVE TO MAKE WILL BE EXCITING TO THE READER TOO.
AND HERE'S A LARGE-SCALE EXAMPLE.
...
TAKE THE BIGGEST BANK IN THE WORLD- LET'S SAY THE BANK WITH THE MOST MONEY IN IT IS THE SWISS BANK.
HE BREAKS INTO THE VAULT AND LEAVES A NOTE...
IT SAYS, "I WAS HERE," BUT HE DOESN'T STEAL ANYTHING.
I WAS HERE.
ISN'T THAT COOL?
YEAH, THAT'S SO COOL!
I LOVE MOVIES ABOUT BANK ROBBERIES AND BREAKOUTS, SO I TOTALLY GET WHAT YOU MEAN!
I THINK IT'S NEAT TOO. GETTING CAUGHT ON PURPOSE JUST TO BREAK OUT OF SOMEWHERE IS SO BADASS. BUT WE CAN'T USE THAT PLOTLINE.
BECAUSE YOU HAVE TO COMMIT AN ACTUAL CRIME TO ENTER PRISON.

READ THIS WAY

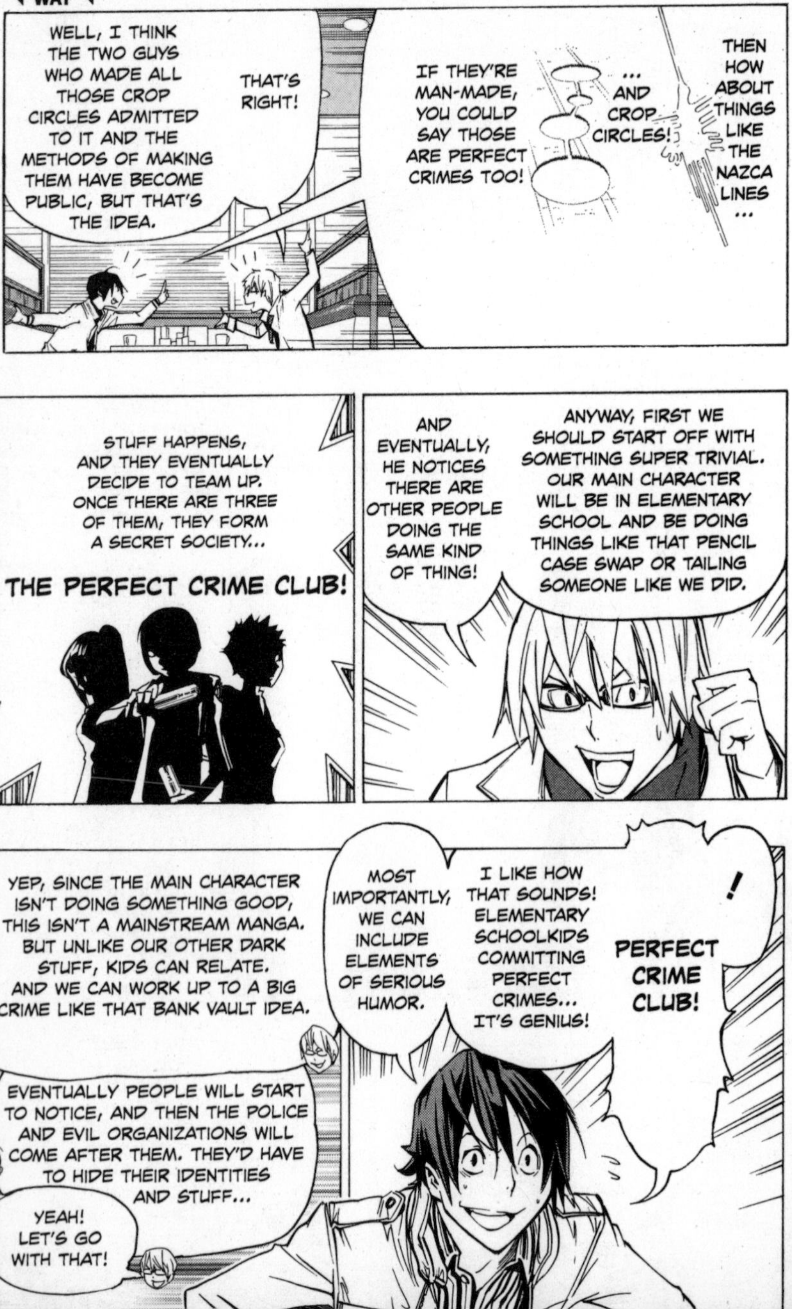
THEN HOW ABOUT THINGS LIKE THE NAZCA LINES...
...AND CROP CIRCLES!
IF THEY'RE MAN-MADE, YOU COULD SAY THOSE ARE PERFECT CRIMES TOO!
WELL, I THINK THE TWO GUYS WHO MADE ALL THOSE CROP CIRCLES ADMITTED TO IT AND THE METHODS OF MAKING THEM HAVE BECOME PUBLIC, BUT THAT'S THE IDEA.
THAT'S RIGHT!
ANYWAY, FIRST WE SHOULD START OFF WITH SOMETHING SUPER TRIVIAL. OUR MAIN CHARACTER WILL BE IN ELEMENTARY SCHOOL AND BE DOING THINGS LIKE THAT PENCIL CASE SWAP OR TAILING SOMEONE LIKE WE DID.
AND EVENTUALLY, HE NOTICES THERE ARE OTHER PEOPLE DOING THE SAME KIND OF THING!
STUFF HAPPENS, AND THEY EVENTUALLY DECIDE TO TEAM UP. ONCE THERE ARE THREE OF THEM, THEY FORM A SECRET SOCIETY...
THE PERFECT CRIME CLUB!
!
PERFECT CRIME CLUB!
I LIKE HOW THAT SOUNDS! ELEMENTARY SCHOOLKIDS COMMITTING PERFECT CRIMES... IT'S GENIUS!
MOST IMPORTANTLY, WE CAN INCLUDE ELEMENTS OF SERIOUS HUMOR.
YEP, SINCE THE MAIN CHARACTER ISN'T DOING SOMETHING GOOD, THIS ISN'T A MAINSTREAM MANGA. BUT UNLIKE OUR OTHER DARK STUFF, KIDS CAN RELATE. AND WE CAN WORK UP TO A BIG CRIME LIKE THAT BANK VAULT IDEA.
EVENTUALLY PEOPLE WILL START TO NOTICE, AND THEN THE POLICE AND EVIL ORGANIZATIONS WILL COME AFTER THEM. THEY'D HAVE TO HIDE THEIR IDENTITIES AND STUFF...
YEAH! LET'S GO WITH THAT!

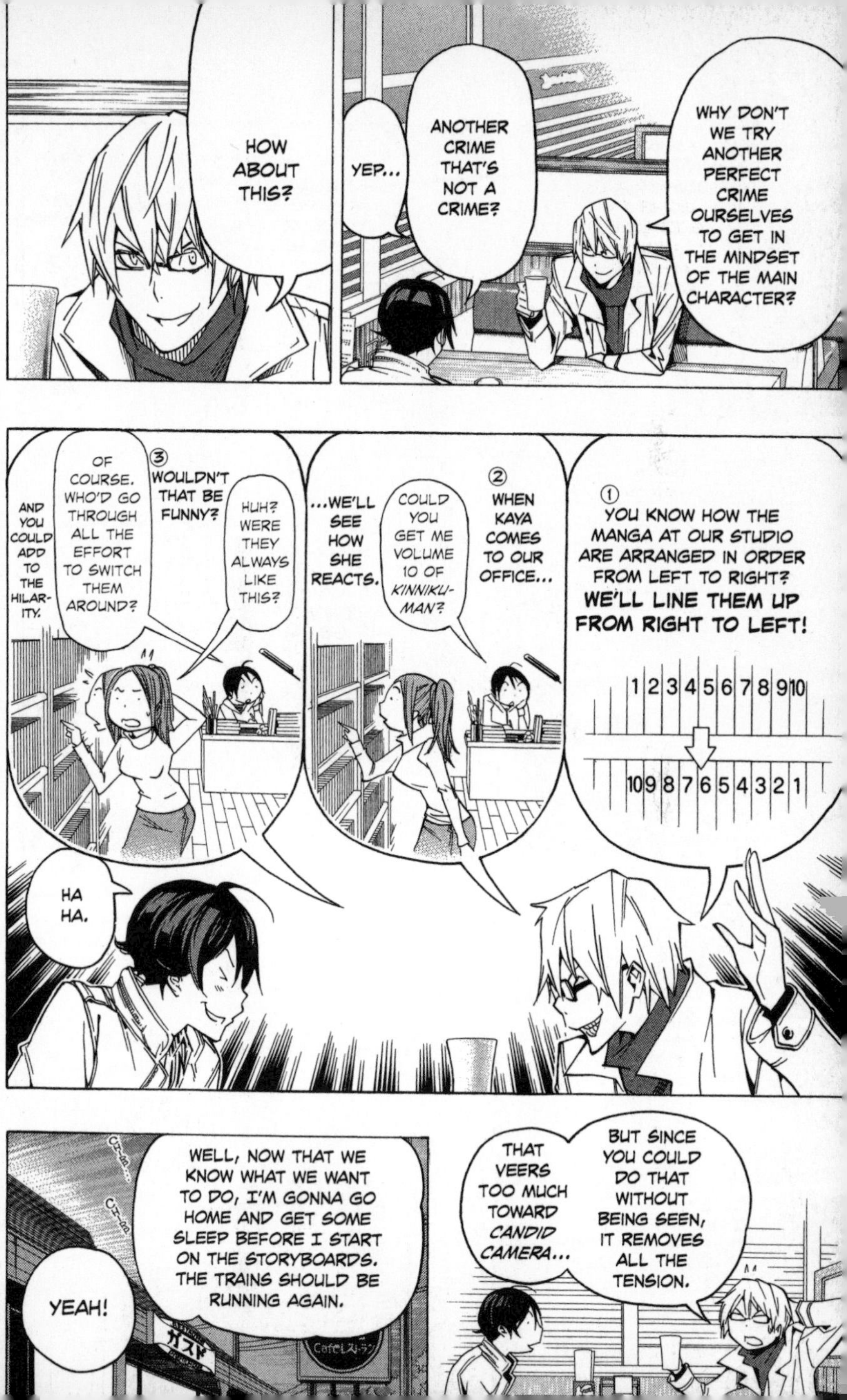
WHY DON'T WE TRY ANOTHER PERFECT CRIME OURSELVES TO GET IN THE MINDSET OF THE MAIN CHARACTER?
ANOTHER CRIME THAT'S NOT A CRIME?
YEP...
HOW ABOUT THIS?
① YOU KNOW HOW THE MANGA AT OUR STUDIO ARE ARRANGED IN ORDER FROM LEFT TO RIGHT? WE'LL LINE THEM UP FROM RIGHT TO LEFT!
1 2 3 4 5 6 7 8 9 10
10 9 8 7 6 5 4 3 2 1
② WHEN KAYA COMES TO OUR OFFICE...
COULD YOU GET ME VOLUME 10 OF *KINNIKU-MAN*?
...WE'LL SEE HOW SHE REACTS.
③ WOULDN'T THAT BE FUNNY?
HUH? WERE THEY ALWAYS LIKE THIS?
OF COURSE. WHO'D GO THROUGH ALL THE EFFORT TO SWITCH THEM AROUND?
AND YOU COULD ADD TO THE HILARITY.
HA HA.
BUT SINCE YOU COULD DO THAT WITHOUT BEING SEEN, IT REMOVES ALL THE TENSION.
THAT VEERS TOO MUCH TOWARD *CANDID CAMERA*...
WELL, NOW THAT WE KNOW WHAT WE WANT TO DO, I'M GONNA GO HOME AND GET SOME SLEEP BEFORE I START ON THE STORYBOARDS. THE TRAINS SHOULD BE RUNNING AGAIN.
YEAH!

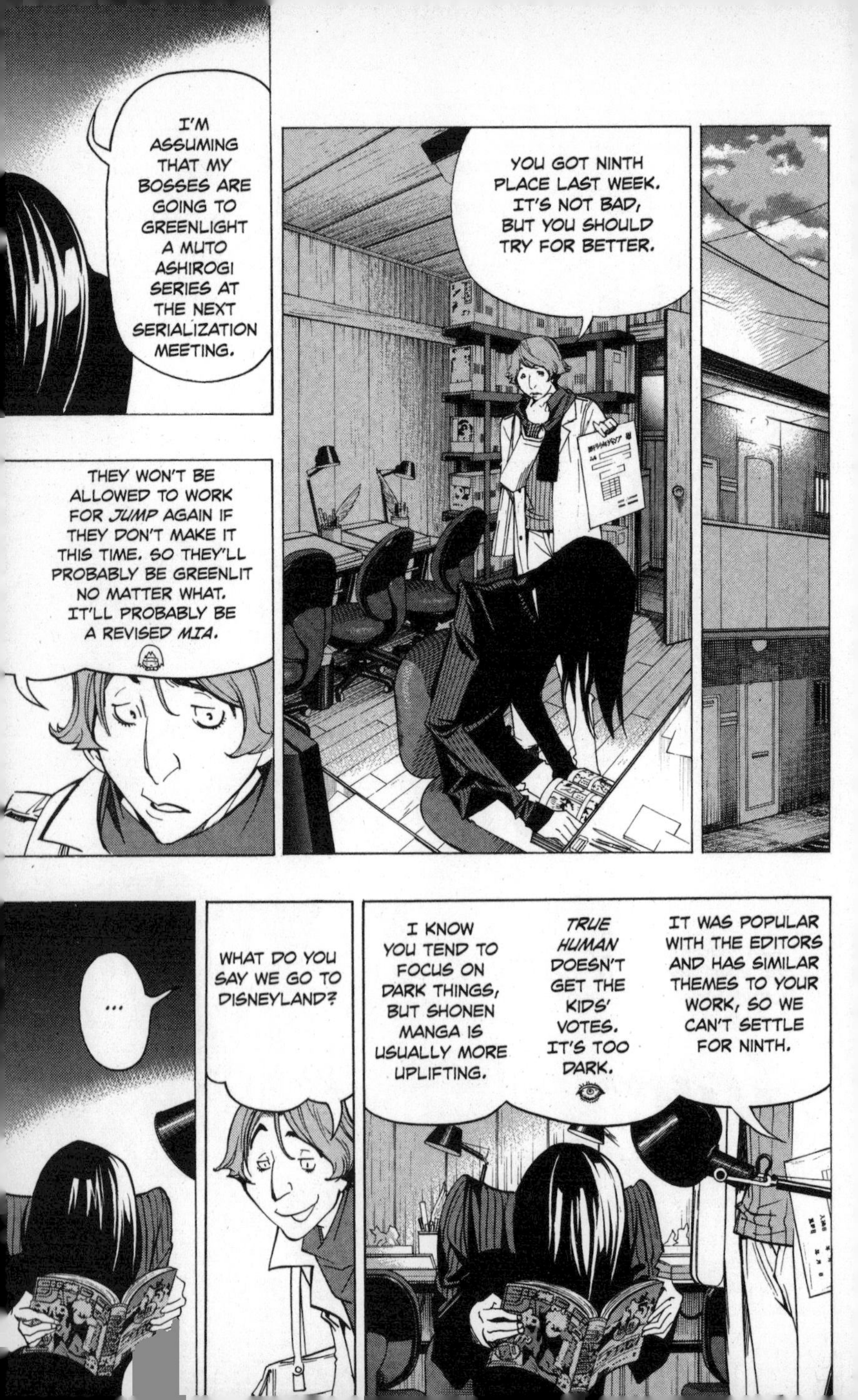
YOU GOT NINTH PLACE LAST WEEK. IT'S NOT BAD, BUT YOU SHOULD TRY FOR BETTER.
I'M ASSUMING THAT MY BOSSES ARE GOING TO GREENLIGHT A MUTO ASHIROGI SERIES AT THE NEXT SERIALIZATION MEETING.
THEY WON'T BE ALLOWED TO WORK FOR *JUMP* AGAIN IF THEY DON'T MAKE IT THIS TIME. SO THEY'LL PROBABLY BE GREENLIT NO MATTER WHAT. IT'LL PROBABLY BE A REVISED *MIA*.
IT WAS POPULAR WITH THE EDITORS AND HAS SIMILAR THEMES TO YOUR WORK, SO WE CAN'T SETTLE FOR NINTH.
TRUE HUMAN DOESN'T GET THE KIDS' VOTES. IT'S TOO DARK.
I KNOW YOU TEND TO FOCUS ON DARK THINGS, BUT SHONEN MANGA IS USUALLY MORE UPLIFTING.
WHAT DO YOU SAY WE GO TO DISNEYLAND?
...

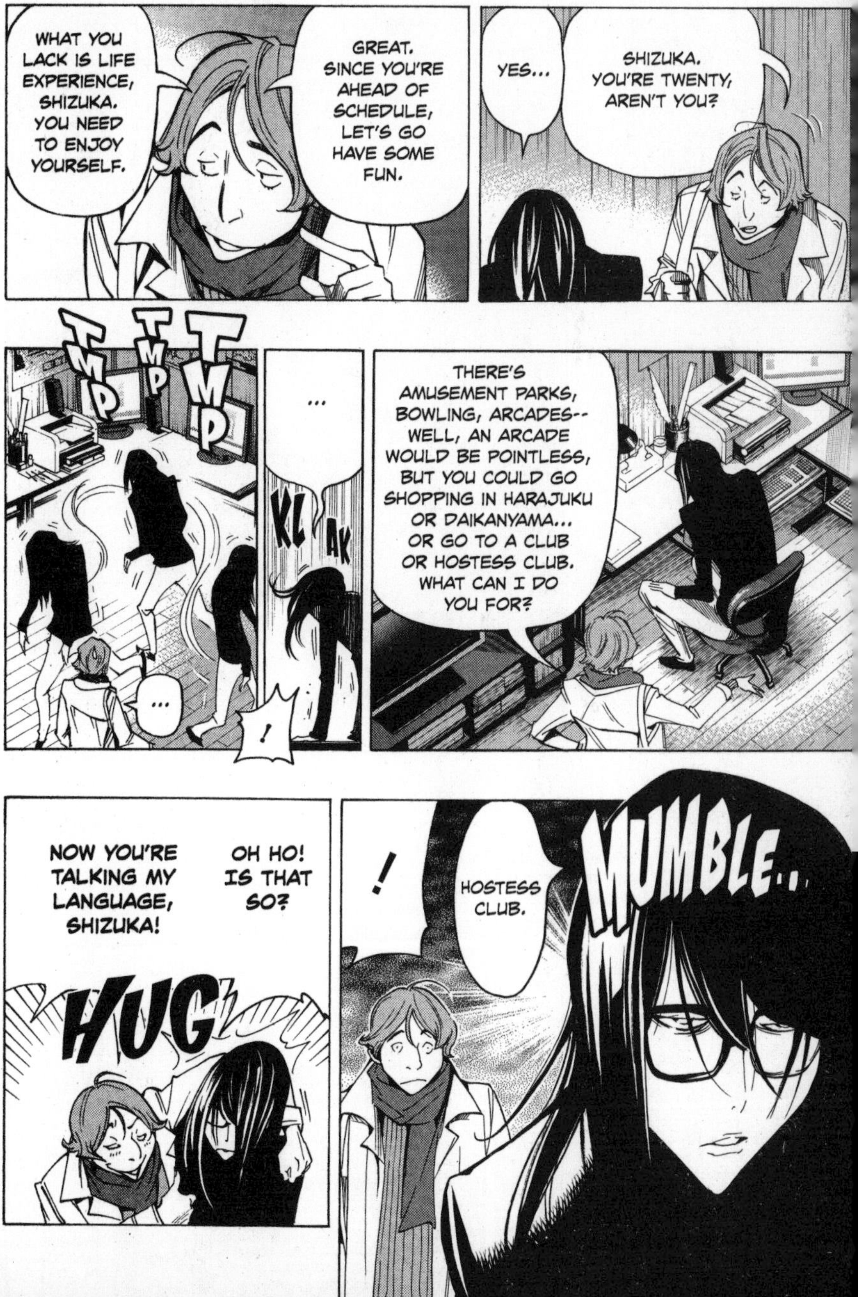
SHIZUKA. YOU'RE TWENTY, AREN'T YOU?
YES...
GREAT. SINCE YOU'RE AHEAD OF SCHEDULE, LET'S GO HAVE SOME FUN.
WHAT YOU LACK IS LIFE EXPERIENCE, SHIZUKA. YOU NEED TO ENJOY YOURSELF.
THERE'S AMUSEMENT PARKS, BOWLING, ARCADES--WELL, AN ARCADE WOULD BE POINTLESS, BUT YOU COULD GO SHOPPING IN HARAJUKU OR DAIKANYAMA... OR GO TO A CLUB OR HOSTESS CLUB. WHAT CAN I DO YOU FOR?
...
KLAK
!
TMP
TMP
TMP
...
MUMBLE...
HOSTESS CLUB.
!
OH HO! IS THAT SO?
NOW YOU'RE TALKING MY LANGUAGE, SHIZUKA!
HUG

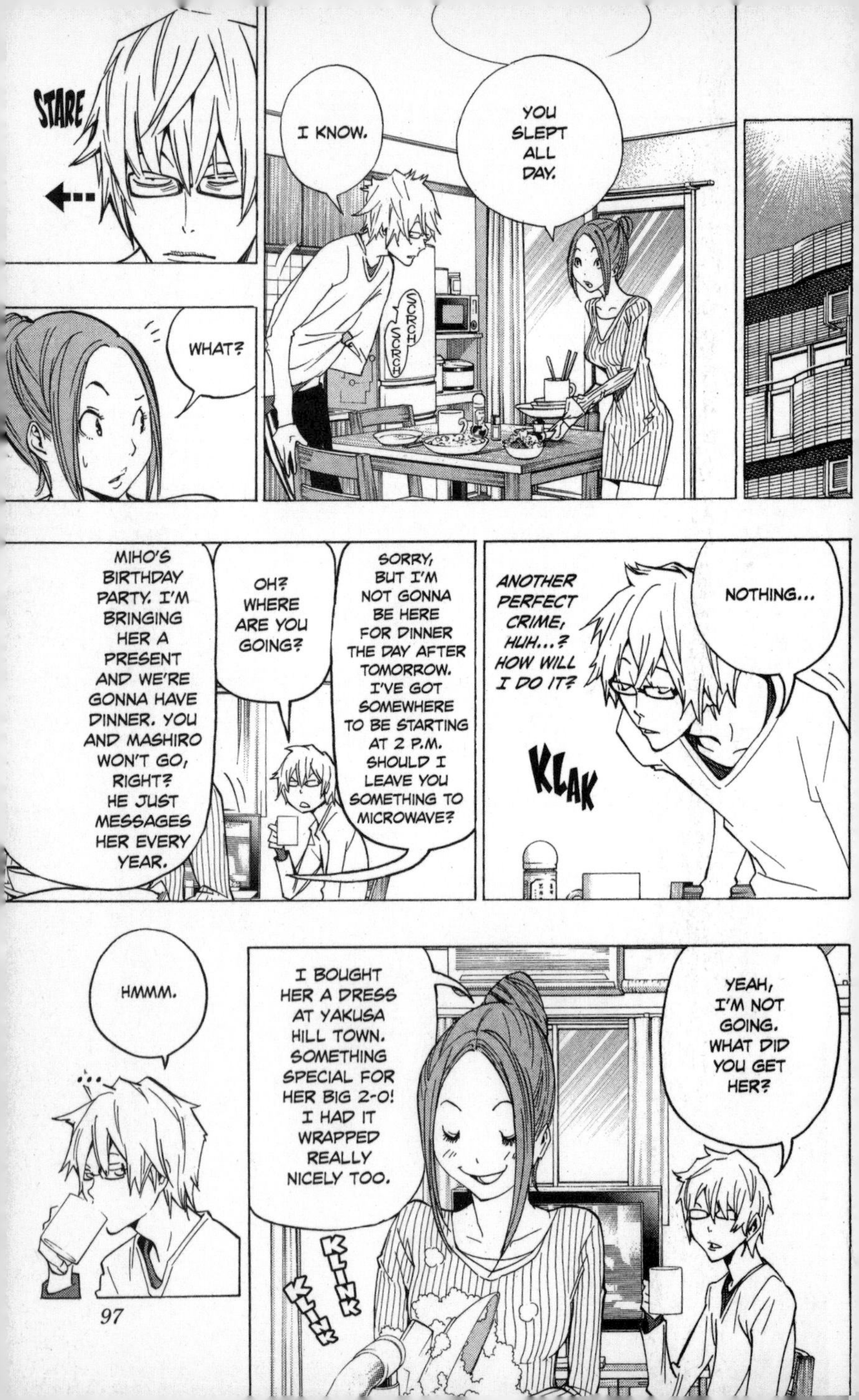
YOU SLEPT ALL DAY.
I KNOW.
SCRCH SCRCH
STARE
WHAT?
NOTHING...
ANOTHER PERFECT CRIME, HUH...? HOW WILL I DO IT?
KLAK
SORRY, BUT I'M NOT GONNA BE HERE FOR DINNER THE DAY AFTER TOMORROW. I'VE GOT SOMEWHERE TO BE STARTING AT 2 P.M. SHOULD I LEAVE YOU SOMETHING TO MICROWAVE?
OH? WHERE ARE YOU GOING?
MIHO'S BIRTHDAY PARTY. I'M BRINGING HER A PRESENT AND WE'RE GONNA HAVE DINNER. YOU AND MASHIRO WON'T GO, RIGHT? HE JUST MESSAGES HER EVERY YEAR.
YEAH, I'M NOT GOING. WHAT DID YOU GET HER?
I BOUGHT HER A DRESS AT YAKUSA HILL TOWN. SOMETHING SPECIAL FOR HER BIG 2-0! I HAD IT WRAPPED REALLY NICELY TOO.
KLINK
KLINK
HMMM.
...

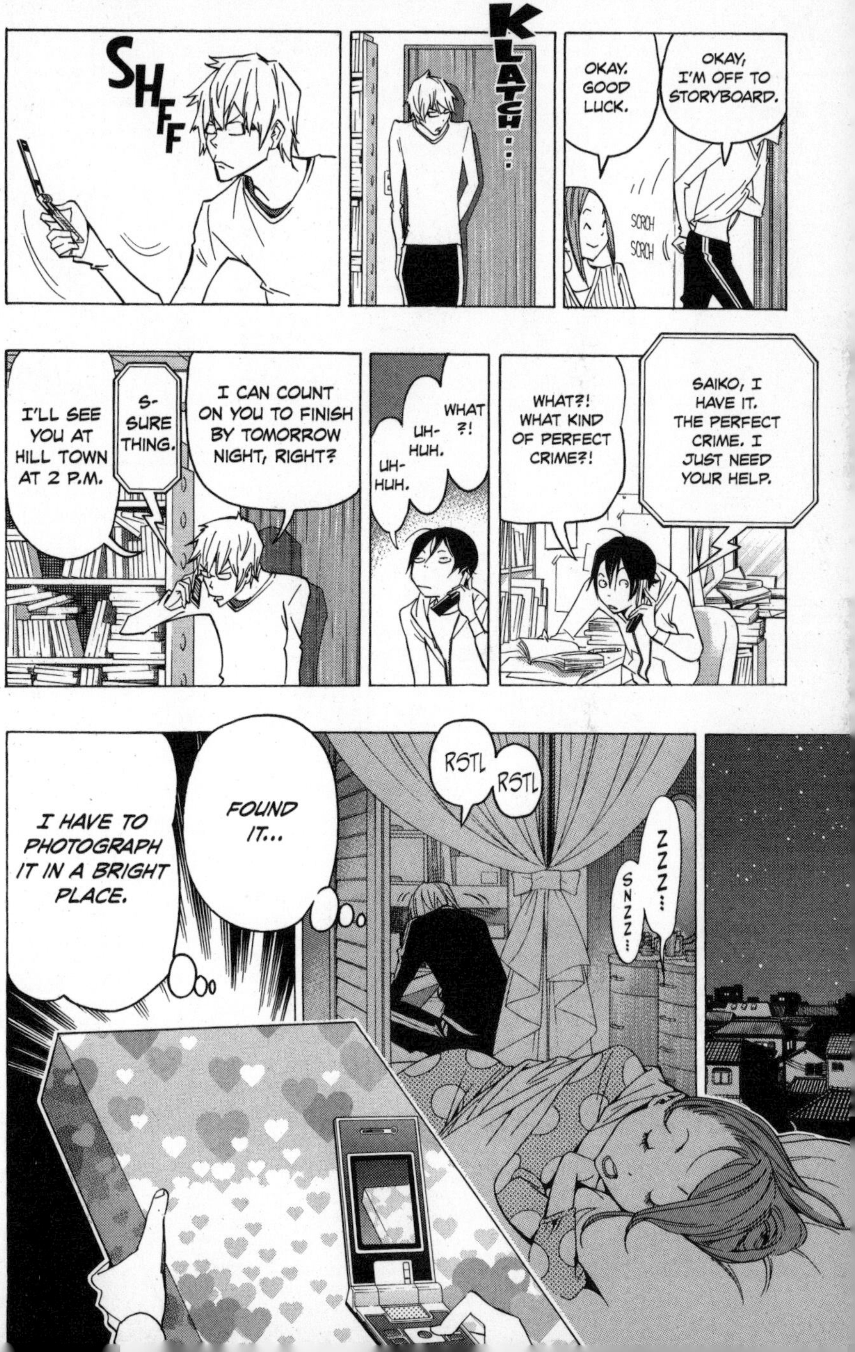
OKAY, I'M OFF TO STORYBOARD.
OKAY. GOOD LUCK.
SCRCH
SCRCH
KLATCH...
SHFF
SAIKO, I HAVE IT. THE PERFECT CRIME. I JUST NEED YOUR HELP.
WHAT?! WHAT KIND OF PERFECT CRIME?!
WHAT?!
UH-HUH.
UH-HUH.
I CAN COUNT ON YOU TO FINISH BY TOMORROW NIGHT, RIGHT?
S-SURE THING.
I'LL SEE YOU AT HILL TOWN AT 2 P.M.
RSTL
RSTL
ZZZ...
SNZZ...
FOUND IT...
I HAVE TO PHOTOGRAPH IT IN A BRIGHT PLACE.

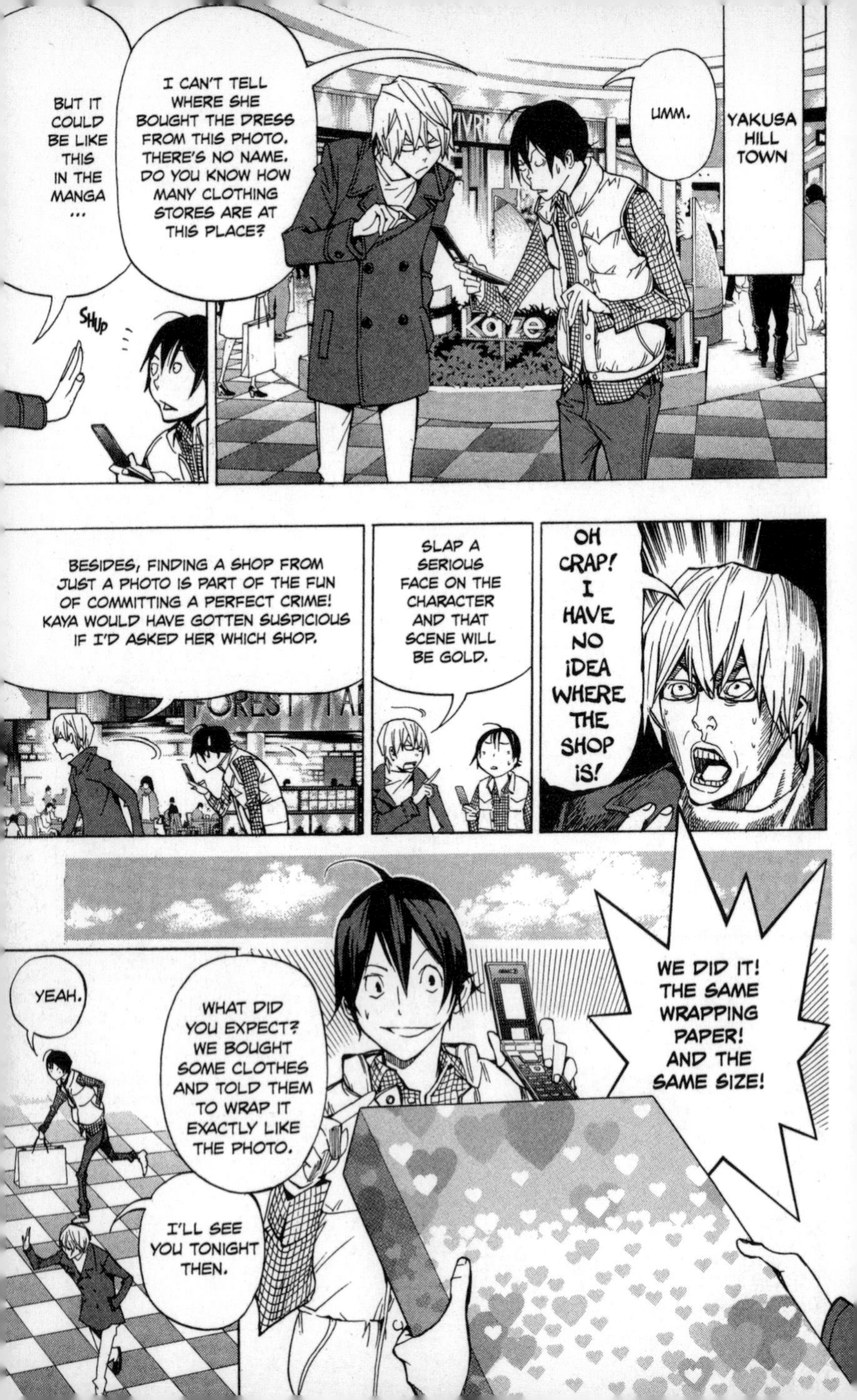
YAKUSA HILL TOWN
UMM.
I CAN'T TELL WHERE SHE BOUGHT THE DRESS FROM THIS PHOTO. THERE'S NO NAME. DO YOU KNOW HOW MANY CLOTHING STORES ARE AT THIS PLACE?
BUT IT COULD BE LIKE THIS IN THE MANGA...
SHUP
OH CRAP! I HAVE NO IDEA WHERE THE SHOP IS!
SLAP A SERIOUS FACE ON THE CHARACTER AND THAT SCENE WILL BE GOLD.
BESIDES, FINDING A SHOP FROM JUST A PHOTO IS PART OF THE FUN OF COMMITTING A PERFECT CRIME! KAYA WOULD HAVE GOTTEN SUSPICIOUS IF I'D ASKED HER WHICH SHOP.
WE DID IT! THE SAME WRAPPING PAPER! AND THE SAME SIZE!
WHAT DID YOU EXPECT? WE BOUGHT SOME CLOTHES AND TOLD THEM TO WRAP IT EXACTLY LIKE THE PHOTO.
YEAH.
I'LL SEE YOU TONIGHT THEN.

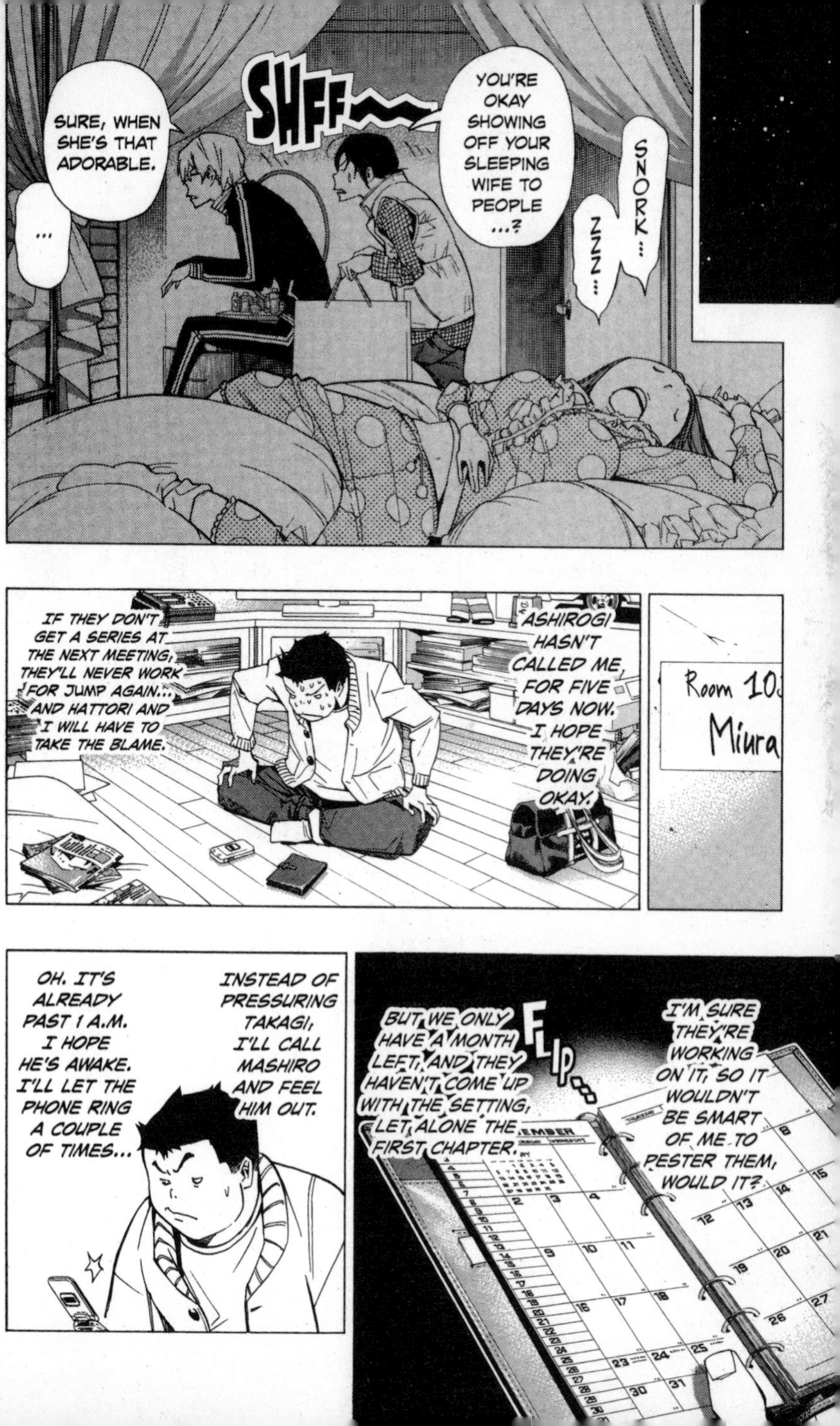
SNORK...
ZZZ...
SHFF
YOU'RE OKAY SHOWING OFF YOUR SLEEPING WIFE TO PEOPLE ...?
SURE, WHEN SHE'S THAT ADORABLE.
...
Room 10
Miura
ASHIROGI HASN'T CALLED ME FOR FIVE DAYS NOW. I HOPE THEY'RE DOING OKAY.
IF THEY DON'T GET A SERIES AT THE NEXT MEETING, THEY'LL NEVER WORK FOR JUMP AGAIN... AND HATTORI AND I WILL HAVE TO TAKE THE BLAME.
I'M SURE THEY'RE WORKING ON IT, SO IT WOULDN'T BE SMART OF ME TO PESTER THEM, WOULD IT?
FLIP...
BUT WE ONLY HAVE A MONTH LEFT, AND THEY HAVEN'T COME UP WITH THE SETTING, LET ALONE THE FIRST CHAPTER.
INSTEAD OF PRESSURING TAKAGI, I'LL CALL MASHIRO AND FEEL HIM OUT.
OH. IT'S ALREADY PAST 1 A.M. I HOPE HE'S AWAKE. I'LL LET THE PHONE RING A COUPLE OF TIMES...

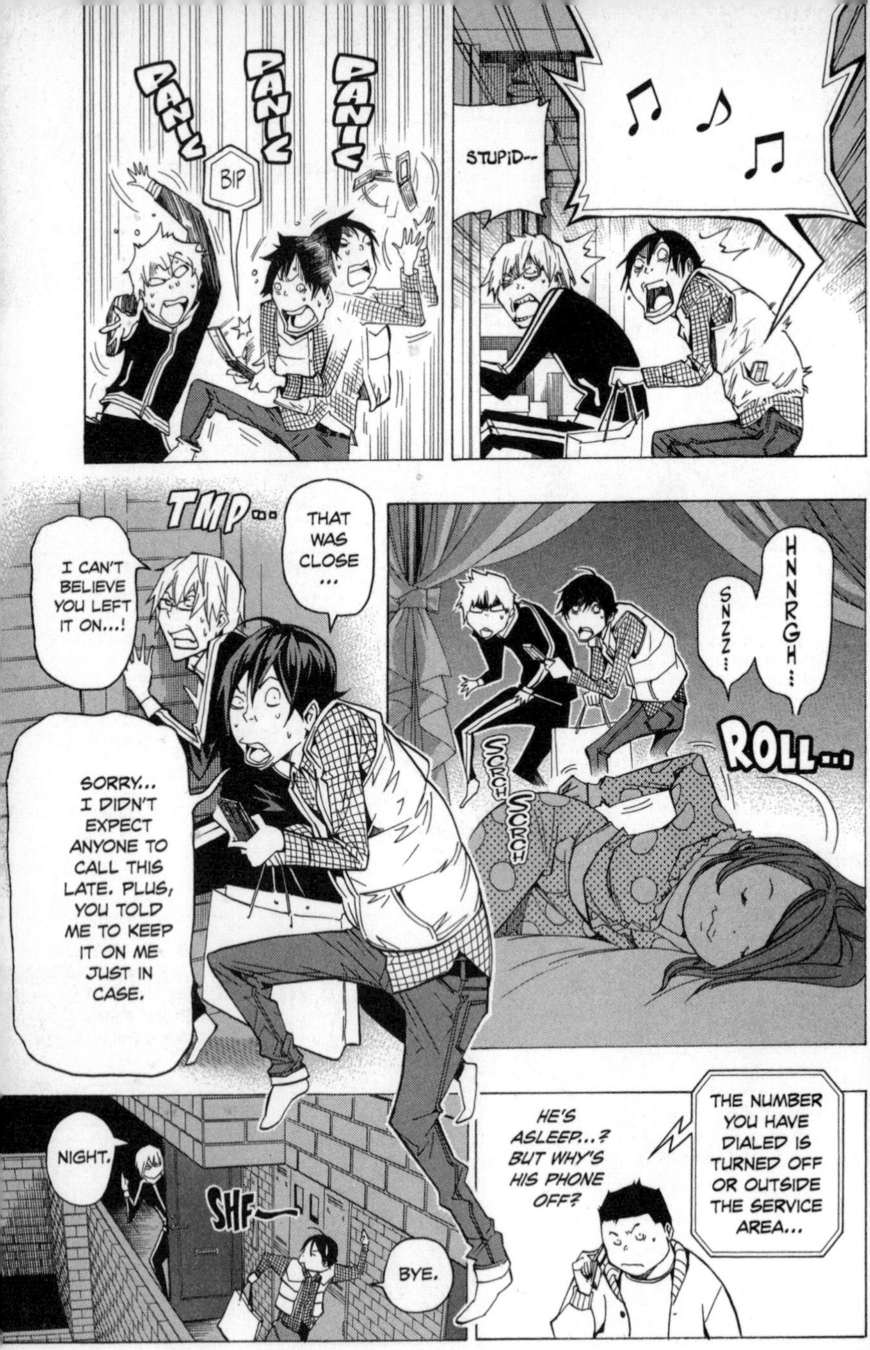
♫ ♪ ♫
STUPID--
PANIC
PANIC
PANIC
BIP
HNNRGH..
SNZZ..
ROLL...
SCRCH SCRCH
THAT WAS CLOSE ...
TMP...
I CAN'T BELIEVE YOU LEFT IT ON...!
SORRY... I DIDN'T EXPECT ANYONE TO CALL THIS LATE. PLUS, YOU TOLD ME TO KEEP IT ON ME JUST IN CASE.
THE NUMBER YOU HAVE DIALED IS TURNED OFF OR OUTSIDE THE SERVICE AREA...
HE'S ASLEEP...? BUT WHY'S HIS PHONE OFF?
NIGHT.
SHF—
BYE.

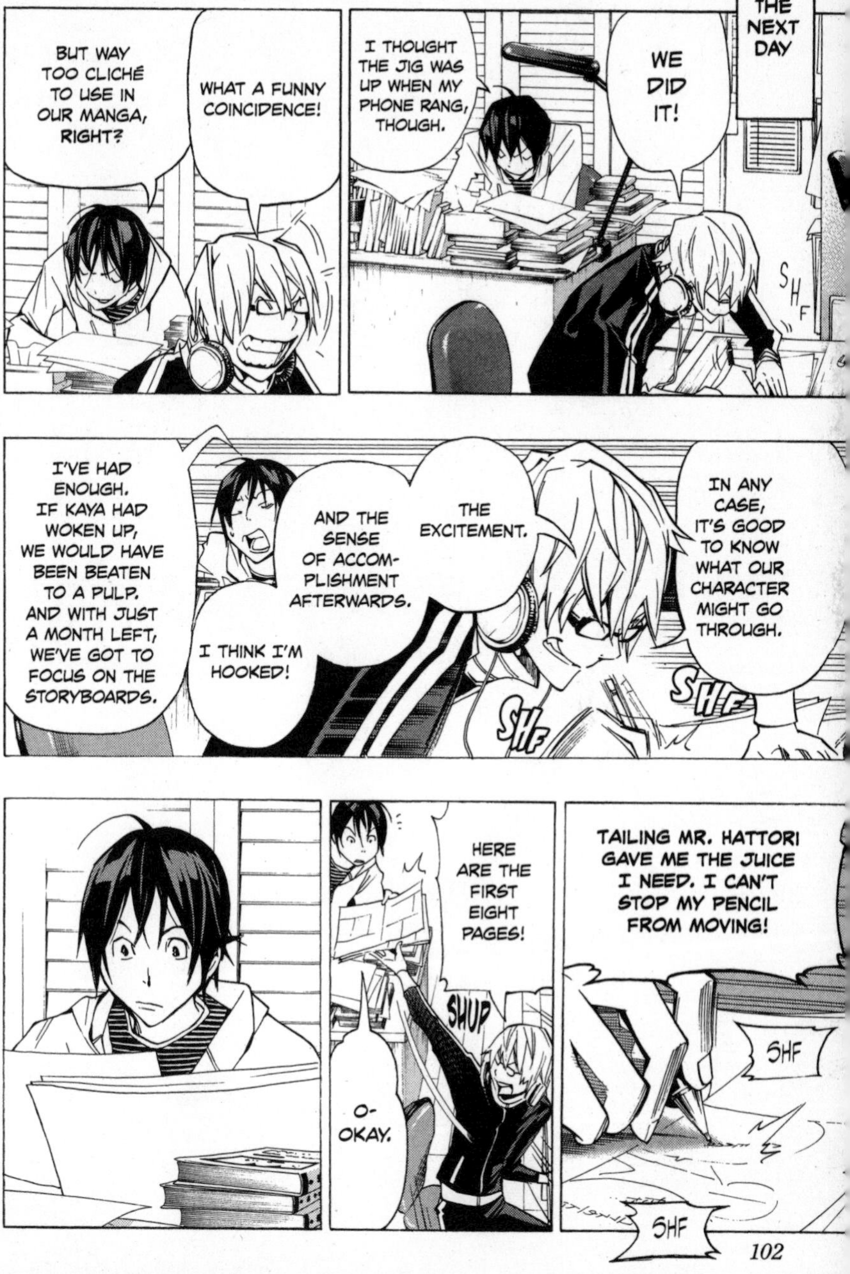
THE NEXT DAY
WE DID IT!
I THOUGHT THE JIG WAS UP WHEN MY PHONE RANG, THOUGH.
SHF
WHAT A FUNNY COINCIDENCE!
BUT WAY TOO CLICHÉ TO USE IN OUR MANGA, RIGHT?
IN ANY CASE, IT'S GOOD TO KNOW WHAT OUR CHARACTER MIGHT GO THROUGH.
SHF
SHF
THE EXCITEMENT.
AND THE SENSE OF ACCOMPLISHMENT AFTERWARDS.
I THINK I'M HOOKED!
I'VE HAD ENOUGH. IF KAYA HAD WOKEN UP, WE WOULD HAVE BEEN BEATEN TO A PULP. AND WITH JUST A MONTH LEFT, WE'VE GOT TO FOCUS ON THE STORYBOARDS.
TAILING MR. HATTORI GAVE ME THE JUICE I NEED. I CAN'T STOP MY PENCIL FROM MOVING!
SHF
SHF
HERE ARE THE FIRST EIGHT PAGES!
SHUP
O-OKAY.

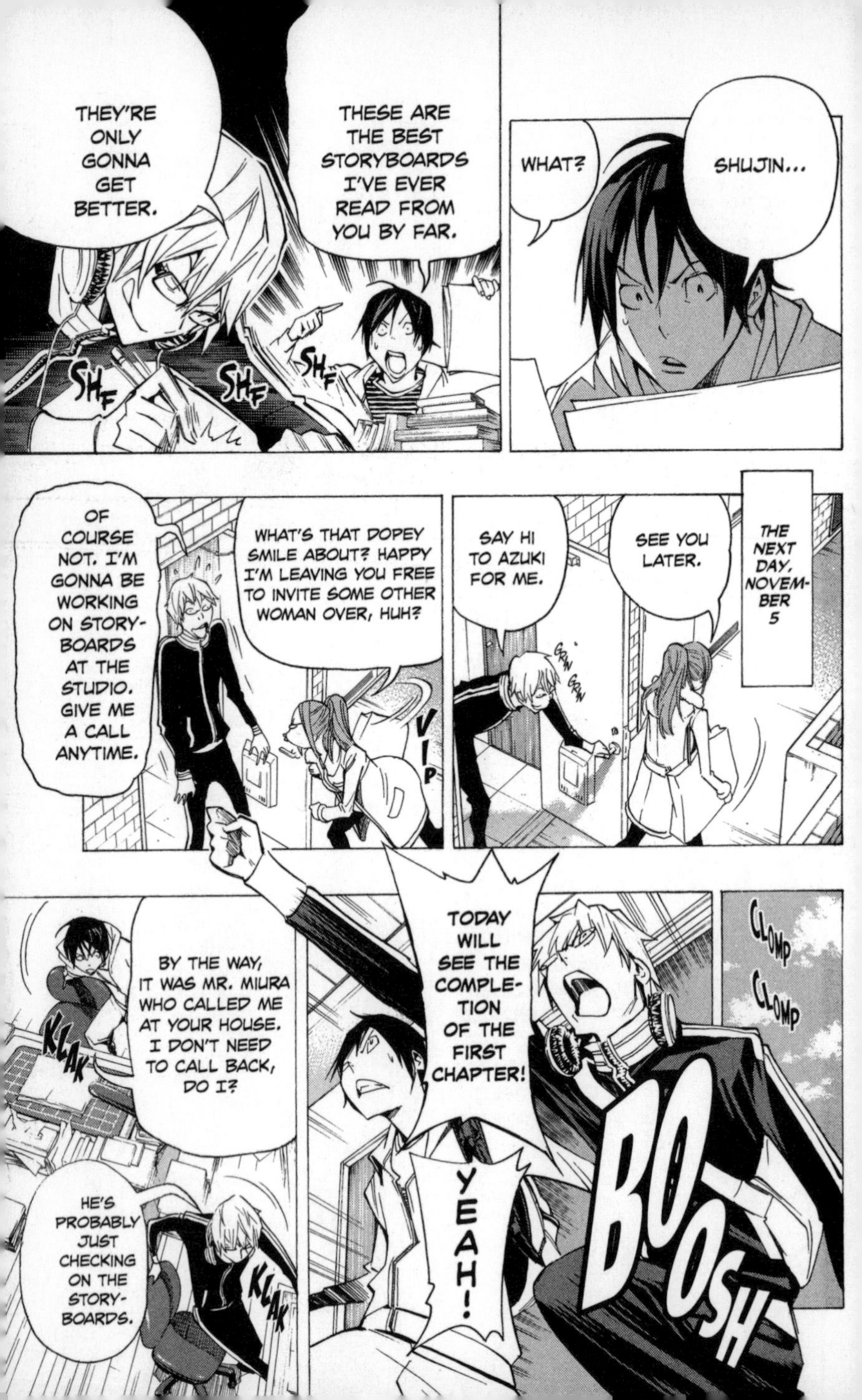
SHUJIN...
WHAT?
THESE ARE THE BEST STORYBOARDS I'VE EVER READ FROM YOU BY FAR.
THEY'RE ONLY GONNA GET BETTER.
SHF
SHF
SHF
THE NEXT DAY, NOVEMBER 5
SEE YOU LATER.
SAY HI TO AZUKI FOR ME.
GRIN GRIN
WHAT'S THAT DOPEY SMILE ABOUT? HAPPY I'M LEAVING YOU FREE TO INVITE SOME OTHER WOMAN OVER, HUH?
OF COURSE NOT. I'M GONNA BE WORKING ON STORYBOARDS AT THE STUDIO. GIVE ME A CALL ANYTIME.
VIP
CLOMP
CLOMP
TODAY WILL SEE THE COMPLETION OF THE FIRST CHAPTER!
YEAH!
BOOSH
BY THE WAY, IT WAS MR. MIURA WHO CALLED ME AT YOUR HOUSE. I DON'T NEED TO CALL BACK, DO I?
KLAK
HE'S PROBABLY JUST CHECKING ON THE STORYBOARDS.
KLAK

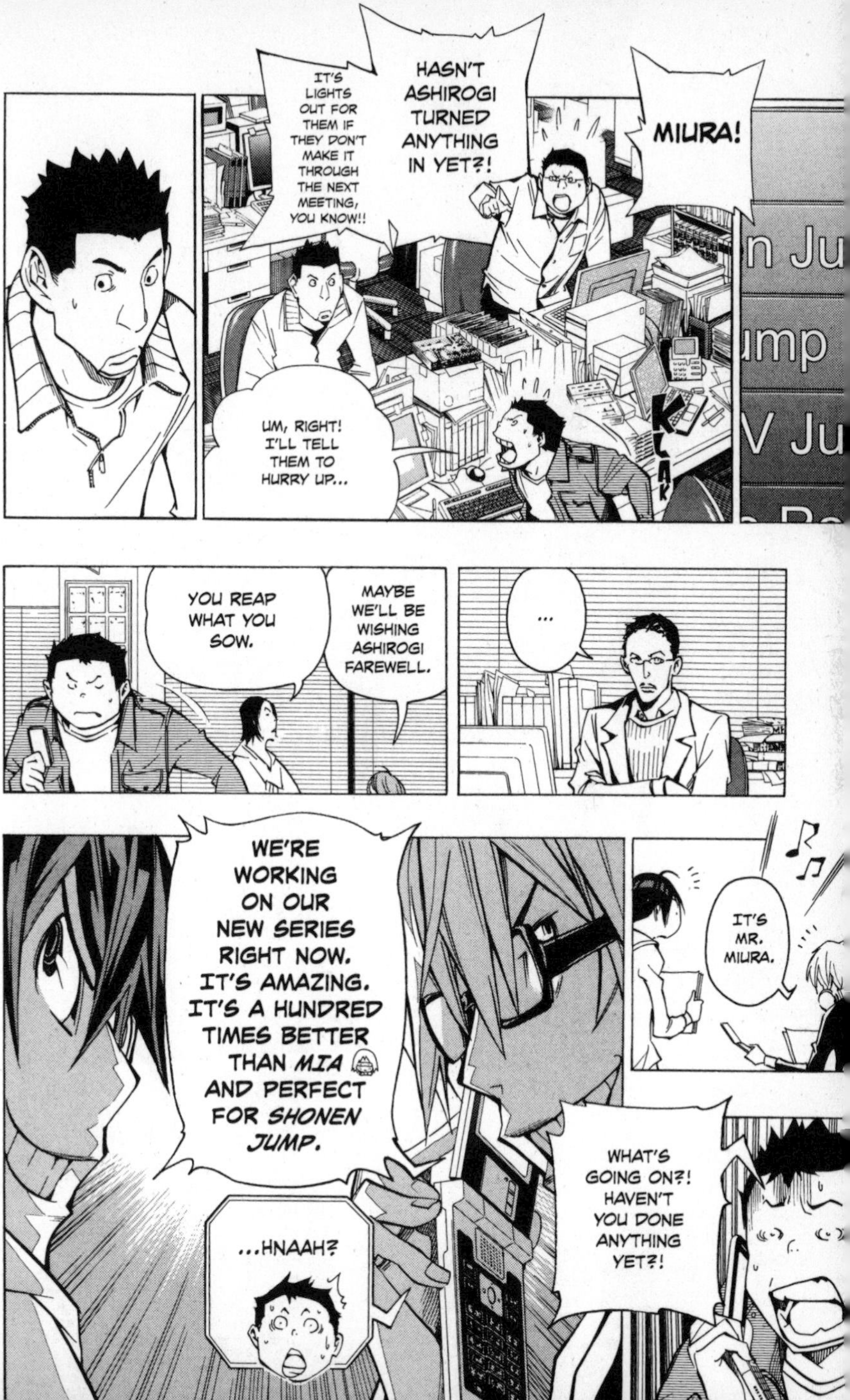
MIURA!
HASN'T ASHIROGI TURNED ANYTHING IN YET?!
IT'S LIGHTS OUT FOR THEM IF THEY DON'T MAKE IT THROUGH THE NEXT MEETING, YOU KNOW!!
KLAK
UM, RIGHT! I'LL TELL THEM TO HURRY UP...
...
MAYBE WE'LL BE WISHING ASHIROGI FAREWELL.
YOU REAP WHAT YOU SOW.
IT'S MR. MIURA.
WHAT'S GOING ON?! HAVEN'T YOU DONE ANYTHING YET?!
WE'RE WORKING ON OUR NEW SERIES RIGHT NOW. IT'S AMAZING. IT'S A HUNDRED TIMES BETTER THAN *MIA* AND PERFECT FOR *SHONEN JUMP*.
...HNAAH?

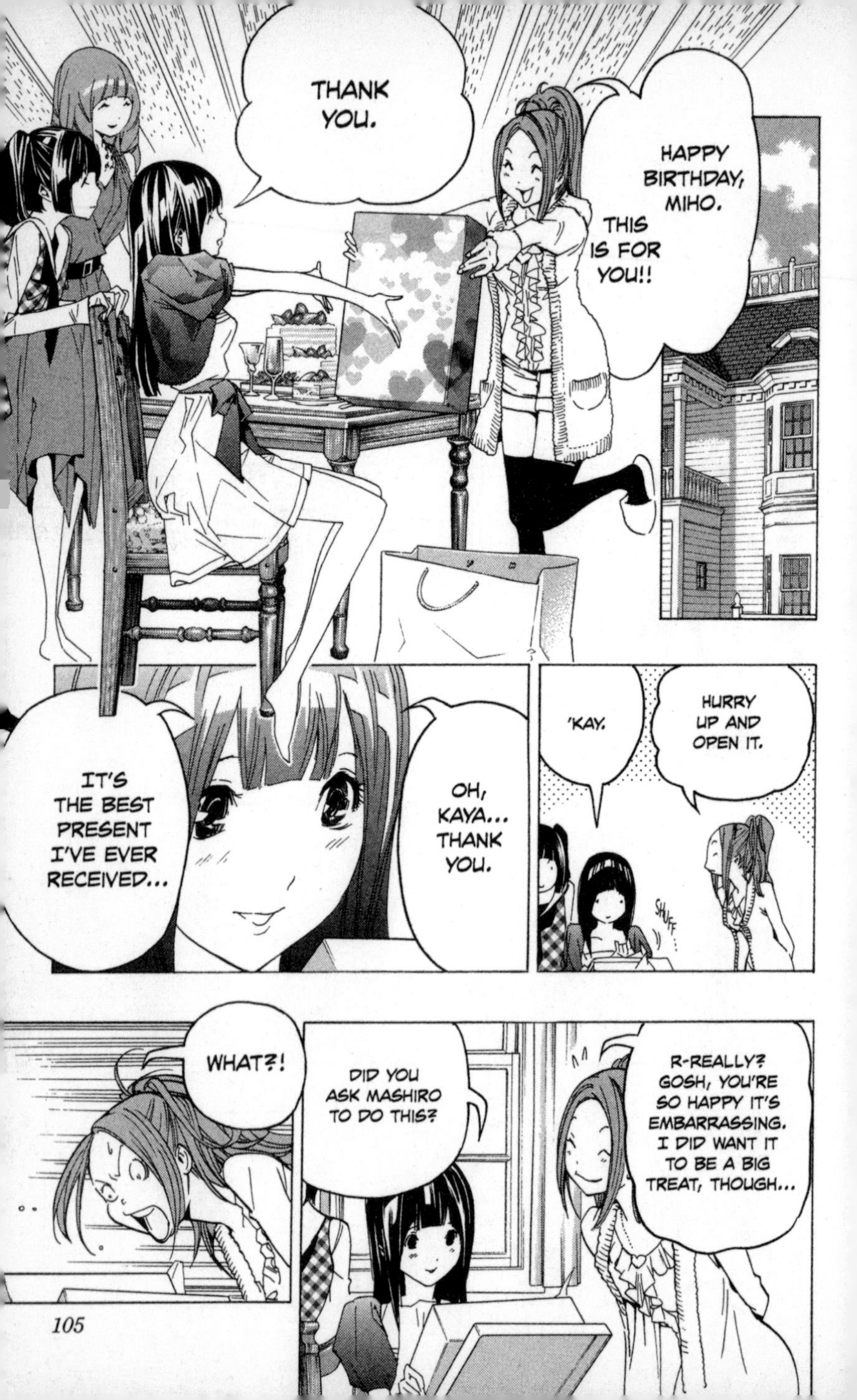
HAPPY BIRTHDAY, MIHO.
THIS IS FOR YOU!!
THANK YOU.
HURRY UP AND OPEN IT.
'KAY.
SHUFF...
OH, KAYA... THANK YOU.
IT'S THE BEST PRESENT I'VE EVER RECEIVED...
R-REALLY? GOSH, YOU'RE SO HAPPY IT'S EMBARRASSING. I DID WANT IT TO BE A BIG TREAT, THOUGH...
DID YOU ASK MASHIRO TO DO THIS?
WHAT?!

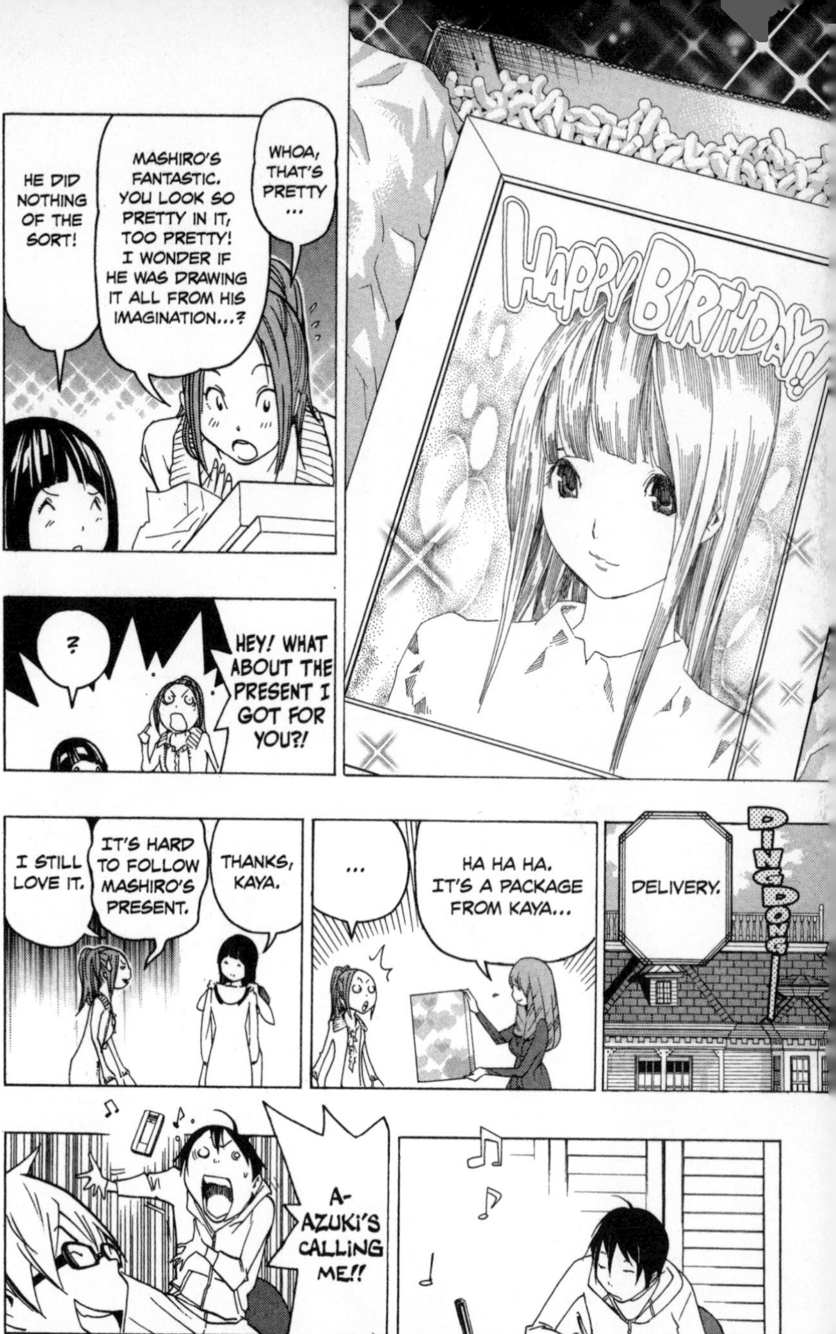
HAPPY BIRTHDAY!!
WHOA, THAT'S PRETTY ...
MASHIRO'S FANTASTIC. YOU LOOK SO PRETTY IN IT, TOO PRETTY! I WONDER IF HE WAS DRAWING IT ALL FROM HIS IMAGINATION...?
HE DID NOTHING OF THE SORT!
HEY! WHAT ABOUT THE PRESENT I GOT FOR YOU?!
?
DING DONG
DELIVERY.
HA HA HA. IT'S A PACKAGE FROM KAYA...
...
THANKS, KAYA.
IT'S HARD TO FOLLOW MASHIRO'S PRESENT.
I STILL LOVE IT.
A-AZUKI'S CALLING ME!!

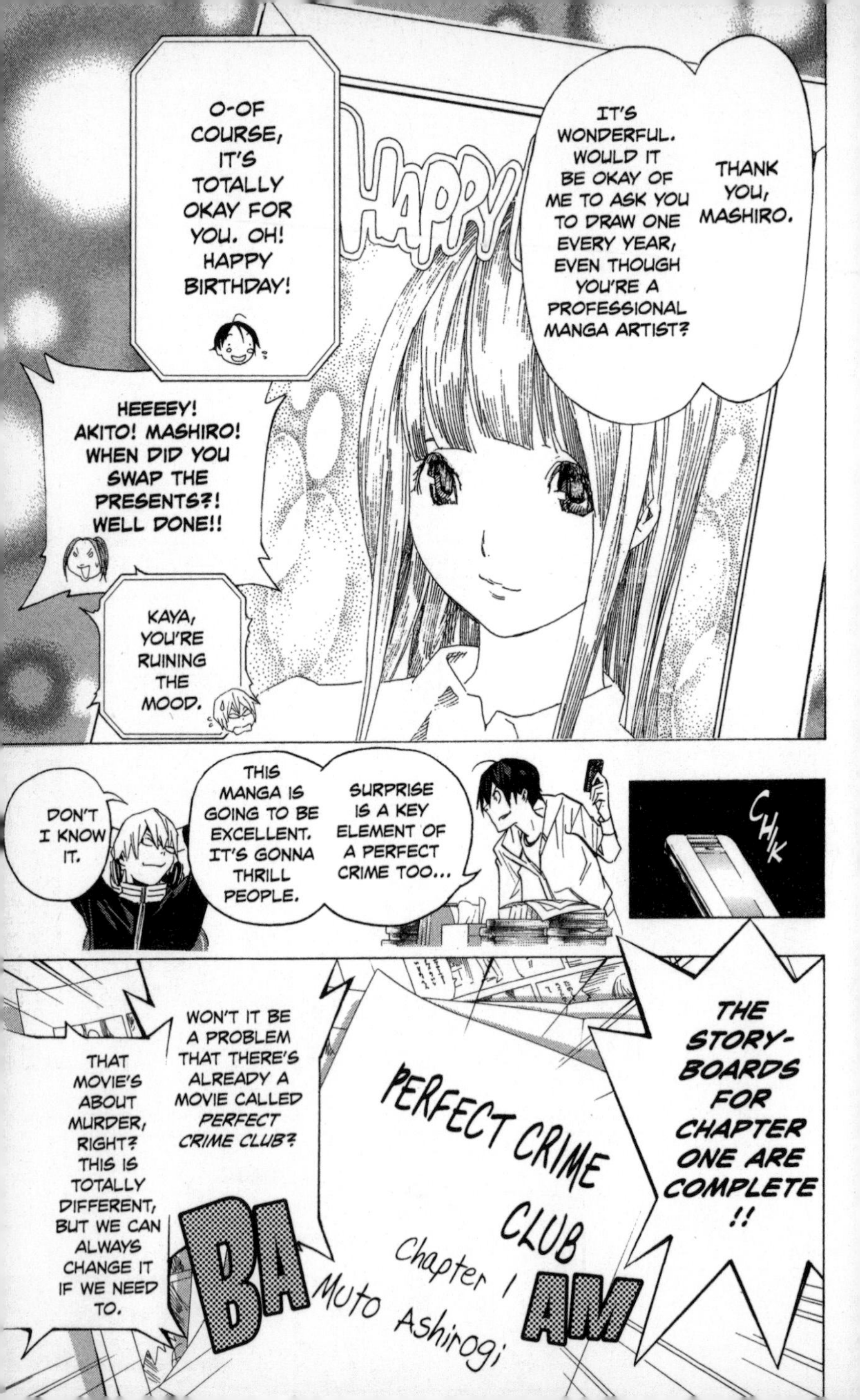
THANK YOU, MASHIRO.
IT'S WONDERFUL. WOULD IT BE OKAY OF ME TO ASK YOU TO DRAW ONE EVERY YEAR, EVEN THOUGH YOU'RE A PROFESSIONAL MANGA ARTIST?
HAPPY
O-OF COURSE, IT'S TOTALLY OKAY FOR YOU. OH! HAPPY BIRTHDAY!
HEEEEY! AKITO! MASHIRO! WHEN DID YOU SWAP THE PRESENTS?! WELL DONE!!
KAYA, YOU'RE RUINING THE MOOD.
CHIK
SURPRISE IS A KEY ELEMENT OF A PERFECT CRIME TOO...
THIS MANGA IS GOING TO BE EXCELLENT. IT'S GONNA THRILL PEOPLE.
DON'T I KNOW IT.
THE STORY-BOARDS FOR CHAPTER ONE ARE COMPLETE!!
PERFECT CRIME CLUB
Chapter 1
Muto Ashirogi
BAAM
WON'T IT BE A PROBLEM THAT THERE'S ALREADY A MOVIE CALLED *PERFECT CRIME CLUB*?
THAT MOVIE'S ABOUT MURDER, RIGHT? THIS IS TOTALLY DIFFERENT, BUT WE CAN ALWAYS CHANGE IT IF WE NEED TO.

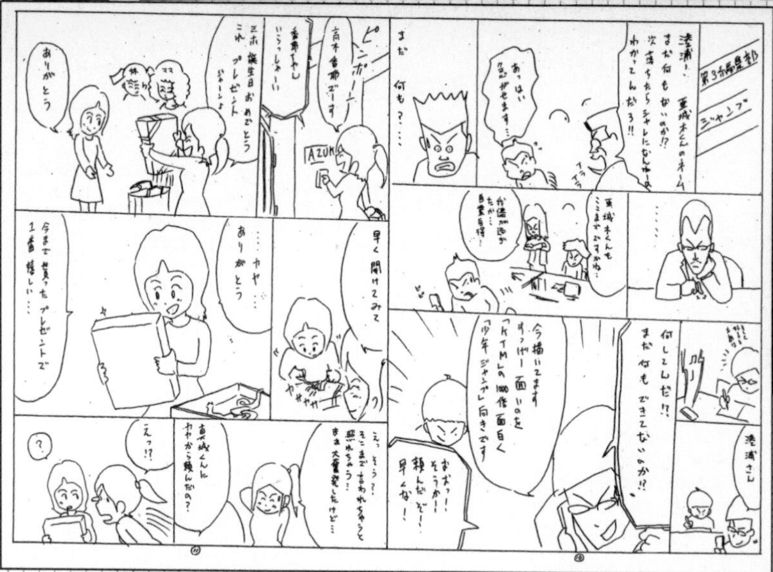
ジャンプ
あっはい 急がせます…
まだ 何も?…
……
港浦さん
何してんだ!? まだ何もできてないのか!?
今描いてます すげー面白いのを 「KTM」の1000倍面白く 「少年ジャンプ」向きです
おおっ! そうか! 頼んだぞ! 早くな!
ピンポーン
高木香耶でーす
香耶ちゃん いらっしゃーい
ミホ 誕生日おめでとう これ プレゼント
ありがとう
早く開けてみて
…カヤ… ありがとう
今まで貰ったプレゼントで 1番嬉しい…
えっ!?
?

OHBA'S STORYBOARD

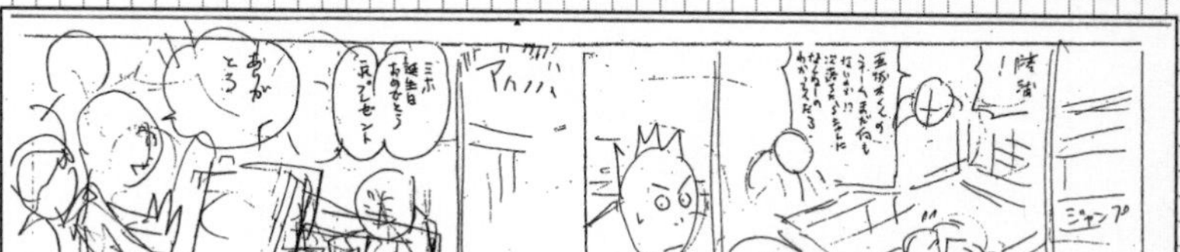

OBATA'S STORYBOARD

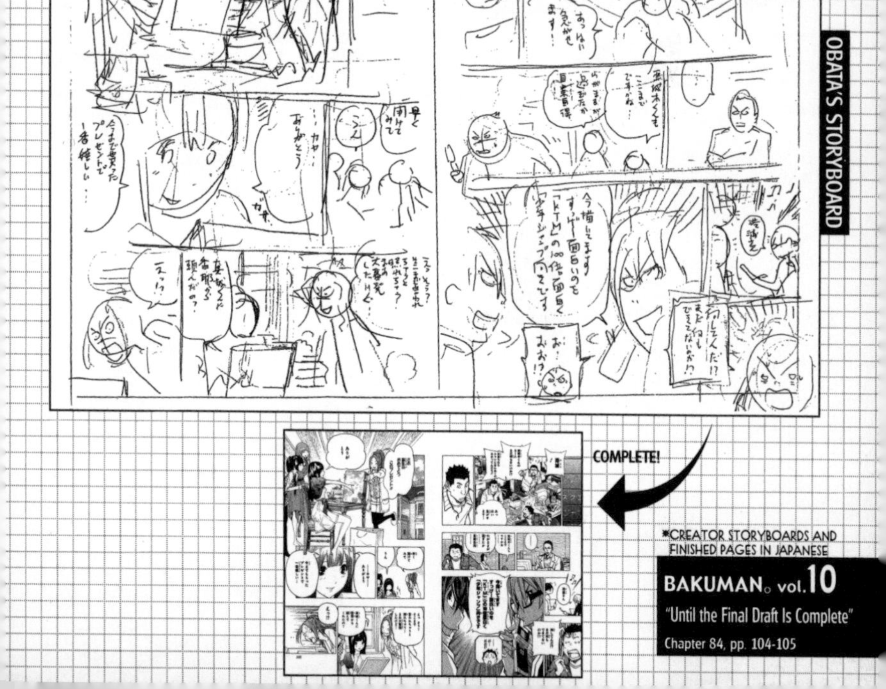

COMPLETE!

*CREATOR STORYBOARDS AND FINISHED PAGES IN JAPANESE

BAKUMAN。 vol.10

"Until the Final Draft Is Complete"

Chapter 84, pp. 104-105

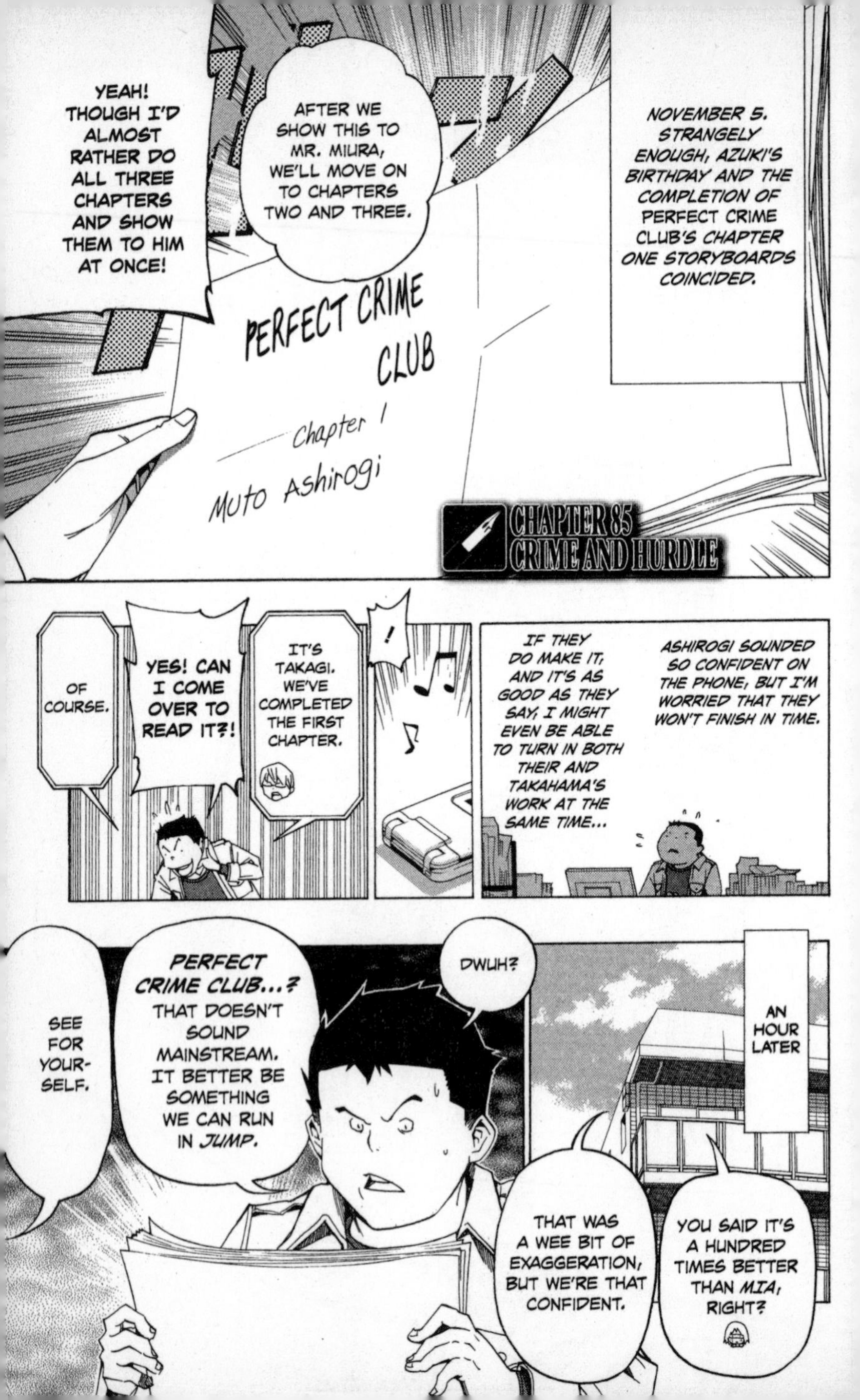
NOVEMBER 5. STRANGELY ENOUGH, AZUKI'S BIRTHDAY AND THE COMPLETION OF PERFECT CRIME CLUB'S CHAPTER ONE STORYBOARDS COINCIDED.
AFTER WE SHOW THIS TO MR. MIURA, WE'LL MOVE ON TO CHAPTERS TWO AND THREE.
YEAH! THOUGH I'D ALMOST RATHER DO ALL THREE CHAPTERS AND SHOW THEM TO HIM AT ONCE!
PERFECT CRIME CLUB
Chapter 1
Muto Ashirogi
CHAPTER 85
CRIME AND HURDLE
ASHIROGI SOUNDED SO CONFIDENT ON THE PHONE, BUT I'M WORRIED THAT THEY WON'T FINISH IN TIME.
IF THEY DO MAKE IT, AND IT'S AS GOOD AS THEY SAY, I MIGHT EVEN BE ABLE TO TURN IN BOTH THEIR AND TAKAHAMA'S WORK AT THE SAME TIME...
!
IT'S TAKAGI. WE'VE COMPLETED THE FIRST CHAPTER.
YES! CAN I COME OVER TO READ IT?!
OF COURSE.
AN HOUR LATER
YOU SAID IT'S A HUNDRED TIMES BETTER THAN MIA, RIGHT?
THAT WAS A WEE BIT OF EXAGGERATION, BUT WE'RE THAT CONFIDENT.
DWUH?
PERFECT CRIME CLUB...? THAT DOESN'T SOUND MAINSTREAM. IT BETTER BE SOMETHING WE CAN RUN IN JUMP.
SEE FOR YOURSELF.

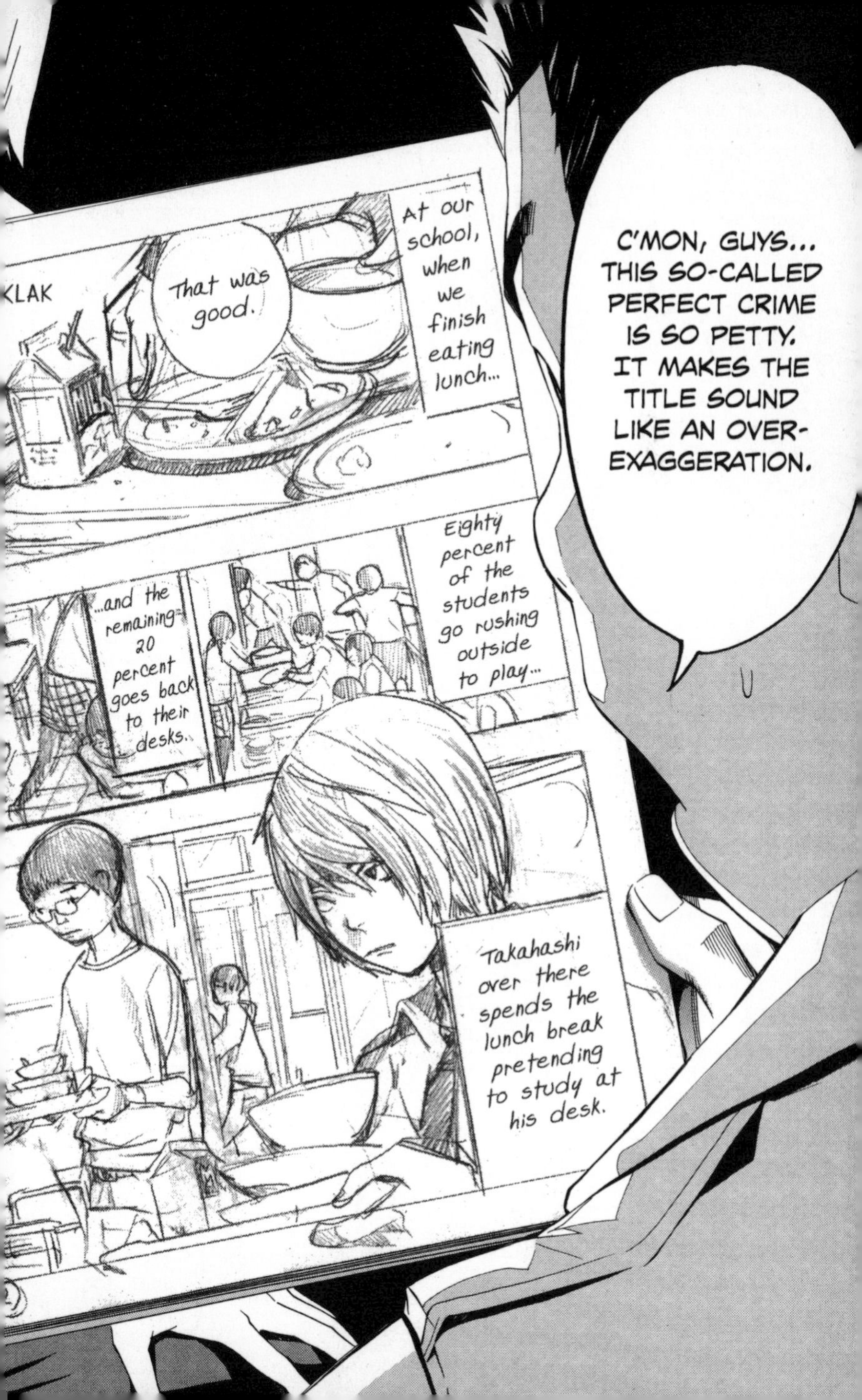

C'MON, GUYS... THIS SO-CALLED PERFECT CRIME IS SO PETTY. IT MAKES THE TITLE SOUND LIKE AN OVER-EXAGGERATION.
At our school, when we finish eating lunch...
That was good.
KLAK
Eighty percent of the students go rushing outside to play...
...and the remaining 20 percent goes back to their desks.
Takahashi over there spends the lunch break pretending to study at his desk.

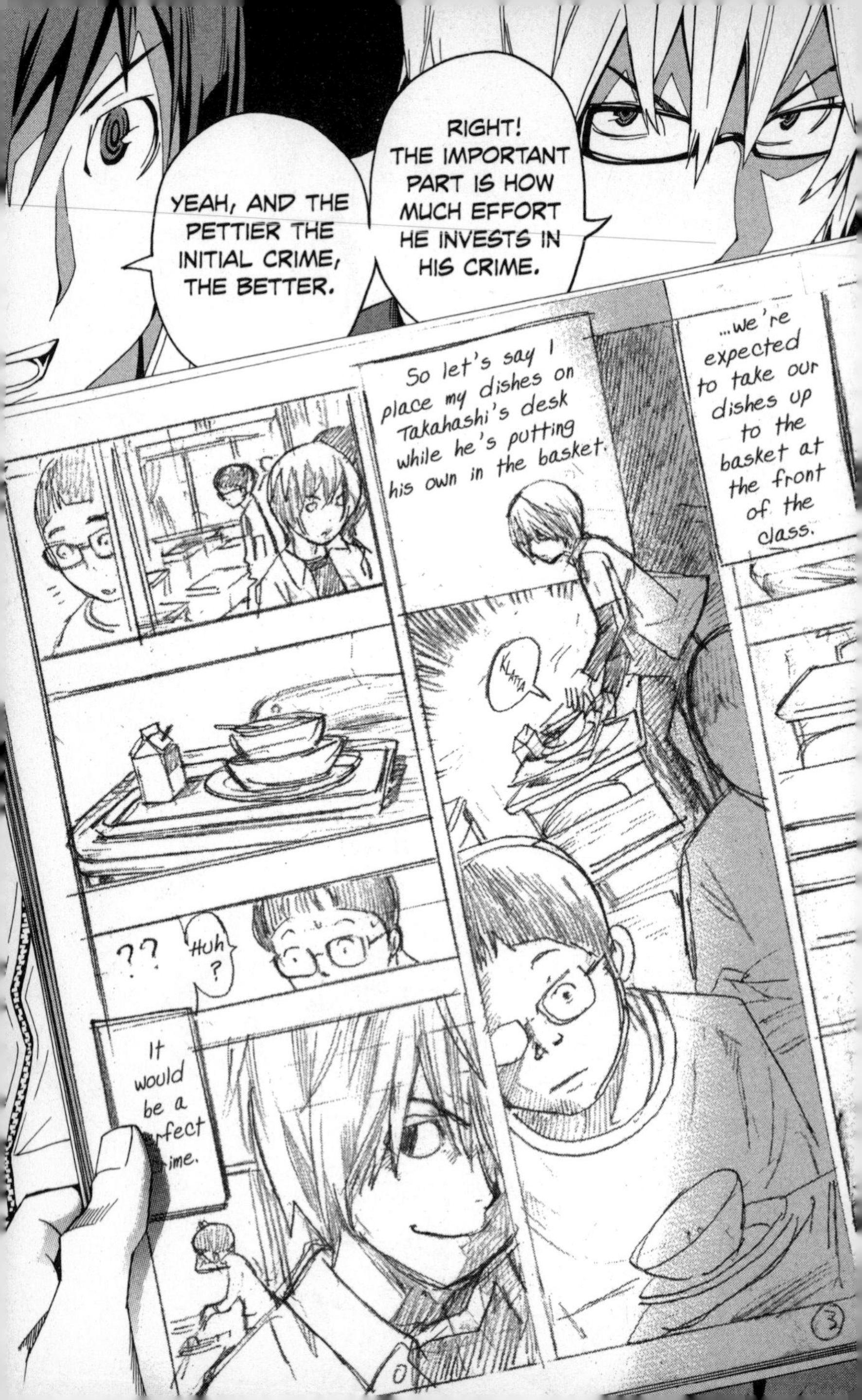
RIGHT! THE IMPORTANT PART IS HOW MUCH EFFORT HE INVESTS IN HIS CRIME.
YEAH, AND THE PETTIER THE INITIAL CRIME, THE BETTER.
...we're expected to take our dishes up to the basket at the front of the class.
So let's say I place my dishes on Takahashi's desk while he's putting his own in the basket.
KLATTA
Huh?
??
It would be a ...rfect ...ime.
3

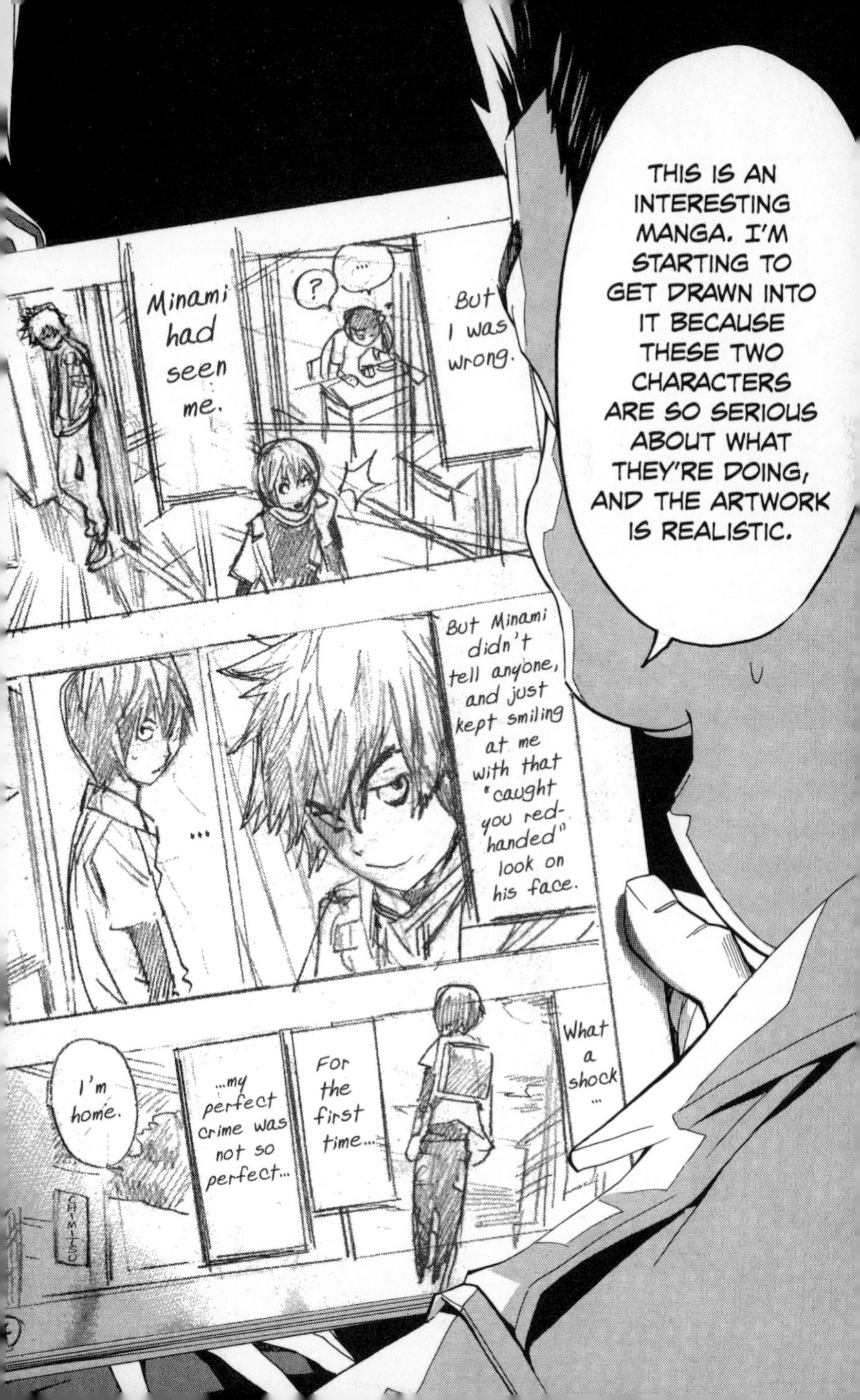
THIS IS AN INTERESTING MANGA. I'M STARTING TO GET DRAWN INTO IT BECAUSE THESE TWO CHARACTERS ARE SO SERIOUS ABOUT WHAT THEY'RE DOING, AND THE ARTWORK IS REALISTIC.
But I was wrong.
?
...
Minami had seen me.
But Minami didn't tell anyone, and just kept smiling at me with that "caught you red-handed" look on his face.
...
What a shock...
For the first time...
...my perfect crime was not so perfect...
I'm home.

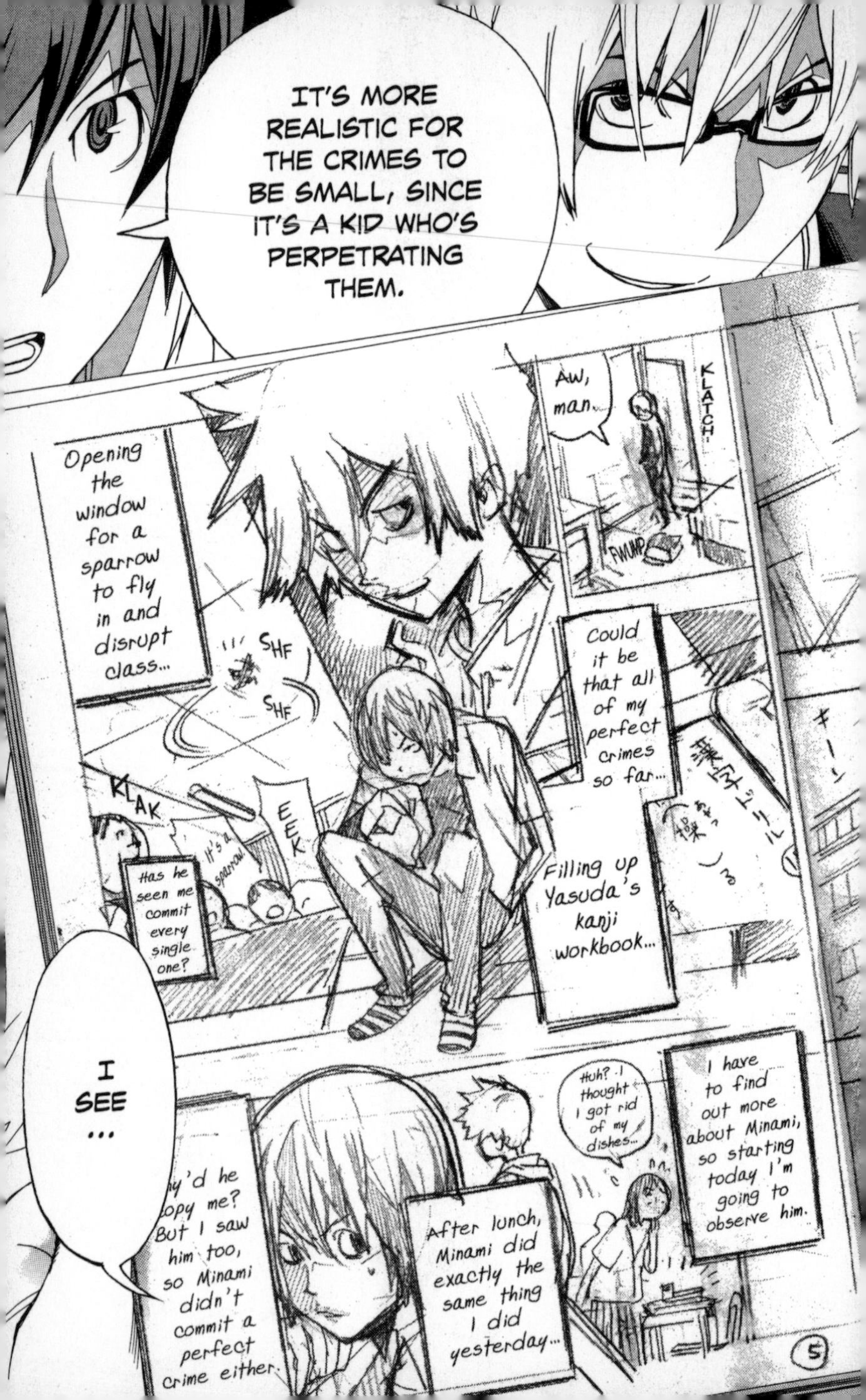
IT'S MORE REALISTIC FOR THE CRIMES TO BE SMALL, SINCE IT'S A KID WHO'S PERPETRATING THEM.
KLATCH!
Aw, man...
FWUMP
Could it be that all of my perfect crimes so far...
Filling up Yasuda's kanji workbook...
Opening the window for a sparrow to fly in and disrupt class...
SHF
SHF
EEK
It's a sparrow!
KLAK
Has he seen me commit every single one?
I have to find out more about Minami, so starting today I'm going to observe him.
Huh? I thought I got rid of my dishes...
After lunch, Minami did exactly the same thing I did yesterday...
...y'd he copy me? But I saw him too, so Minami didn't commit a perfect crime either.
I SEE...
5

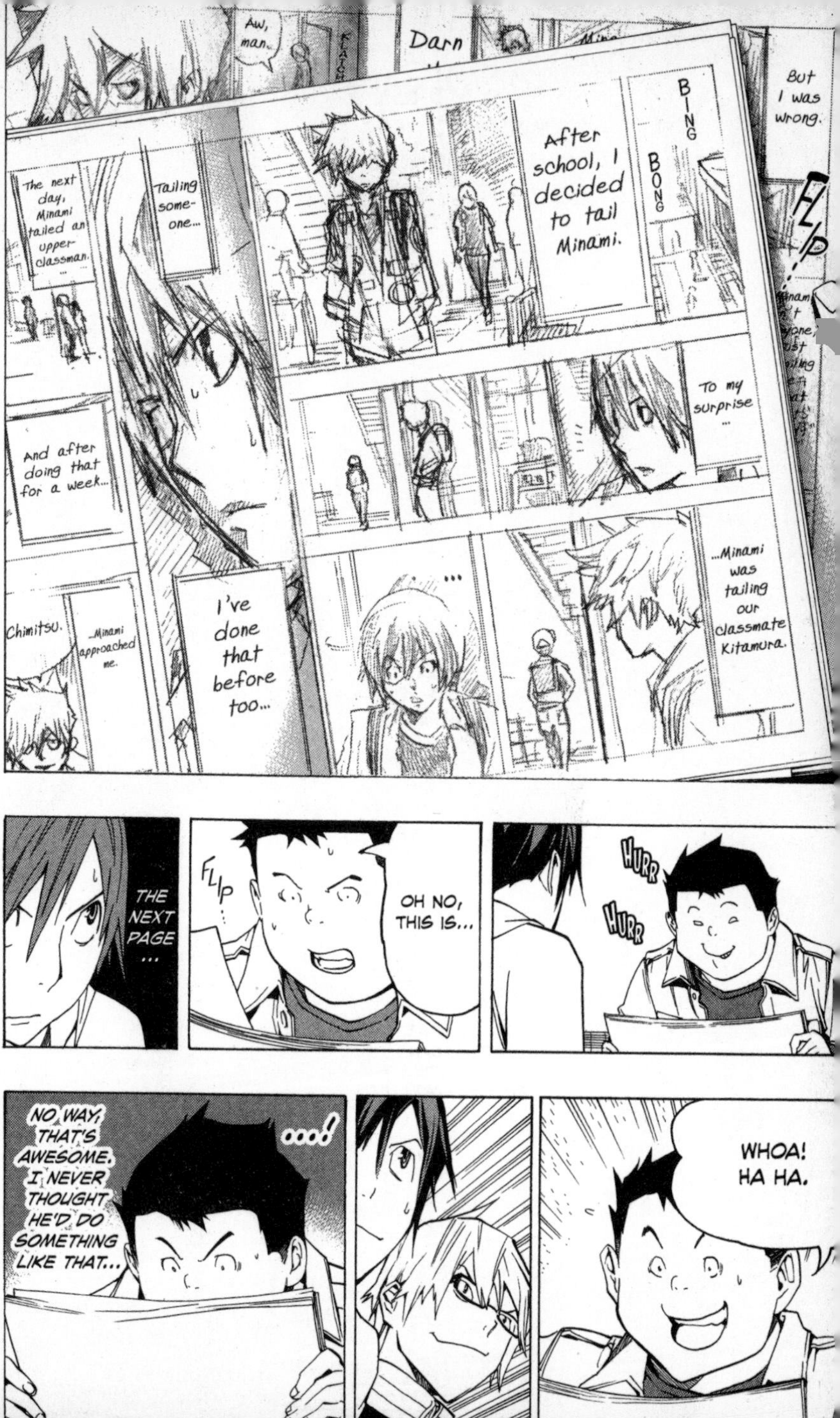
Darn
Aw, man...
But I was wrong.
FLIP
BING
BONG
After school, I decided to tail Minami.
To my surprise...
...Minami was tailing our classmate Kitamura.
...
Tailing someone...
The next day, Minami tailed an upperclassman...
And after doing that for a week...
I've done that before too...
...Minami approached me.
Chimitsu.
HURR
HURR
OH NO, THIS IS...
FLIP...
THE NEXT PAGE...
WHOA! HA HA.
...!
NO WAY, THAT'S AWESOME. I NEVER THOUGHT HE'D DO SOMETHING LIKE THAT...

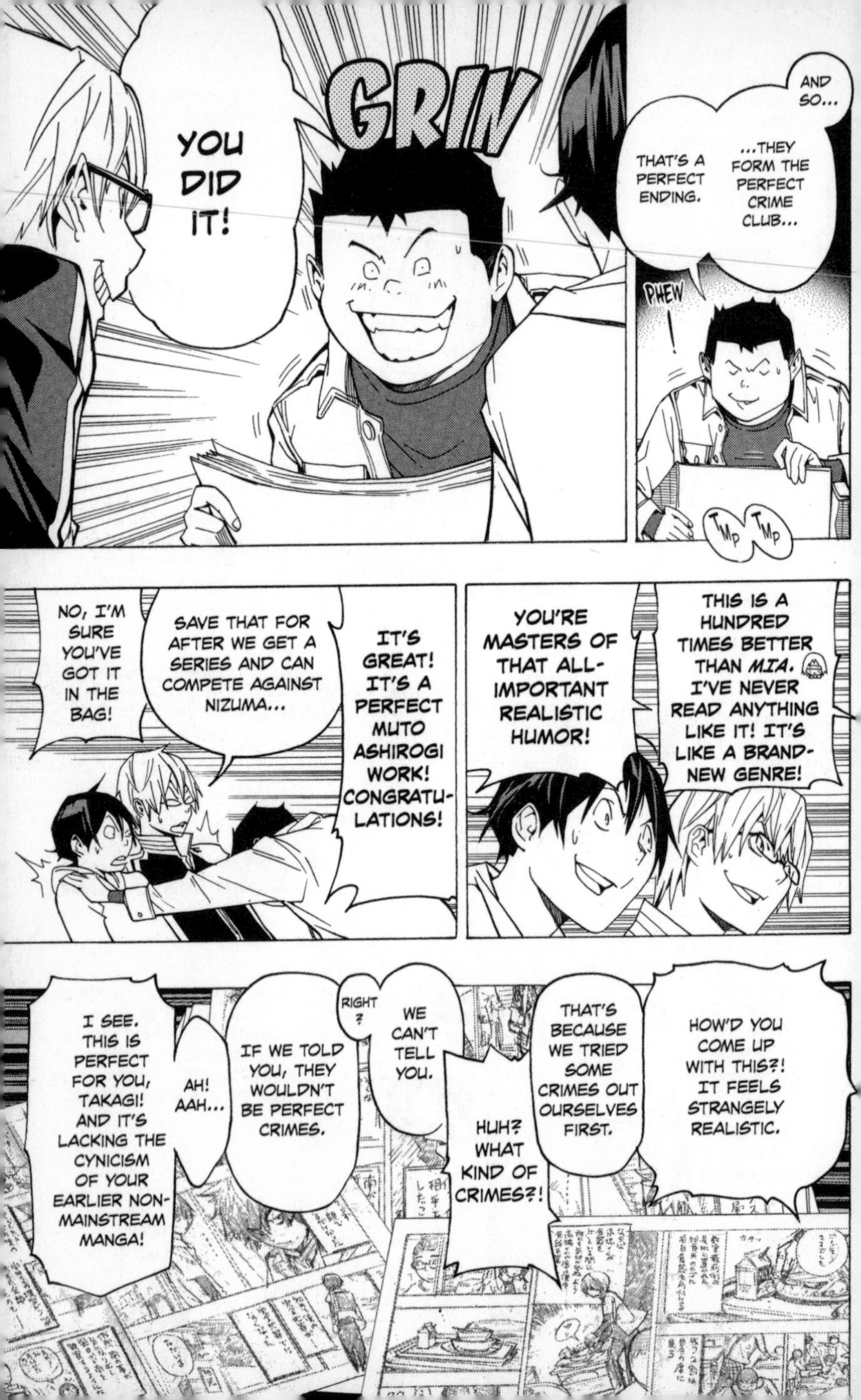
AND SO...
...THEY FORM THE PERFECT CRIME CLUB...
THAT'S A PERFECT ENDING.
PHEW!
TMP TMP
GRIN
YOU DID IT!
THIS IS A HUNDRED TIMES BETTER THAN MIA. I'VE NEVER READ ANYTHING LIKE IT! IT'S LIKE A BRAND-NEW GENRE!
YOU'RE MASTERS OF THAT ALL-IMPORTANT REALISTIC HUMOR!
IT'S GREAT! IT'S A PERFECT MUTO ASHIROGI WORK! CONGRATULATIONS!
SAVE THAT FOR AFTER WE GET A SERIES AND CAN COMPETE AGAINST NIZUMA...
NO, I'M SURE YOU'VE GOT IT IN THE BAG!
HOW'D YOU COME UP WITH THIS?! IT FEELS STRANGELY REALISTIC.
THAT'S BECAUSE WE TRIED SOME CRIMES OUT OURSELVES FIRST.
HUH? WHAT KIND OF CRIMES?!
WE CAN'T TELL YOU.
RIGHT?
IF WE TOLD YOU, THEY WOULDN'T BE PERFECT CRIMES.
AH! AAH...
I SEE. THIS IS PERFECT FOR YOU, TAKAGI! AND IT'S LACKING THE CYNICISM OF YOUR EARLIER NON-MAINSTREAM MANGA!

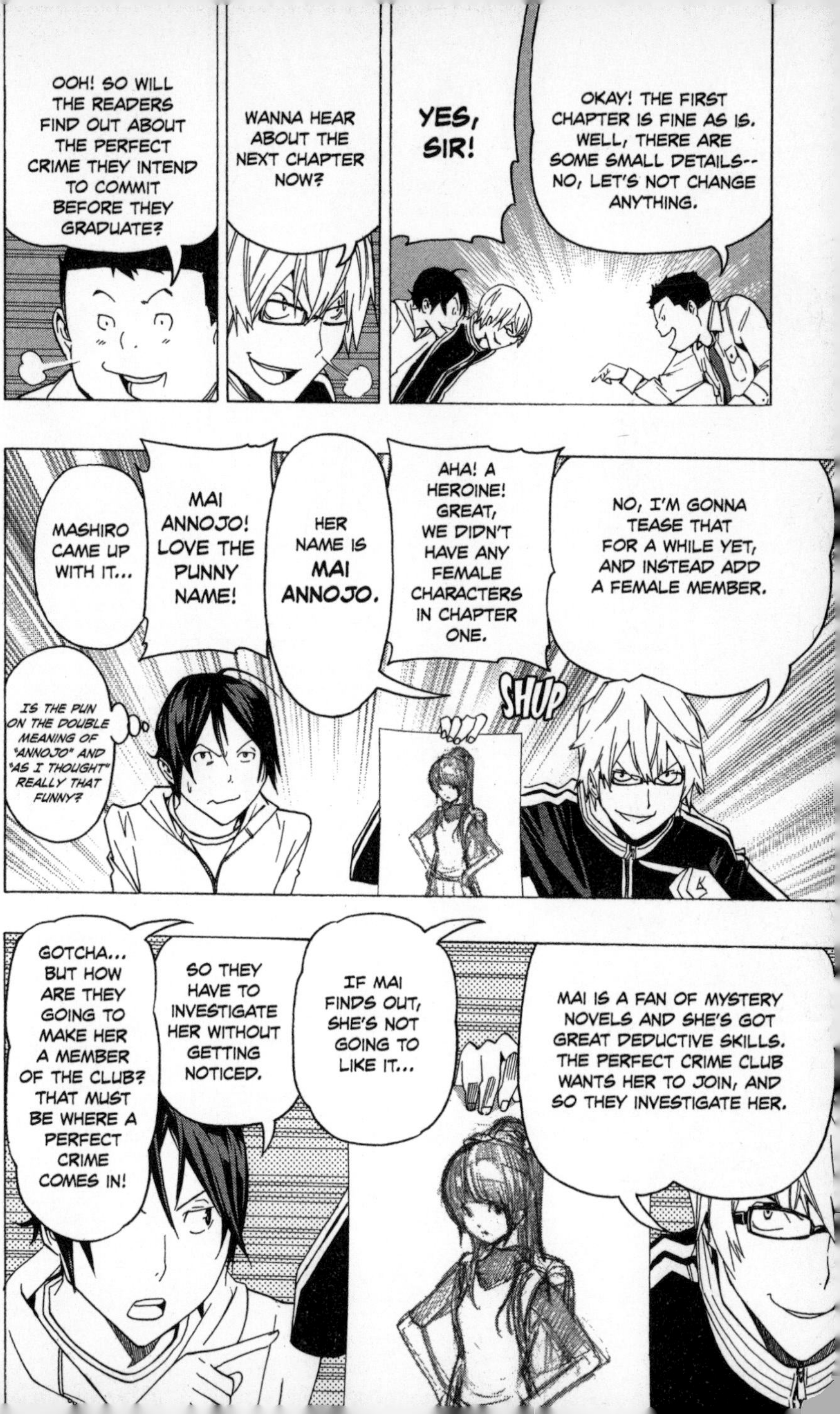
OKAY! THE FIRST CHAPTER IS FINE AS IS. WELL, THERE ARE SOME SMALL DETAILS-- NO, LET'S NOT CHANGE ANYTHING.
YES, SIR!
WANNA HEAR ABOUT THE NEXT CHAPTER NOW?
OOH! SO WILL THE READERS FIND OUT ABOUT THE PERFECT CRIME THEY INTEND TO COMMIT BEFORE THEY GRADUATE?
NO, I'M GONNA TEASE THAT FOR A WHILE YET, AND INSTEAD ADD A FEMALE MEMBER.
AHA! A HEROINE! GREAT, WE DIDN'T HAVE ANY FEMALE CHARACTERS IN CHAPTER ONE.
HER NAME IS MAI ANNOJO.
MAI ANNOJO! LOVE THE PUNNY NAME!
MASHIRO CAME UP WITH IT...
SHUP
IS THE PUN ON THE DOUBLE MEANING OF "ANNOJO" AND "AS I THOUGHT" REALLY THAT FUNNY?
MAI IS A FAN OF MYSTERY NOVELS AND SHE'S GOT GREAT DEDUCTIVE SKILLS. THE PERFECT CRIME CLUB WANTS HER TO JOIN, AND SO THEY INVESTIGATE HER.
IF MAI FINDS OUT, SHE'S NOT GOING TO LIKE IT...
SO THEY HAVE TO INVESTIGATE HER WITHOUT GETTING NOTICED.
GOTCHA... BUT HOW ARE THEY GOING TO MAKE HER A MEMBER OF THE CLUB? THAT MUST BE WHERE A PERFECT CRIME COMES IN!

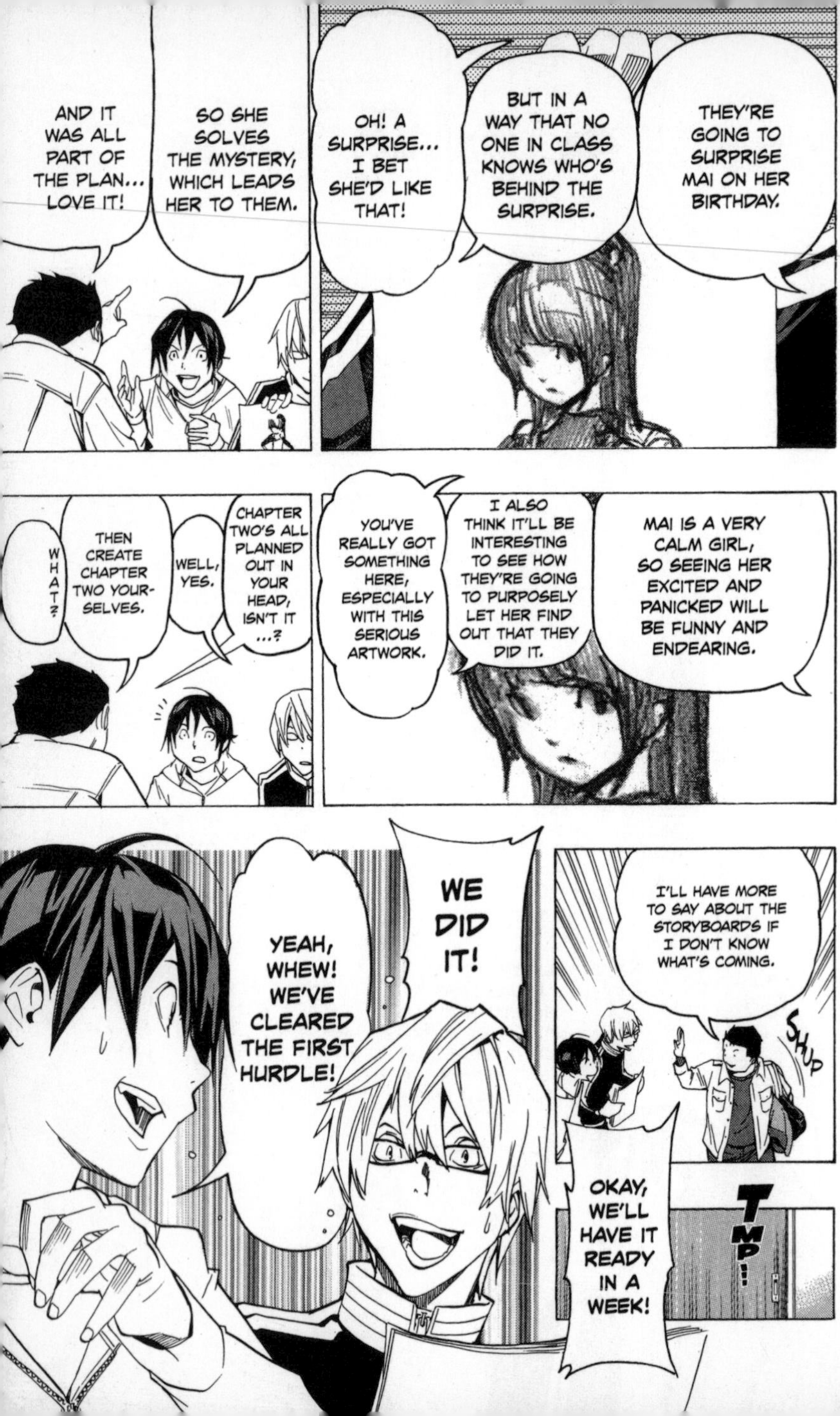
THEY'RE GOING TO SURPRISE MAI ON HER BIRTHDAY.
BUT IN A WAY THAT NO ONE IN CLASS KNOWS WHO'S BEHIND THE SURPRISE.
OH! A SURPRISE... I BET SHE'D LIKE THAT!
SO SHE SOLVES THE MYSTERY, WHICH LEADS HER TO THEM.
AND IT WAS ALL PART OF THE PLAN... LOVE IT!
MAI IS A VERY CALM GIRL, SO SEEING HER EXCITED AND PANICKED WILL BE FUNNY AND ENDEARING.
I ALSO THINK IT'LL BE INTERESTING TO SEE HOW THEY'RE GOING TO PURPOSELY LET HER FIND OUT THAT THEY DID IT.
YOU'VE REALLY GOT SOMETHING HERE, ESPECIALLY WITH THIS SERIOUS ARTWORK.
CHAPTER TWO'S ALL PLANNED OUT IN YOUR HEAD, ISN'T IT ...?
WELL, YES.
THEN CREATE CHAPTER TWO YOUR-SELVES.
WHAT?
I'LL HAVE MORE TO SAY ABOUT THE STORYBOARDS IF I DON'T KNOW WHAT'S COMING.
SHUP
OKAY, WE'LL HAVE IT READY IN A WEEK!
TMP!!
WE DID IT!
YEAH, WHEW! WE'VE CLEARED THE FIRST HURDLE!

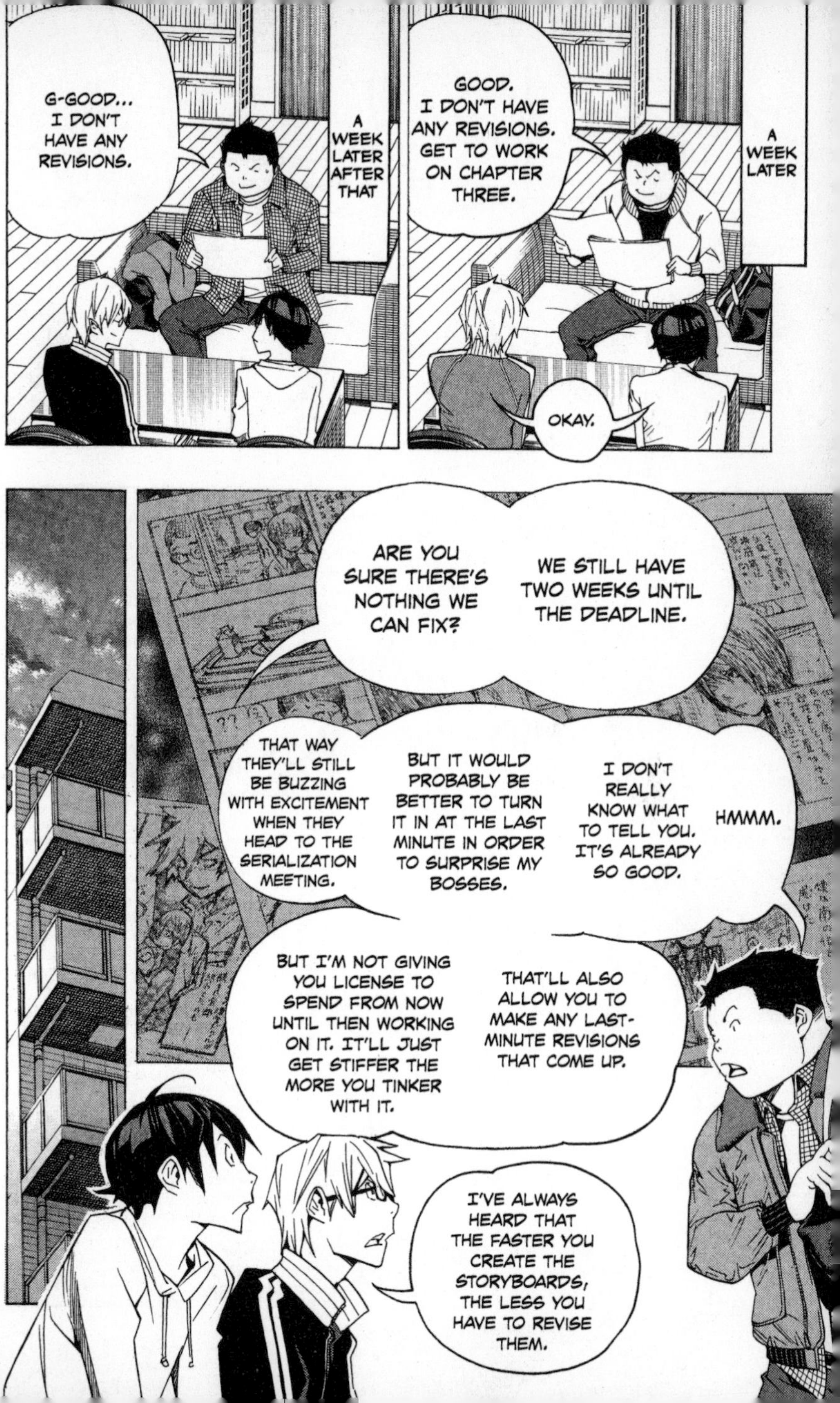
A WEEK LATER
GOOD. I DON'T HAVE ANY REVISIONS. GET TO WORK ON CHAPTER THREE.
OKAY.
A WEEK LATER AFTER THAT
G-GOOD... I DON'T HAVE ANY REVISIONS.
ARE YOU SURE THERE'S NOTHING WE CAN FIX?
WE STILL HAVE TWO WEEKS UNTIL THE DEADLINE.
HMMM.
I DON'T REALLY KNOW WHAT TO TELL YOU. IT'S ALREADY SO GOOD.
BUT IT WOULD PROBABLY BE BETTER TO TURN IT IN AT THE LAST MINUTE IN ORDER TO SURPRISE MY BOSSES.
THAT WAY THEY'LL STILL BE BUZZING WITH EXCITEMENT WHEN THEY HEAD TO THE SERIALIZATION MEETING.
THAT'LL ALSO ALLOW YOU TO MAKE ANY LAST-MINUTE REVISIONS THAT COME UP.
BUT I'M NOT GIVING YOU LICENSE TO SPEND FROM NOW UNTIL THEN WORKING ON IT. IT'LL JUST GET STIFFER THE MORE YOU TINKER WITH IT.
I'VE ALWAYS HEARD THAT THE FASTER YOU CREATE THE STORYBOARDS, THE LESS YOU HAVE TO REVISE THEM.

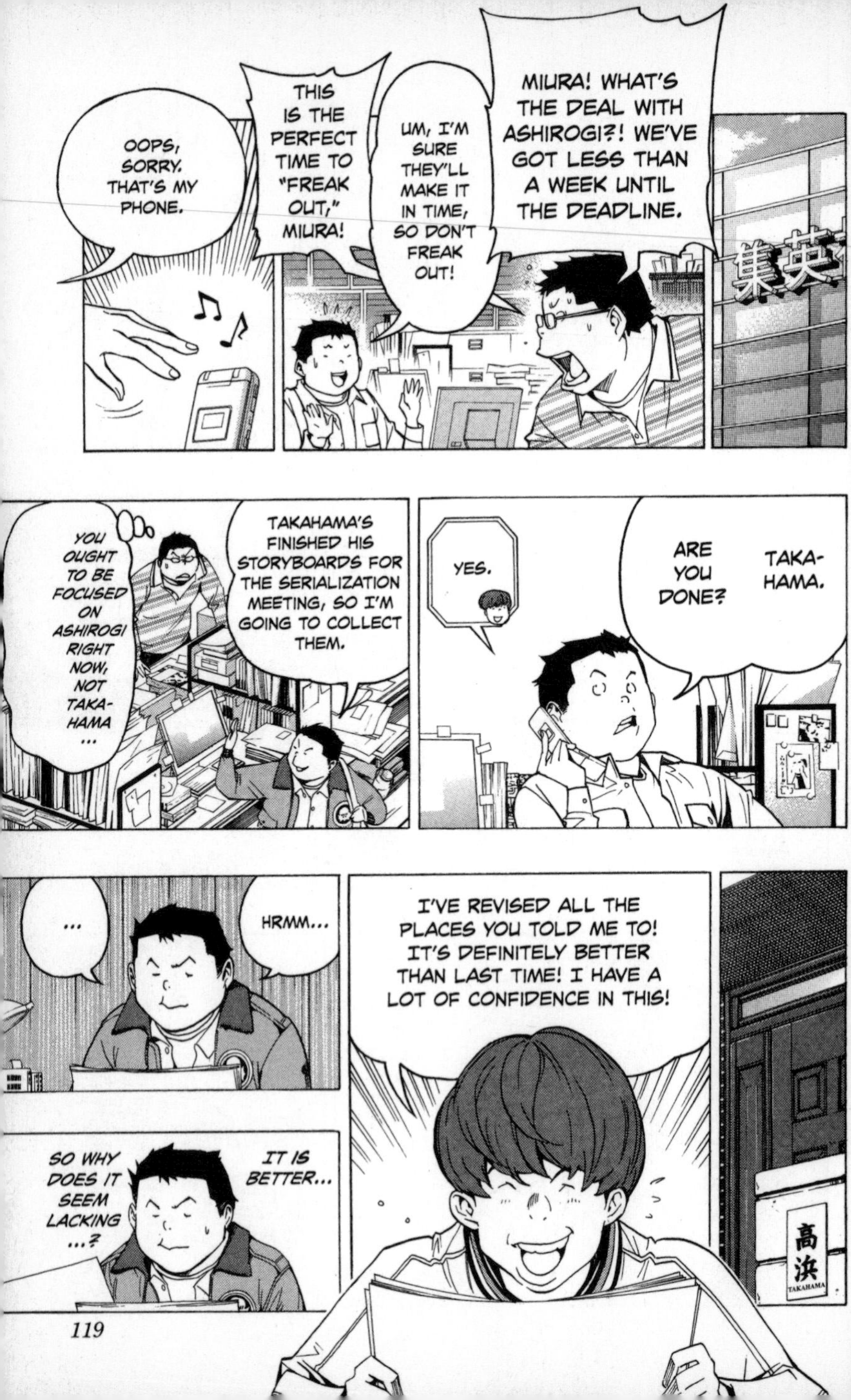
集英
MIURA! WHAT'S THE DEAL WITH ASHIROGI?! WE'VE GOT LESS THAN A WEEK UNTIL THE DEADLINE.
UM, I'M SURE THEY'LL MAKE IT IN TIME, SO DON'T FREAK OUT!
THIS IS THE PERFECT TIME TO "FREAK OUT," MIURA!
OOPS, SORRY. THAT'S MY PHONE.
TAKA-HAMA.
ARE YOU DONE?
YES.
TAKAHAMA'S FINISHED HIS STORYBOARDS FOR THE SERIALIZATION MEETING, SO I'M GOING TO COLLECT THEM.
YOU OUGHT TO BE FOCUSED ON ASHIROGI RIGHT NOW, NOT TAKA-HAMA...
高浜
TAKAHAMA
I'VE REVISED ALL THE PLACES YOU TOLD ME TO! IT'S DEFINITELY BETTER THAN LAST TIME! I HAVE A LOT OF CONFIDENCE IN THIS!
HRMM...
...
IT IS BETTER...
SO WHY DOES IT SEEM LACKING...?

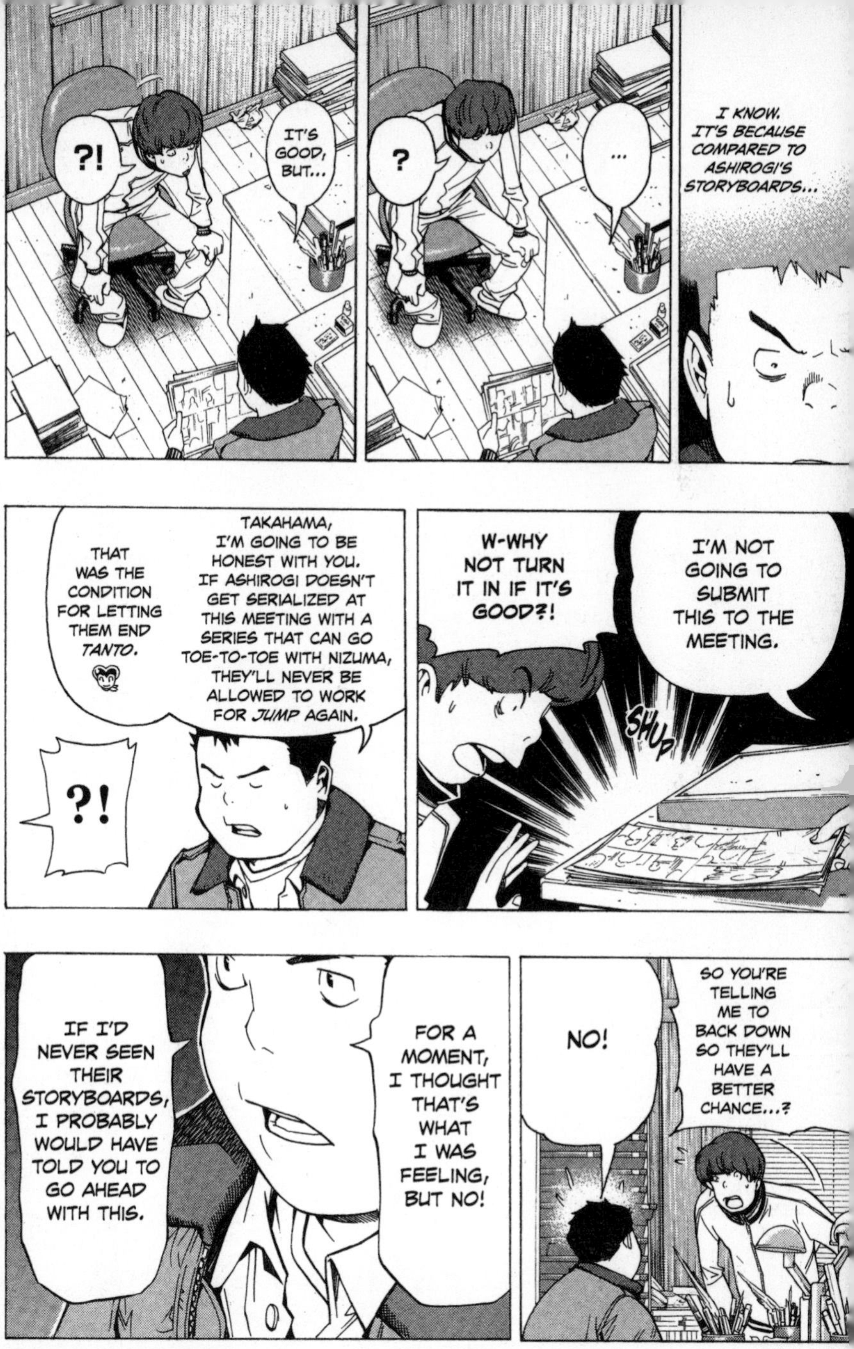
I KNOW. IT'S BECAUSE COMPARED TO ASHIROGI'S STORYBOARDS...
...
?
IT'S GOOD, BUT...
?!
I'M NOT GOING TO SUBMIT THIS TO THE MEETING.
W-WHY NOT TURN IT IN IF IT'S GOOD?!
SHUP
TAKAHAMA, I'M GOING TO BE HONEST WITH YOU. IF ASHIROGI DOESN'T GET SERIALIZED AT THIS MEETING WITH A SERIES THAT CAN GO TOE-TO-TOE WITH NIZUMA, THEY'LL NEVER BE ALLOWED TO WORK FOR *JUMP* AGAIN.
THAT WAS THE CONDITION FOR LETTING THEM END *TANTO*.
?!
SO YOU'RE TELLING ME TO BACK DOWN SO THEY'LL HAVE A BETTER CHANCE...?
NO!
FOR A MOMENT, I THOUGHT THAT'S WHAT I WAS FEELING, BUT NO!
IF I'D NEVER SEEN THEIR STORYBOARDS, I PROBABLY WOULD HAVE TOLD YOU TO GO AHEAD WITH THIS.

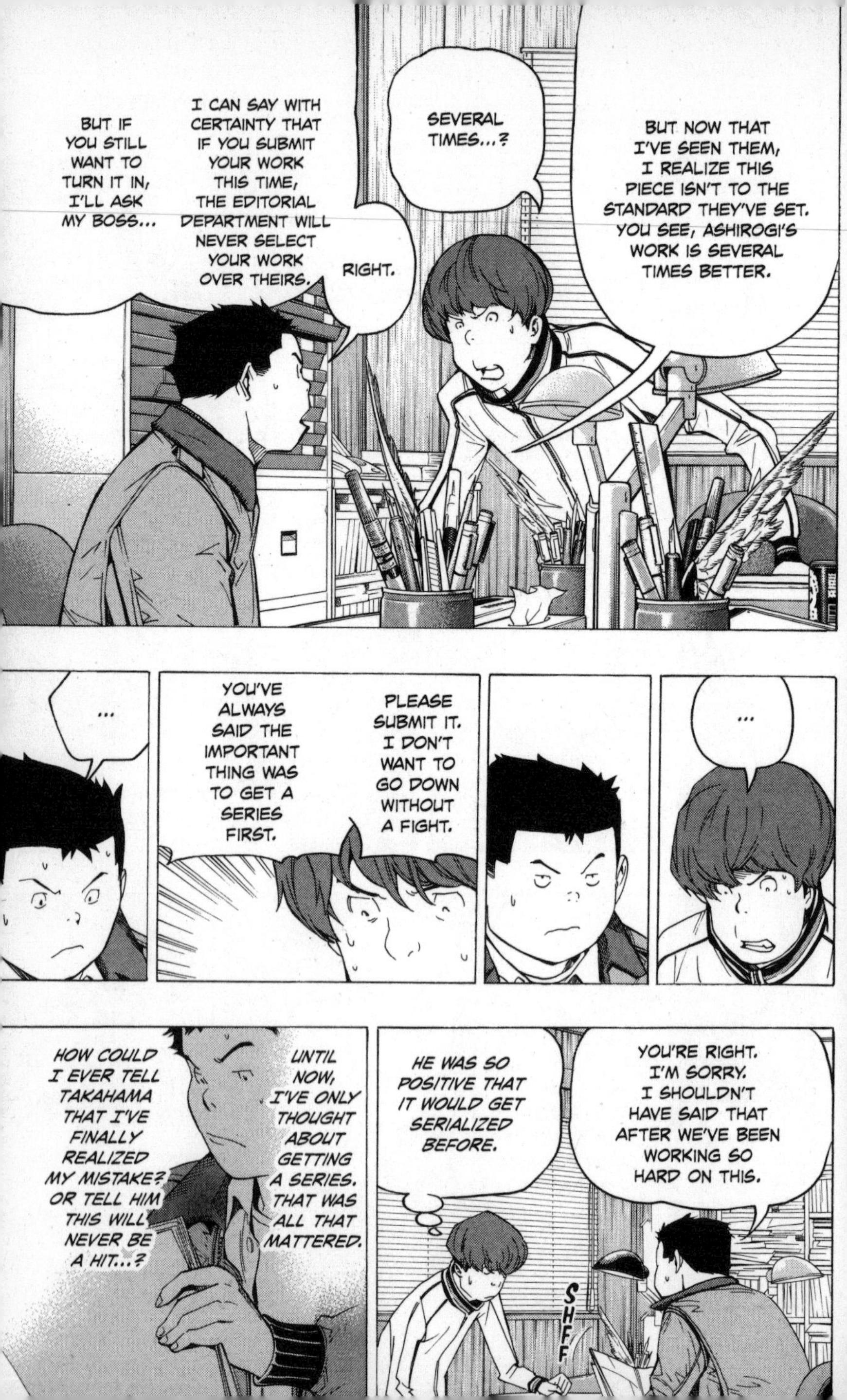
BUT NOW THAT I'VE SEEN THEM, I REALIZE THIS PIECE ISN'T TO THE STANDARD THEY'VE SET. YOU SEE, ASHIROGI'S WORK IS SEVERAL TIMES BETTER.
SEVERAL TIMES...?
RIGHT.
I CAN SAY WITH CERTAINTY THAT IF YOU SUBMIT YOUR WORK THIS TIME, THE EDITORIAL DEPARTMENT WILL NEVER SELECT YOUR WORK OVER THEIRS.
BUT IF YOU STILL WANT TO TURN IT IN, I'LL ASK MY BOSS...
...
YOU'VE ALWAYS SAID THE IMPORTANT THING WAS TO GET A SERIES FIRST.
PLEASE SUBMIT IT. I DON'T WANT TO GO DOWN WITHOUT A FIGHT.
...
YOU'RE RIGHT. I'M SORRY. I SHOULDN'T HAVE SAID THAT AFTER WE'VE BEEN WORKING SO HARD ON THIS.
HE WAS SO POSITIVE THAT IT WOULD GET SERIALIZED BEFORE.
SHFF
UNTIL NOW, I'VE ONLY THOUGHT ABOUT GETTING A SERIES. THAT WAS ALL THAT MATTERED.
HOW COULD I EVER TELL TAKAHAMA THAT I'VE FINALLY REALIZED MY MISTAKE? OR TELL HIM THIS WILL NEVER BE A HIT...?

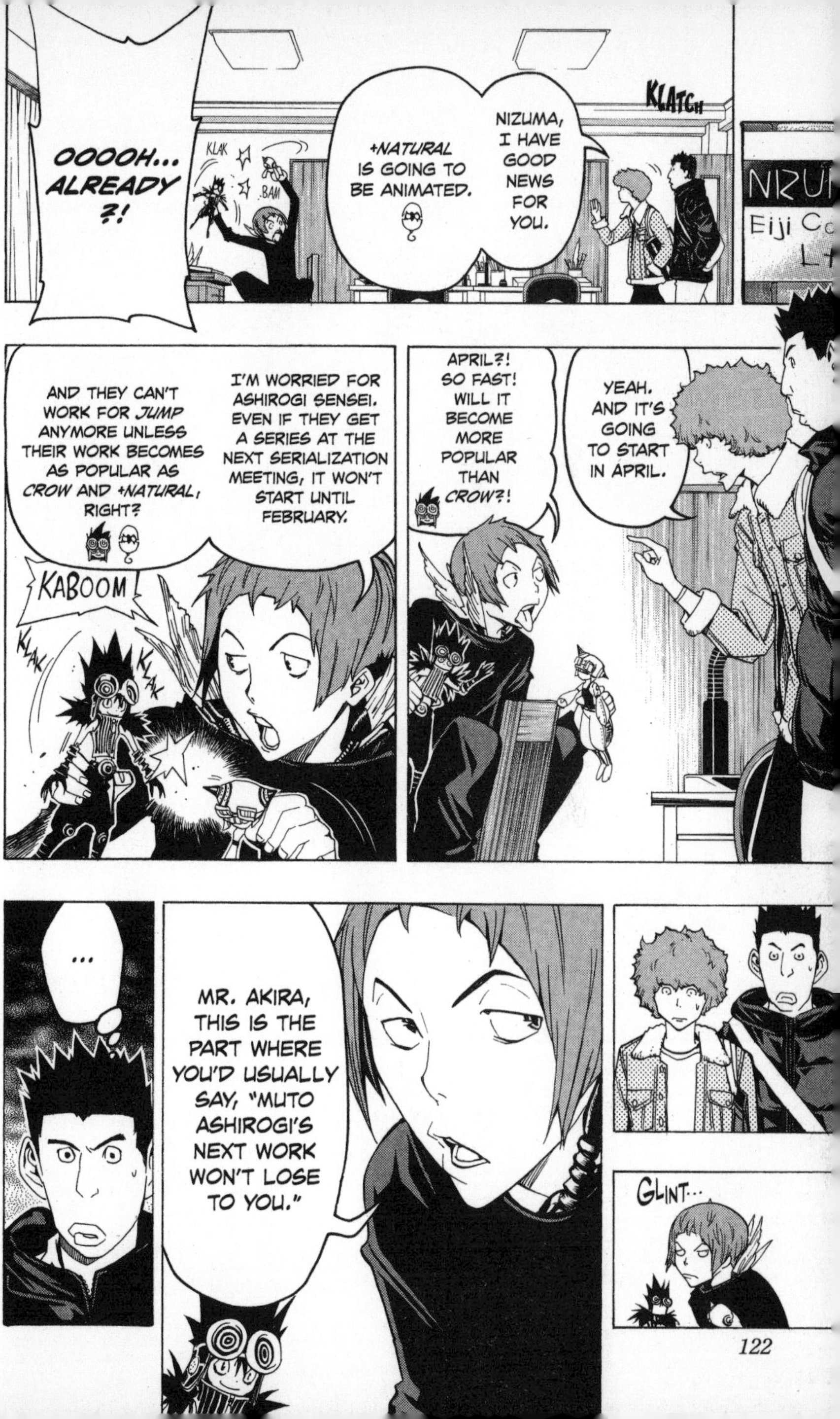
KLATCH
NIZUMA, I HAVE GOOD NEWS FOR YOU.
+NATURAL IS GOING TO BE ANIMATED.
KLAK
BAM
OOOOH... ALREADY?!
YEAH. AND IT'S GOING TO START IN APRIL.
APRIL?! SO FAST! WILL IT BECOME MORE POPULAR THAN CROW?!
I'M WORRIED FOR ASHIROGI SENSEI. EVEN IF THEY GET A SERIES AT THE NEXT SERIALIZATION MEETING, IT WON'T START UNTIL FEBRUARY.
AND THEY CAN'T WORK FOR JUMP ANYMORE UNLESS THEIR WORK BECOMES AS POPULAR AS CROW AND +NATURAL, RIGHT?
KABOOM
KLAK
KLAK
GLINT...
MR. AKIRA, THIS IS THE PART WHERE YOU'D USUALLY SAY, "MUTO ASHIROGI'S NEXT WORK WON'T LOSE TO YOU."
...

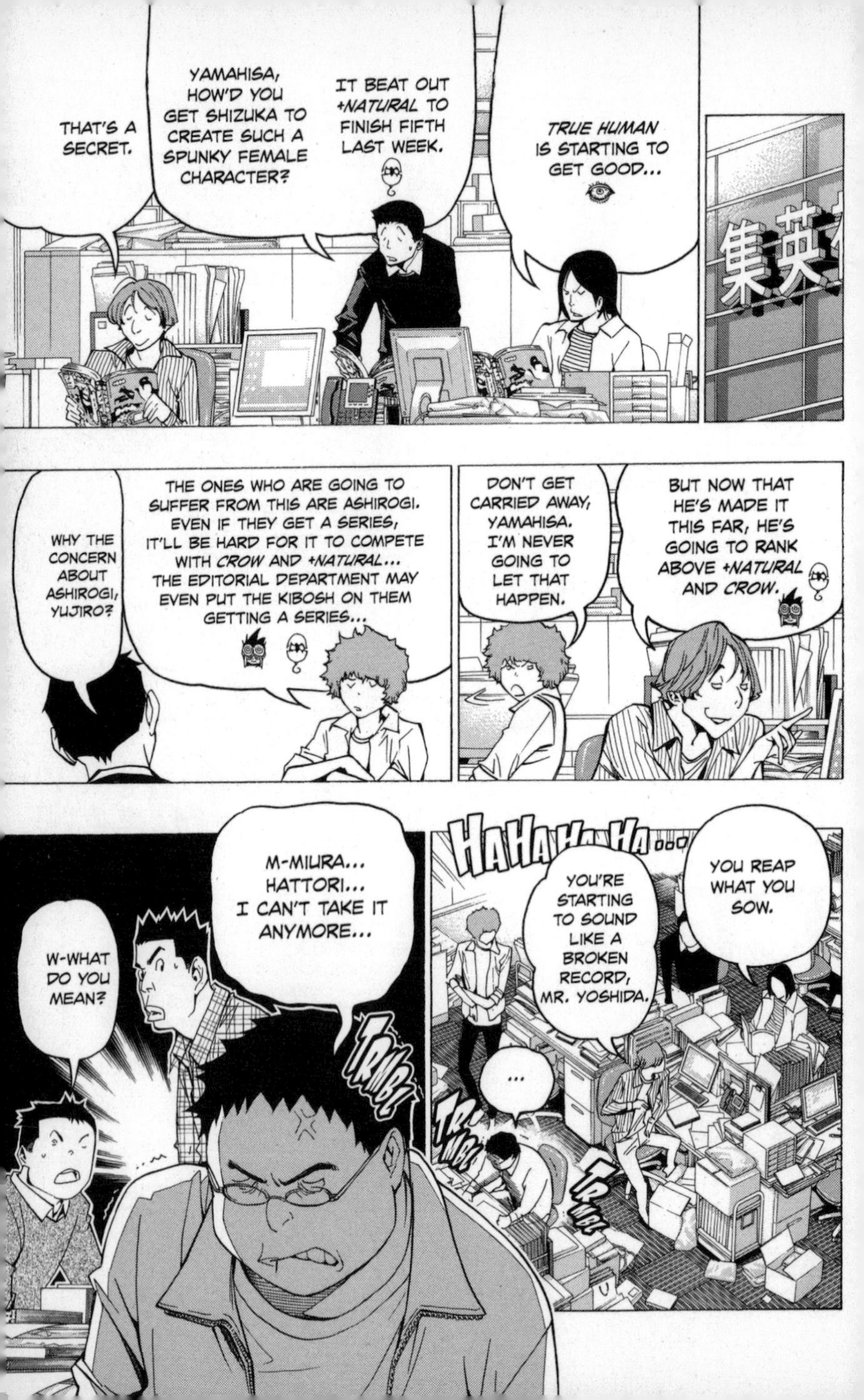
集英
TRUE HUMAN IS STARTING TO GET GOOD...
IT BEAT OUT +NATURAL TO FINISH FIFTH LAST WEEK.
YAMAHISA, HOW'D YOU GET SHIZUKA TO CREATE SUCH A SPUNKY FEMALE CHARACTER?
THAT'S A SECRET.
BUT NOW THAT HE'S MADE IT THIS FAR, HE'S GOING TO RANK ABOVE +NATURAL AND CROW.
DON'T GET CARRIED AWAY, YAMAHISA. I'M NEVER GOING TO LET THAT HAPPEN.
THE ONES WHO ARE GOING TO SUFFER FROM THIS ARE ASHIROGI. EVEN IF THEY GET A SERIES, IT'LL BE HARD FOR IT TO COMPETE WITH CROW AND +NATURAL... THE EDITORIAL DEPARTMENT MAY EVEN PUT THE KIBOSH ON THEM GETTING A SERIES...
WHY THE CONCERN ABOUT ASHIROGI, YUJIRO?
HAHAHAHAHA...
YOU REAP WHAT YOU SOW.
YOU'RE STARTING TO SOUND LIKE A BROKEN RECORD, MR. YOSHIDA.
...
TRMBL
TRMBL
M-MIURA... HATTORI... I CAN'T TAKE IT ANYMORE...
TRMBL
W-WHAT DO YOU MEAN?
...

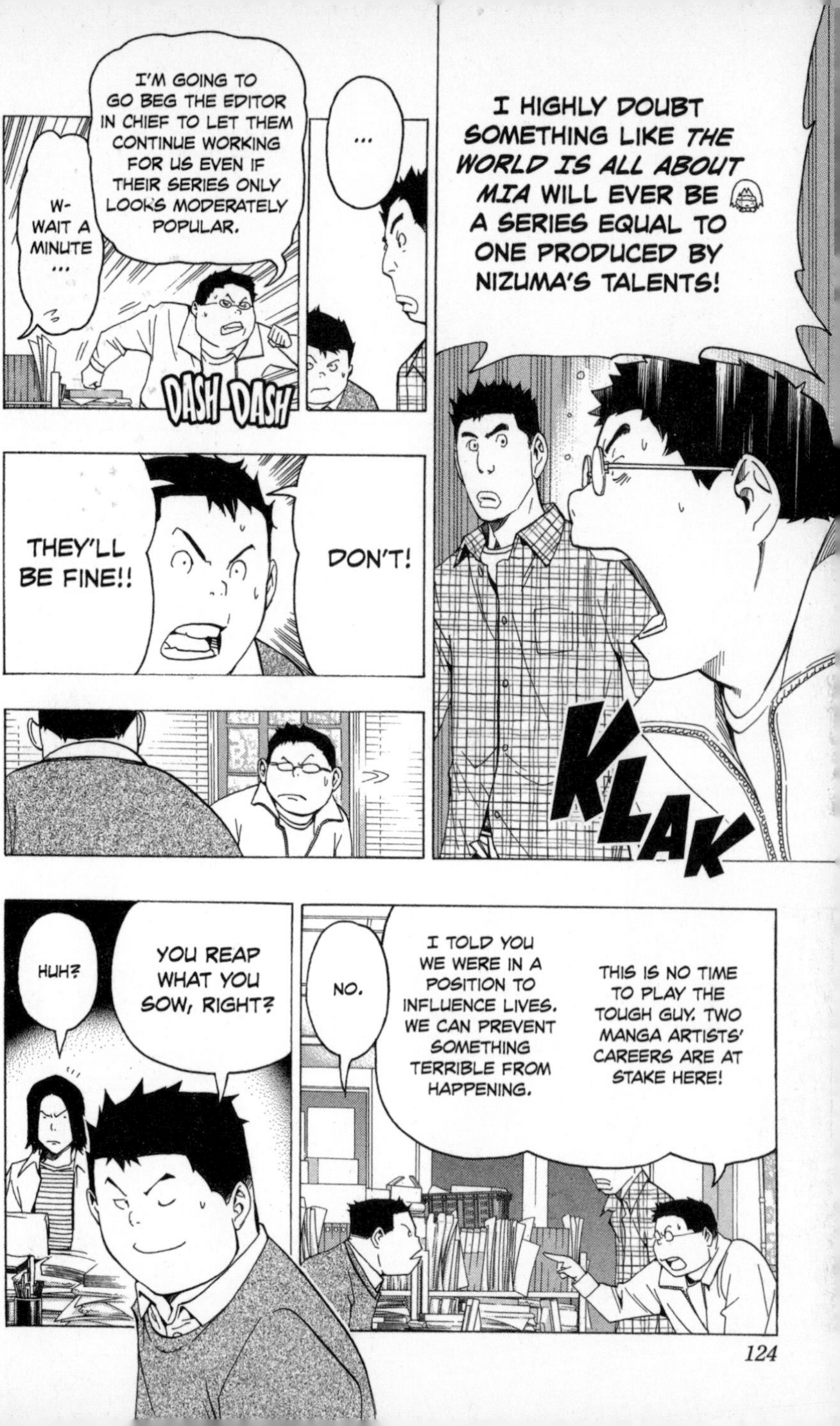
I HIGHLY DOUBT SOMETHING LIKE *THE WORLD IS ALL ABOUT MIA* WILL EVER BE A SERIES EQUAL TO ONE PRODUCED BY NIZUMA'S TALENTS!
KLAK
...
I'M GOING TO GO BEG THE EDITOR IN CHIEF TO LET THEM CONTINUE WORKING FOR US EVEN IF THEIR SERIES ONLY LOOKS MODERATELY POPULAR.
W-WAIT A MINUTE...
DASH DASH
DON'T!
THEY'LL BE FINE!!
THIS IS NO TIME TO PLAY THE TOUGH GUY. TWO MANGA ARTISTS' CAREERS ARE AT STAKE HERE!
I TOLD YOU WE WERE IN A POSITION TO INFLUENCE LIVES. WE CAN PREVENT SOMETHING TERRIBLE FROM HAPPENING.
NO.
YOU REAP WHAT YOU SOW, RIGHT?
HUH?

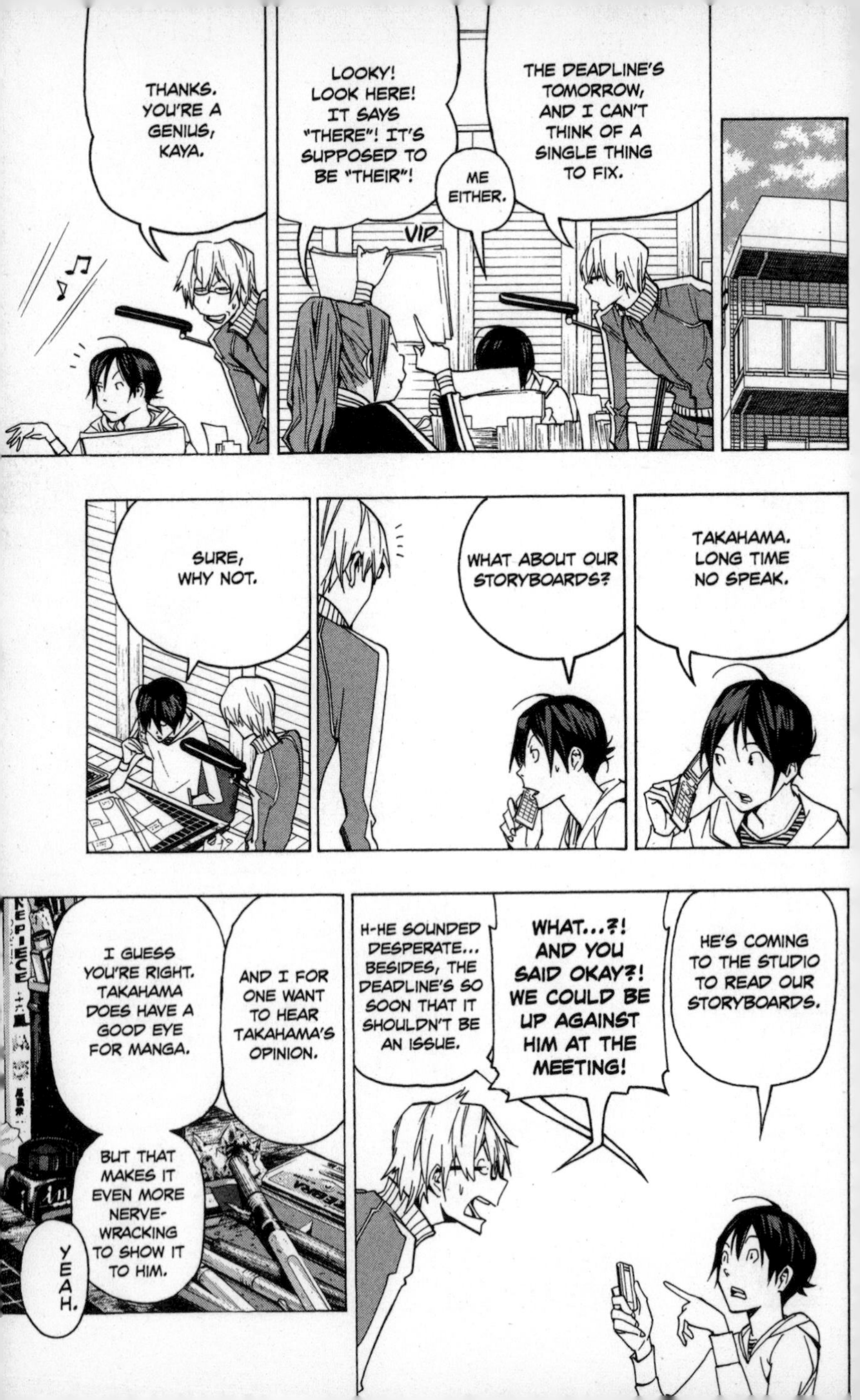
THE DEADLINE'S TOMORROW, AND I CAN'T THINK OF A SINGLE THING TO FIX.
ME EITHER.
LOOKY! LOOK HERE! IT SAYS "THERE"! IT'S SUPPOSED TO BE "THEIR"!
VIP
THANKS. YOU'RE A GENIUS, KAYA.
TAKAHAMA. LONG TIME NO SPEAK.
WHAT ABOUT OUR STORYBOARDS?
SURE, WHY NOT.
HE'S COMING TO THE STUDIO TO READ OUR STORYBOARDS.
WHAT...?! AND YOU SAID OKAY?! WE COULD BE UP AGAINST HIM AT THE MEETING!
H-HE SOUNDED DESPERATE... BESIDES, THE DEADLINE'S SO SOON THAT IT SHOULDN'T BE AN ISSUE.
AND I FOR ONE WANT TO HEAR TAKAHAMA'S OPINION.
I GUESS YOU'RE RIGHT. TAKAHAMA DOES HAVE A GOOD EYE FOR MANGA.
BUT THAT MAKES IT EVEN MORE NERVE-WRACKING TO SHOW IT TO HIM.
YEAH.

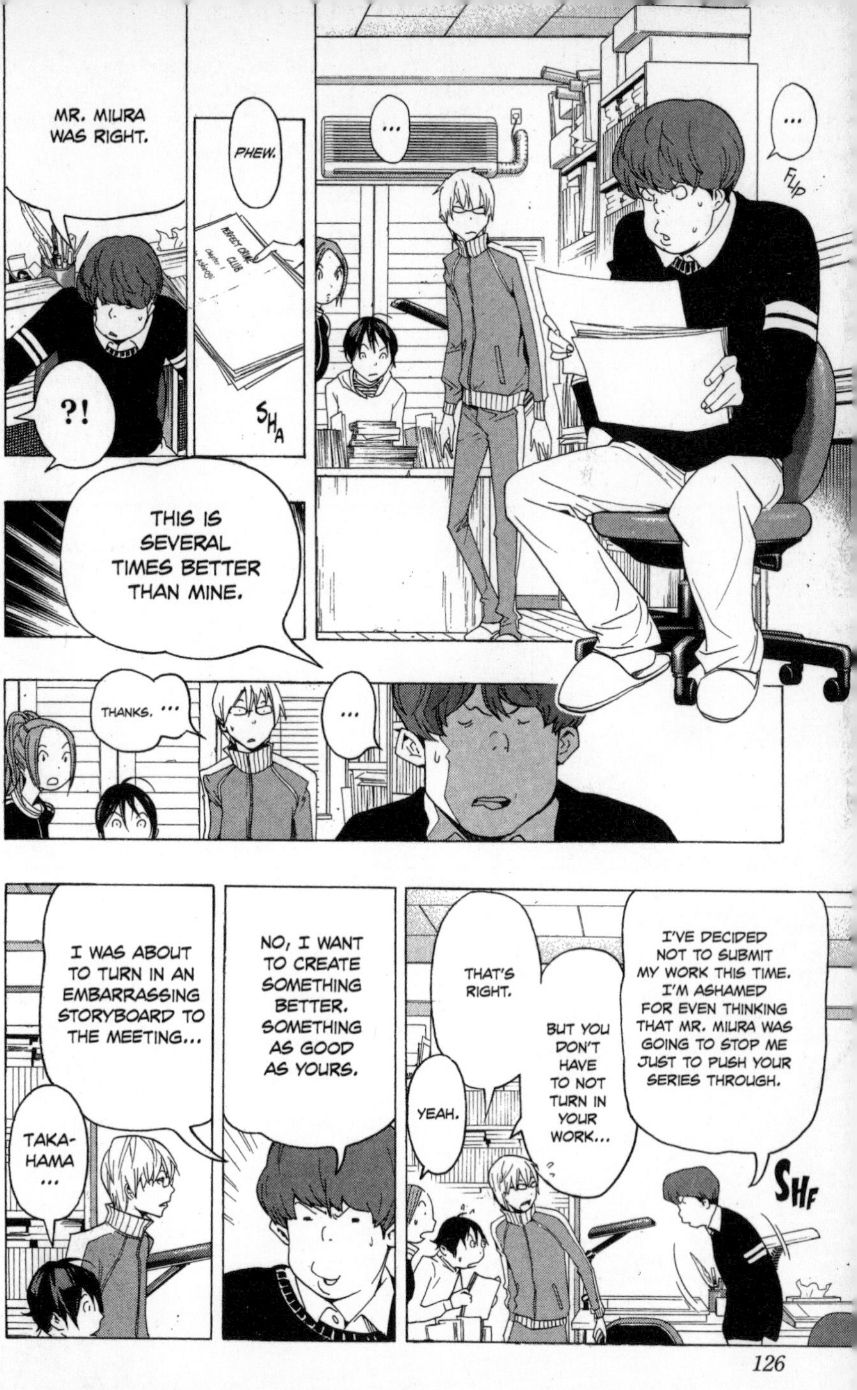
...
FLIP
...
PHEW.
SHA
MR. MIURA WAS RIGHT.
?!
THIS IS SEVERAL TIMES BETTER THAN MINE.
...
THANKS. ...
I'VE DECIDED NOT TO SUBMIT MY WORK THIS TIME. I'M ASHAMED FOR EVEN THINKING THAT MR. MIURA WAS GOING TO STOP ME JUST TO PUSH YOUR SERIES THROUGH.
SHF
BUT YOU DON'T HAVE TO NOT TURN IN YOUR WORK...
THAT'S RIGHT.
YEAH.
NO, I WANT TO CREATE SOMETHING BETTER. SOMETHING AS GOOD AS YOURS.
I WAS ABOUT TO TURN IN AN EMBARRASSING STORYBOARD TO THE MEETING...
TAKA-HAMA ...

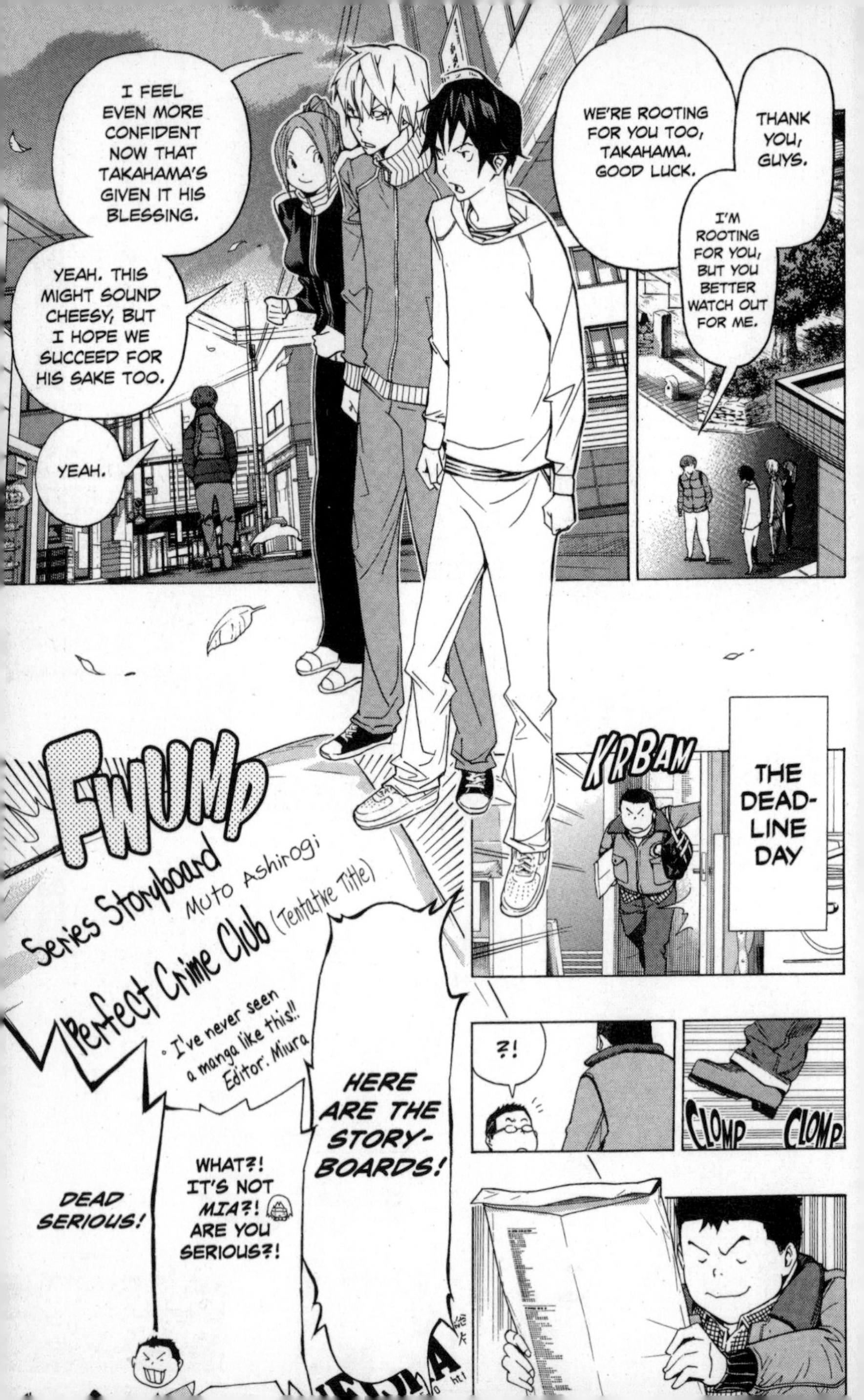
WE'RE ROOTING FOR YOU TOO, TAKAHAMA. GOOD LUCK.
THANK YOU, GUYS.
I'M ROOTING FOR YOU, BUT YOU BETTER WATCH OUT FOR ME.
I FEEL EVEN MORE CONFIDENT NOW THAT TAKAHAMA'S GIVEN IT HIS BLESSING.
YEAH. THIS MIGHT SOUND CHEESY, BUT I HOPE WE SUCCEED FOR HIS SAKE TOO.
YEAH.
THE DEAD-LINE DAY
KRBAM
?!
CLOMP
CLOMP
HERE ARE THE STORY-BOARDS!
WHAT?! IT'S NOT MIA?! ARE YOU SERIOUS?!
DEAD SERIOUS!
FWUMP
Series Storyboard
Muto Ashirogi
Perfect Crime Club (Tentative Title)
I've never seen a manga like this!! Editor: Miura

OHBA'S STORYBOARD

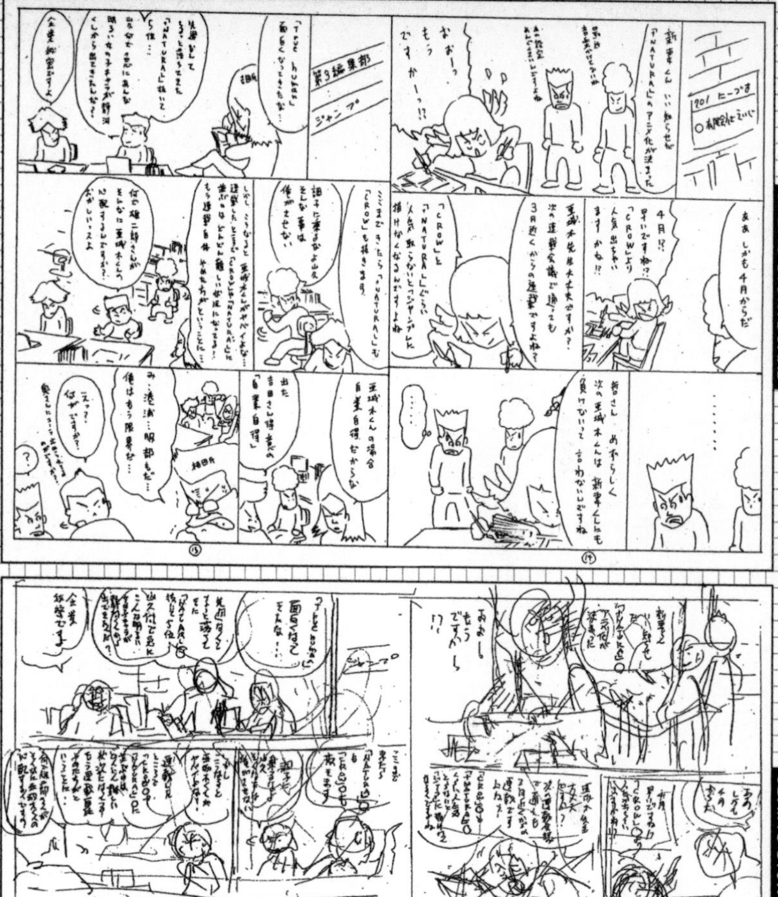
新妻くん いい知らせだ 「NATURAL」のアニメ化が決まった
おぉーっ もうですかーっ!?
第3編集部
ジャンプ
ああ しかも4月からだ
4月!? 早いですね!? 「CROW」より人気出ちゃいますかね!?
......
雄二郎さん めずらしく 次の亜城木くんは新妻くんにも負けないって言わないんですね
亜城木くんの場合 自業自得だからな
出た 吉田さん得意の「自業自得」

OBATA'S STORYBOARD

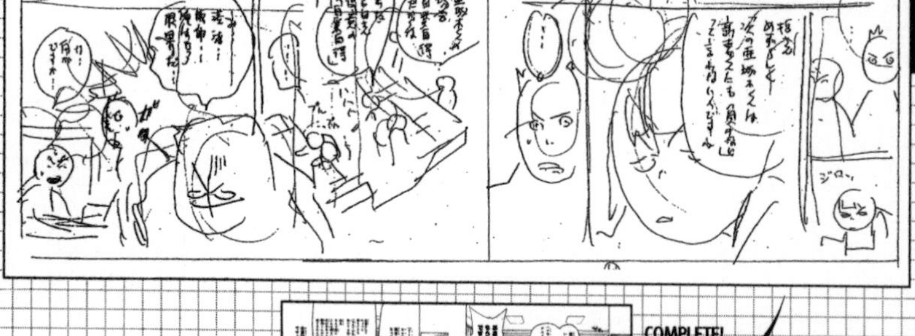

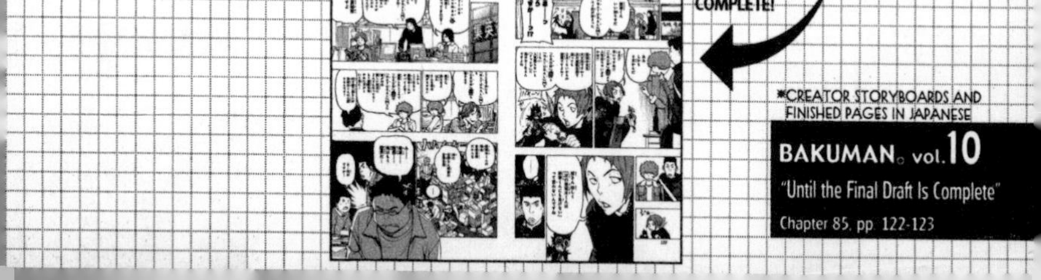

COMPLETE!

*CREATOR STORYBOARDS AND FINISHED PAGES IN JAPANESE

BAKUMAN。 vol.10

"Until the Final Draft Is Complete"

Chapter 85, pp. 122-123

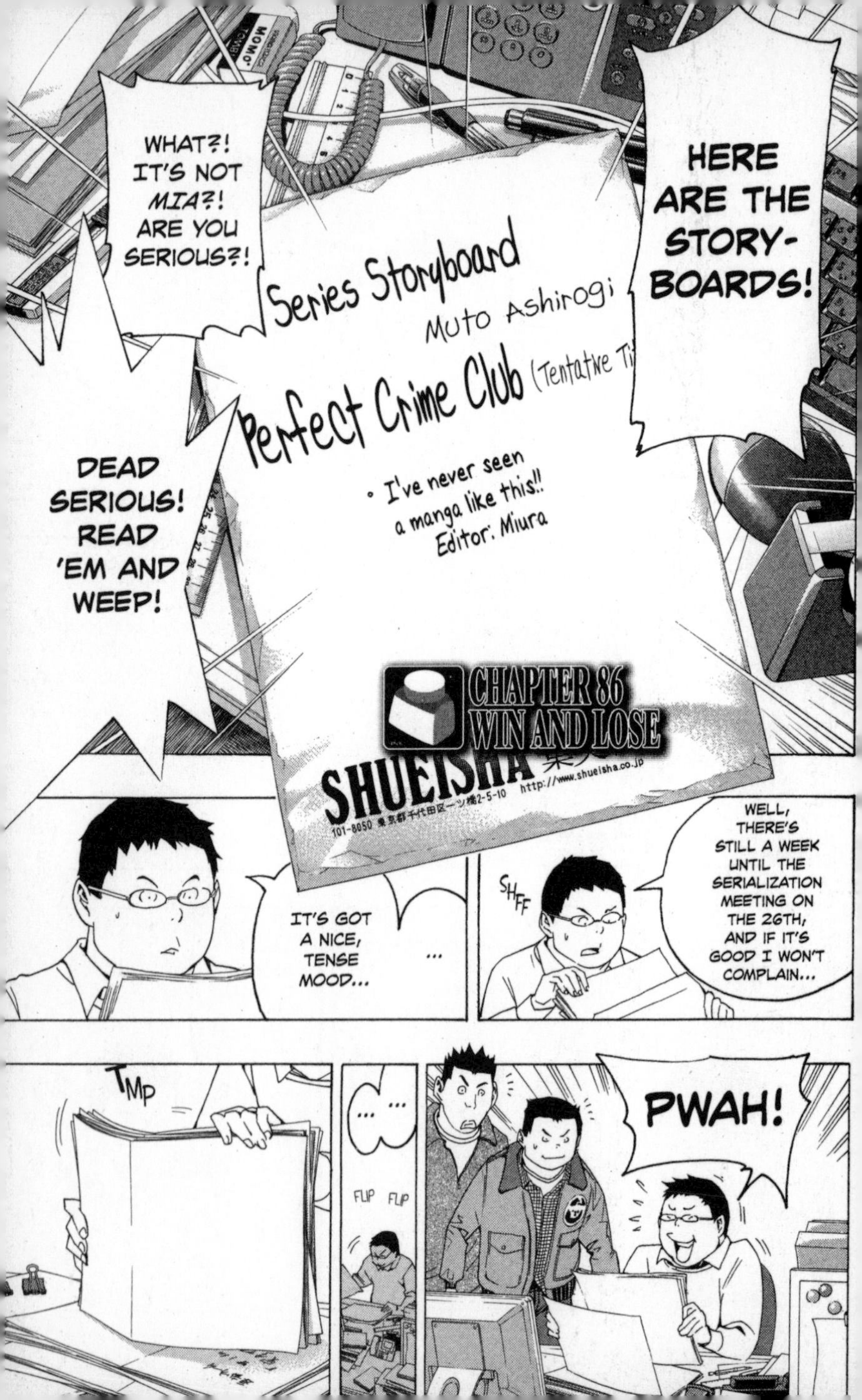
HERE ARE THE STORY-BOARDS!
WHAT?! IT'S NOT MIA?! ARE YOU SERIOUS?!
Series Storyboard
Muto Ashirogi
Perfect Crime Club (Tentative Ti
• I've never seen a manga like this!! Editor: Miura
DEAD SERIOUS! READ 'EM AND WEEP!
CHAPTER 86 WIN AND LOSE
SHUEISHA http://www.shueisha.co.jp
101-8050 東京都千代田区一ツ橋2-5-10
SHFF
WELL, THERE'S STILL A WEEK UNTIL THE SERIALIZATION MEETING ON THE 26TH, AND IF IT'S GOOD I WON'T COMPLAIN...
...
IT'S GOT A NICE, TENSE MOOD...
PWAH!
... ...
FLIP FLIP
TMP

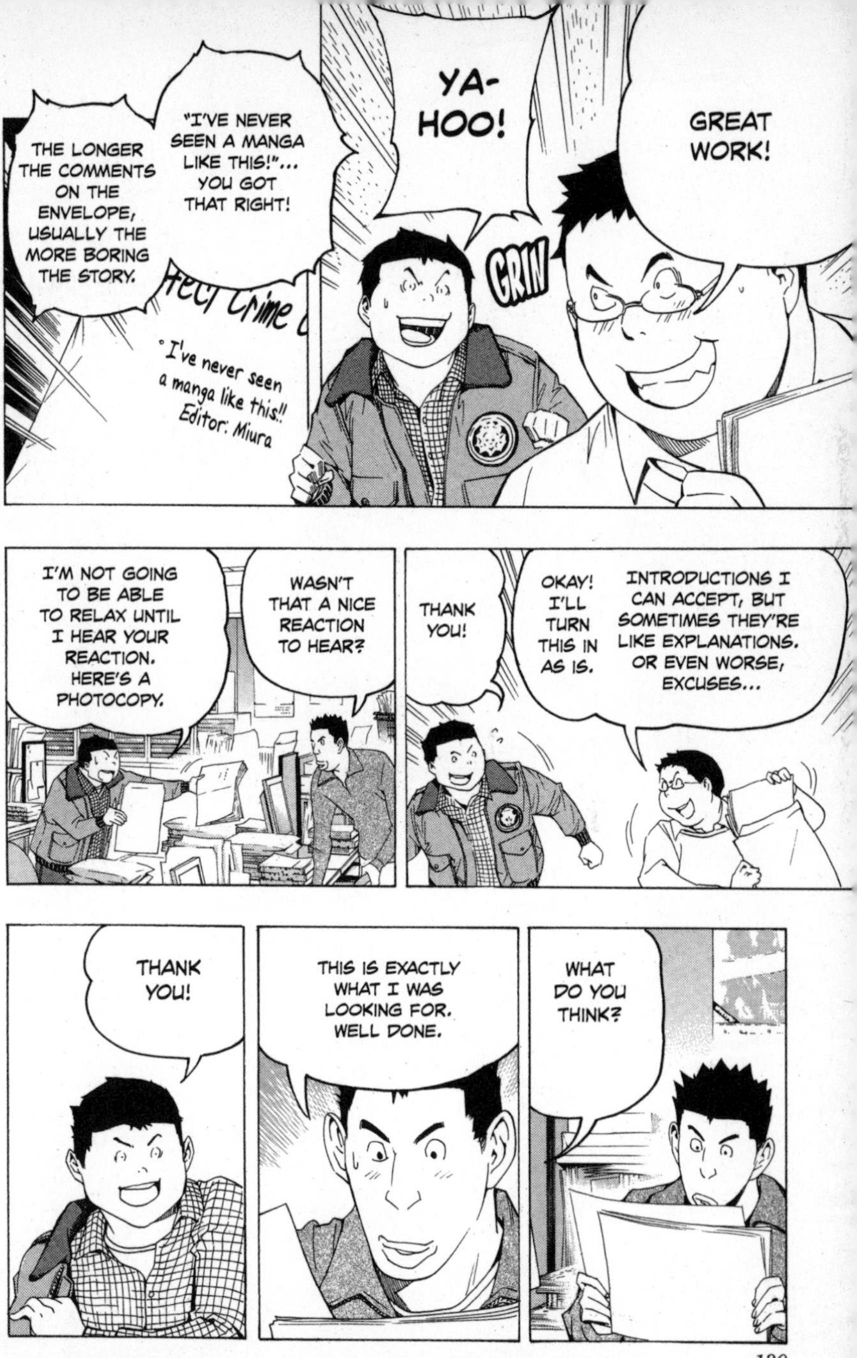
GREAT WORK!
YA-HOO!
GRIN
"I'VE NEVER SEEN A MANGA LIKE THIS!"... YOU GOT THAT RIGHT!
THE LONGER THE COMMENTS ON THE ENVELOPE, USUALLY THE MORE BORING THE STORY.
°I've never seen a manga like this!! Editor: Miura
INTRODUCTIONS I CAN ACCEPT, BUT SOMETIMES THEY'RE LIKE EXPLANATIONS. OR EVEN WORSE, EXCUSES...
OKAY! I'LL TURN THIS IN AS IS.
THANK YOU!
WASN'T THAT A NICE REACTION TO HEAR?
I'M NOT GOING TO BE ABLE TO RELAX UNTIL I HEAR YOUR REACTION. HERE'S A PHOTOCOPY.
WHAT DO YOU THINK?
THIS IS EXACTLY WHAT I WAS LOOKING FOR. WELL DONE.
THANK YOU!

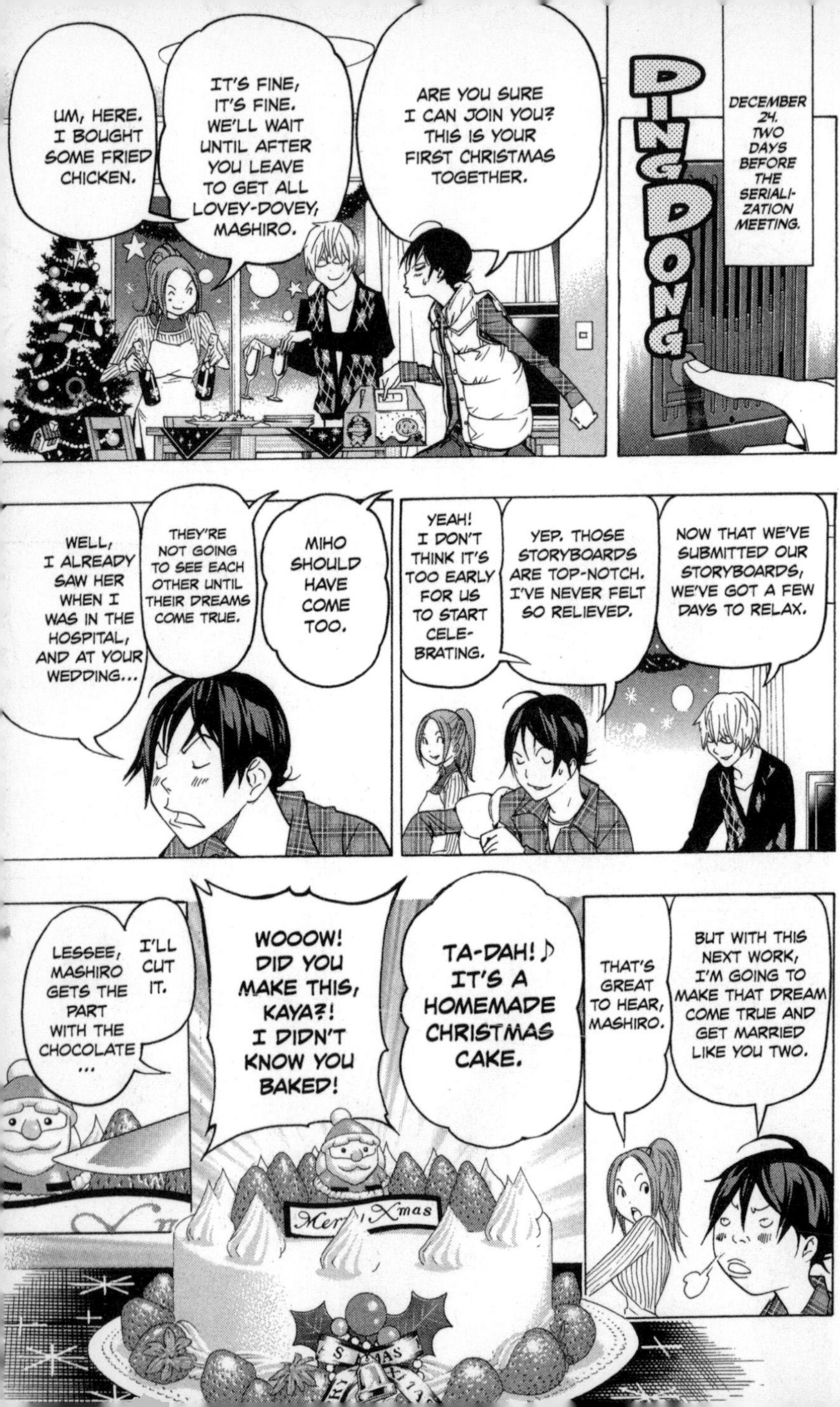
DECEMBER 24. TWO DAYS BEFORE THE SERIALIZATION MEETING.
DING DONG
ARE YOU SURE I CAN JOIN YOU? THIS IS YOUR FIRST CHRISTMAS TOGETHER.
IT'S FINE, IT'S FINE. WE'LL WAIT UNTIL AFTER YOU LEAVE TO GET ALL LOVEY-DOVEY, MASHIRO.
UM, HERE. I BOUGHT SOME FRIED CHICKEN.
NOW THAT WE'VE SUBMITTED OUR STORYBOARDS, WE'VE GOT A FEW DAYS TO RELAX.
YEP. THOSE STORYBOARDS ARE TOP-NOTCH. I'VE NEVER FELT SO RELIEVED.
YEAH! I DON'T THINK IT'S TOO EARLY FOR US TO START CELEBRATING.
MIHO SHOULD HAVE COME TOO.
THEY'RE NOT GOING TO SEE EACH OTHER UNTIL THEIR DREAMS COME TRUE.
WELL, I ALREADY SAW HER WHEN I WAS IN THE HOSPITAL, AND AT YOUR WEDDING...
BUT WITH THIS NEXT WORK, I'M GOING TO MAKE THAT DREAM COME TRUE AND GET MARRIED LIKE YOU TWO.
THAT'S GREAT TO HEAR, MASHIRO.
TA-DAH!♪ IT'S A HOMEMADE CHRISTMAS CAKE.
WOOOW! DID YOU MAKE THIS, KAYA?! I DIDN'T KNOW YOU BAKED!
I'LL CUT IT.
LESSEE, MASHIRO GETS THE PART WITH THE CHOCOLATE...

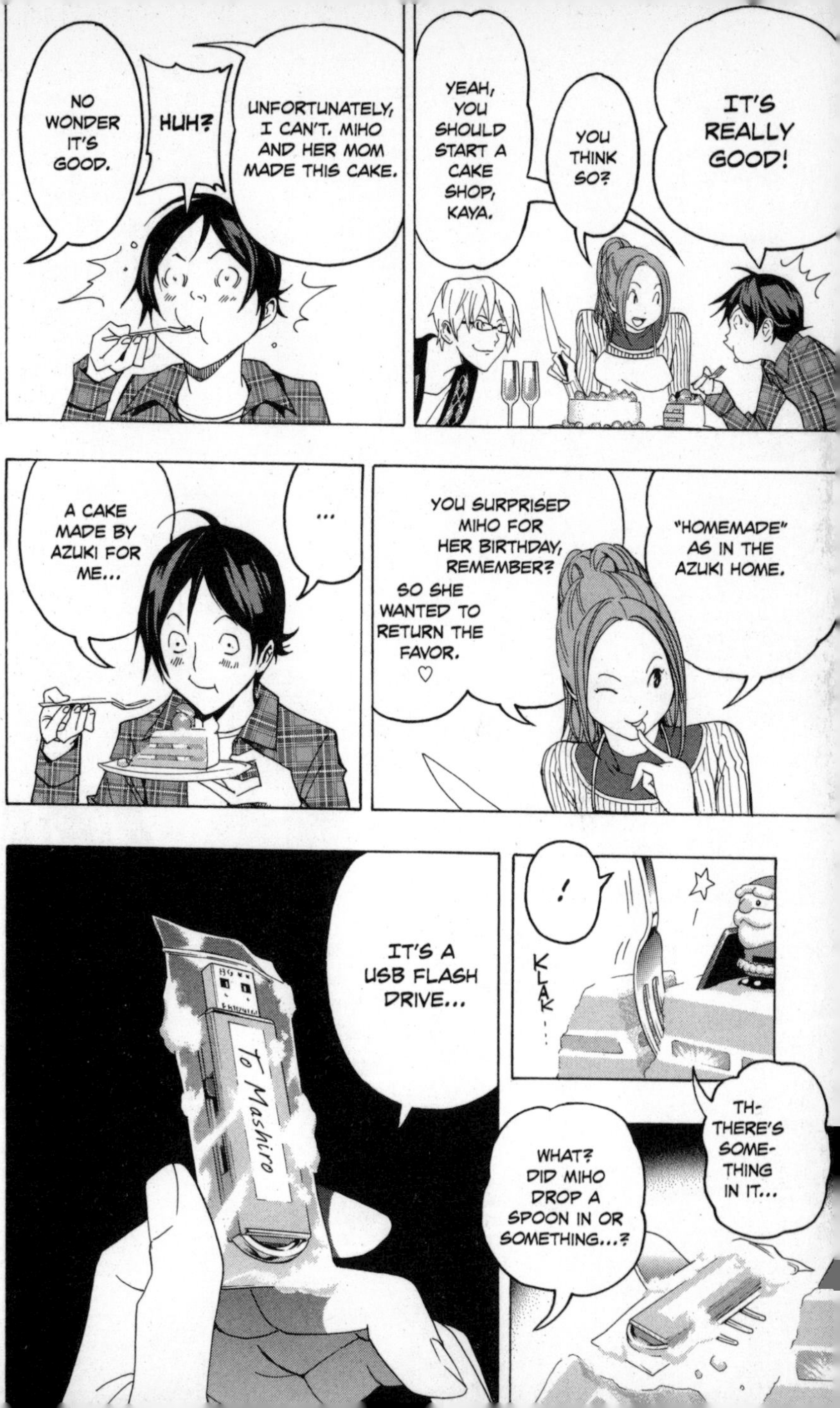
IT'S REALLY GOOD!
YOU THINK SO?
YEAH, YOU SHOULD START A CAKE SHOP, KAYA.
UNFORTUNATELY, I CAN'T. MIHO AND HER MOM MADE THIS CAKE.
HUH?
NO WONDER IT'S GOOD.
"HOMEMADE" AS IN THE AZUKI HOME.
YOU SURPRISED MIHO FOR HER BIRTHDAY, REMEMBER?
SO SHE WANTED TO RETURN THE FAVOR. ♡
...
A CAKE MADE BY AZUKI FOR ME...
!
KLAK...
TH- THERE'S SOMETHING IN IT...
WHAT? DID MIHO DROP A SPOON IN OR SOMETHING...?
IT'S A USB FLASH DRIVE...
To Mashiro

READ THIS WAY

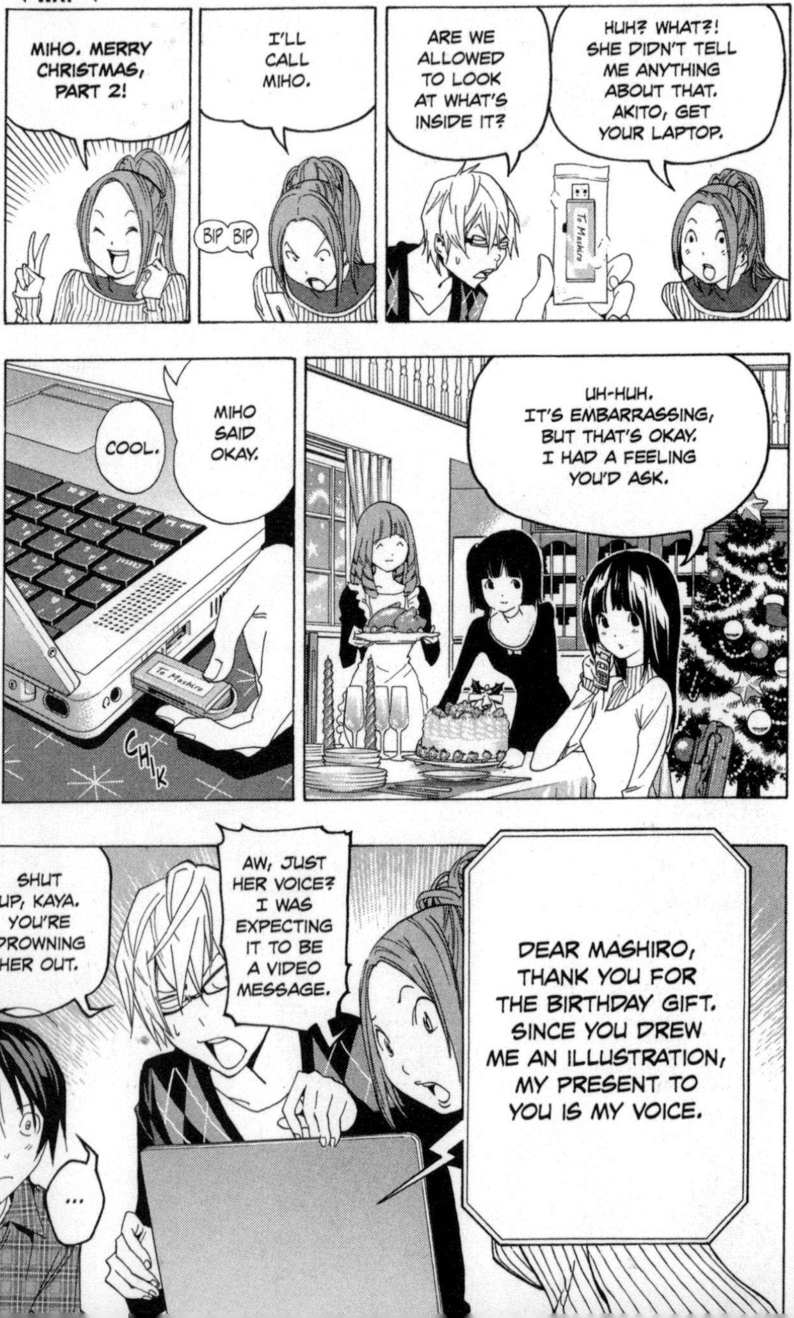
HUH? WHAT?! SHE DIDN'T TELL ME ANYTHING ABOUT THAT. AKITO, GET YOUR LAPTOP.
ARE WE ALLOWED TO LOOK AT WHAT'S INSIDE IT?
To Mashiro
I'LL CALL MIHO.
BIP BIP
MIHO. MERRY CHRISTMAS, PART 2!
UH-HUH. IT'S EMBARRASSING, BUT THAT'S OKAY. I HAD A FEELING YOU'D ASK.
MIHO SAID OKAY.
COOL.
To Mashiro
CHIK
DEAR MASHIRO, THANK YOU FOR THE BIRTHDAY GIFT. SINCE YOU DREW ME AN ILLUSTRATION, MY PRESENT TO YOU IS MY VOICE.
AW, JUST HER VOICE? I WAS EXPECTING IT TO BE A VIDEO MESSAGE.
SHUT UP, KAYA. YOU'RE DROWNING HER OUT.
...

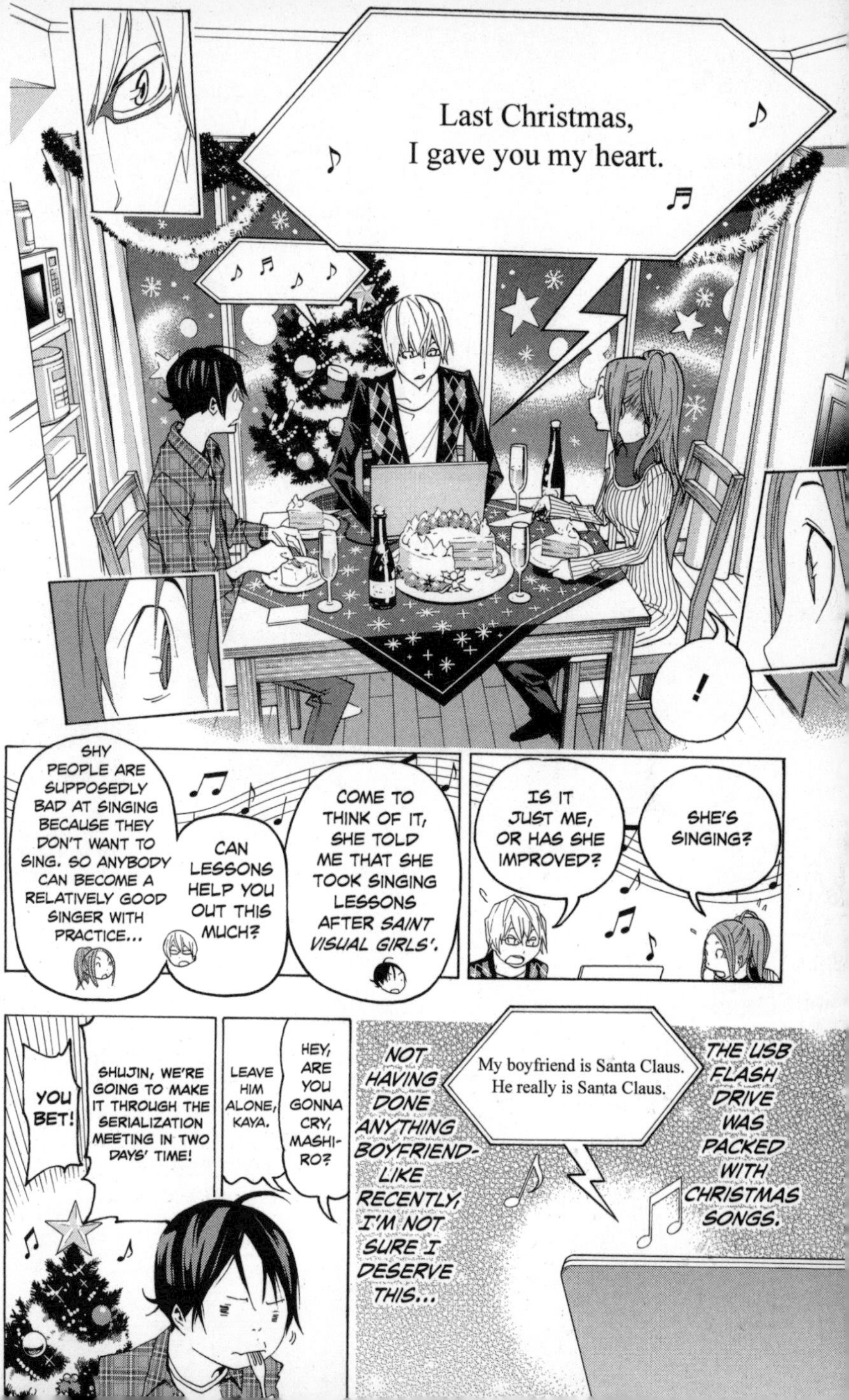
Last Christmas,
I gave you my heart.
!
SHE'S SINGING?
IS IT JUST ME, OR HAS SHE IMPROVED?
COME TO THINK OF IT, SHE TOLD ME THAT SHE TOOK SINGING LESSONS AFTER *SAINT VISUAL GIRLS'.*
CAN LESSONS HELP YOU OUT THIS MUCH?
SHY PEOPLE ARE SUPPOSEDLY BAD AT SINGING BECAUSE THEY DON'T WANT TO SING. SO ANYBODY CAN BECOME A RELATIVELY GOOD SINGER WITH PRACTICE...
THE USB FLASH DRIVE WAS PACKED WITH CHRISTMAS SONGS.
My boyfriend is Santa Claus. He really is Santa Claus.
NOT HAVING DONE ANYTHING BOYFRIEND-LIKE RECENTLY, I'M NOT SURE I DESERVE THIS...
HEY, ARE YOU GONNA CRY, MASHIRO?
LEAVE HIM ALONE, KAYA.
SHUJIN, WE'RE GOING TO MAKE IT THROUGH THE SERIALIZATION MEETING IN TWO DAYS' TIME!
YOU BET!

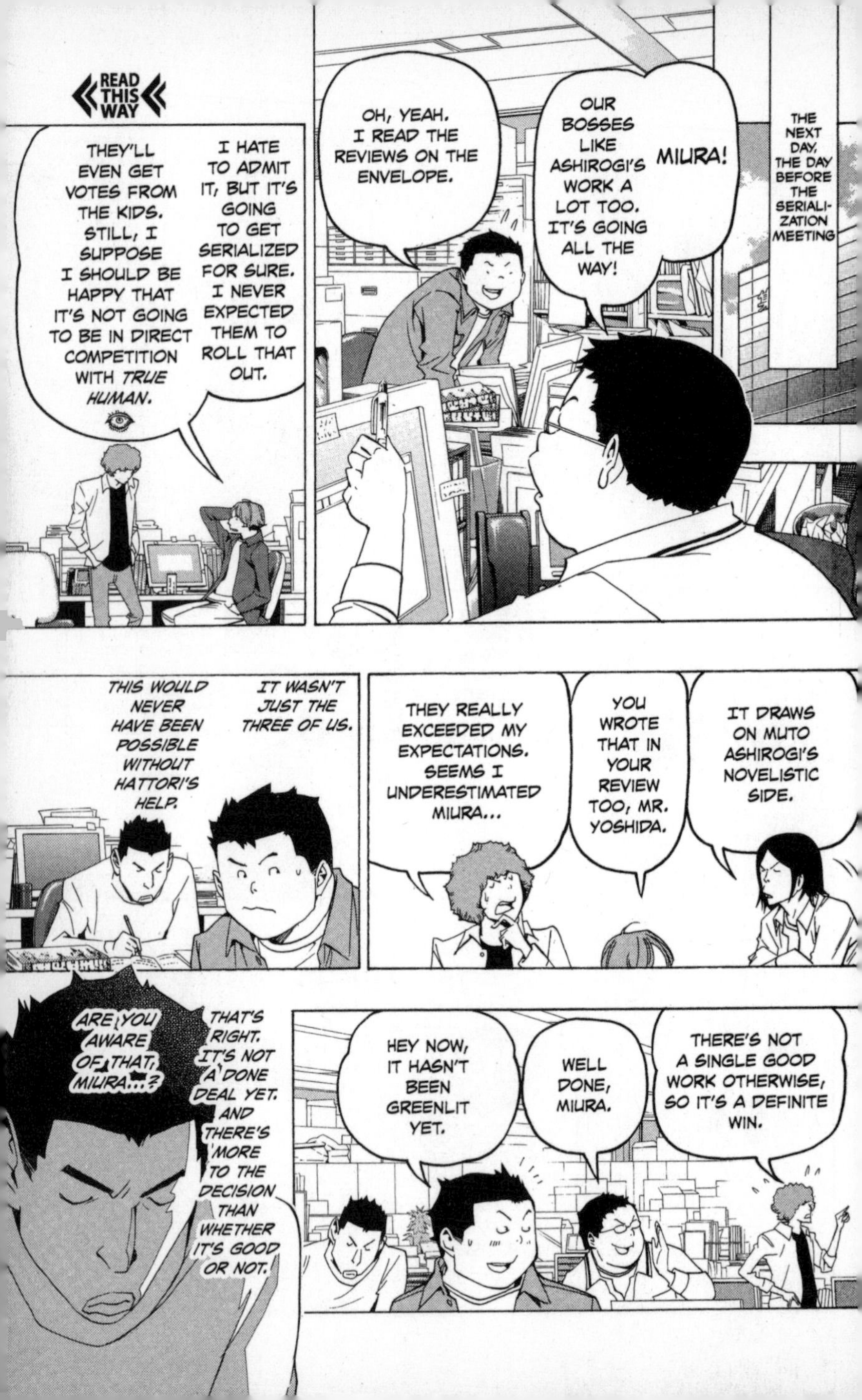
READ THIS WAY
THE NEXT DAY, THE DAY BEFORE THE SERIALIZATION MEETING
MIURA!
OUR BOSSES LIKE ASHIROGI'S WORK A LOT TOO. IT'S GOING ALL THE WAY!
OH, YEAH. I READ THE REVIEWS ON THE ENVELOPE.
I HATE TO ADMIT IT, BUT IT'S GOING TO GET SERIALIZED FOR SURE. I NEVER EXPECTED THEM TO ROLL THAT OUT.
THEY'LL EVEN GET VOTES FROM THE KIDS. STILL, I SUPPOSE I SHOULD BE HAPPY THAT IT'S NOT GOING TO BE IN DIRECT COMPETITION WITH *TRUE HUMAN*.
IT DRAWS ON MUTO ASHIROGI'S NOVELISTIC SIDE.
YOU WROTE THAT IN YOUR REVIEW TOO, MR. YOSHIDA.
THEY REALLY EXCEEDED MY EXPECTATIONS. SEEMS I UNDERESTIMATED MIURA...
IT WASN'T JUST THE THREE OF US.
THIS WOULD NEVER HAVE BEEN POSSIBLE WITHOUT HATTORI'S HELP.
THERE'S NOT A SINGLE GOOD WORK OTHERWISE, SO IT'S A DEFINITE WIN.
WELL DONE, MIURA.
HEY NOW, IT HASN'T BEEN GREENLIT YET.
THAT'S RIGHT. IT'S NOT A DONE DEAL YET. AND THERE'S MORE TO THE DECISION THAN WHETHER IT'S GOOD OR NOT.
ARE YOU AWARE OF THAT, MIURA...?

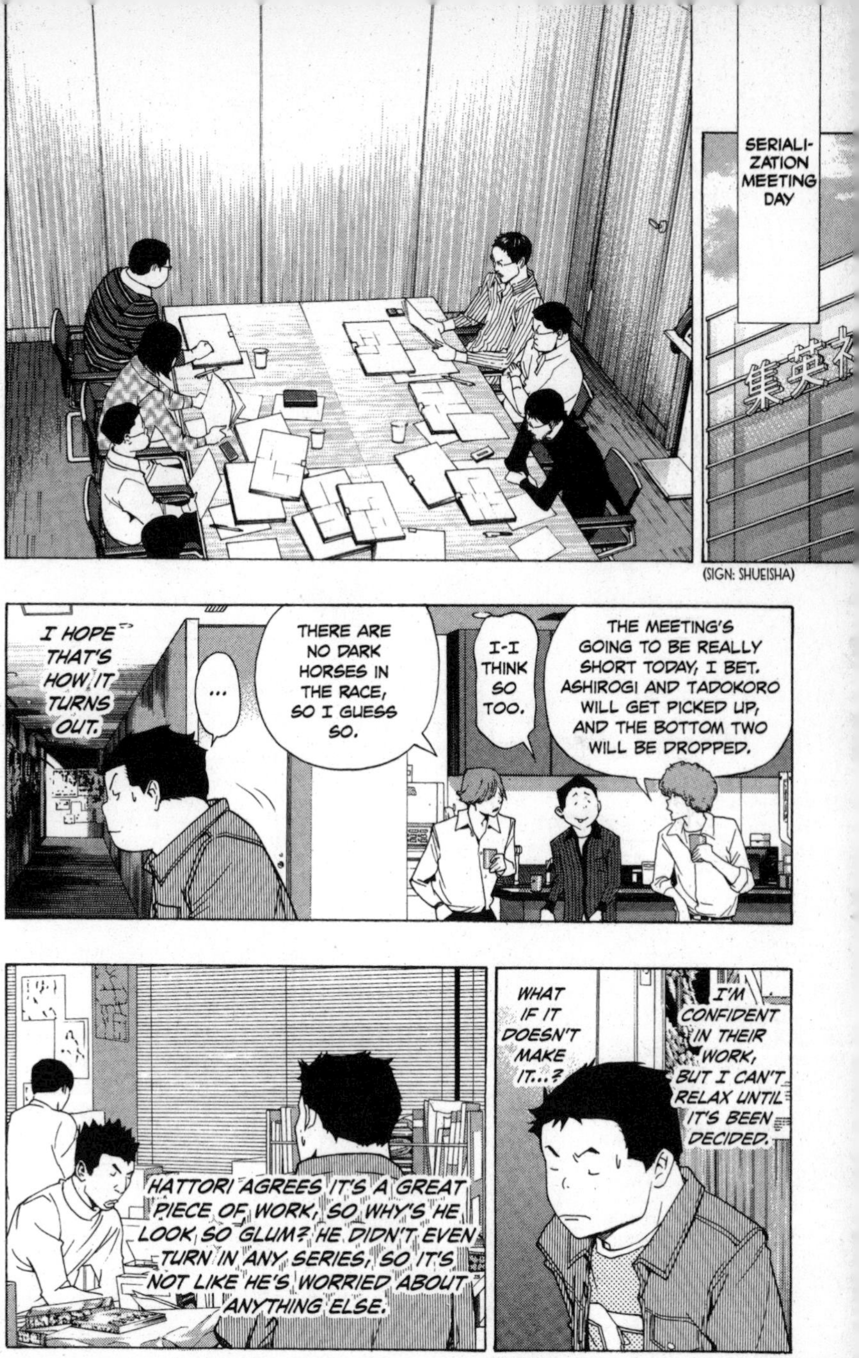
SERIALI-ZATION MEETING DAY
(SIGN: SHUEISHA)
THE MEETING'S GOING TO BE REALLY SHORT TODAY, I BET. ASHIROGI AND TADOKORO WILL GET PICKED UP, AND THE BOTTOM TWO WILL BE DROPPED.
I-I THINK SO TOO.
THERE ARE NO DARK HORSES IN THE RACE, SO I GUESS SO.
...
I HOPE THAT'S HOW IT TURNS OUT.
I'M CONFIDENT IN THEIR WORK, BUT I CAN'T RELAX UNTIL IT'S BEEN DECIDED.
WHAT IF IT DOESN'T MAKE IT...?
HATTORI AGREES IT'S A GREAT PIECE OF WORK, SO WHY'S HE LOOK SO GLUM? HE DIDN'T EVEN TURN IN ANY SERIES, SO IT'S NOT LIKE HE'S WORRIED ABOUT ANYTHING ELSE.

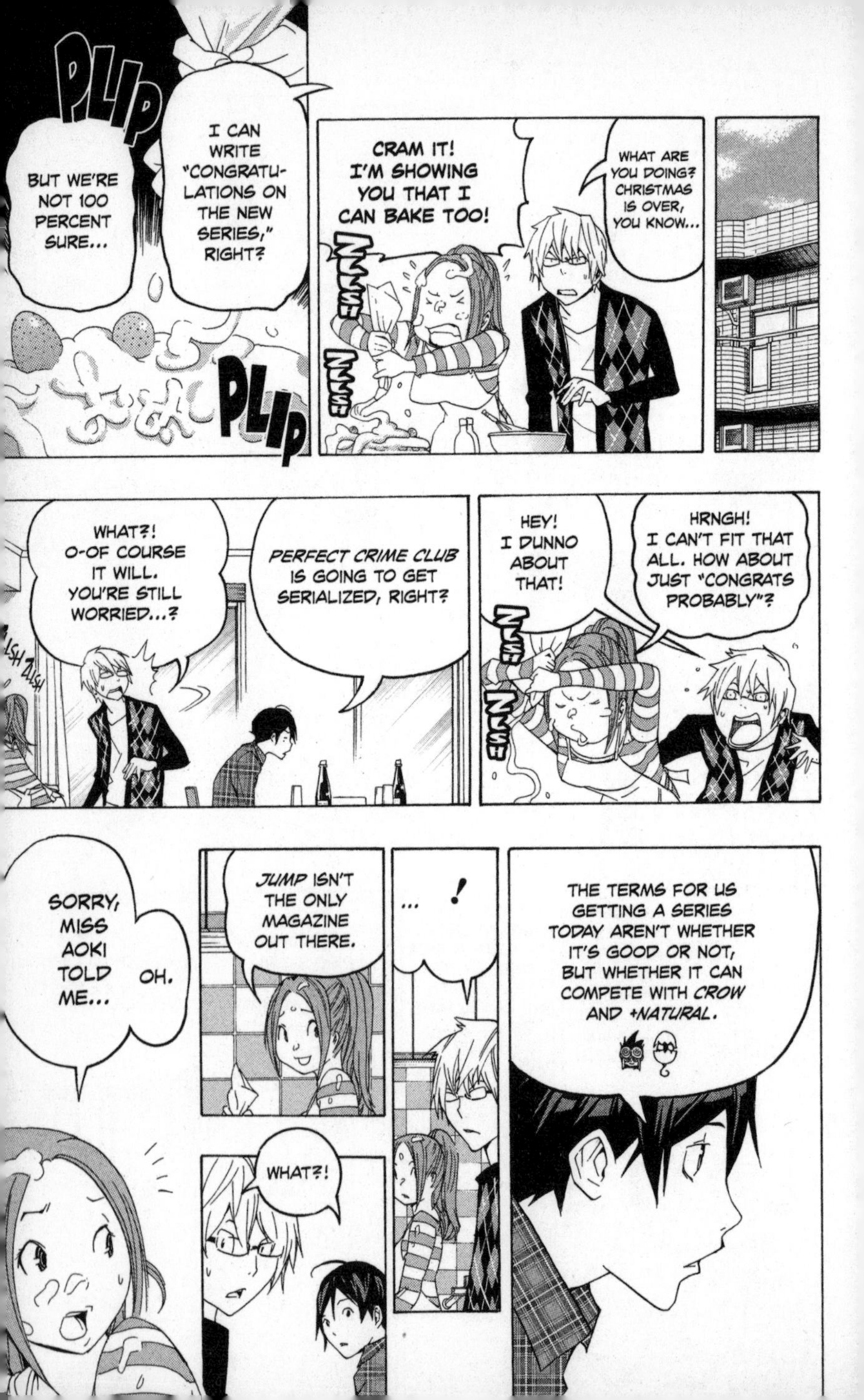
WHAT ARE YOU DOING? CHRISTMAS IS OVER, YOU KNOW...
CRAM IT! I'M SHOWING YOU THAT I CAN BAKE TOO!
ZLLSH
ZLLSH
I CAN WRITE "CONGRATULATIONS ON THE NEW SERIES," RIGHT?
BUT WE'RE NOT 100 PERCENT SURE...
PLIP
PLIP
HRNGH! I CAN'T FIT THAT ALL. HOW ABOUT JUST "CONGRATS PROBABLY"?
HEY! I DUNNO ABOUT THAT!
ZLLSH
ZLLSH
PERFECT CRIME CLUB IS GOING TO GET SERIALIZED, RIGHT?
WHAT?! O-OF COURSE IT WILL. YOU'RE STILL WORRIED...?
THE TERMS FOR US GETTING A SERIES TODAY AREN'T WHETHER IT'S GOOD OR NOT, BUT WHETHER IT CAN COMPETE WITH *CROW* AND *+NATURAL*.
...
!
JUMP ISN'T THE ONLY MAGAZINE OUT THERE.
WHAT?!
SORRY, MISS AOKI TOLD ME...
OH.

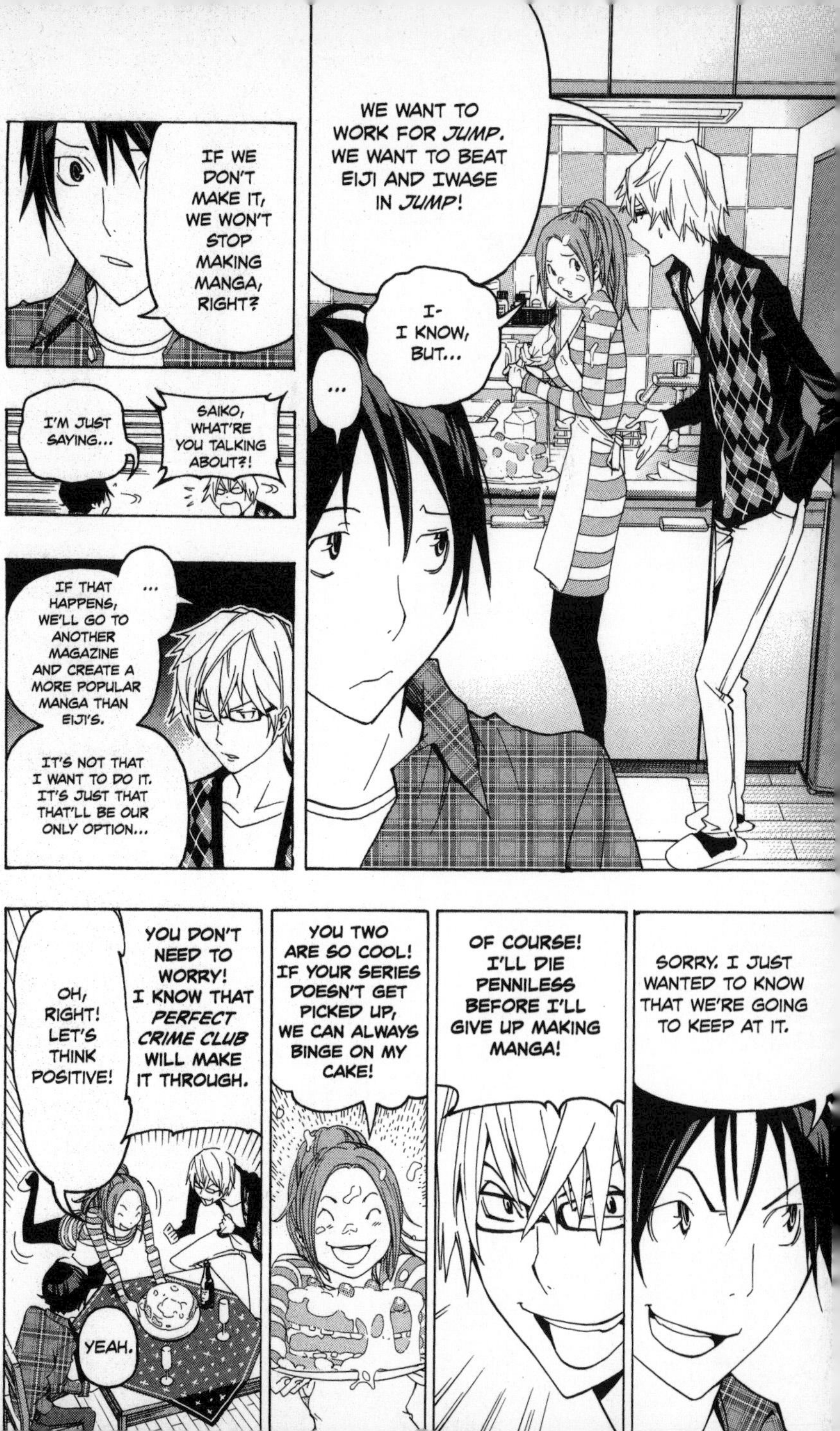
WE WANT TO WORK FOR *JUMP*. WE WANT TO BEAT EIJI AND IWASE IN *JUMP*!
I- I KNOW, BUT...
...
IF WE DON'T MAKE IT, WE WON'T STOP MAKING MANGA, RIGHT?
SAIKO, WHAT'RE YOU TALKING ABOUT?!
I'M JUST SAYING...
...
IF THAT HAPPENS, WE'LL GO TO ANOTHER MAGAZINE AND CREATE A MORE POPULAR MANGA THAN EIJI'S.
IT'S NOT THAT I WANT TO DO IT. IT'S JUST THAT THAT'LL BE OUR ONLY OPTION...
SORRY. I JUST WANTED TO KNOW THAT WE'RE GOING TO KEEP AT IT.
OF COURSE! I'LL DIE PENNILESS BEFORE I'LL GIVE UP MAKING MANGA!
YOU TWO ARE SO COOL! IF YOUR SERIES DOESN'T GET PICKED UP, WE CAN ALWAYS BINGE ON MY CAKE!
YOU DON'T NEED TO WORRY! I KNOW THAT *PERFECT CRIME CLUB* WILL MAKE IT THROUGH.
OH, RIGHT! LET'S THINK POSITIVE!
YEAH.

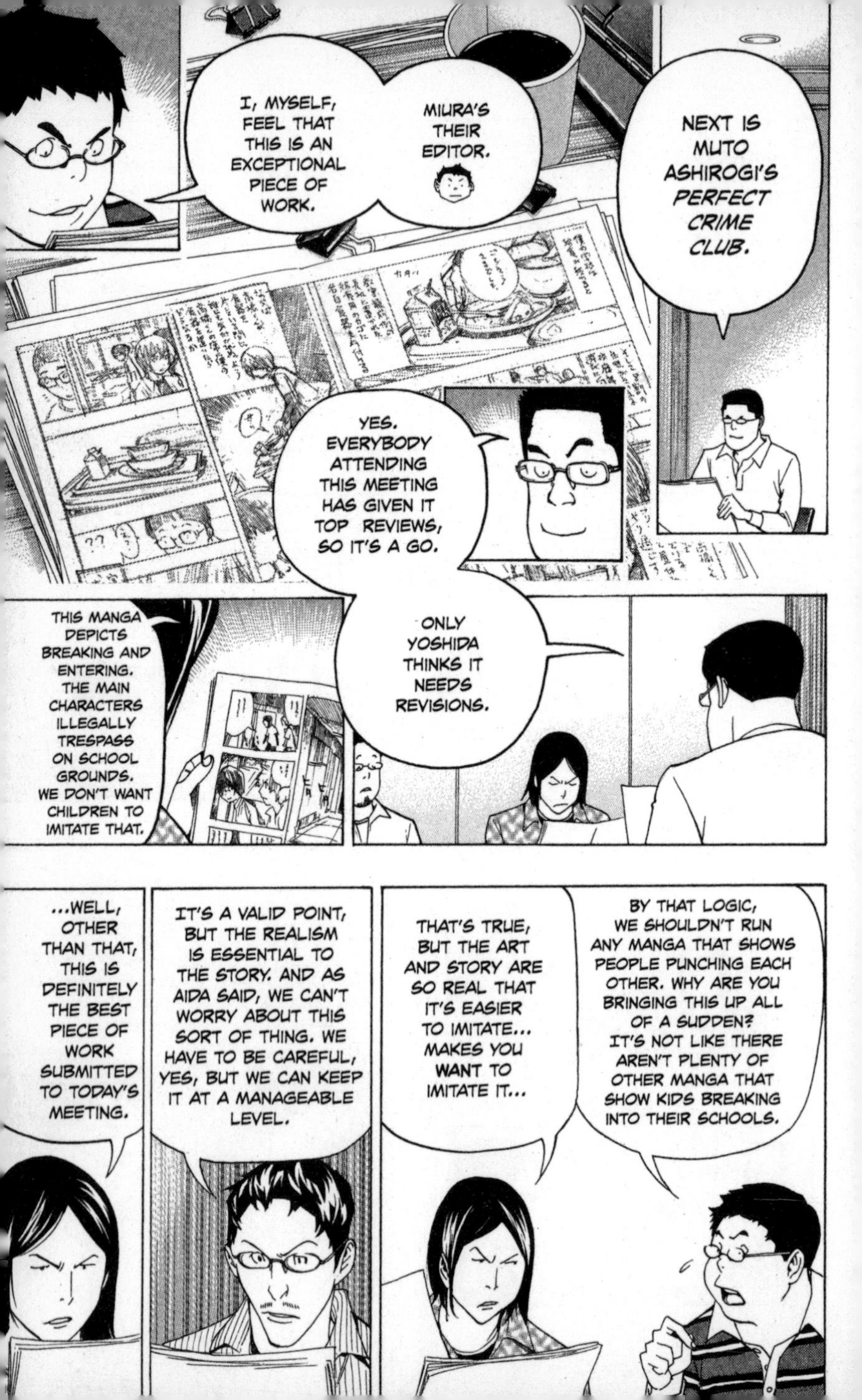
NEXT IS MUTO ASHIROGI'S *PERFECT CRIME CLUB*.
MIURA'S THEIR EDITOR.
I, MYSELF, FEEL THAT THIS IS AN EXCEPTIONAL PIECE OF WORK.
YES. EVERYBODY ATTENDING THIS MEETING HAS GIVEN IT TOP REVIEWS, SO IT'S A GO.
ONLY YOSHIDA THINKS IT NEEDS REVISIONS.
THIS MANGA DEPICTS BREAKING AND ENTERING. THE MAIN CHARACTERS ILLEGALLY TRESPASS ON SCHOOL GROUNDS. WE DON'T WANT CHILDREN TO IMITATE THAT.
BY THAT LOGIC, WE SHOULDN'T RUN ANY MANGA THAT SHOWS PEOPLE PUNCHING EACH OTHER. WHY ARE YOU BRINGING THIS UP ALL OF A SUDDEN? IT'S NOT LIKE THERE AREN'T PLENTY OF OTHER MANGA THAT SHOW KIDS BREAKING INTO THEIR SCHOOLS.
THAT'S TRUE, BUT THE ART AND STORY ARE SO REAL THAT IT'S EASIER TO IMITATE... MAKES YOU WANT TO IMITATE IT...
IT'S A VALID POINT, BUT THE REALISM IS ESSENTIAL TO THE STORY. AND AS AIDA SAID, WE CAN'T WORRY ABOUT THIS SORT OF THING. WE HAVE TO BE CAREFUL, YES, BUT WE CAN KEEP IT AT A MANAGEABLE LEVEL.
...WELL, OTHER THAN THAT, THIS IS DEFINITELY THE BEST PIECE OF WORK SUBMITTED TO TODAY'S MEETING.

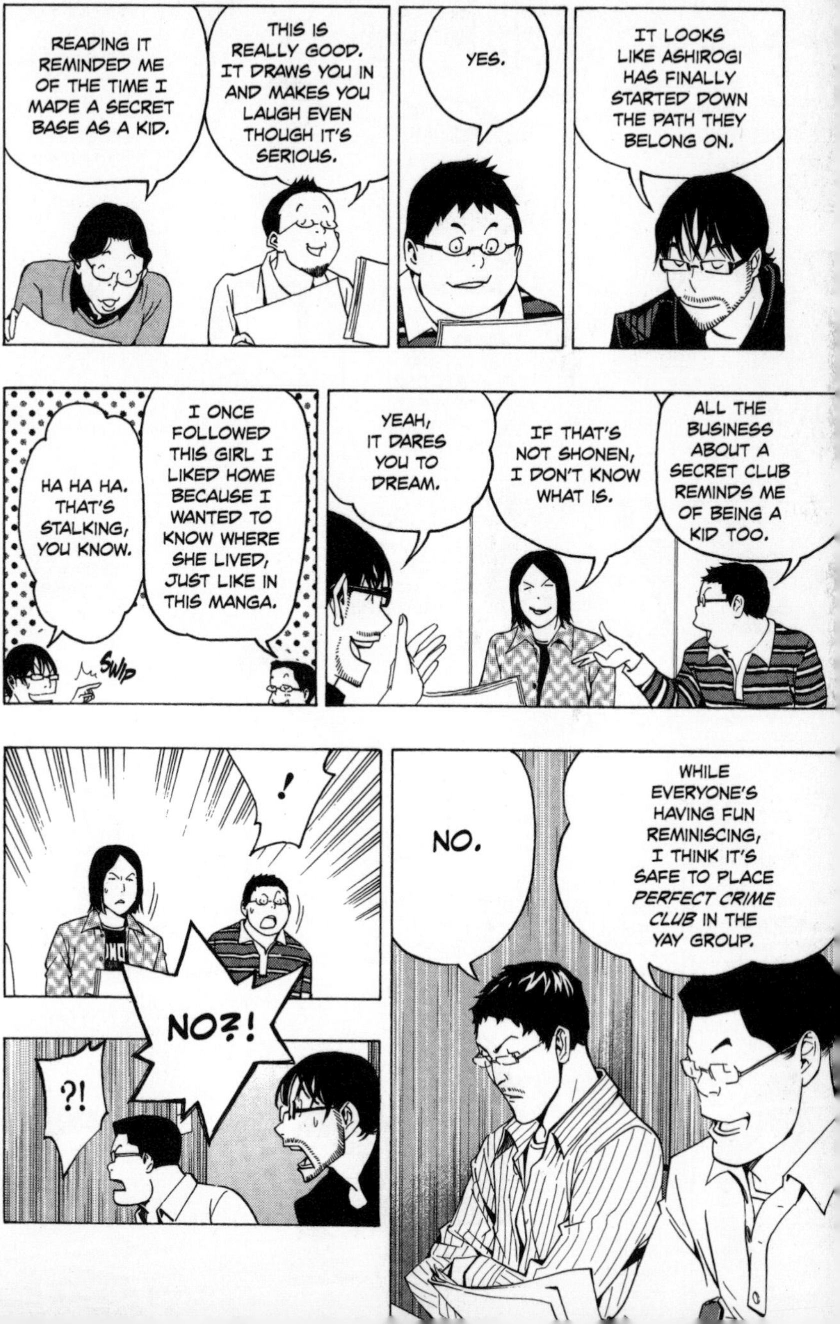

IT LOOKS LIKE ASHIROGI HAS FINALLY STARTED DOWN THE PATH THEY BELONG ON.
YES.
THIS IS REALLY GOOD. IT DRAWS YOU IN AND MAKES YOU LAUGH EVEN THOUGH IT'S SERIOUS.
READING IT REMINDED ME OF THE TIME I MADE A SECRET BASE AS A KID.
ALL THE BUSINESS ABOUT A SECRET CLUB REMINDS ME OF BEING A KID TOO.
IF THAT'S NOT SHONEN, I DON'T KNOW WHAT IS.
YEAH, IT DARES YOU TO DREAM.
I ONCE FOLLOWED THIS GIRL I LIKED HOME BECAUSE I WANTED TO KNOW WHERE SHE LIVED, JUST LIKE IN THIS MANGA.
HA HA HA. THAT'S STALKING, YOU KNOW.
SWIP
WHILE EVERYONE'S HAVING FUN REMINISCING, I THINK IT'S SAFE TO PLACE *PERFECT CRIME CLUB* IN THE YAY GROUP.
NO.
!
NO?!
?!

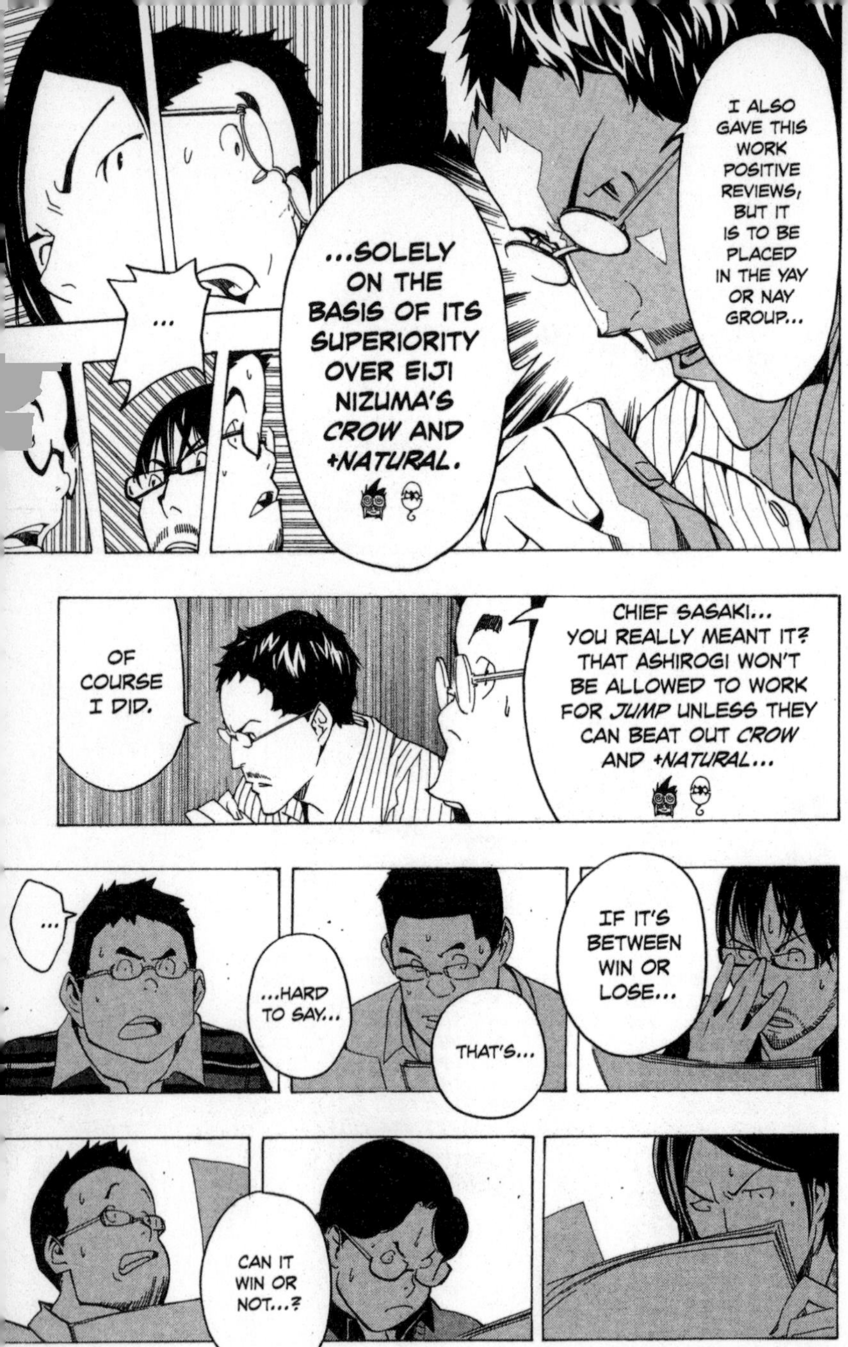
I ALSO GAVE THIS WORK POSITIVE REVIEWS, BUT IT IS TO BE PLACED IN THE YAY OR NAY GROUP...
...SOLELY ON THE BASIS OF ITS SUPERIORITY OVER EIJI NIZUMA'S *CROW* AND *+NATURAL*.
...
CHIEF SASAKI... YOU REALLY MEANT IT? THAT ASHIROGI WON'T BE ALLOWED TO WORK FOR *JUMP* UNLESS THEY CAN BEAT OUT *CROW* AND *+NATURAL*...
OF COURSE I DID.
IF IT'S BETWEEN WIN OR LOSE...
THAT'S...
...HARD TO SAY...
...
CAN IT WIN OR NOT...?

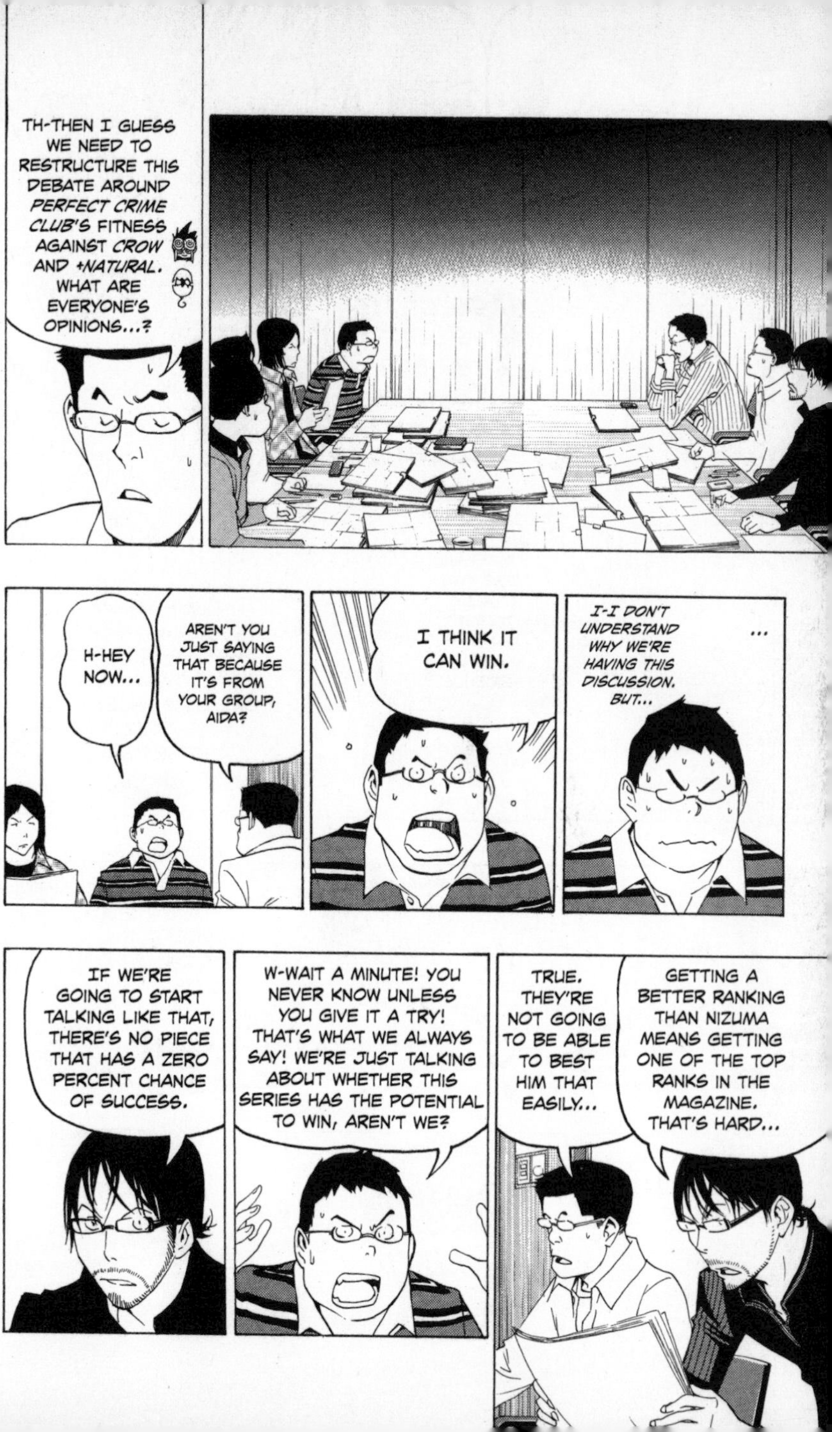
TH-THEN I GUESS WE NEED TO RESTRUCTURE THIS DEBATE AROUND *PERFECT CRIME CLUB*'S FITNESS AGAINST *CROW* AND *+NATURAL*. WHAT ARE EVERYONE'S OPINIONS...?
...
I-I DON'T UNDERSTAND WHY WE'RE HAVING THIS DISCUSSION. BUT...
I THINK IT CAN WIN.
AREN'T YOU JUST SAYING THAT BECAUSE IT'S FROM YOUR GROUP, AIDA?
H-HEY NOW...
GETTING A BETTER RANKING THAN NIZUMA MEANS GETTING ONE OF THE TOP RANKS IN THE MAGAZINE. THAT'S HARD...
TRUE. THEY'RE NOT GOING TO BE ABLE TO BEST HIM THAT EASILY...
W-WAIT A MINUTE! YOU NEVER KNOW UNLESS YOU GIVE IT A TRY! THAT'S WHAT WE ALWAYS SAY! WE'RE JUST TALKING ABOUT WHETHER THIS SERIES HAS THE POTENTIAL TO WIN, AREN'T WE?
IF WE'RE GOING TO START TALKING LIKE THAT, THERE'S NO PIECE THAT HAS A ZERO PERCENT CHANCE OF SUCCESS.

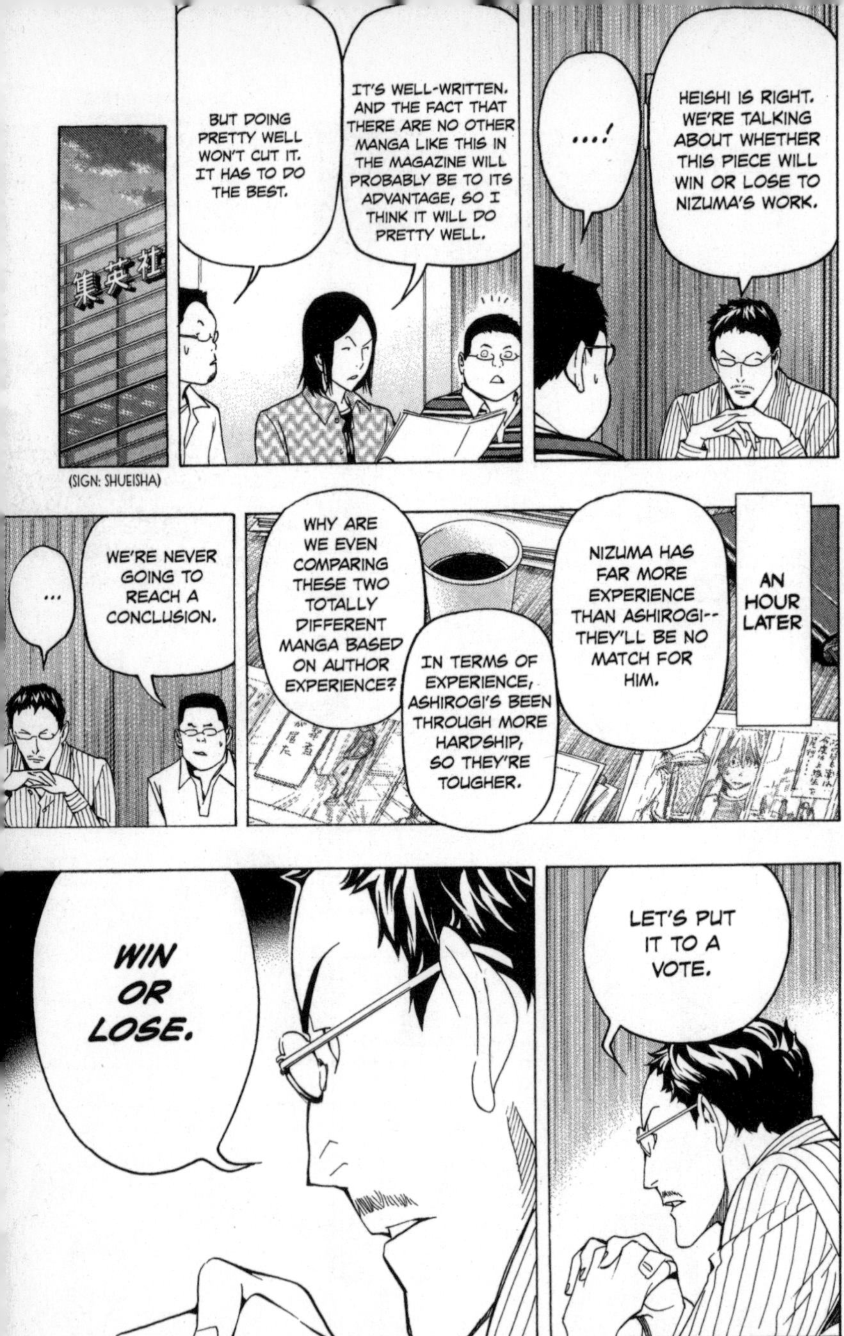
HEISHI IS RIGHT. WE'RE TALKING ABOUT WHETHER THIS PIECE WILL WIN OR LOSE TO NIZUMA'S WORK.
...!
IT'S WELL-WRITTEN. AND THE FACT THAT THERE ARE NO OTHER MANGA LIKE THIS IN THE MAGAZINE WILL PROBABLY BE TO ITS ADVANTAGE, SO I THINK IT WILL DO PRETTY WELL.
BUT DOING PRETTY WELL WON'T CUT IT. IT HAS TO DO THE BEST.
集英社
(SIGN: SHUEISHA)
AN HOUR LATER
NIZUMA HAS FAR MORE EXPERIENCE THAN ASHIROGI-- THEY'LL BE NO MATCH FOR HIM.
IN TERMS OF EXPERIENCE, ASHIROGI'S BEEN THROUGH MORE HARDSHIP, SO THEY'RE TOUGHER.
WHY ARE WE EVEN COMPARING THESE TWO TOTALLY DIFFERENT MANGA BASED ON AUTHOR EXPERIENCE?
WE'RE NEVER GOING TO REACH A CONCLUSION.
...
LET'S PUT IT TO A VOTE.
WIN OR LOSE.

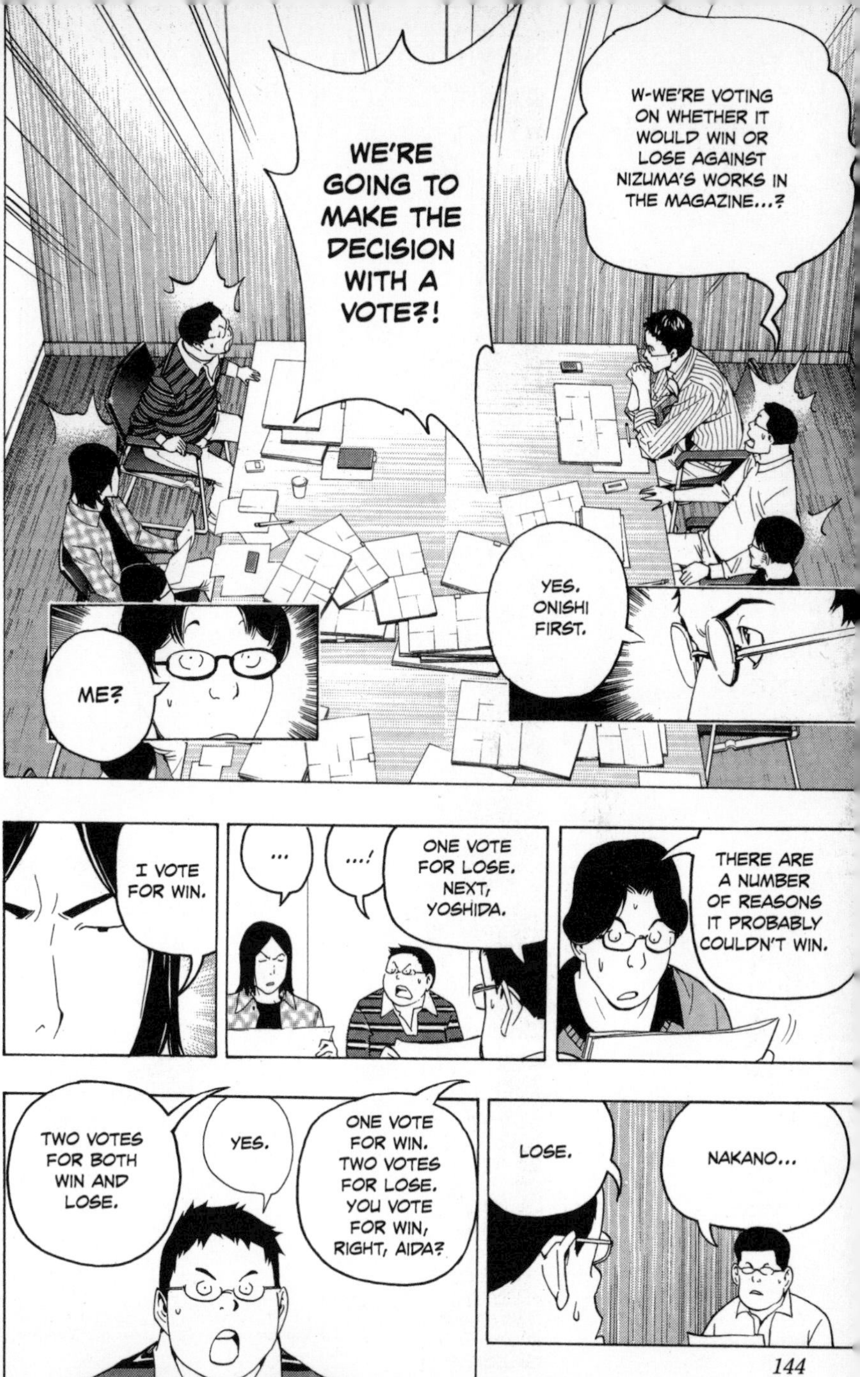
W-WE'RE VOTING ON WHETHER IT WOULD WIN OR LOSE AGAINST NIZUMA'S WORKS IN THE MAGAZINE...?
WE'RE GOING TO MAKE THE DECISION WITH A VOTE?!
YES. ONISHI FIRST.
ME?
THERE ARE A NUMBER OF REASONS IT PROBABLY COULDN'T WIN.
ONE VOTE FOR LOSE. NEXT, YOSHIDA.
...!
...
I VOTE FOR WIN.
NAKANO...
LOSE.
ONE VOTE FOR WIN. TWO VOTES FOR LOSE. YOU VOTE FOR WIN, RIGHT, AIDA?
YES.
TWO VOTES FOR BOTH WIN AND LOSE.

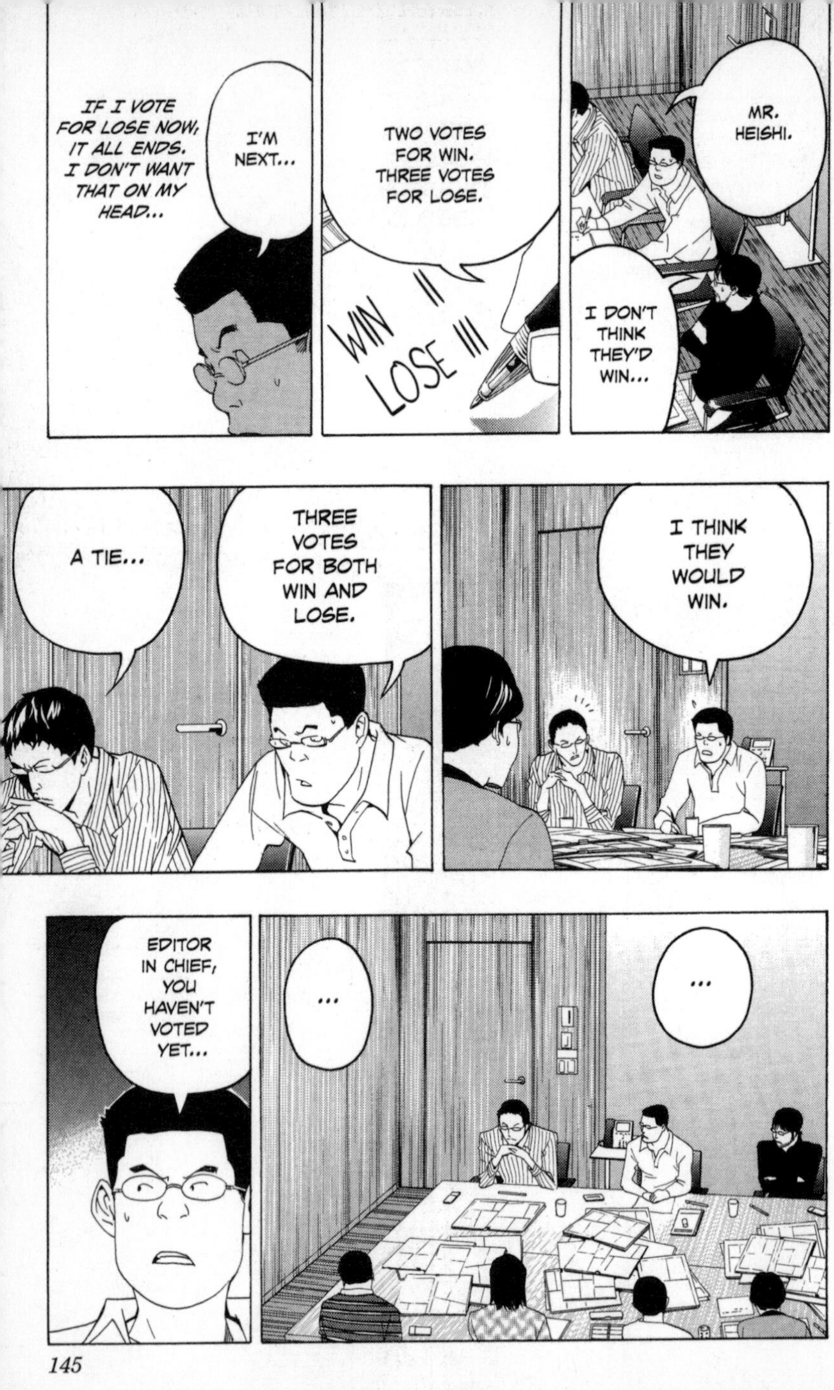
MR. HEISHI.
I DON'T THINK THEY'D WIN...
TWO VOTES FOR WIN. THREE VOTES FOR LOSE.
WIN
LOSE
I'M NEXT...
IF I VOTE FOR LOSE NOW, IT ALL ENDS. I DON'T WANT THAT ON MY HEAD...
I THINK THEY WOULD WIN.
THREE VOTES FOR BOTH WIN AND LOSE.
A TIE...
...
...
EDITOR IN CHIEF, YOU HAVEN'T VOTED YET...

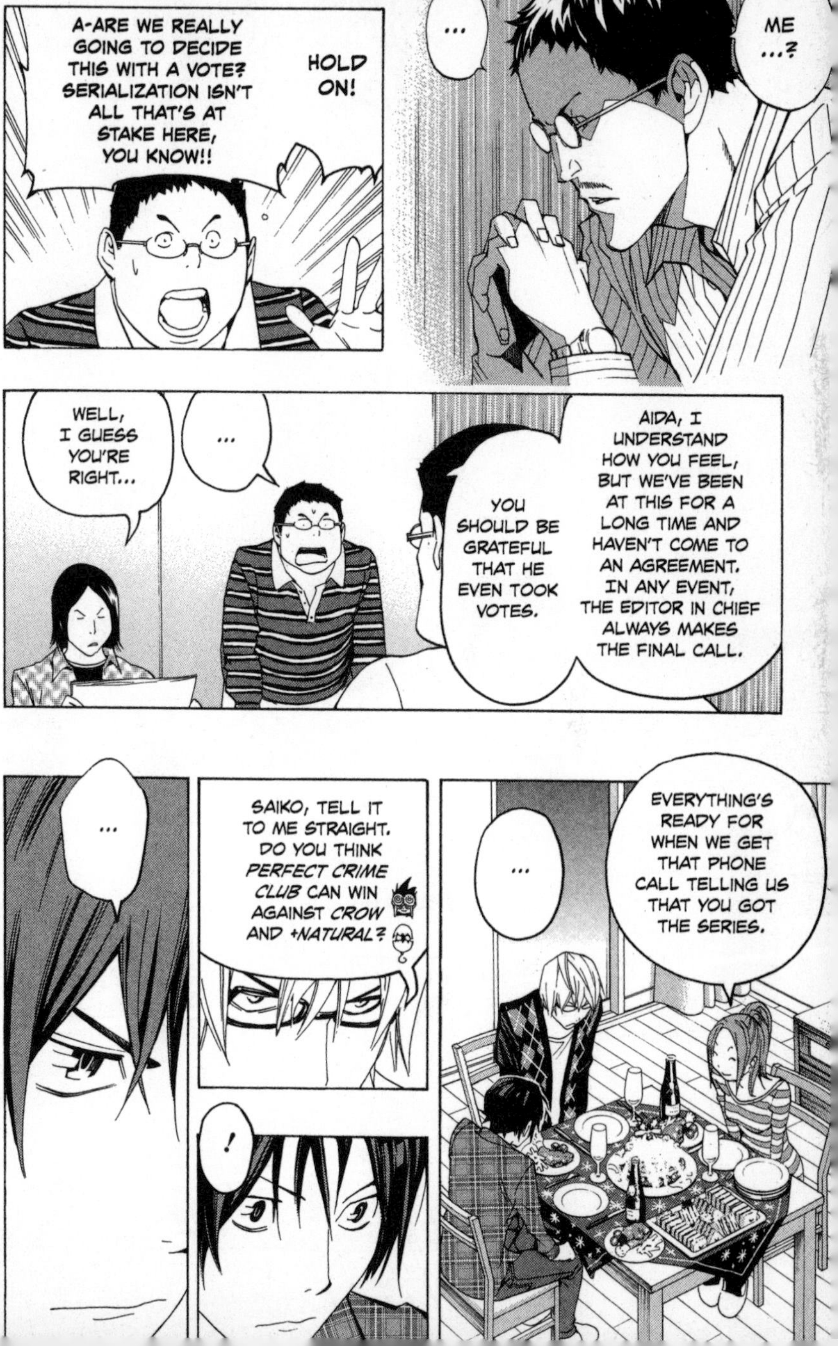
ME ...?
...
HOLD ON!
A-ARE WE REALLY GOING TO DECIDE THIS WITH A VOTE? SERIALIZATION ISN'T ALL THAT'S AT STAKE HERE, YOU KNOW!!
AIDA, I UNDERSTAND HOW YOU FEEL, BUT WE'VE BEEN AT THIS FOR A LONG TIME AND HAVEN'T COME TO AN AGREEMENT. IN ANY EVENT, THE EDITOR IN CHIEF ALWAYS MAKES THE FINAL CALL.
YOU SHOULD BE GRATEFUL THAT HE EVEN TOOK VOTES.
...
WELL, I GUESS YOU'RE RIGHT...
EVERYTHING'S READY FOR WHEN WE GET THAT PHONE CALL TELLING US THAT YOU GOT THE SERIES.
...
SAIKO, TELL IT TO ME STRAIGHT. DO YOU THINK *PERFECT CRIME CLUB* CAN WIN AGAINST *CROW* AND *+NATURAL*?
!
...

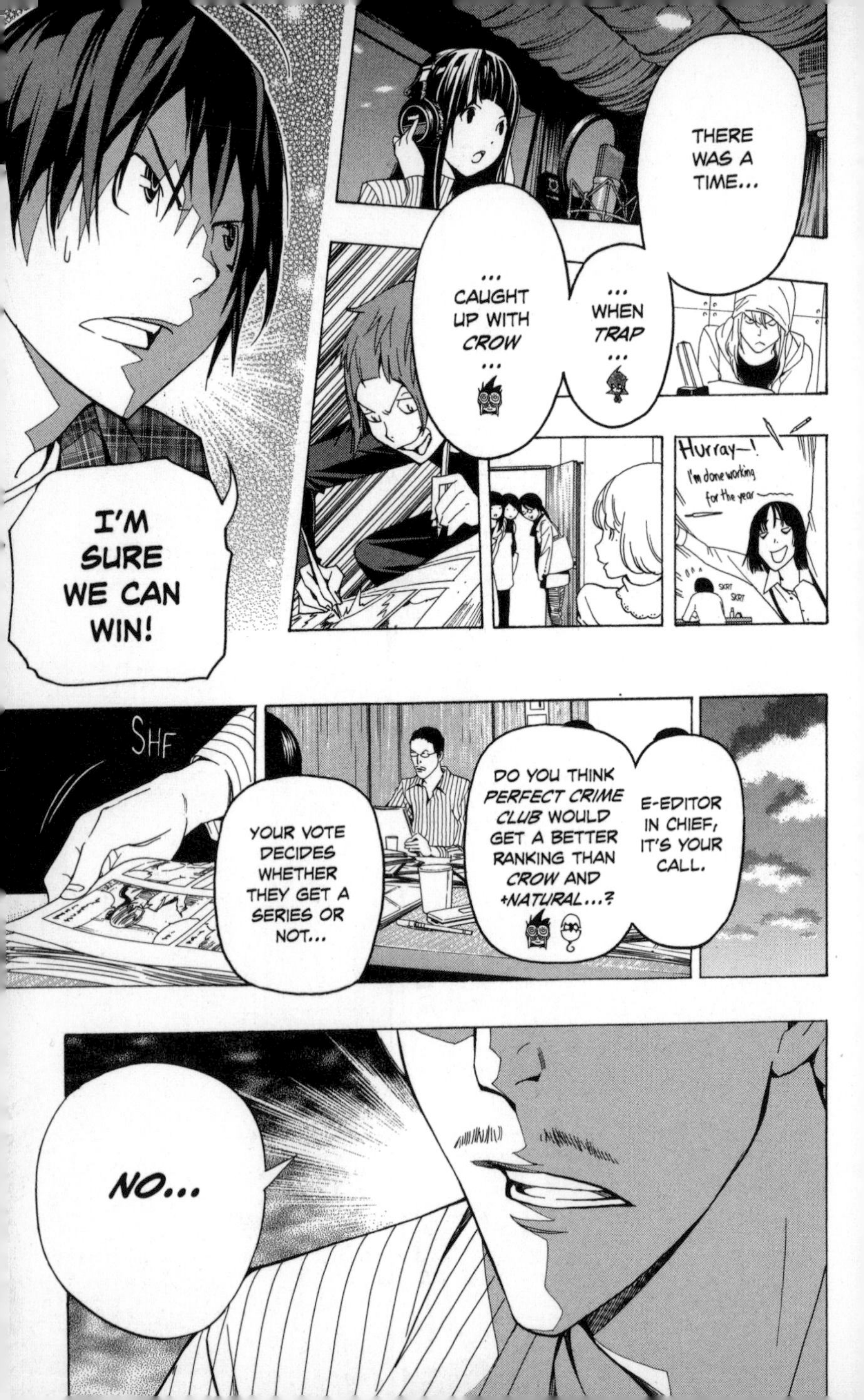
THERE WAS A TIME...
...WHEN TRAP...
...CAUGHT UP WITH CROW...
Hurray—! I'm done working for the year ~~~
SKRT SKRT
I'M SURE WE CAN WIN!
E-EDITOR IN CHIEF, IT'S YOUR CALL.
DO YOU THINK PERFECT CRIME CLUB WOULD GET A BETTER RANKING THAN CROW AND +NATURAL...?
YOUR VOTE DECIDES WHETHER THEY GET A SERIES OR NOT...
SHF
NO...

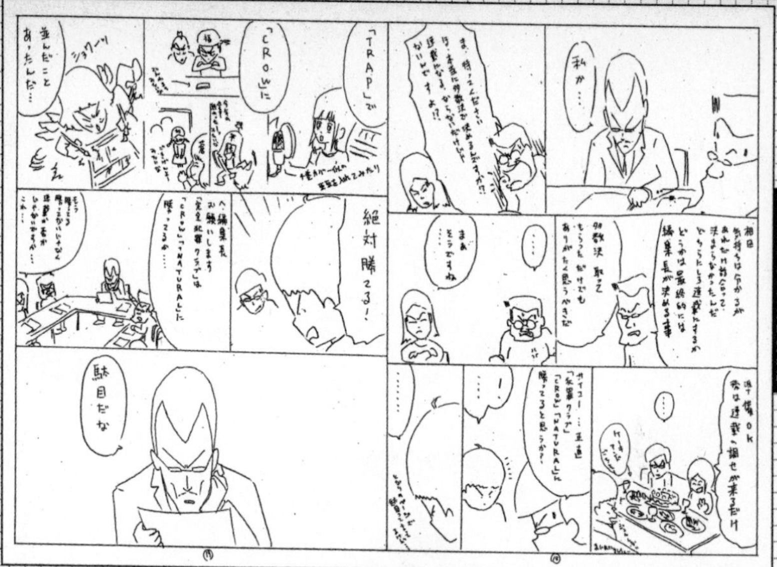

私か…
まあ そうですね
「TRAP」で
絶対勝てる!
駄目だな

OHBA'S STORYBOARD

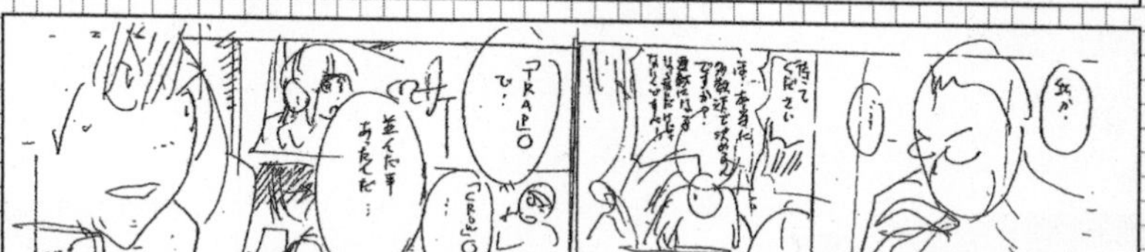

絶対勝てる!
駄目だな

OBATA'S STORYBOARD

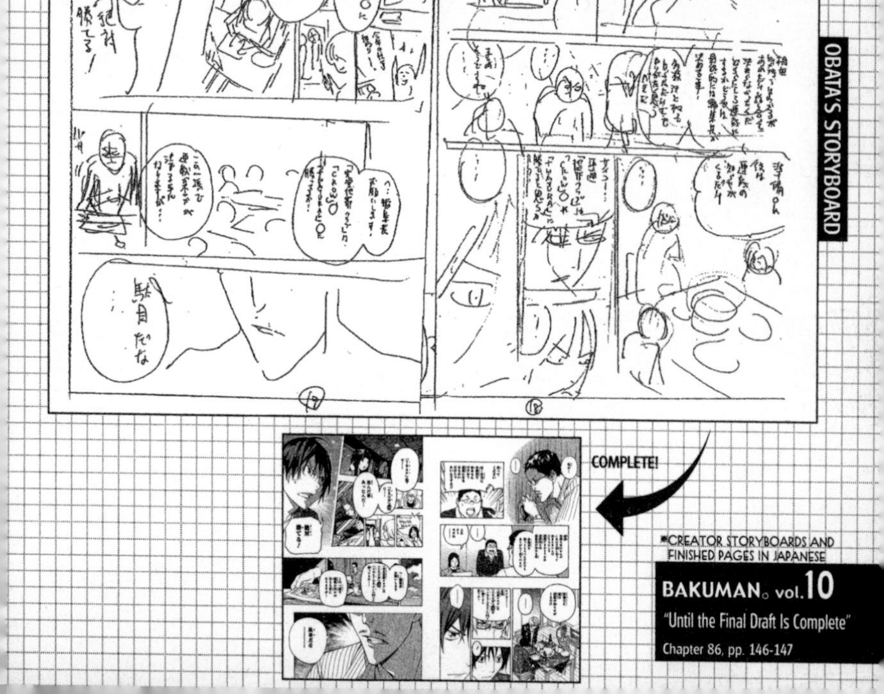

COMPLETE!

*CREATOR STORYBOARDS AND FINISHED PAGES IN JAPANESE

BAKUMAN。 vol.10

"Until the Final Draft Is Complete"

Chapter 86, pp. 146-147

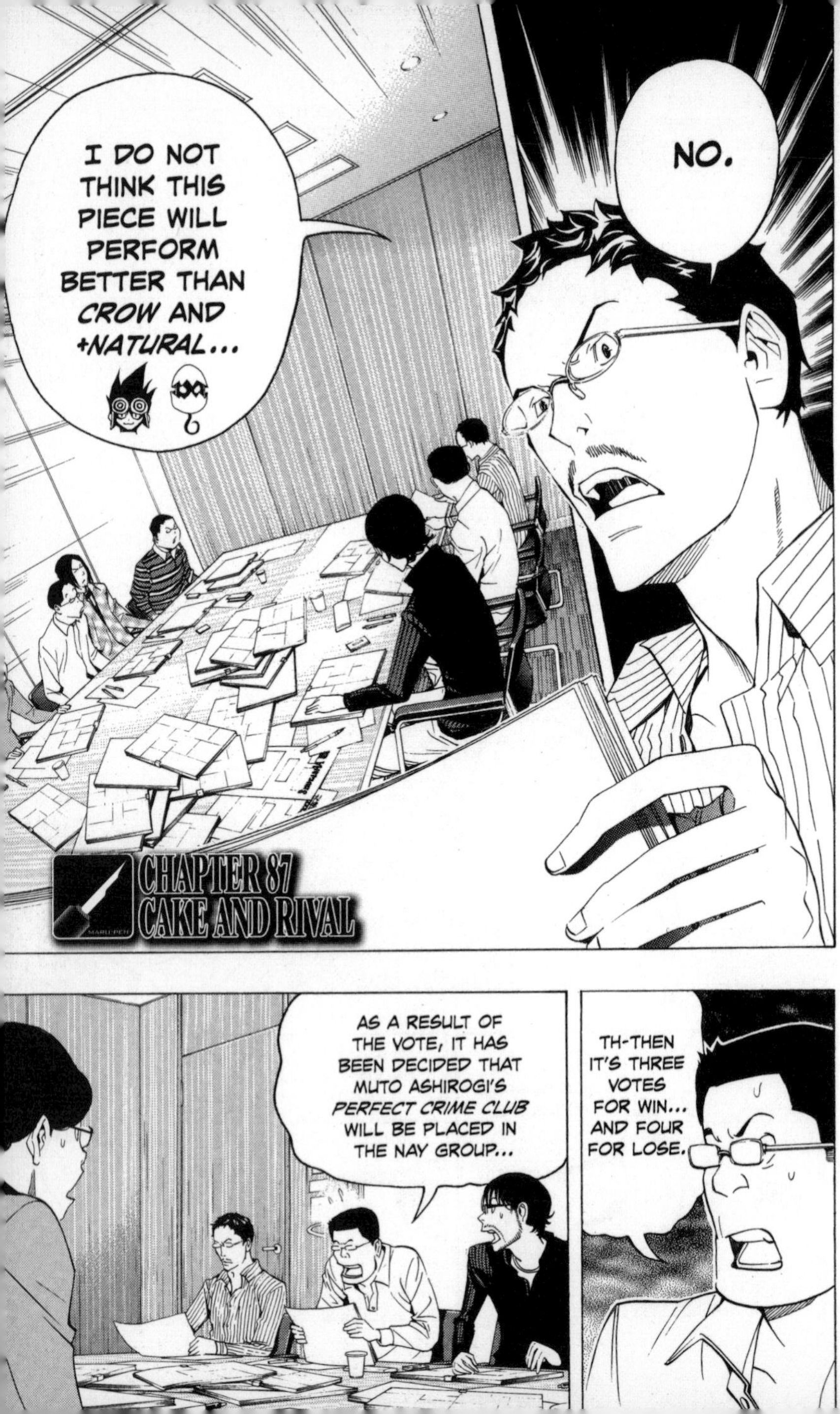
NO.
I DO NOT THINK THIS PIECE WILL PERFORM BETTER THAN *CROW* AND *+NATURAL*...
CHAPTER 87
CAKE AND RIVAL
TH-THEN IT'S THREE VOTES FOR WIN... AND FOUR FOR LOSE.
AS A RESULT OF THE VOTE, IT HAS BEEN DECIDED THAT MUTO ASHIROGI'S *PERFECT CRIME CLUB* WILL BE PLACED IN THE NAY GROUP...

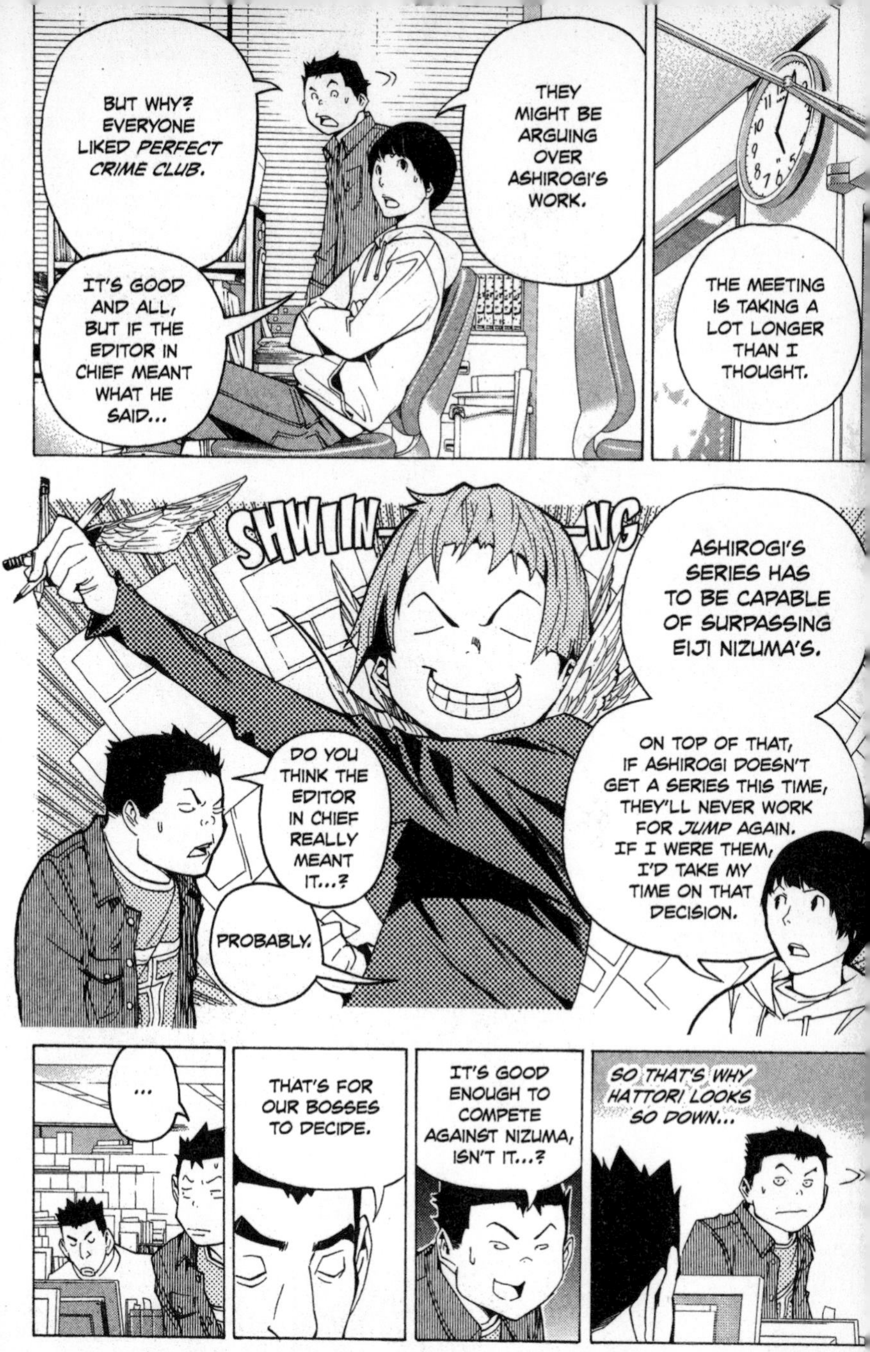
THE MEETING IS TAKING A LOT LONGER THAN I THOUGHT.
THEY MIGHT BE ARGUING OVER ASHIROGI'S WORK.
BUT WHY? EVERYONE LIKED *PERFECT CRIME CLUB.*
IT'S GOOD AND ALL, BUT IF THE EDITOR IN CHIEF MEANT WHAT HE SAID...
SHWIIN—NG
ASHIROGI'S SERIES HAS TO BE CAPABLE OF SURPASSING EIJI NIZUMA'S.
ON TOP OF THAT, IF ASHIROGI DOESN'T GET A SERIES THIS TIME, THEY'LL NEVER WORK FOR *JUMP* AGAIN. IF I WERE THEM, I'D TAKE MY TIME ON THAT DECISION.
DO YOU THINK THE EDITOR IN CHIEF REALLY MEANT IT...?
PROBABLY.
SO THAT'S WHY HATTORI LOOKS SO DOWN...
IT'S GOOD ENOUGH TO COMPETE AGAINST NIZUMA, ISN'T IT...?
THAT'S FOR OUR BOSSES TO DECIDE.
...

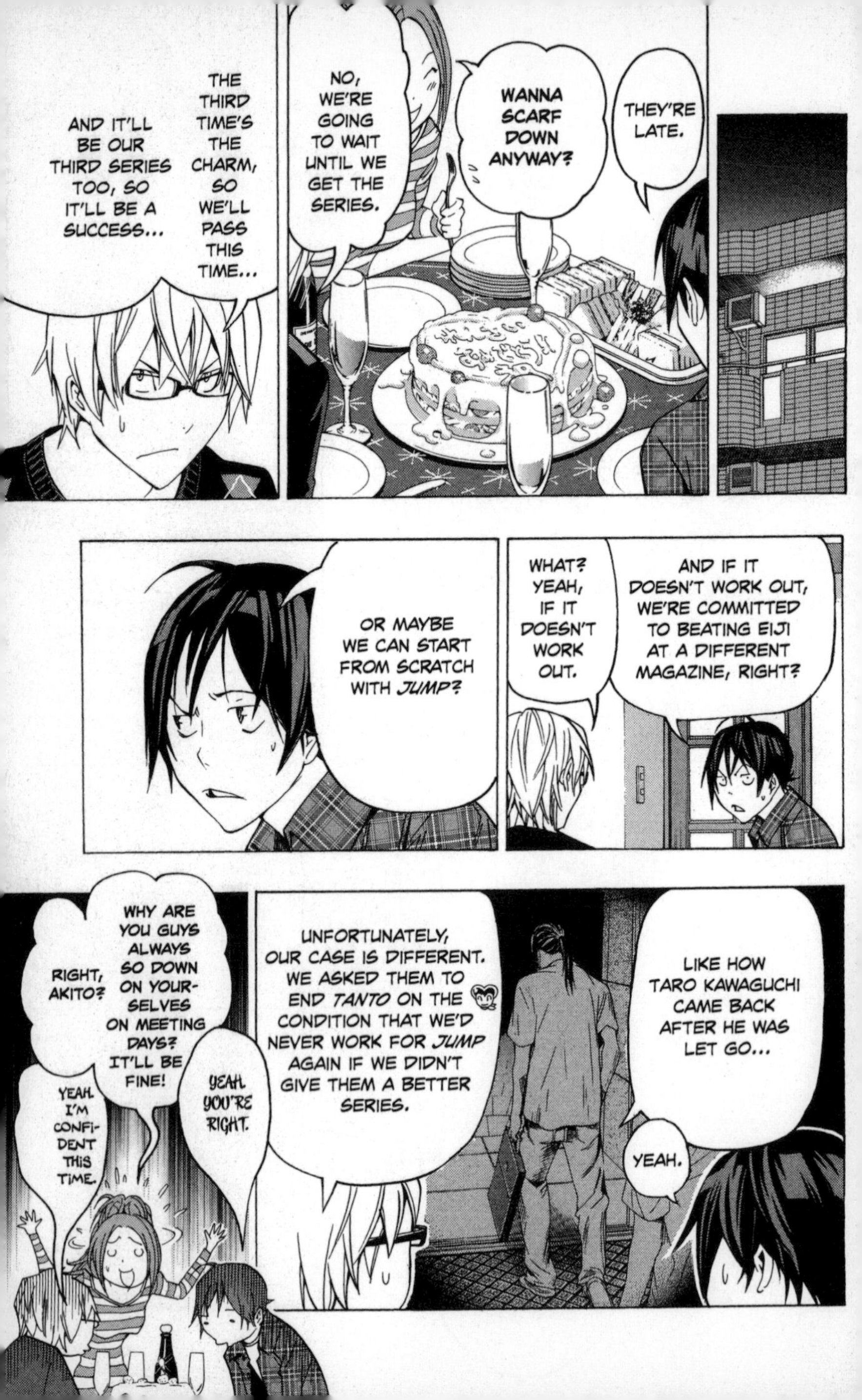
THEY'RE LATE.
WANNA SCARF DOWN ANYWAY?
NO, WE'RE GOING TO WAIT UNTIL WE GET THE SERIES.
THE THIRD TIME'S THE CHARM, SO WE'LL PASS THIS TIME...
AND IT'LL BE OUR THIRD SERIES TOO, SO IT'LL BE A SUCCESS...
AND IF IT DOESN'T WORK OUT, WE'RE COMMITTED TO BEATING EIJI AT A DIFFERENT MAGAZINE, RIGHT?
WHAT? YEAH, IF IT DOESN'T WORK OUT.
OR MAYBE WE CAN START FROM SCRATCH WITH *JUMP*?
LIKE HOW TARO KAWAGUCHI CAME BACK AFTER HE WAS LET GO...
YEAH.
UNFORTUNATELY, OUR CASE IS DIFFERENT. WE ASKED THEM TO END *TANTO* ON THE CONDITION THAT WE'D NEVER WORK FOR *JUMP* AGAIN IF WE DIDN'T GIVE THEM A BETTER SERIES.
WHY ARE YOU GUYS ALWAYS SO DOWN ON YOUR-SELVES ON MEETING DAYS? IT'LL BE FINE!
RIGHT, AKITO?
YEAH. YOU'RE RIGHT.
YEAH. I'M CONFI-DENT THIS TIME.

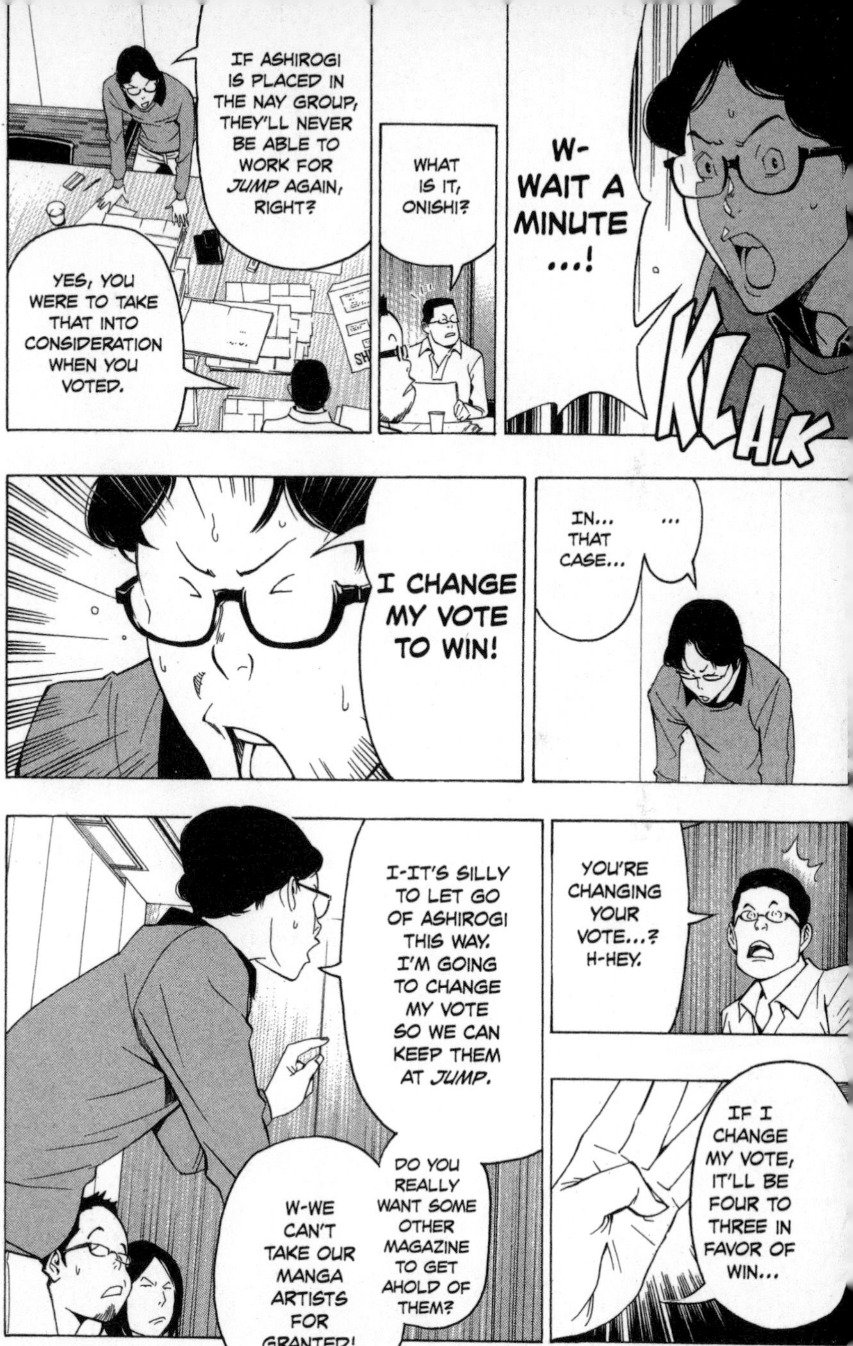
W-WAIT A MINUTE...!
KLAK
WHAT IS IT, ONISHI?
IF ASHIROGI IS PLACED IN THE NAY GROUP, THEY'LL NEVER BE ABLE TO WORK FOR *JUMP* AGAIN, RIGHT?
YES, YOU WERE TO TAKE THAT INTO CONSIDERATION WHEN YOU VOTED.
...
IN... THAT CASE...
I CHANGE MY VOTE TO WIN!
YOU'RE CHANGING YOUR VOTE...? H-HEY.
IF I CHANGE MY VOTE, IT'LL BE FOUR TO THREE IN FAVOR OF WIN...
I-IT'S SILLY TO LET GO OF ASHIROGI THIS WAY. I'M GOING TO CHANGE MY VOTE SO WE CAN KEEP THEM AT *JUMP*.
DO YOU REALLY WANT SOME OTHER MAGAZINE TO GET AHOLD OF THEM?
W-WE CAN'T TAKE OUR MANGA ARTISTS FOR GRANTED!

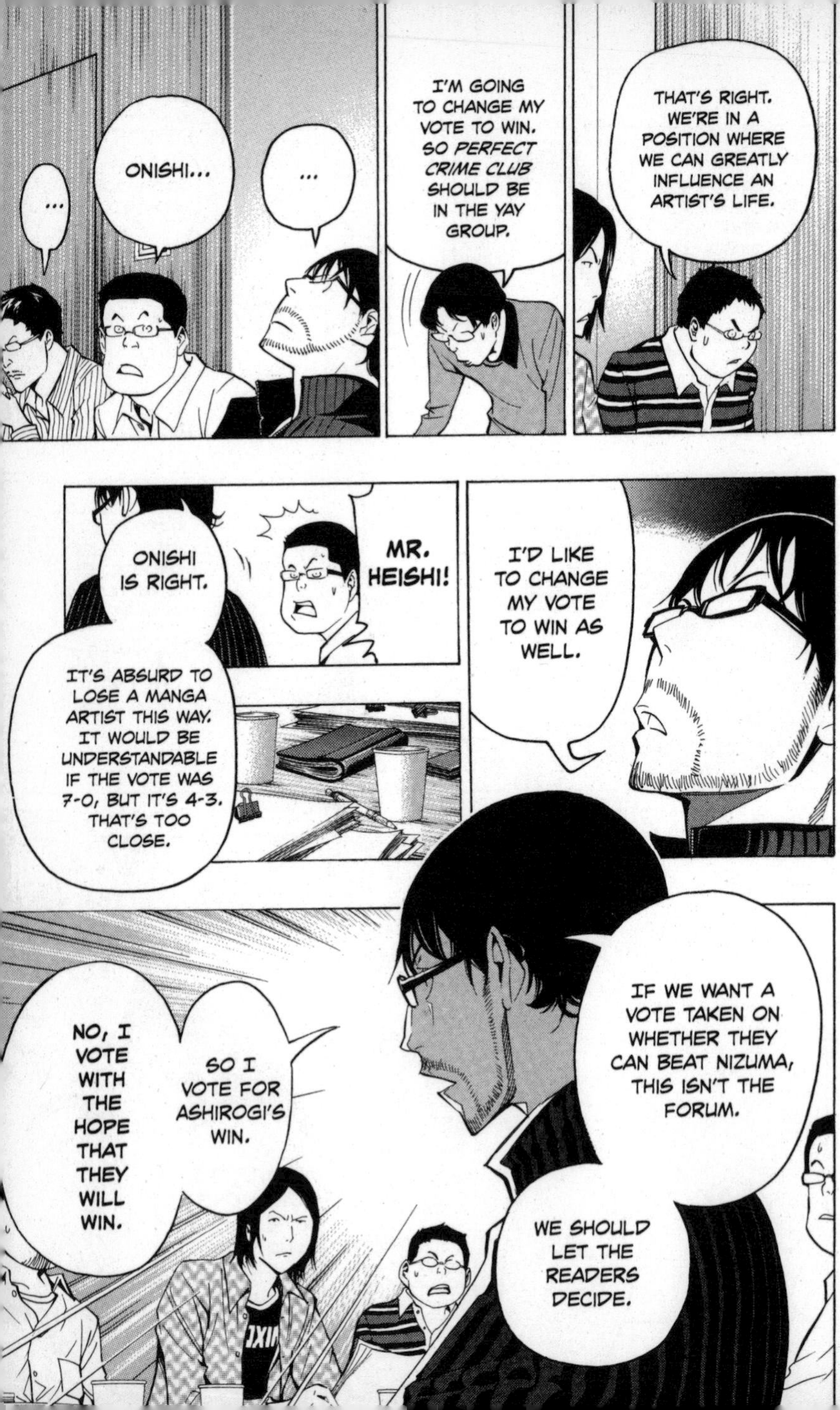
THAT'S RIGHT. WE'RE IN A POSITION WHERE WE CAN GREATLY INFLUENCE AN ARTIST'S LIFE.
I'M GOING TO CHANGE MY VOTE TO WIN. SO *PERFECT CRIME CLUB* SHOULD BE IN THE YAY GROUP.
...
ONISHI...
...
I'D LIKE TO CHANGE MY VOTE TO WIN AS WELL.
MR. HEISHI!
ONISHI IS RIGHT.
IT'S ABSURD TO LOSE A MANGA ARTIST THIS WAY. IT WOULD BE UNDERSTANDABLE IF THE VOTE WAS 7-0, BUT IT'S 4-3. THAT'S TOO CLOSE.
IF WE WANT A VOTE TAKEN ON WHETHER THEY CAN BEAT NIZUMA, THIS ISN'T THE FORUM.
WE SHOULD LET THE READERS DECIDE.
SO I VOTE FOR ASHIROGI'S WIN.
NO, I VOTE WITH THE HOPE THAT THEY WILL WIN.

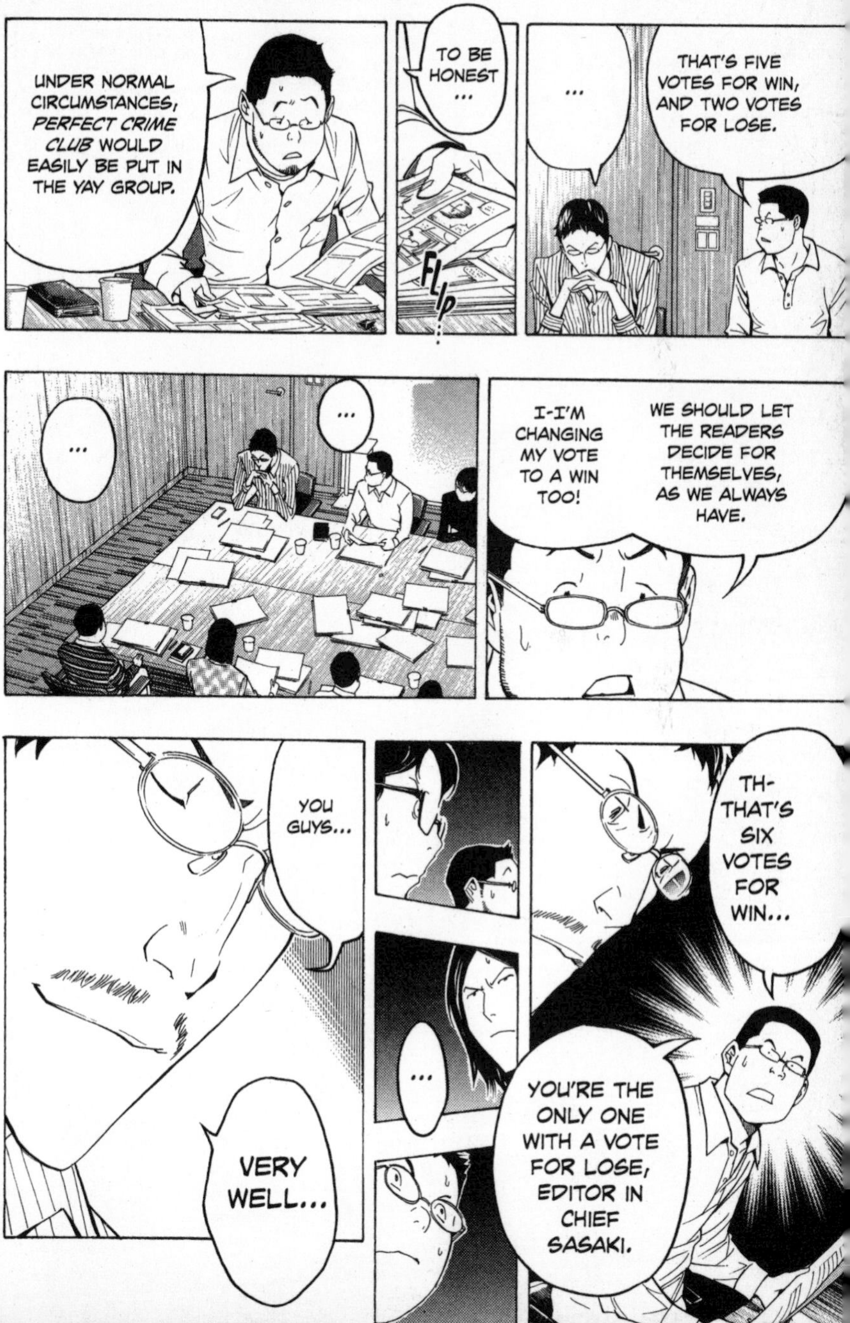
THAT'S FIVE VOTES FOR WIN, AND TWO VOTES FOR LOSE.
...
TO BE HONEST ...
FLIP...
UNDER NORMAL CIRCUMSTANCES, *PERFECT CRIME CLUB* WOULD EASILY BE PUT IN THE YAY GROUP.
WE SHOULD LET THE READERS DECIDE FOR THEMSELVES, AS WE ALWAYS HAVE.
I-I'M CHANGING MY VOTE TO A WIN TOO!
...
...
TH-THAT'S SIX VOTES FOR WIN...
YOU'RE THE ONLY ONE WITH A VOTE FOR LOSE, EDITOR IN CHIEF SASAKI.
...
YOU GUYS...
VERY WELL...

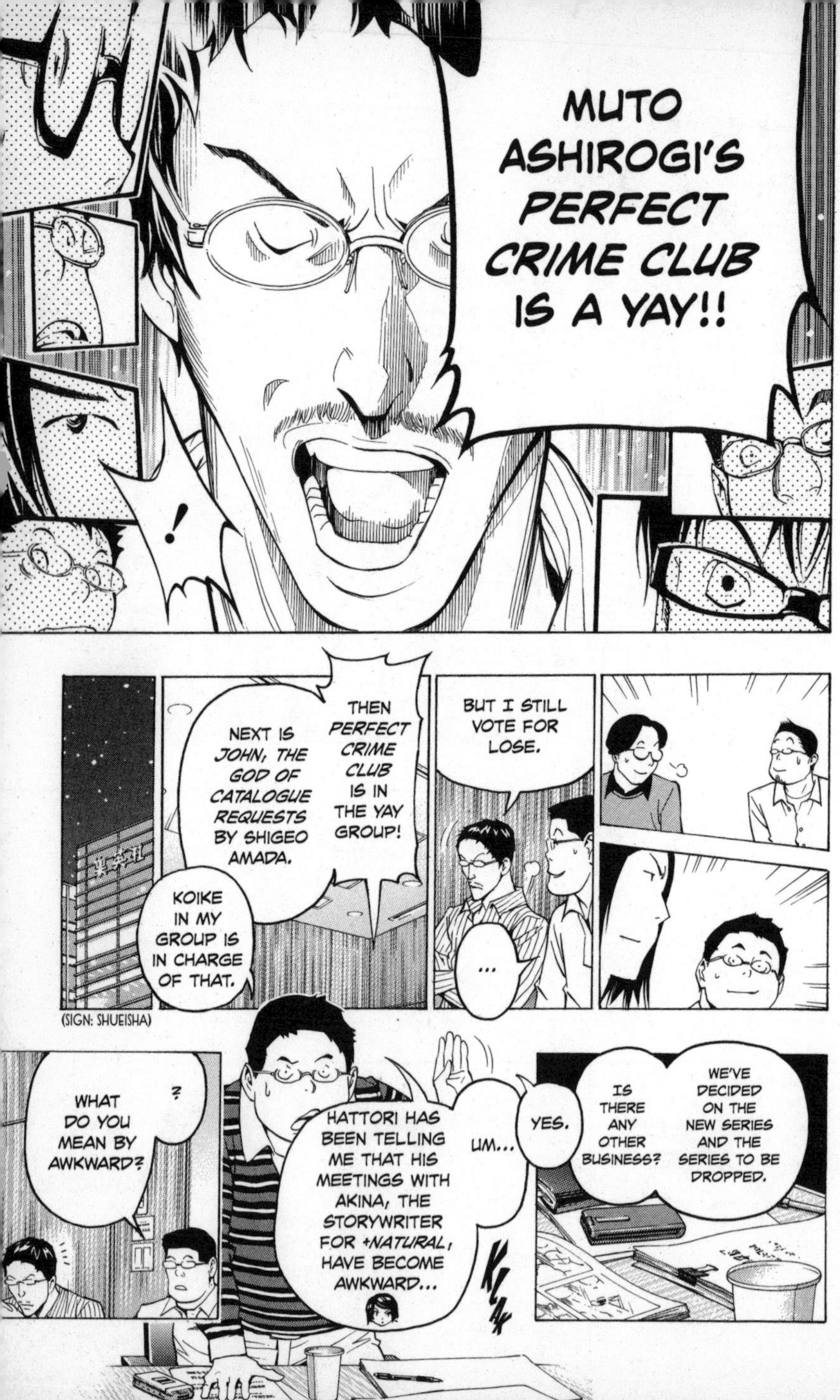
MUTO ASHIROGI'S *PERFECT CRIME CLUB* IS A YAY!!
!
BUT I STILL VOTE FOR *LOSE*.
...
THEN *PERFECT CRIME CLUB* IS IN THE YAY GROUP!
NEXT IS *JOHN, THE GOD OF CATALOGUE REQUESTS* BY SHIGEO AMADA.
KOIKE IN MY GROUP IS IN CHARGE OF THAT.
(SIGN: SHUEISHA)
WE'VE DECIDED ON THE NEW SERIES AND THE SERIES TO BE DROPPED.
IS THERE ANY OTHER BUSINESS?
YES.
UM...
HATTORI HAS BEEN TELLING ME THAT HIS MEETINGS WITH AKINA, THE STORYWRITER FOR *+NATURAL*, HAVE BECOME AWKWARD...
KLAK
?
WHAT DO YOU MEAN BY AWKWARD?

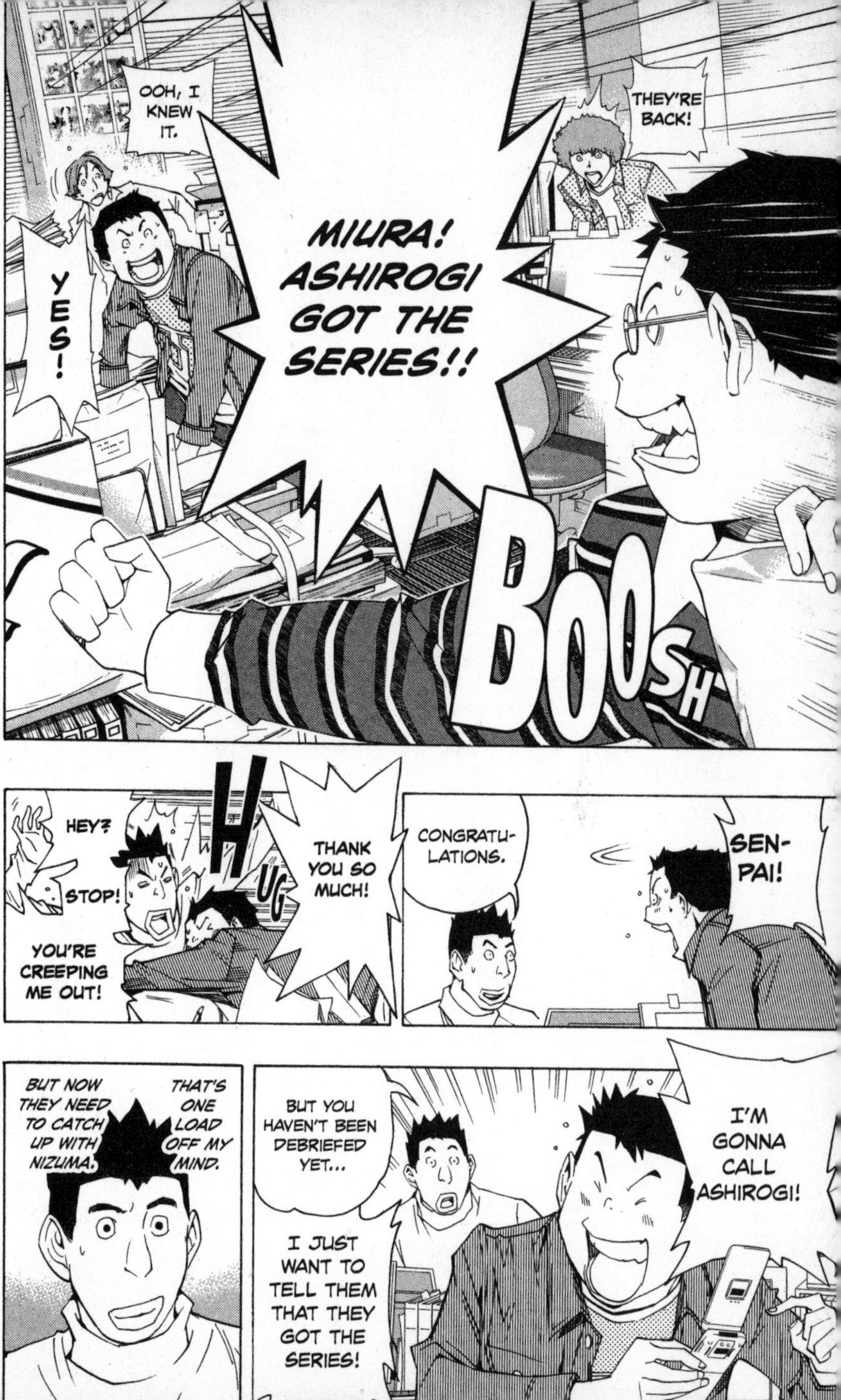
THEY'RE BACK!
MIURA! ASHIROGI GOT THE SERIES!!
OOH, I KNEW IT.
YES!
BOOSH
SEN-PAI!
CONGRATU-LATIONS.
THANK YOU SO MUCH!
HUG
HEY?
STOP!
YOU'RE CREEPING ME OUT!
I'M GONNA CALL ASHIROGI!
BUT YOU HAVEN'T BEEN DEBRIEFED YET...
I JUST WANT TO TELL THEM THAT THEY GOT THE SERIES!
THAT'S ONE LOAD OFF MY MIND.
BUT NOW THEY NEED TO CATCH UP WITH NIZUMA.

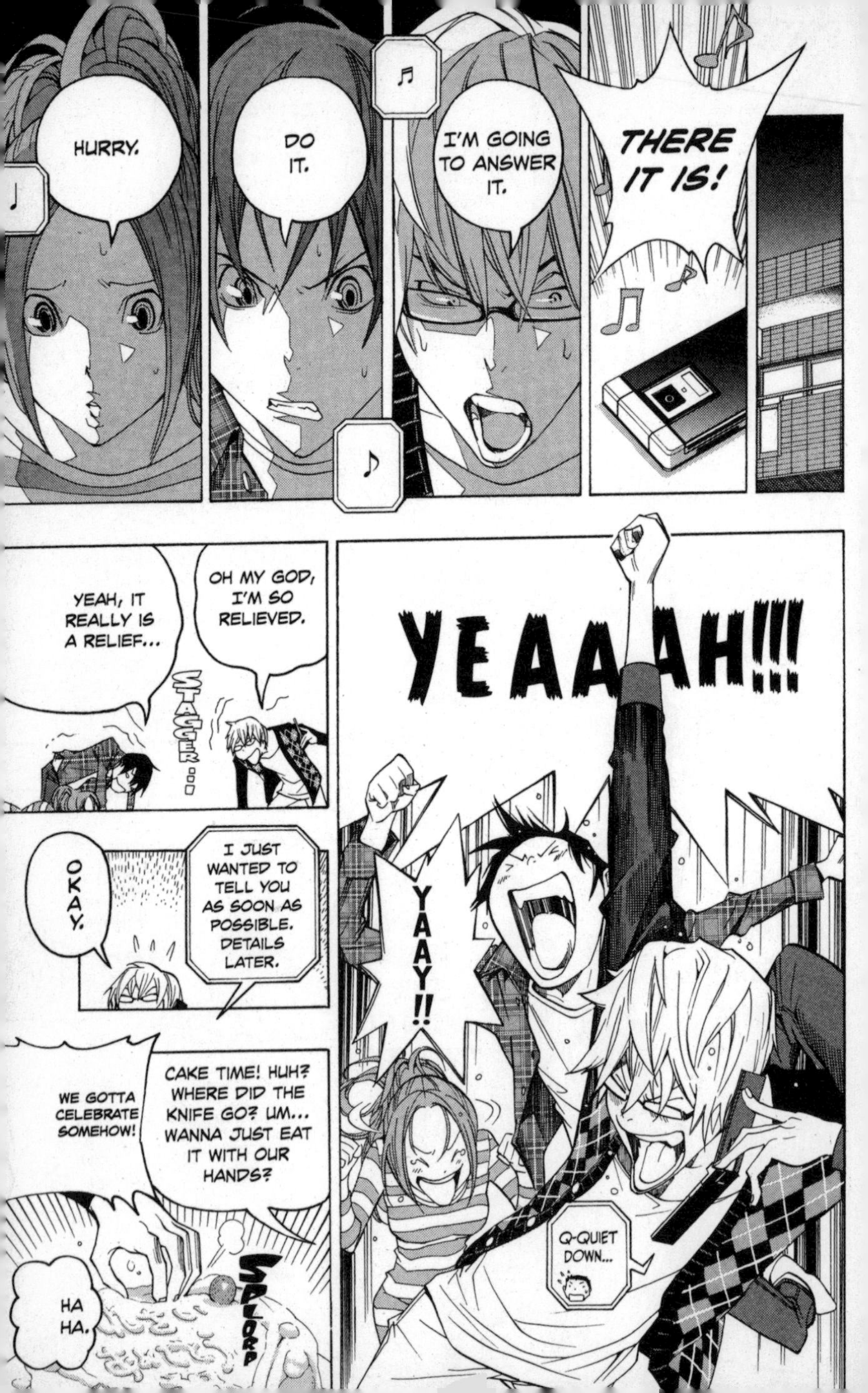
THERE IT IS!
I'M GOING TO ANSWER IT.
DO IT.
HURRY.
YEAAAH!!!
YAAY!!
Q-QUIET DOWN...
OH MY GOD, I'M SO RELIEVED.
YEAH, IT REALLY IS A RELIEF...
STAGGER...
I JUST WANTED TO TELL YOU AS SOON AS POSSIBLE. DETAILS LATER.
OKAY.
CAKE TIME! HUH? WHERE DID THE KNIFE GO? UM... WANNA JUST EAT IT WITH OUR HANDS?
WE GOTTA CELEBRATE SOMEHOW!
SPLORP
HA HA.

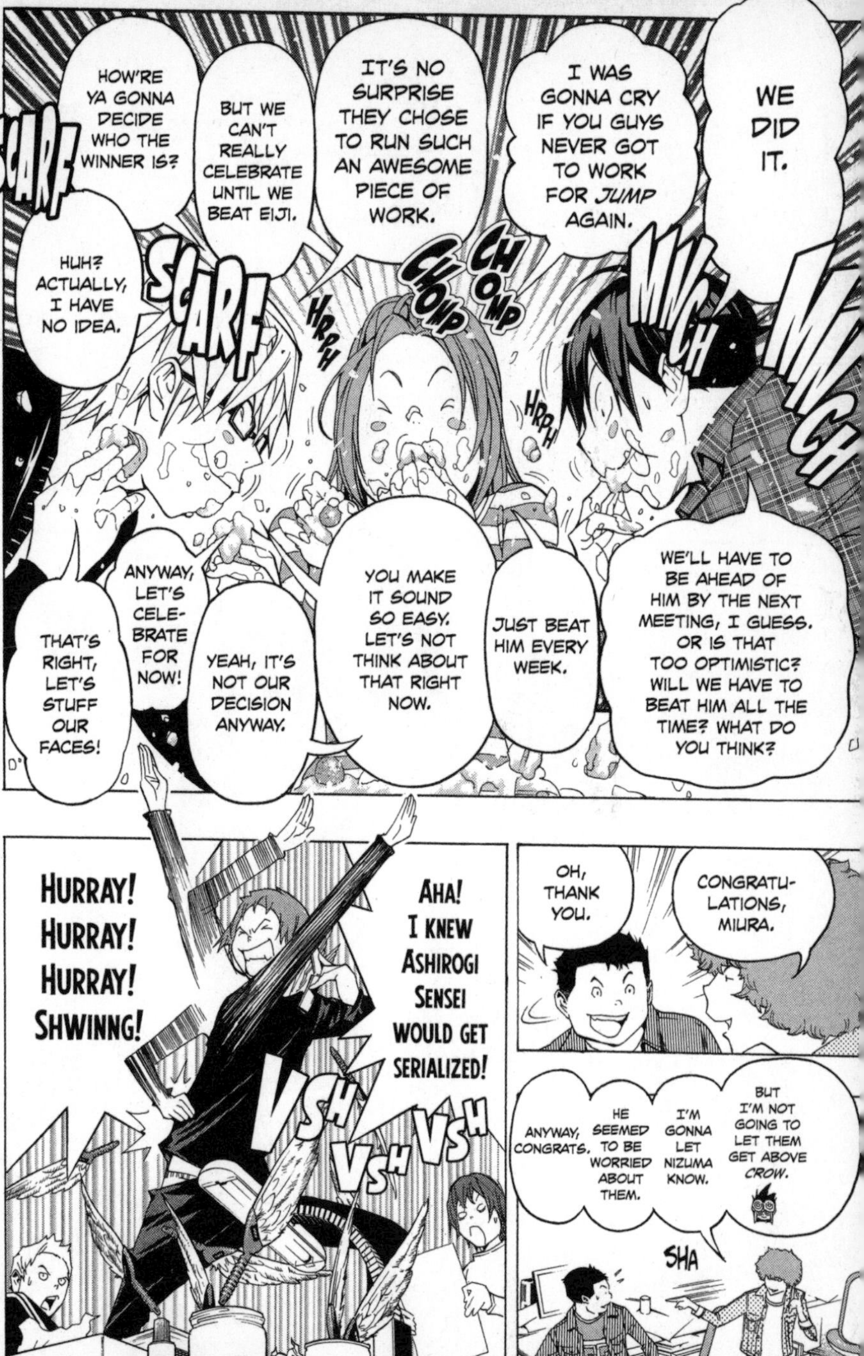
WE DID IT.
I WAS GONNA CRY IF YOU GUYS NEVER GOT TO WORK FOR *JUMP* AGAIN.
IT'S NO SURPRISE THEY CHOSE TO RUN SUCH AN AWESOME PIECE OF WORK.
BUT WE CAN'T REALLY CELEBRATE UNTIL WE BEAT EIJI.
HOW'RE YA GONNA DECIDE WHO THE WINNER IS?
HUH? ACTUALLY, I HAVE NO IDEA.
MUNCH
MUNCH
CHOMP
CHOMP
HRPH
HRPH
SCARF
SCARF
WE'LL HAVE TO BE AHEAD OF HIM BY THE NEXT MEETING, I GUESS. OR IS THAT TOO OPTIMISTIC? WILL WE HAVE TO BEAT HIM ALL THE TIME? WHAT DO YOU THINK?
JUST BEAT HIM EVERY WEEK.
YOU MAKE IT SOUND SO EASY. LET'S NOT THINK ABOUT THAT RIGHT NOW.
YEAH, IT'S NOT OUR DECISION ANYWAY.
ANYWAY, LET'S CELE-BRATE FOR NOW!
THAT'S RIGHT, LET'S STUFF OUR FACES!
CONGRATU-LATIONS, MIURA.
OH, THANK YOU.
BUT I'M NOT GOING TO LET THEM GET ABOVE *CROW*.
I'M GONNA LET NIZUMA KNOW.
HE SEEMED TO BE WORRIED ABOUT THEM.
ANYWAY, CONGRATS.
SHA
AHA! I KNEW ASHIROGI SENSEI WOULD GET SERIALIZED!
HURRAY! HURRAY! HURRAY! SHWINNG!
VSH
VSH
VSH

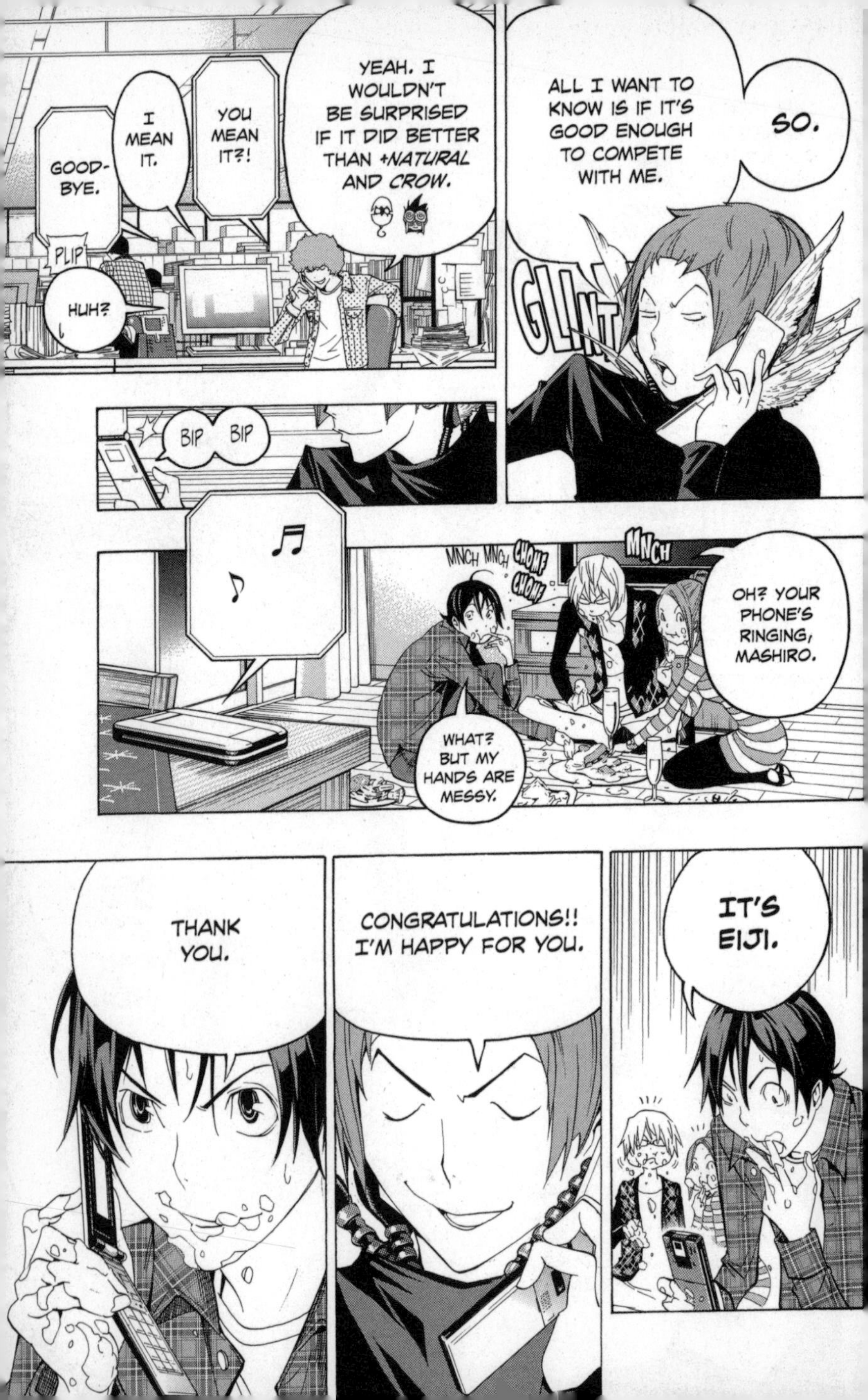
SO.
ALL I WANT TO KNOW IS IF IT'S GOOD ENOUGH TO COMPETE WITH ME.
GLINT
YEAH. I WOULDN'T BE SURPRISED IF IT DID BETTER THAN +NATURAL AND CROW.
YOU MEAN IT?!
I MEAN IT.
GOOD-BYE.
PLIP
HUH?
BIP BIP
OH? YOUR PHONE'S RINGING, MASHIRO.
MNCH
CHOMF CHOMF
MNCH MNCH
♫ ♪
WHAT? BUT MY HANDS ARE MESSY.
IT'S EIJI.
CONGRATULATIONS!! I'M HAPPY FOR YOU.
THANK YOU.

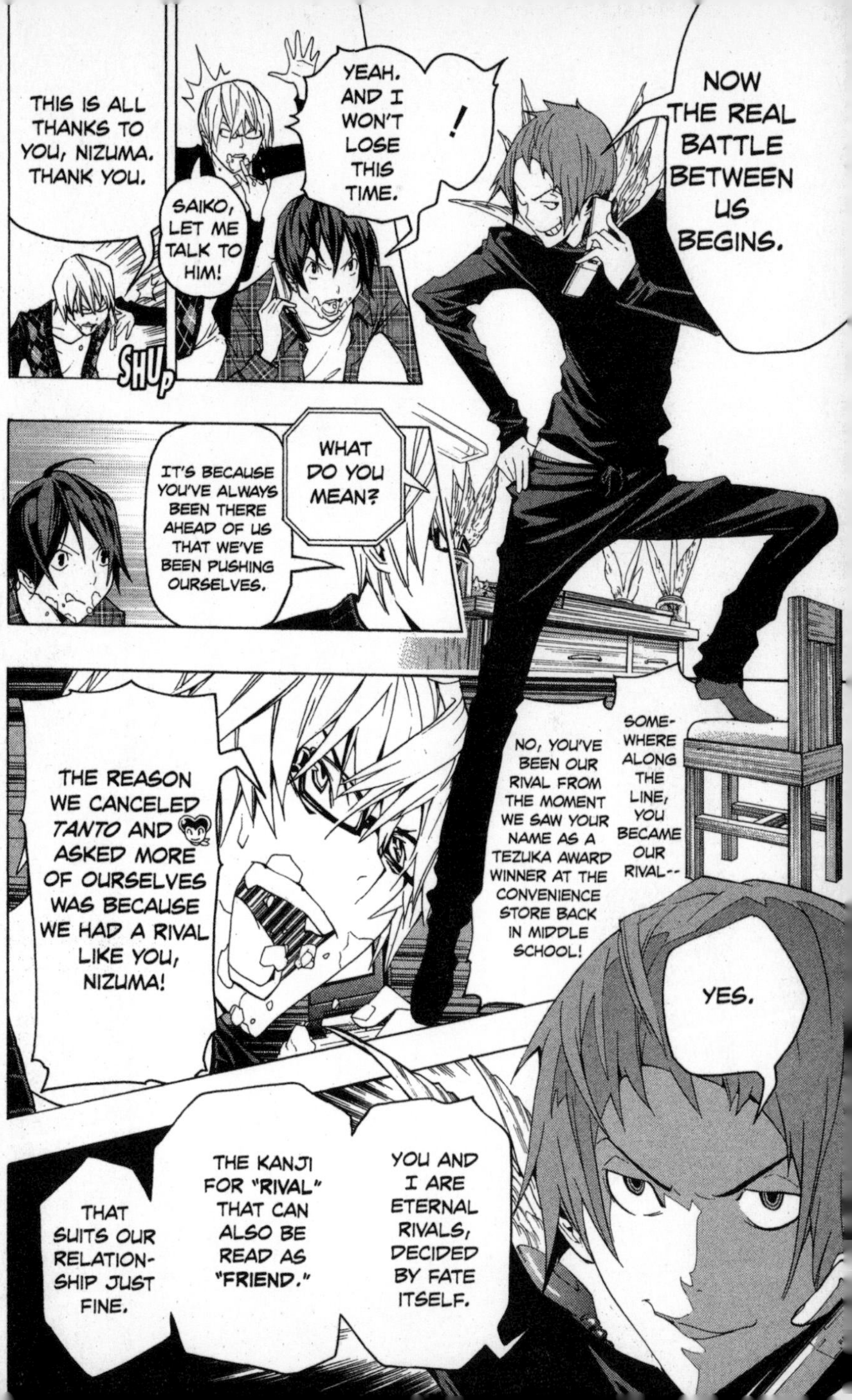

NOW THE REAL BATTLE BETWEEN US BEGINS.
YEAH. AND I WON'T LOSE THIS TIME.
!
THIS IS ALL THANKS TO YOU, NIZUMA. THANK YOU.
SAIKO, LET ME TALK TO HIM!
SHUP
WHAT DO YOU MEAN?
IT'S BECAUSE YOU'VE ALWAYS BEEN THERE AHEAD OF US THAT WE'VE BEEN PUSHING OURSELVES.
SOME-WHERE ALONG THE LINE, YOU BECAME OUR RIVAL--
NO, YOU'VE BEEN OUR RIVAL FROM THE MOMENT WE SAW YOUR NAME AS A TEZUKA AWARD WINNER AT THE CONVENIENCE STORE BACK IN MIDDLE SCHOOL!
THE REASON WE CANCELED *TANTO* AND ASKED MORE OF OURSELVES WAS BECAUSE WE HAD A RIVAL LIKE YOU, NIZUMA!
YES.
YOU AND I ARE ETERNAL RIVALS, DECIDED BY FATE ITSELF.
THE KANJI FOR "RIVAL" THAT CAN ALSO BE READ AS "FRIEND."
THAT SUITS OUR RELATIONSHIP JUST FINE.

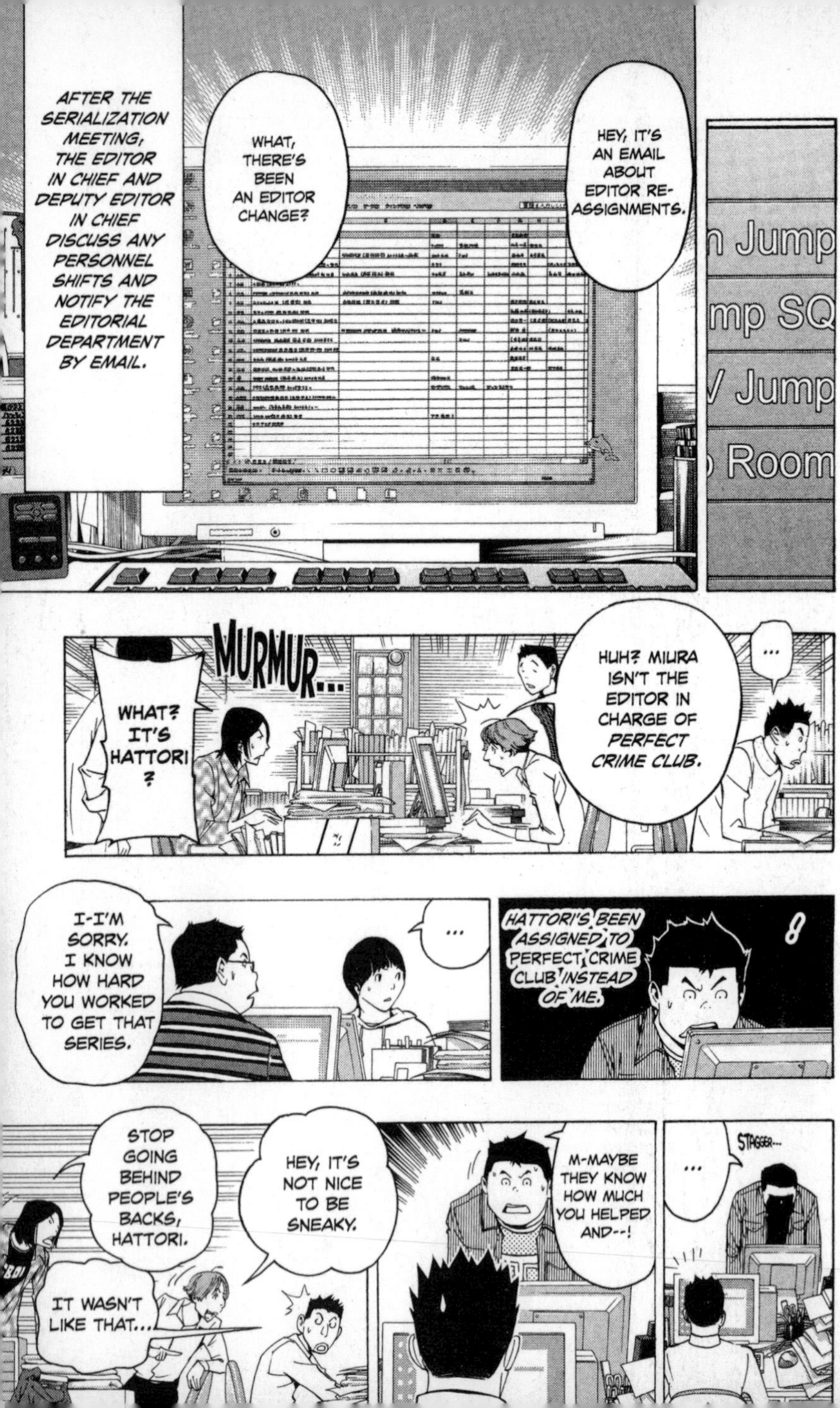
n Jump
mp SQ
V Jump
o Room
HEY, IT'S AN EMAIL ABOUT EDITOR RE-ASSIGNMENTS.
WHAT, THERE'S BEEN AN EDITOR CHANGE?
AFTER THE SERIALIZATION MEETING, THE EDITOR IN CHIEF AND DEPUTY EDITOR IN CHIEF DISCUSS ANY PERSONNEL SHIFTS AND NOTIFY THE EDITORIAL DEPARTMENT BY EMAIL.
...
HUH? MIURA ISN'T THE EDITOR IN CHARGE OF PERFECT CRIME CLUB.
MURMUR...
WHAT? IT'S HATTORI?
HATTORI'S BEEN ASSIGNED TO PERFECT CRIME CLUB INSTEAD OF ME.
...
I-I'M SORRY. I KNOW HOW HARD YOU WORKED TO GET THAT SERIES.
STAGGER...
...
M-MAYBE THEY KNOW HOW MUCH YOU HELPED AND--!
HEY, IT'S NOT NICE TO BE SNEAKY.
STOP GOING BEHIND PEOPLE'S BACKS, HATTORI.
IT WASN'T LIKE THAT...

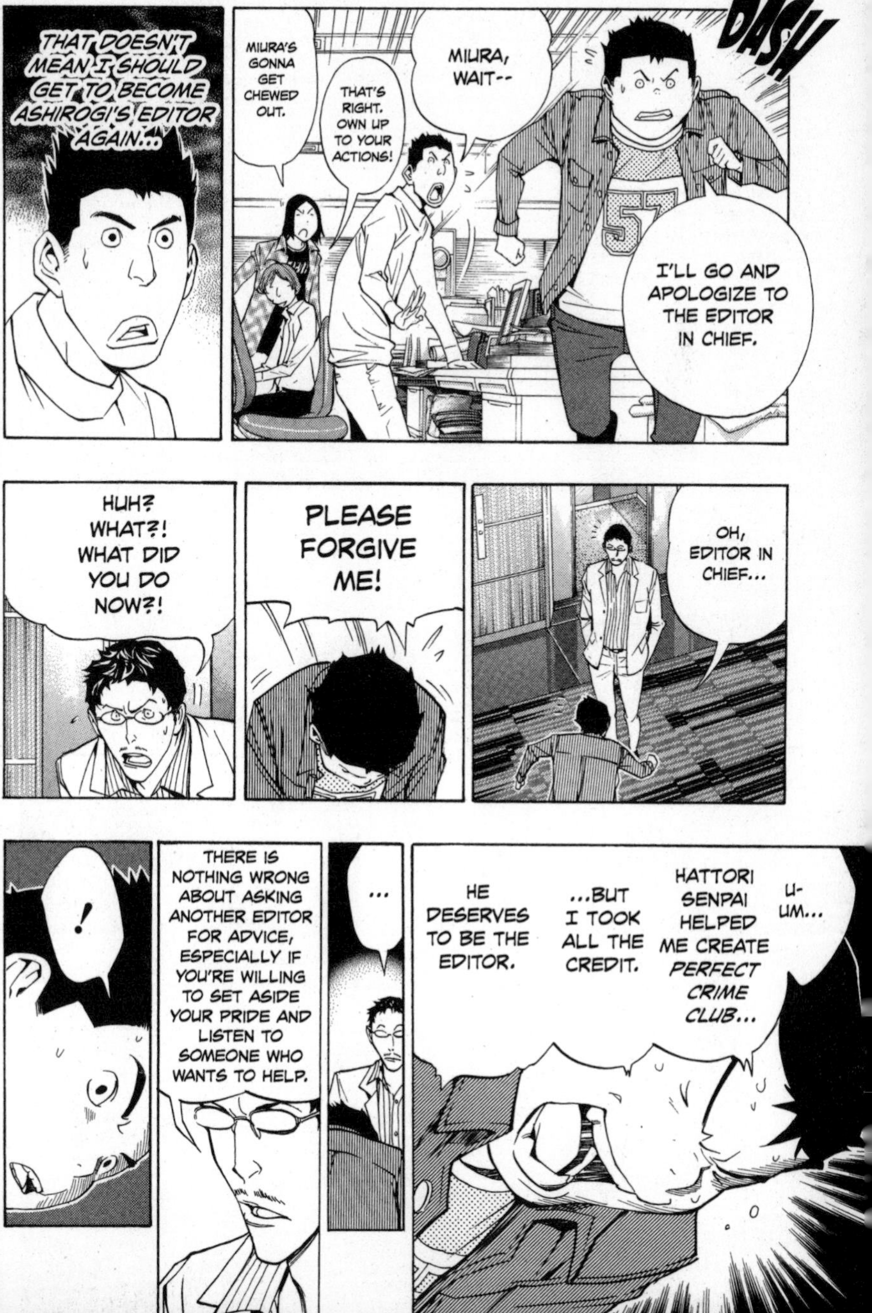
DASH
MIURA, WAIT--
MIURA'S GONNA GET CHEWED OUT.
THAT'S RIGHT. OWN UP TO YOUR ACTIONS!
I'LL GO AND APOLOGIZE TO THE EDITOR IN CHIEF.
THAT DOESN'T MEAN I SHOULD GET TO BECOME ASHIROGI'S EDITOR AGAIN...
OH, EDITOR IN CHIEF...
PLEASE FORGIVE ME!
HUH? WHAT?! WHAT DID YOU DO NOW?!
U-UM...
HATTORI SENPAI HELPED ME CREATE *PERFECT CRIME CLUB*...
...BUT I TOOK ALL THE CREDIT.
HE DESERVES TO BE THE EDITOR.
...
THERE IS NOTHING WRONG ABOUT ASKING ANOTHER EDITOR FOR ADVICE, ESPECIALLY IF YOU'RE WILLING TO SET ASIDE YOUR PRIDE AND LISTEN TO SOMEONE WHO WANTS TO HELP.
!

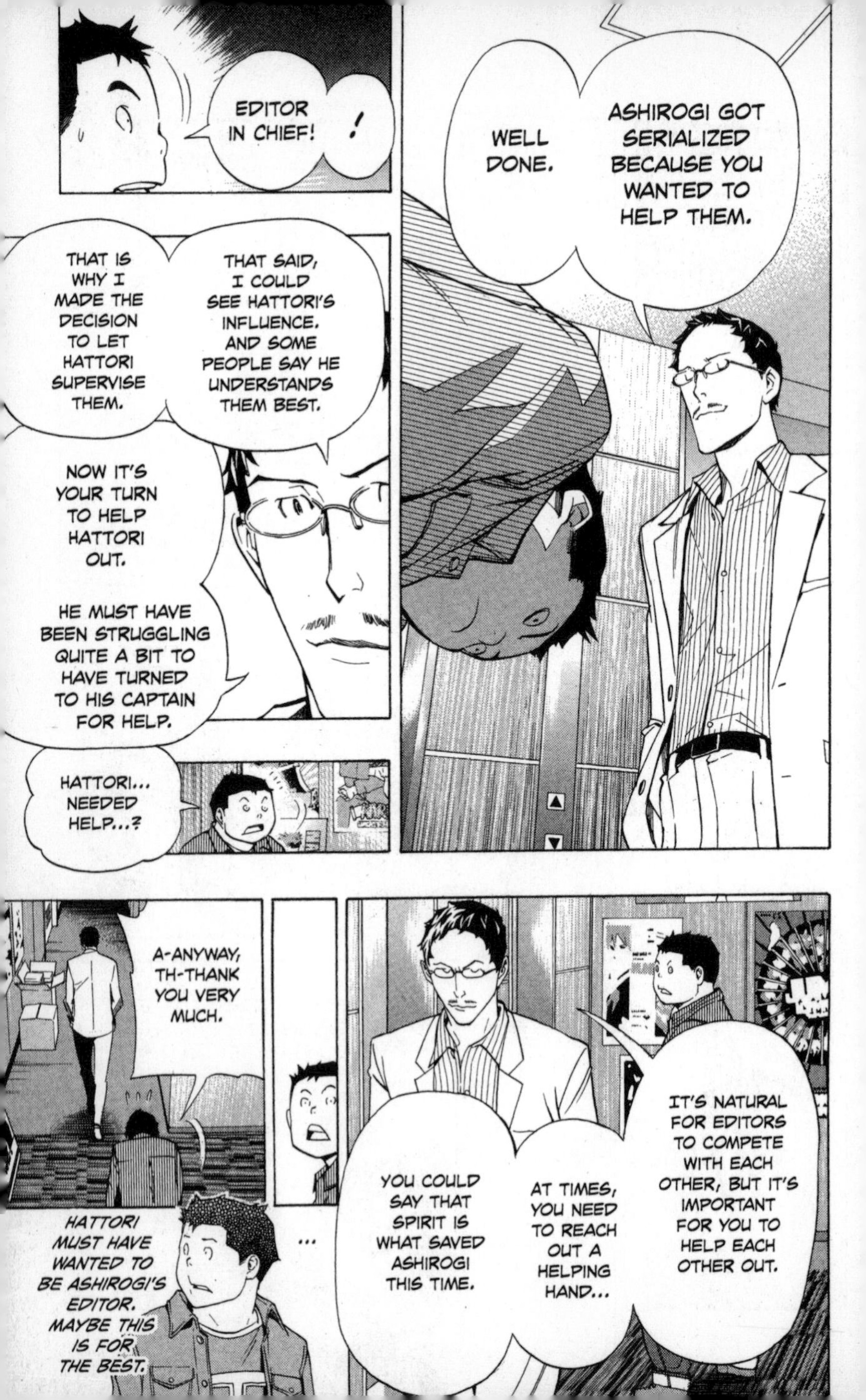
ASHIROGI GOT SERIALIZED BECAUSE YOU WANTED TO HELP THEM.
WELL DONE.
!
EDITOR IN CHIEF!
THAT SAID, I COULD SEE HATTORI'S INFLUENCE. AND SOME PEOPLE SAY HE UNDERSTANDS THEM BEST.
THAT IS WHY I MADE THE DECISION TO LET HATTORI SUPERVISE THEM.
NOW IT'S YOUR TURN TO HELP HATTORI OUT.
HE MUST HAVE BEEN STRUGGLING QUITE A BIT TO HAVE TURNED TO HIS CAPTAIN FOR HELP.
HATTORI... NEEDED HELP...?
IT'S NATURAL FOR EDITORS TO COMPETE WITH EACH OTHER, BUT IT'S IMPORTANT FOR YOU TO HELP EACH OTHER OUT.
AT TIMES, YOU NEED TO REACH OUT A HELPING HAND...
YOU COULD SAY THAT SPIRIT IS WHAT SAVED ASHIROGI THIS TIME.
...
HATTORI MUST HAVE WANTED TO BE ASHIROGI'S EDITOR. MAYBE THIS IS FOR THE BEST.
A-ANYWAY, TH-THANK YOU VERY MUCH.

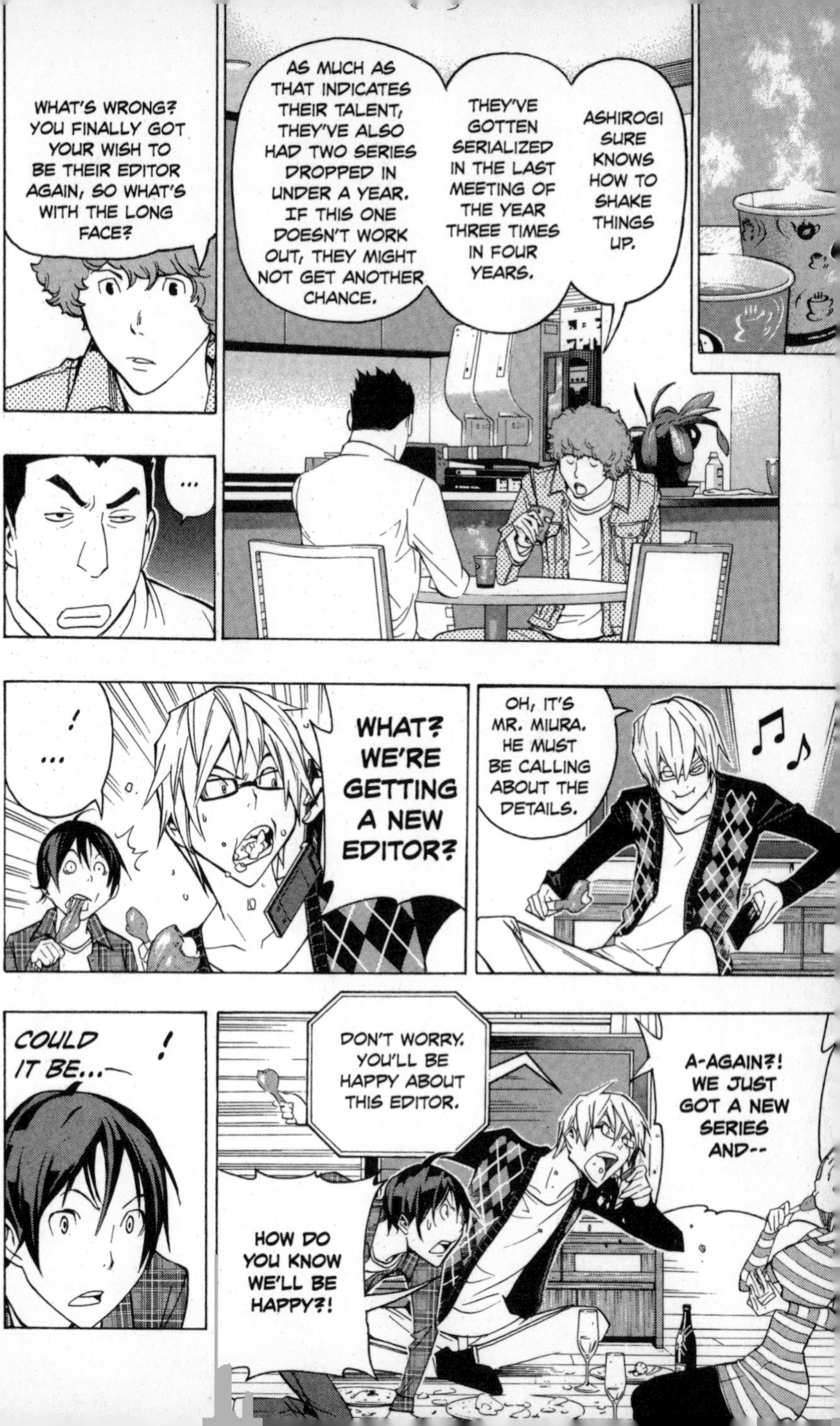

ASHIROGI SURE KNOWS HOW TO SHAKE THINGS UP.
THEY'VE GOTTEN SERIALIZED IN THE LAST MEETING OF THE YEAR THREE TIMES IN FOUR YEARS.
AS MUCH AS THAT INDICATES THEIR TALENT, THEY'VE ALSO HAD TWO SERIES DROPPED IN UNDER A YEAR. IF THIS ONE DOESN'T WORK OUT, THEY MIGHT NOT GET ANOTHER CHANCE.
WHAT'S WRONG? YOU FINALLY GOT YOUR WISH TO BE THEIR EDITOR AGAIN, SO WHAT'S WITH THE LONG FACE?
...
OH, IT'S MR. MIURA. HE MUST BE CALLING ABOUT THE DETAILS.
WHAT? WE'RE GETTING A NEW EDITOR?
!
...
A-AGAIN?! WE JUST GOT A NEW SERIES AND--
DON'T WORRY. YOU'LL BE HAPPY ABOUT THIS EDITOR.
HOW DO YOU KNOW WE'LL BE HAPPY?!
COULD IT BE...
!

READ THIS WAY

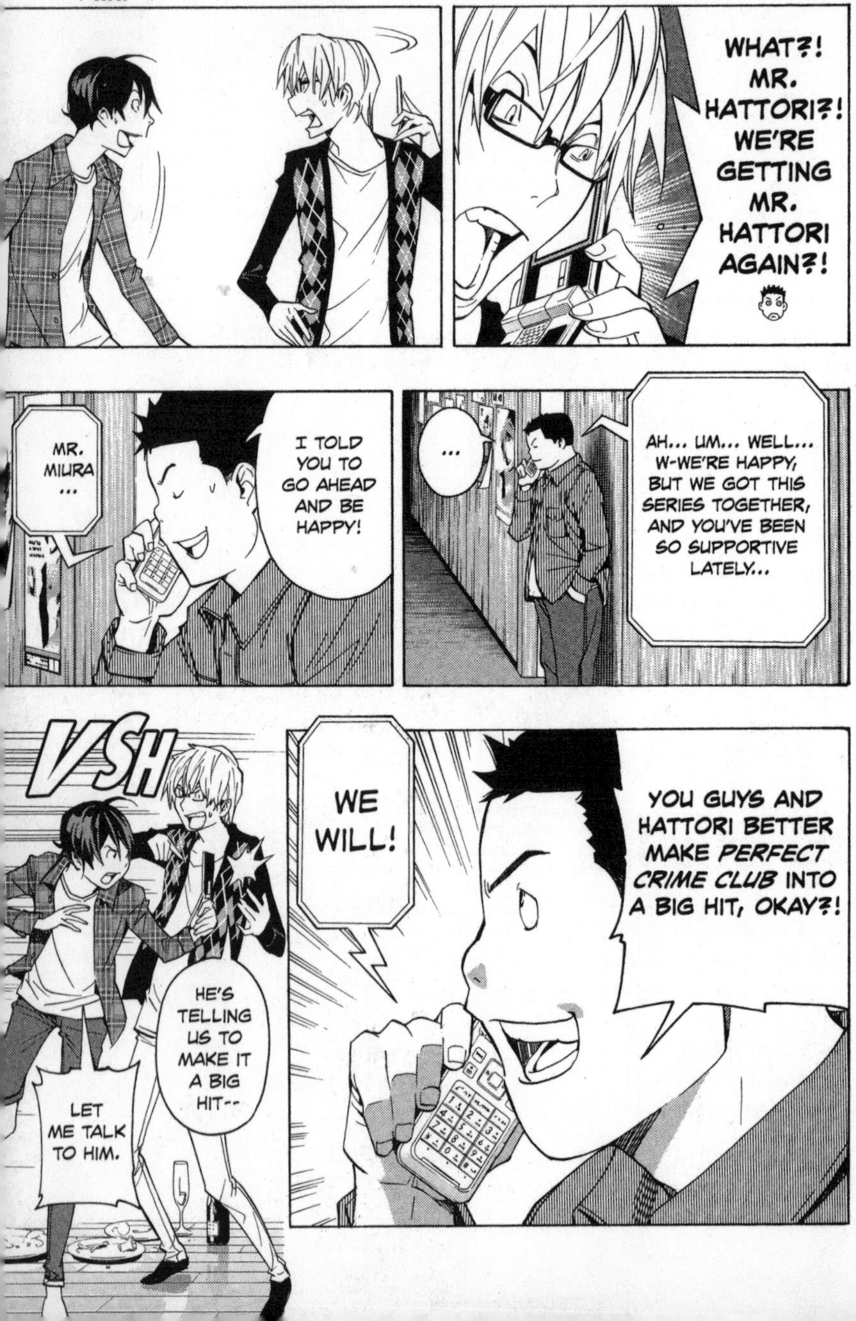
WHAT?! MR. HATTORI?! WE'RE GETTING MR. HATTORI AGAIN?!
AH... UM... WELL... W-WE'RE HAPPY, BUT WE GOT THIS SERIES TOGETHER, AND YOU'VE BEEN SO SUPPORTIVE LATELY...
...
I TOLD YOU TO GO AHEAD AND BE HAPPY!
MR. MIURA ...
YOU GUYS AND HATTORI BETTER MAKE *PERFECT CRIME CLUB* INTO A BIG HIT, OKAY?!
WE WILL!
VSH
HE'S TELLING US TO MAKE IT A BIG HIT--
LET ME TALK TO HIM.

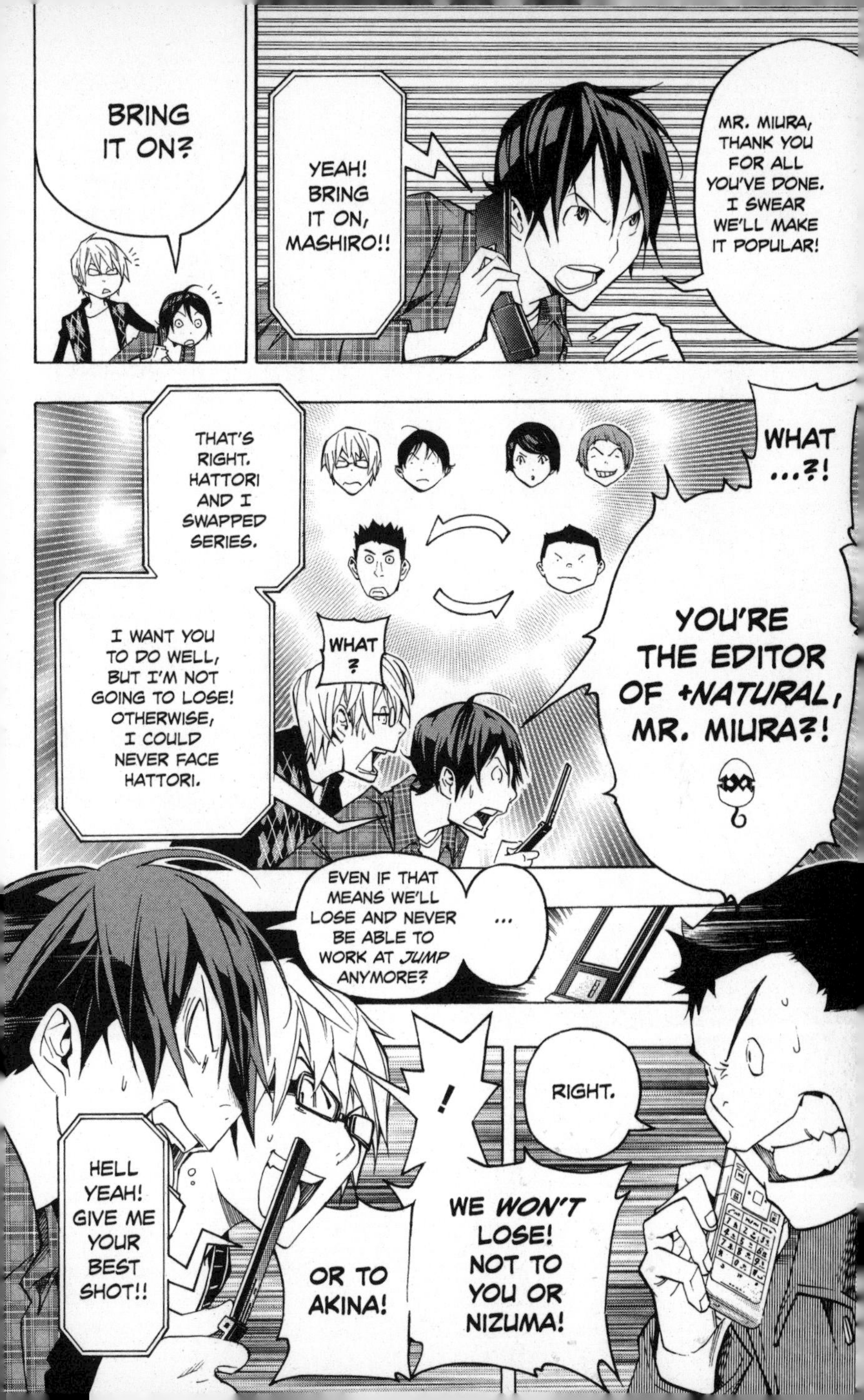
MR. MIURA, THANK YOU FOR ALL YOU'VE DONE. I SWEAR WE'LL MAKE IT POPULAR!
YEAH! BRING IT ON, MASHIRO!!
BRING IT ON?
WHAT ...?!
YOU'RE THE EDITOR OF +*NATURAL*, MR. MIURA?!
THAT'S RIGHT. HATTORI AND I SWAPPED SERIES.
WHAT?
I WANT YOU TO DO WELL, BUT I'M NOT GOING TO LOSE! OTHERWISE, I COULD NEVER FACE HATTORI.
...
EVEN IF THAT MEANS WE'LL LOSE AND NEVER BE ABLE TO WORK AT *JUMP* ANYMORE?
RIGHT.
WE *WON'T* LOSE! NOT TO YOU OR NIZUMA!
OR TO AKINA!
!
HELL YEAH! GIVE ME YOUR BEST SHOT!!

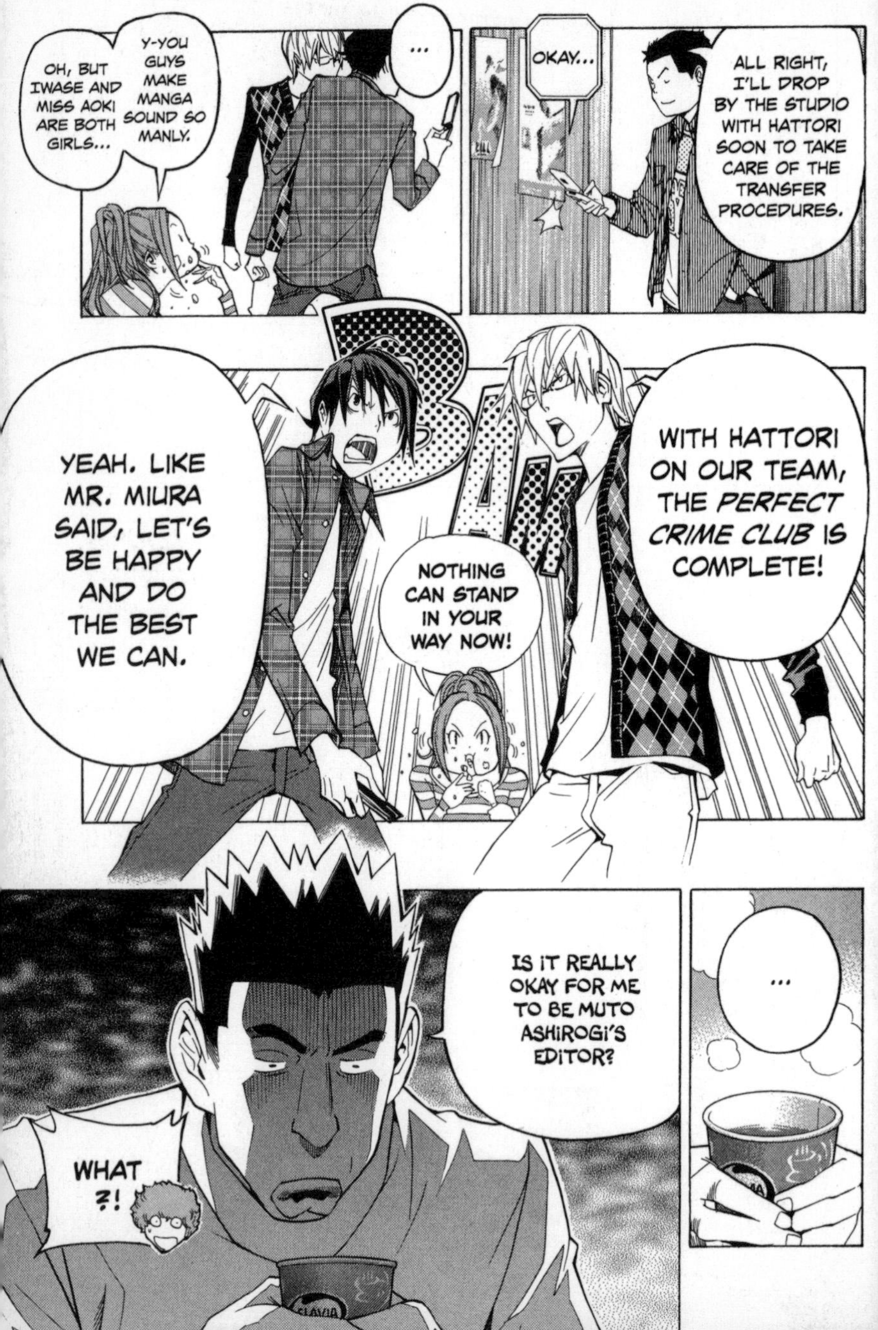
ALL RIGHT, I'LL DROP BY THE STUDIO WITH HATTORI SOON TO TAKE CARE OF THE TRANSFER PROCEDURES.
OKAY...
...
Y-YOU GUYS MAKE MANGA SOUND SO MANLY.
OH, BUT IWASE AND MISS AOKI ARE BOTH GIRLS...
BAM
WITH HATTORI ON OUR TEAM, THE *PERFECT CRIME CLUB* IS COMPLETE!
NOTHING CAN STAND IN YOUR WAY NOW!
YEAH. LIKE MR. MIURA SAID, LET'S BE HAPPY AND DO THE BEST WE CAN.
...
IS IT REALLY OKAY FOR ME TO BE MUTO ASHIROGI'S EDITOR?
WHAT?!

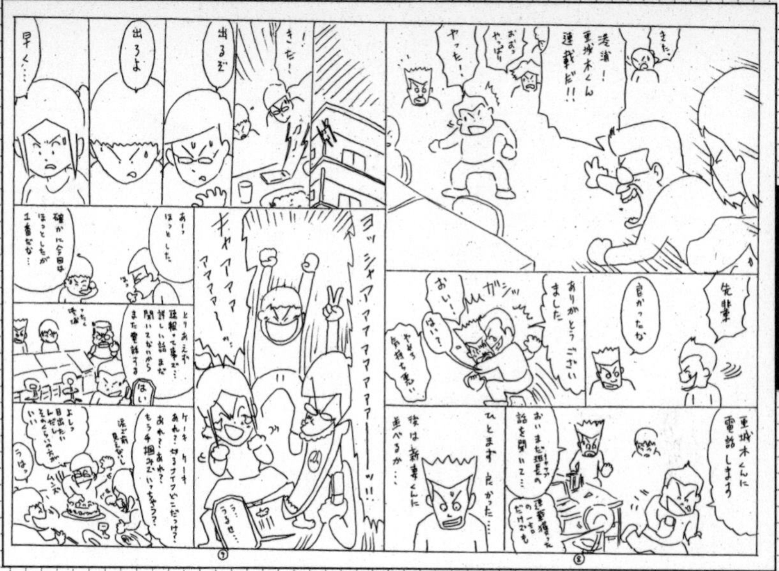
きた…
港浦！亜城木くん連載だ!!
おおっやっぱり
やった！
先輩
良かったな
ありがとうございました
ガシッ
おい！
はい？
やめろ気持ち悪い
亜城木くんに電話します
おいまだ班長の話を聞いて…
ひとまず良かった…
後は新妻くんに並べるか…
きた！
出るぞ
出るよ
早く…
ヨッシャアアアアアアアアア――ッ!!
キャアアアアアアー…
あーっほっとした
とりあえず速報で嬉しい話また電話する
はい
うっ…うるせ…
うはっ

OHBA'S STORYBOARD

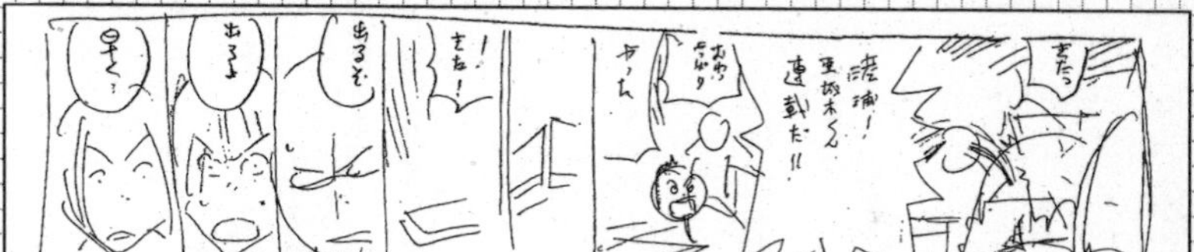

OBATA'S STORYBOARD

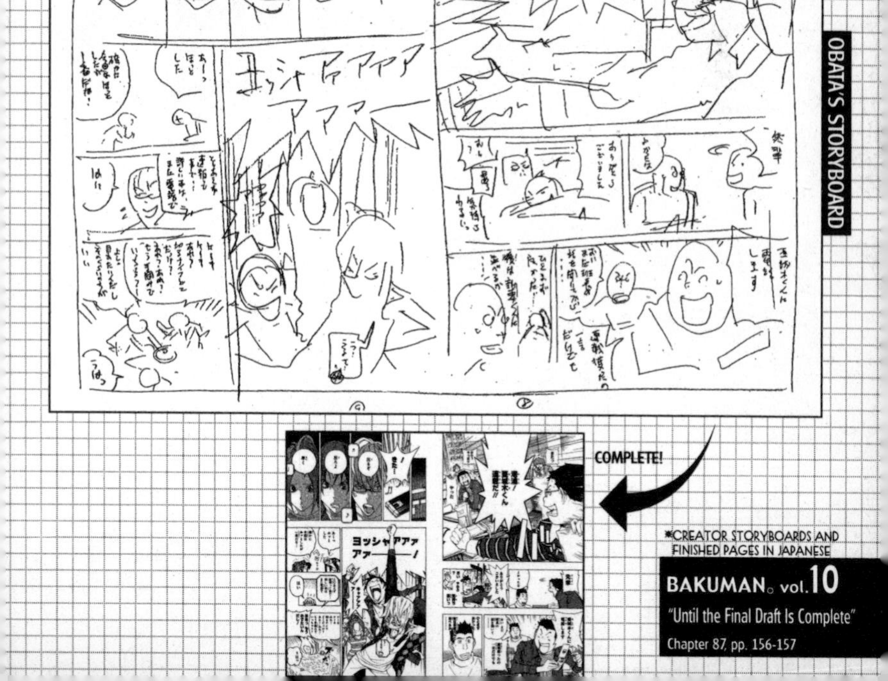
ヨッシャアァアアー！
港浦！亜城木くん連載だ!!

COMPLETE!

*CREATOR STORYBOARDS AND FINISHED PAGES IN JAPANESE

BAKUMAN。vol.10

"Until the Final Draft Is Complete"

Chapter 87, pp. 156-157

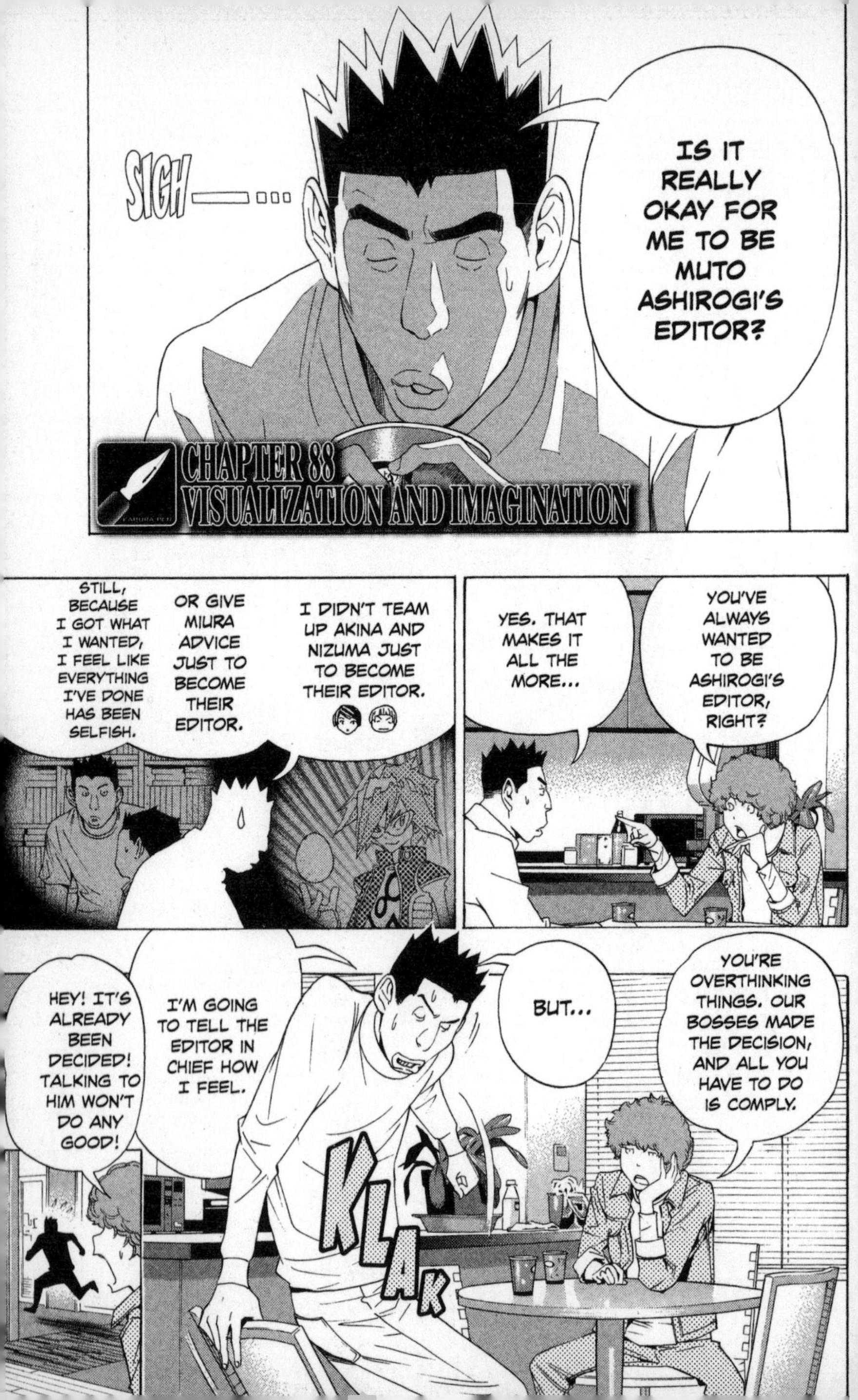
IS IT REALLY OKAY FOR ME TO BE MUTO ASHIROGI'S EDITOR?
SIGH—...
CHAPTER 88
VISUALIZATION AND IMAGINATION
YOU'VE ALWAYS WANTED TO BE ASHIROGI'S EDITOR, RIGHT?
YES. THAT MAKES IT ALL THE MORE...
I DIDN'T TEAM UP AKINA AND NIZUMA JUST TO BECOME THEIR EDITOR.
OR GIVE MIURA ADVICE JUST TO BECOME THEIR EDITOR.
STILL, BECAUSE I GOT WHAT I WANTED, I FEEL LIKE EVERYTHING I'VE DONE HAS BEEN SELFISH.
YOU'RE OVERTHINKING THINGS. OUR BOSSES MADE THE DECISION, AND ALL YOU HAVE TO DO IS COMPLY.
BUT...
I'M GOING TO TELL THE EDITOR IN CHIEF HOW I FEEL.
KLAK
HEY! IT'S ALREADY BEEN DECIDED! TALKING TO HIM WON'T DO ANY GOOD!

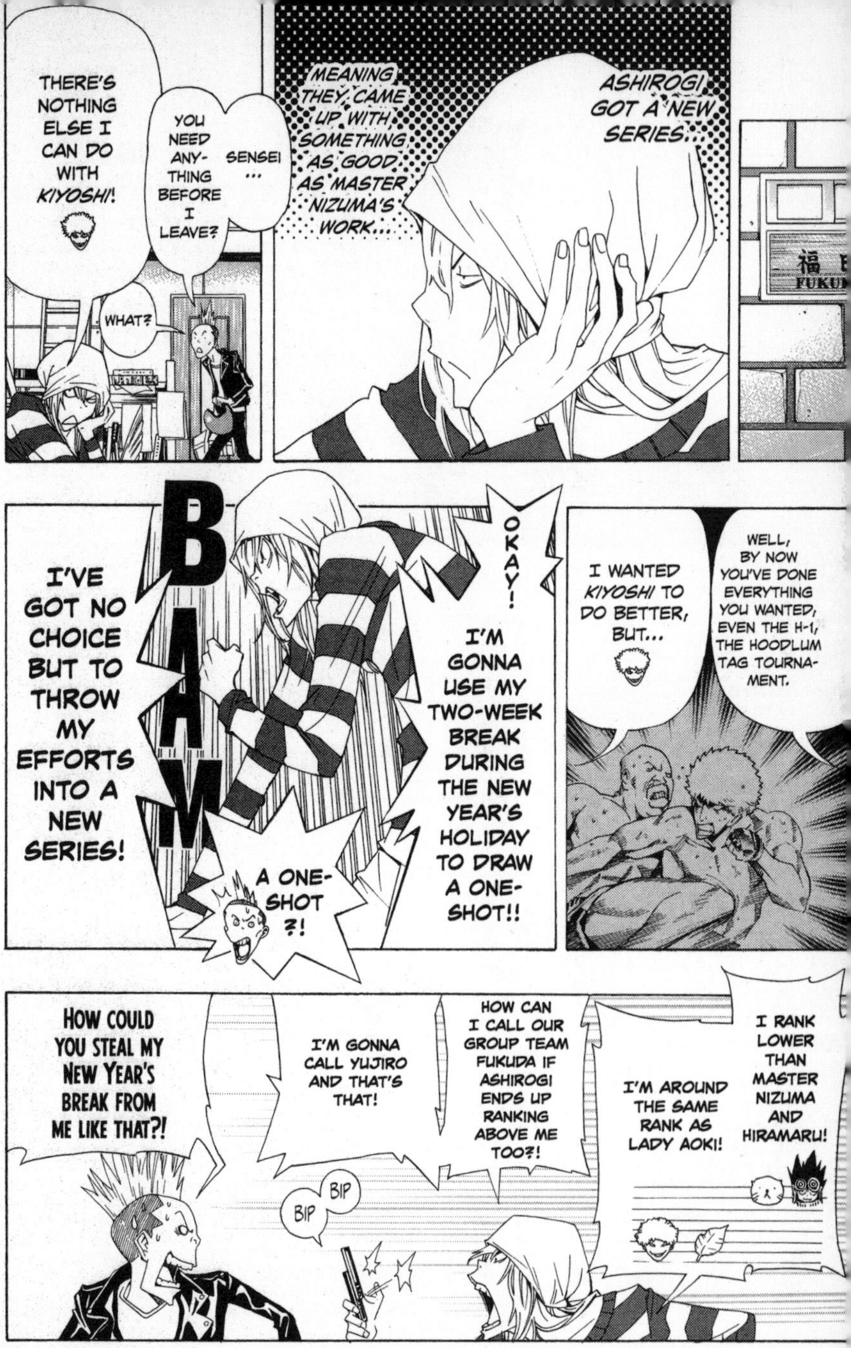

福 田
FUKU
ASHIROGI GOT A NEW SERIES...
MEANING THEY CAME UP WITH SOMETHING AS GOOD AS MASTER NIZUMA'S WORK...
SENSEI...
YOU NEED ANYTHING BEFORE I LEAVE?
THERE'S NOTHING ELSE I CAN DO WITH *KIYOSHI*!
WHAT?
WELL, BY NOW YOU'VE DONE EVERYTHING YOU WANTED, EVEN THE H-1, THE HOODLUM TAG TOURNAMENT.
I WANTED *KIYOSHI* TO DO BETTER, BUT...
OKAY!
I'M GONNA USE MY TWO-WEEK BREAK DURING THE NEW YEAR'S HOLIDAY TO DRAW A ONE-SHOT!!
BAM
I'VE GOT NO CHOICE BUT TO THROW MY EFFORTS INTO A NEW SERIES!
A ONE-SHOT ?!
I RANK LOWER THAN MASTER NIZUMA AND HIRAMARU!
I'M AROUND THE SAME RANK AS LADY AOKI!
HOW CAN I CALL OUR GROUP TEAM FUKUDA IF ASHIROGI ENDS UP RANKING ABOVE ME TOO?!
I'M GONNA CALL YUJIRO AND THAT'S THAT!
BIP
BIP
HOW COULD YOU STEAL MY NEW YEAR'S BREAK FROM ME LIKE THAT?!

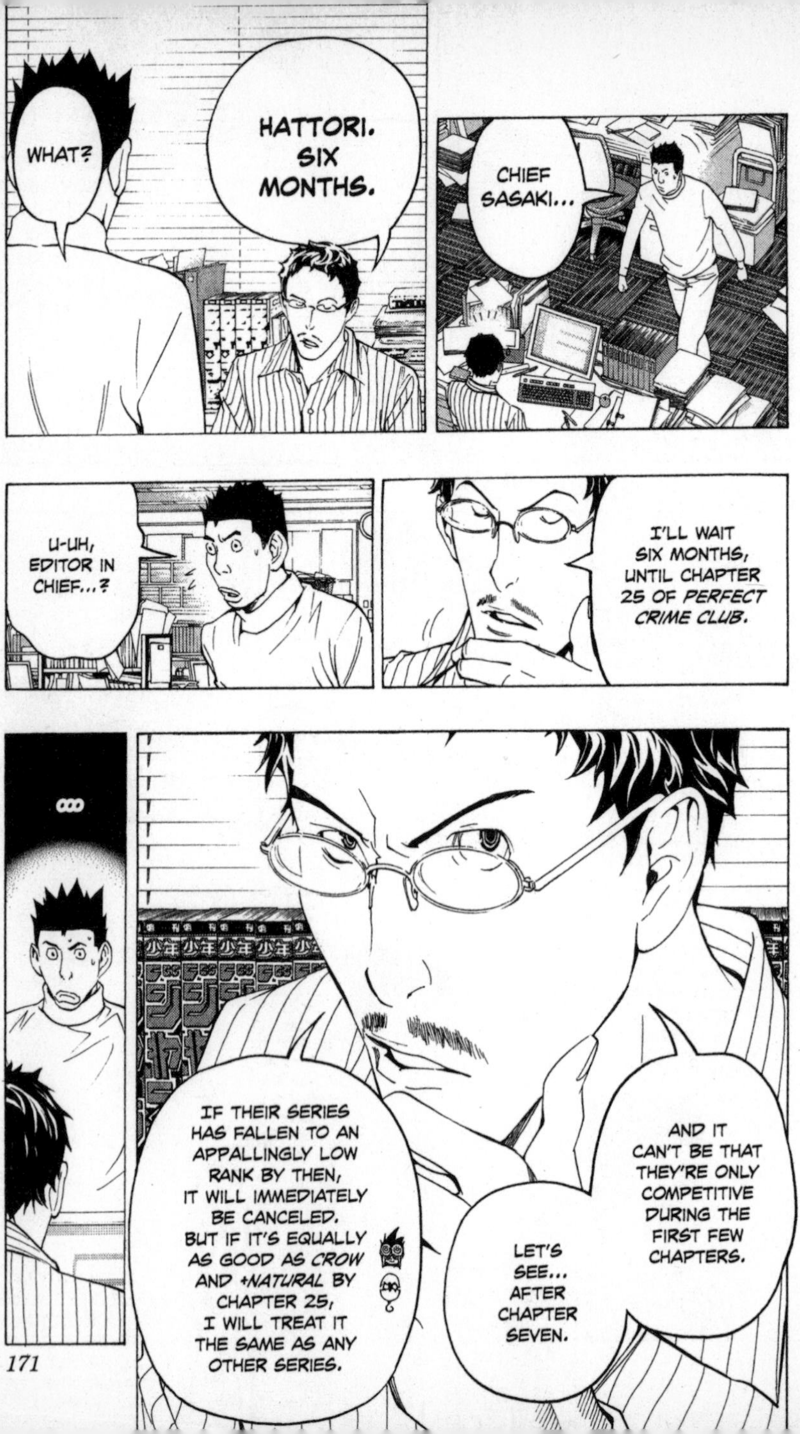
CHIEF SASAKI...
HATTORI. SIX MONTHS.
WHAT?
I'LL WAIT SIX MONTHS, UNTIL CHAPTER 25 OF *PERFECT CRIME CLUB.*
U-UH, EDITOR IN CHIEF...?
AND IT CAN'T BE THAT THEY'RE ONLY COMPETITIVE DURING THE FIRST FEW CHAPTERS.
LET'S SEE... AFTER CHAPTER SEVEN.
IF THEIR SERIES HAS FALLEN TO AN APPALLINGLY LOW RANK BY THEN, IT WILL IMMEDIATELY BE CANCELED. BUT IF IT'S EQUALLY AS GOOD AS *CROW* AND *+NATURAL* BY CHAPTER 25, I WILL TREAT IT THE SAME AS ANY OTHER SERIES.
...

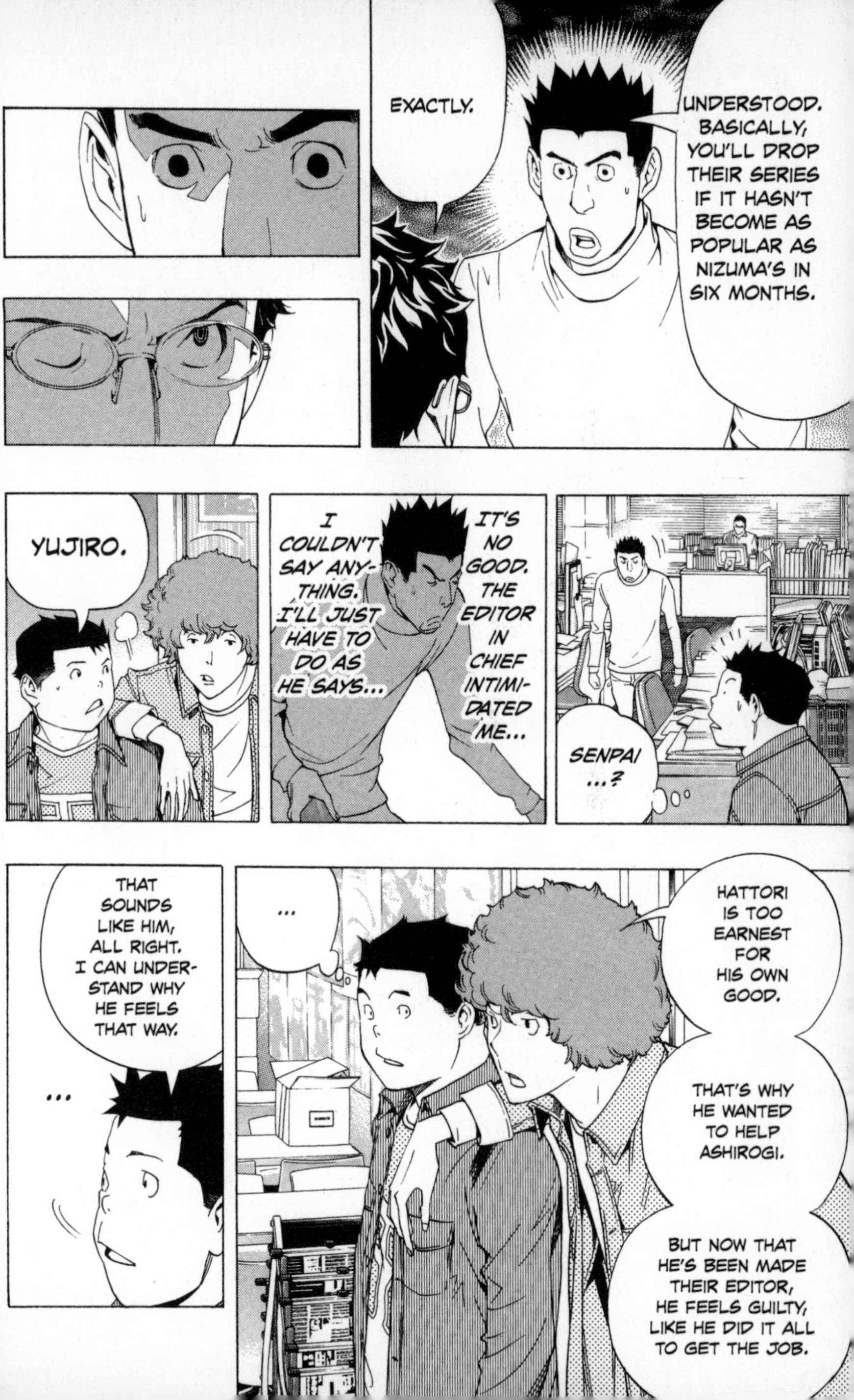
UNDERSTOOD. BASICALLY, YOU'LL DROP THEIR SERIES IF IT HASN'T BECOME AS POPULAR AS NIZUMA'S IN SIX MONTHS.
EXACTLY.
SENPAI ...?
IT'S NO GOOD. THE EDITOR IN CHIEF INTIMIDATED ME...
I COULDN'T SAY ANYTHING. I'LL JUST HAVE TO DO AS HE SAYS...
YUJIRO.
HATTORI IS TOO EARNEST FOR HIS OWN GOOD.
THAT'S WHY HE WANTED TO HELP ASHIROGI.
BUT NOW THAT HE'S BEEN MADE THEIR EDITOR, HE FEELS GUILTY, LIKE HE DID IT ALL TO GET THE JOB.
...
THAT SOUNDS LIKE HIM, ALL RIGHT. I CAN UNDERSTAND WHY HE FEELS THAT WAY.
...

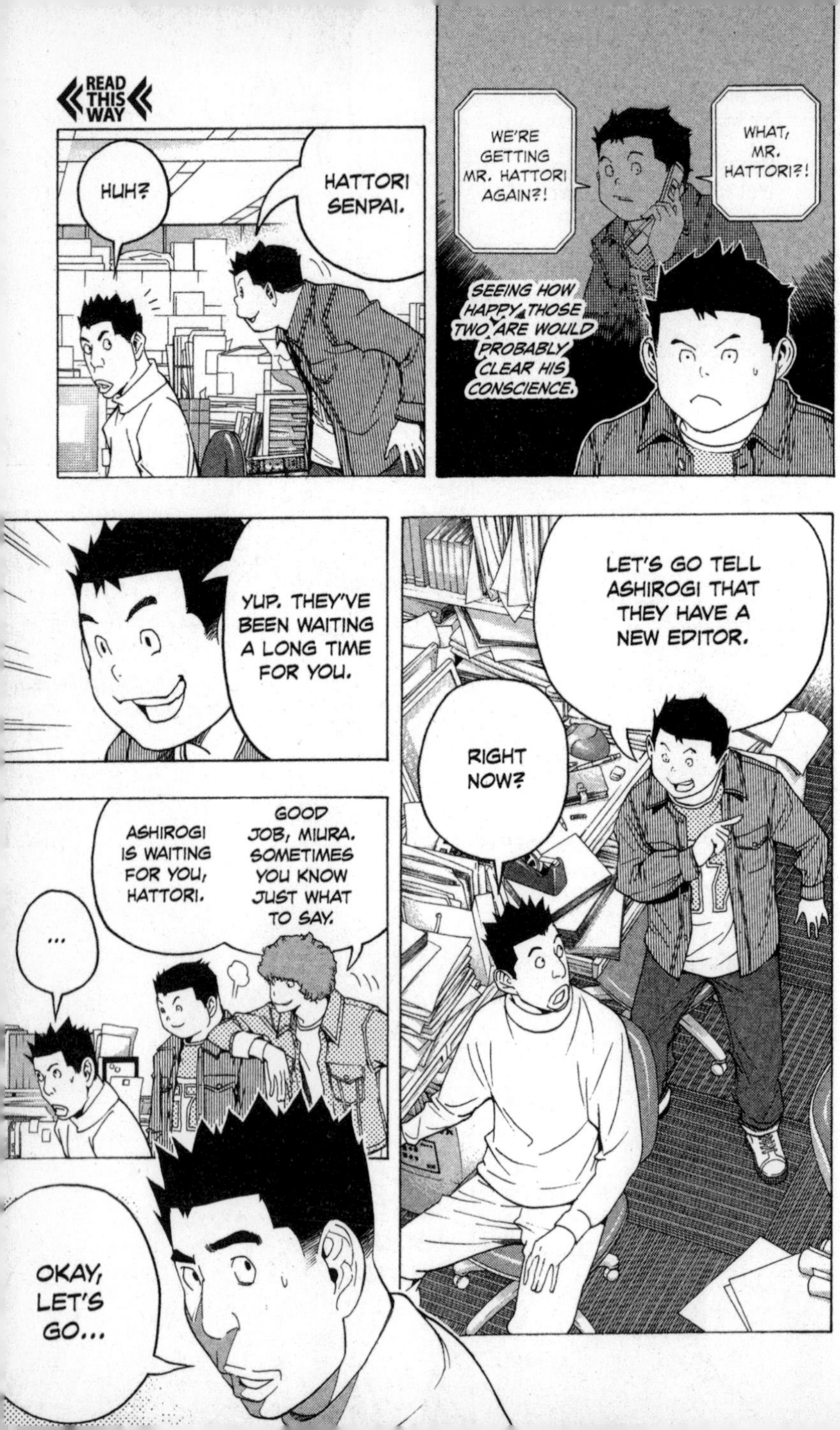
READ THIS WAY
WHAT, MR. HATTORI?!
WE'RE GETTING MR. HATTORI AGAIN?!
SEEING HOW HAPPY THOSE TWO ARE WOULD PROBABLY CLEAR HIS CONSCIENCE.
HATTORI SENPAI.
HUH?
LET'S GO TELL ASHIROGI THAT THEY HAVE A NEW EDITOR.
RIGHT NOW?
YUP. THEY'VE BEEN WAITING A LONG TIME FOR YOU.
GOOD JOB, MIURA. SOMETIMES YOU KNOW JUST WHAT TO SAY.
ASHIROGI IS WAITING FOR YOU, HATTORI.
...
OKAY, LET'S GO...

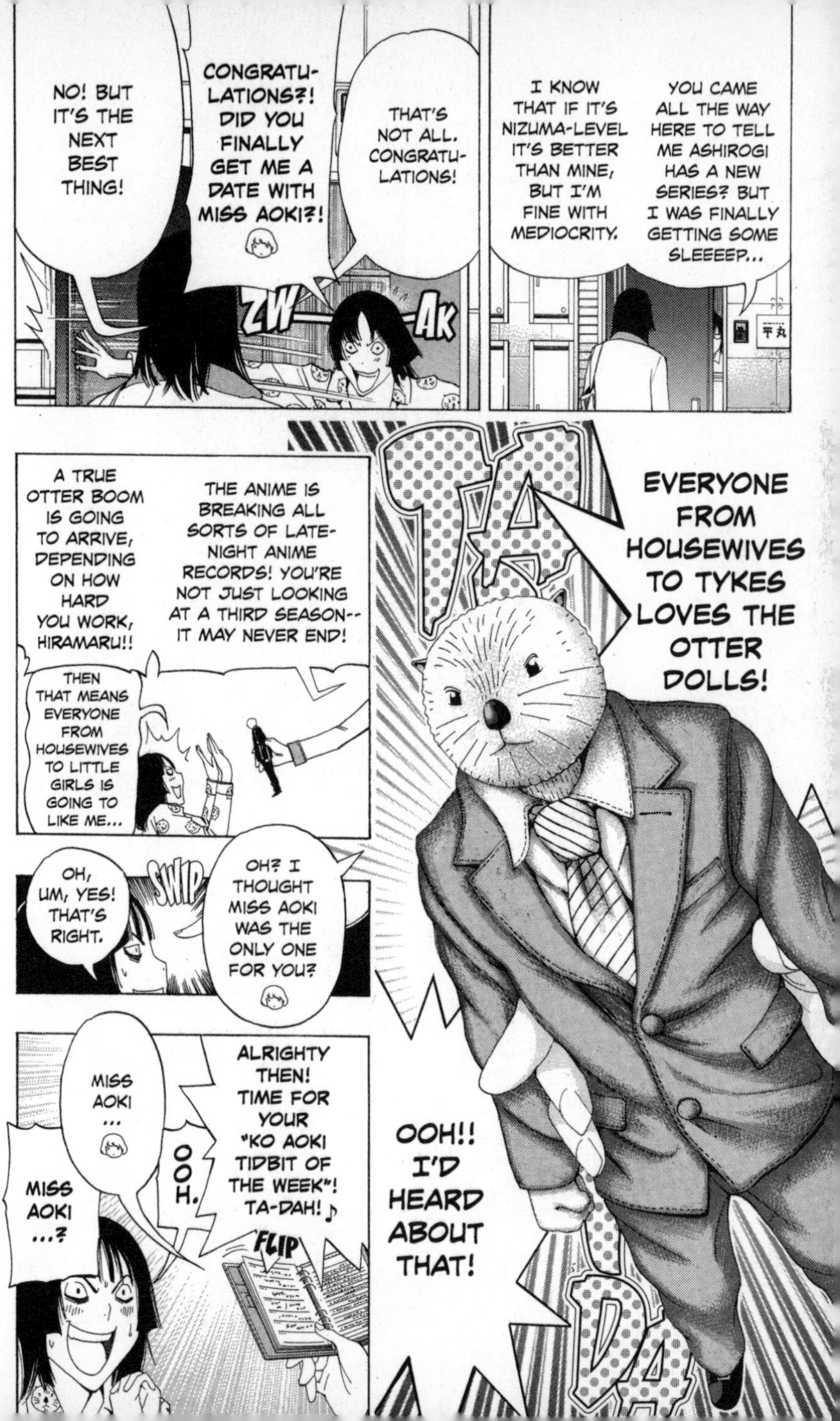
YOU CAME ALL THE WAY HERE TO TELL ME ASHIROGI HAS A NEW SERIES? BUT I WAS FINALLY GETTING SOME SLEEEEP...
I KNOW THAT IF IT'S NIZUMA-LEVEL IT'S BETTER THAN MINE, BUT I'M FINE WITH MEDIOCRITY.
THAT'S NOT ALL. CONGRATULATIONS!
CONGRATULATIONS?! DID YOU FINALLY GET ME A DATE WITH MISS AOKI?!
ZW-AK
NO! BUT IT'S THE NEXT BEST THING!
EVERYONE FROM HOUSEWIVES TO TYKES LOVES THE OTTER DOLLS!
OOH!! I'D HEARD ABOUT THAT!
THE ANIME IS BREAKING ALL SORTS OF LATE-NIGHT ANIME RECORDS! YOU'RE NOT JUST LOOKING AT A THIRD SEASON-- IT MAY NEVER END!
A TRUE OTTER BOOM IS GOING TO ARRIVE, DEPENDING ON HOW HARD YOU WORK, HIRAMARU!!
THEN THAT MEANS EVERYONE FROM HOUSEWIVES TO LITTLE GIRLS IS GOING TO LIKE ME...
OH? I THOUGHT MISS AOKI WAS THE ONLY ONE FOR YOU?
SWIP
OH, UM, YES! THAT'S RIGHT.
ALRIGHTY THEN! TIME FOR YOUR "KO AOKI TIDBIT OF THE WEEK"! TA-DAH! ♪
OOH.
MISS AOKI ...
MISS AOKI ...?
FLIP

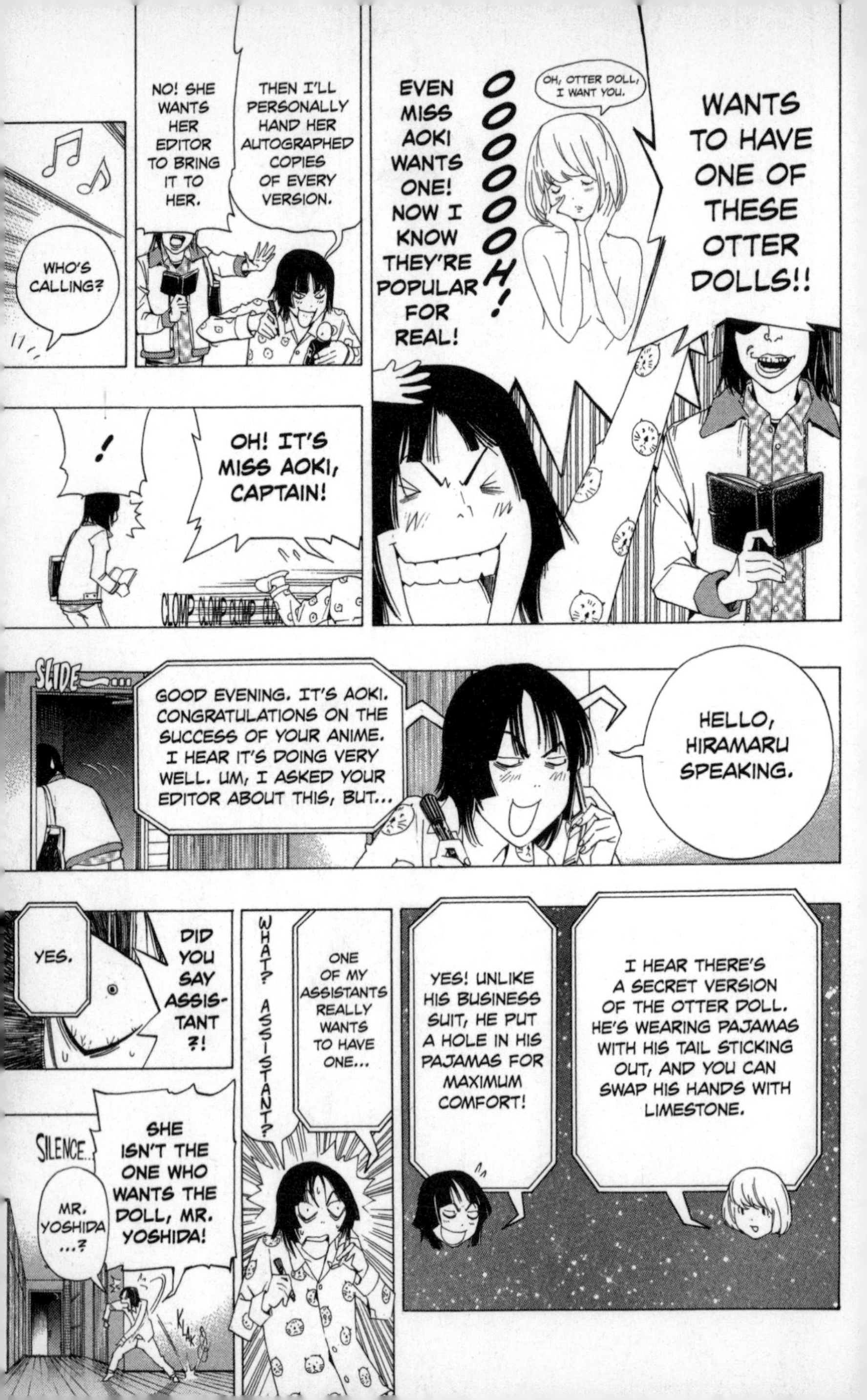

WANTS TO HAVE ONE OF THESE OTTER DOLLS!!
OH, OTTER DOLL, I WANT YOU.
OOOOOOOH!
EVEN MISS AOKI WANTS ONE! NOW I KNOW THEY'RE POPULAR FOR REAL!
THEN I'LL PERSONALLY HAND HER AUTOGRAPHED COPIES OF EVERY VERSION.
NO! SHE WANTS HER EDITOR TO BRING IT TO HER.
WHO'S CALLING?
OH! IT'S MISS AOKI, CAPTAIN!
!
CLOMP CLOMP CLOMP CLO
HELLO, HIRAMARU SPEAKING.
GOOD EVENING. IT'S AOKI. CONGRATULATIONS ON THE SUCCESS OF YOUR ANIME. I HEAR IT'S DOING VERY WELL. UM, I ASKED YOUR EDITOR ABOUT THIS, BUT...
SLIDE...
I HEAR THERE'S A SECRET VERSION OF THE OTTER DOLL. HE'S WEARING PAJAMAS WITH HIS TAIL STICKING OUT, AND YOU CAN SWAP HIS HANDS WITH LIMESTONE.
YES! UNLIKE HIS BUSINESS SUIT, HE PUT A HOLE IN HIS PAJAMAS FOR MAXIMUM COMFORT!
ONE OF MY ASSISTANTS REALLY WANTS TO HAVE ONE...
WHAT? ASSISTANT?
DID YOU SAY ASSISTANT?!
YES.
SHE ISN'T THE ONE WHO WANTS THE DOLL, MR. YOSHIDA!
SILENCE...
MR. YOSHIDA...?
KLAK

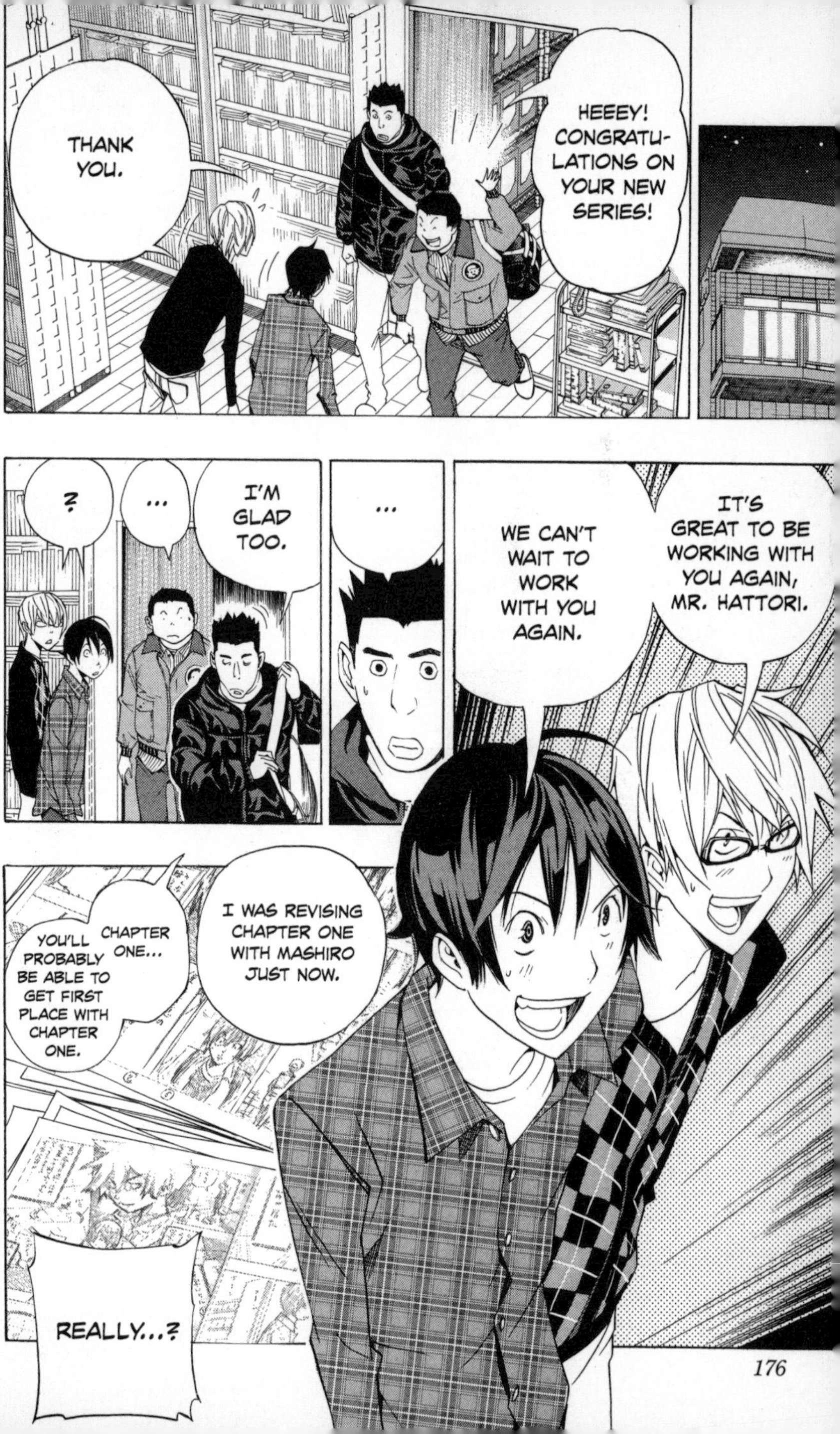
HEEEY! CONGRATULATIONS ON YOUR NEW SERIES!
THANK YOU.
IT'S GREAT TO BE WORKING WITH YOU AGAIN, MR. HATTORI.
WE CAN'T WAIT TO WORK WITH YOU AGAIN.
...
I'M GLAD TOO.
...
?
I WAS REVISING CHAPTER ONE WITH MASHIRO JUST NOW.
CHAPTER ONE...
YOU'LL PROBABLY BE ABLE TO GET FIRST PLACE WITH CHAPTER ONE.
REALLY...?

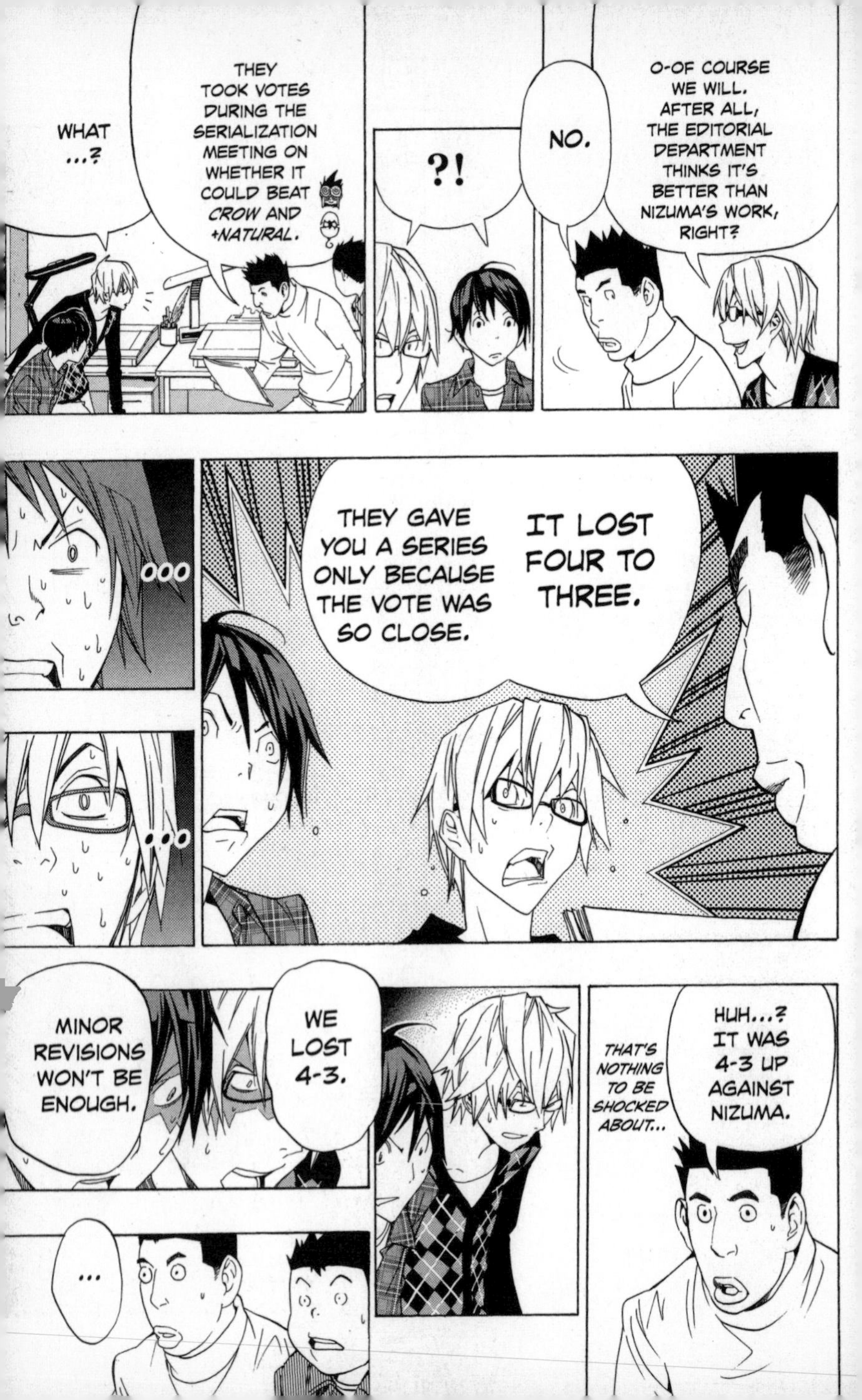
O-OF COURSE WE WILL. AFTER ALL, THE EDITORIAL DEPARTMENT THINKS IT'S BETTER THAN NIZUMA'S WORK, RIGHT?
NO.
?!
THEY TOOK VOTES DURING THE SERIALIZATION MEETING ON WHETHER IT COULD BEAT *CROW* AND *+NATURAL*.
WHAT ...?
IT LOST FOUR TO THREE.
THEY GAVE YOU A SERIES ONLY BECAUSE THE VOTE WAS SO CLOSE.
HUH...? IT WAS 4-3 UP AGAINST NIZUMA.
THAT'S NOTHING TO BE SHOCKED ABOUT...
WE LOST 4-3.
MINOR REVISIONS WON'T BE ENOUGH.
...

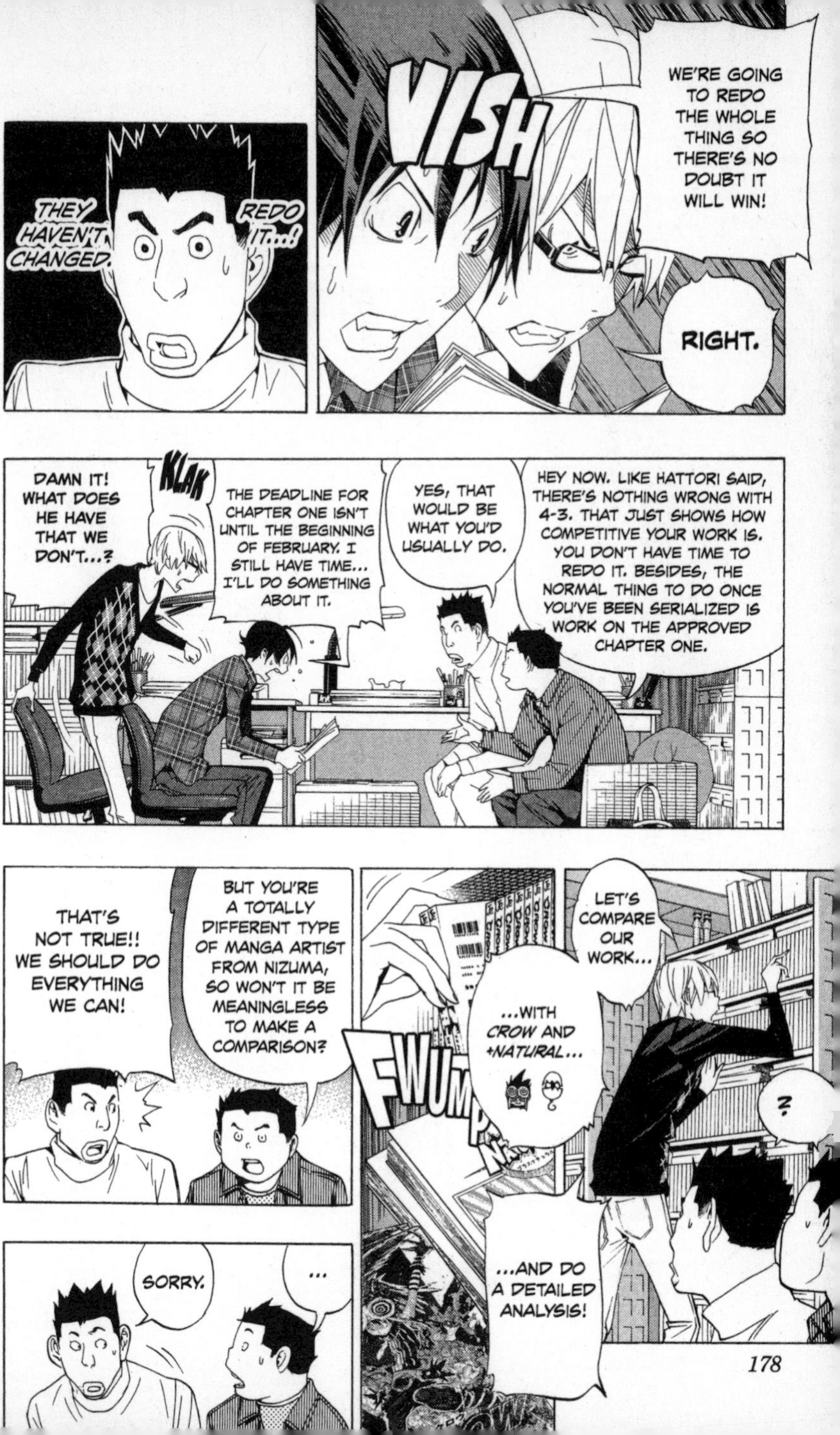
VISH
WE'RE GOING TO REDO THE WHOLE THING SO THERE'S NO DOUBT IT WILL WIN!
RIGHT.
REDO IT...!
THEY HAVEN'T CHANGED.
HEY NOW. LIKE HATTORI SAID, THERE'S NOTHING WRONG WITH 4-3. THAT JUST SHOWS HOW COMPETITIVE YOUR WORK IS. YOU DON'T HAVE TIME TO REDO IT. BESIDES, THE NORMAL THING TO DO ONCE YOU'VE BEEN SERIALIZED IS WORK ON THE APPROVED CHAPTER ONE.
YES, THAT WOULD BE WHAT YOU'D USUALLY DO.
THE DEADLINE FOR CHAPTER ONE ISN'T UNTIL THE BEGINNING OF FEBRUARY. I STILL HAVE TIME... I'LL DO SOMETHING ABOUT IT.
KLAK
DAMN IT! WHAT DOES HE HAVE THAT WE DON'T...?
LET'S COMPARE OUR WORK...
...WITH *CROW* AND *+NATURAL*...
FWUMP
?
...AND DO A DETAILED ANALYSIS!
BUT YOU'RE A TOTALLY DIFFERENT TYPE OF MANGA ARTIST FROM NIZUMA, SO WON'T IT BE MEANINGLESS TO MAKE A COMPARISON?
THAT'S NOT TRUE!! WE SHOULD DO EVERYTHING WE CAN!
...
SORRY.

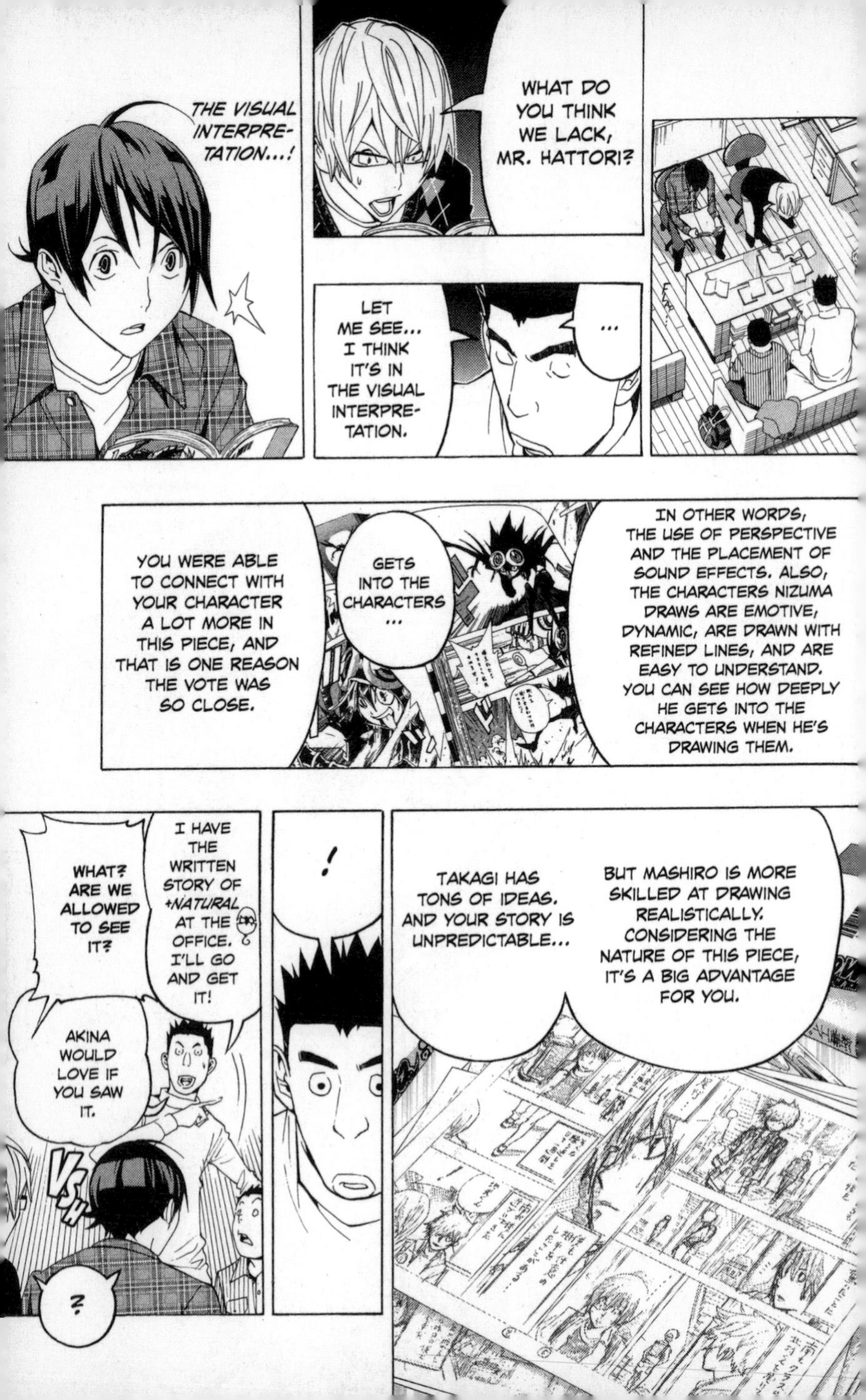
WHAT DO YOU THINK WE LACK, MR. HATTORI?
...
LET ME SEE... I THINK IT'S IN THE VISUAL INTERPRETATION.
THE VISUAL INTERPRETATION...!
IN OTHER WORDS, THE USE OF PERSPECTIVE AND THE PLACEMENT OF SOUND EFFECTS. ALSO, THE CHARACTERS NIZUMA DRAWS ARE EMOTIVE, DYNAMIC, ARE DRAWN WITH REFINED LINES, AND ARE EASY TO UNDERSTAND. YOU CAN SEE HOW DEEPLY HE GETS INTO THE CHARACTERS WHEN HE'S DRAWING THEM.
GETS INTO THE CHARACTERS ...
YOU WERE ABLE TO CONNECT WITH YOUR CHARACTER A LOT MORE IN THIS PIECE, AND THAT IS ONE REASON THE VOTE WAS SO CLOSE.
TAKAGI HAS TONS OF IDEAS. AND YOUR STORY IS UNPREDICTABLE...
BUT MASHIRO IS MORE SKILLED AT DRAWING REALISTICALLY. CONSIDERING THE NATURE OF THIS PIECE, IT'S A BIG ADVANTAGE FOR YOU.
!
I HAVE THE WRITTEN STORY OF +NATURAL AT THE OFFICE. I'LL GO AND GET IT!
WHAT? ARE WE ALLOWED TO SEE IT?
AKINA WOULD LOVE IF YOU SAW IT.
VSH
?

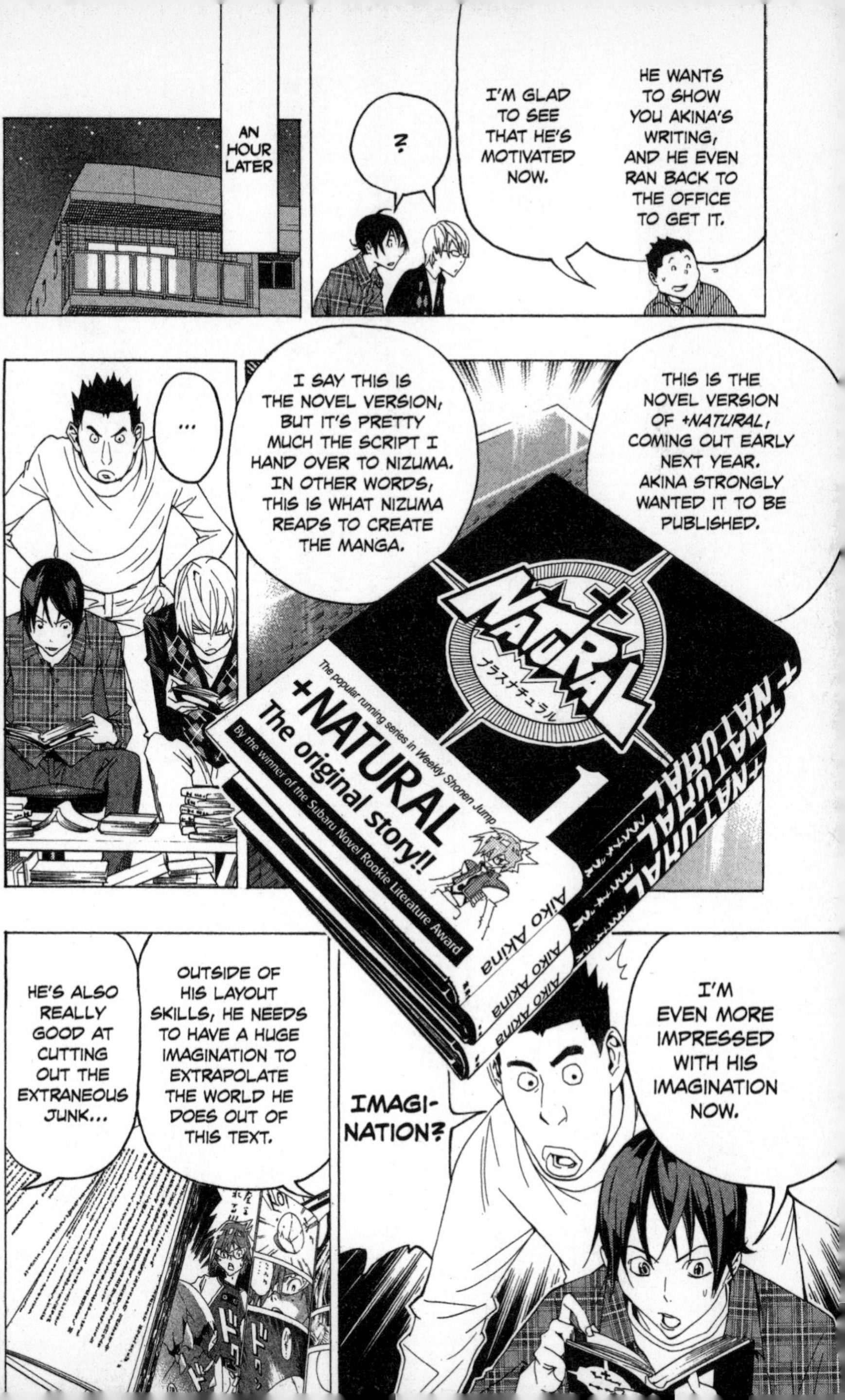
HE WANTS TO SHOW YOU AKINA'S WRITING, AND HE EVEN RAN BACK TO THE OFFICE TO GET IT.
I'M GLAD TO SEE THAT HE'S MOTIVATED NOW.
?
AN HOUR LATER
THIS IS THE NOVEL VERSION OF +NATURAL, COMING OUT EARLY NEXT YEAR. AKINA STRONGLY WANTED IT TO BE PUBLISHED.
I SAY THIS IS THE NOVEL VERSION, BUT IT'S PRETTY MUCH THE SCRIPT I HAND OVER TO NIZUMA. IN OTHER WORDS, THIS IS WHAT NIZUMA READS TO CREATE THE MANGA.
+NATURAL
プラスナチュラル
1
The popular running series in Weekly Shonen Jump
+NATURAL
The original story!!
By the winner of the Subaru Novel Rookie Literature Award
Aiko Akina
...
I'M EVEN MORE IMPRESSED WITH HIS IMAGINATION NOW.
IMAGI-NATION?
OUTSIDE OF HIS LAYOUT SKILLS, HE NEEDS TO HAVE A HUGE IMAGINATION TO EXTRAPOLATE THE WORLD HE DOES OUT OF THIS TEXT.
HE'S ALSO REALLY GOOD AT CUTTING OUT THE EXTRANEOUS JUNK...

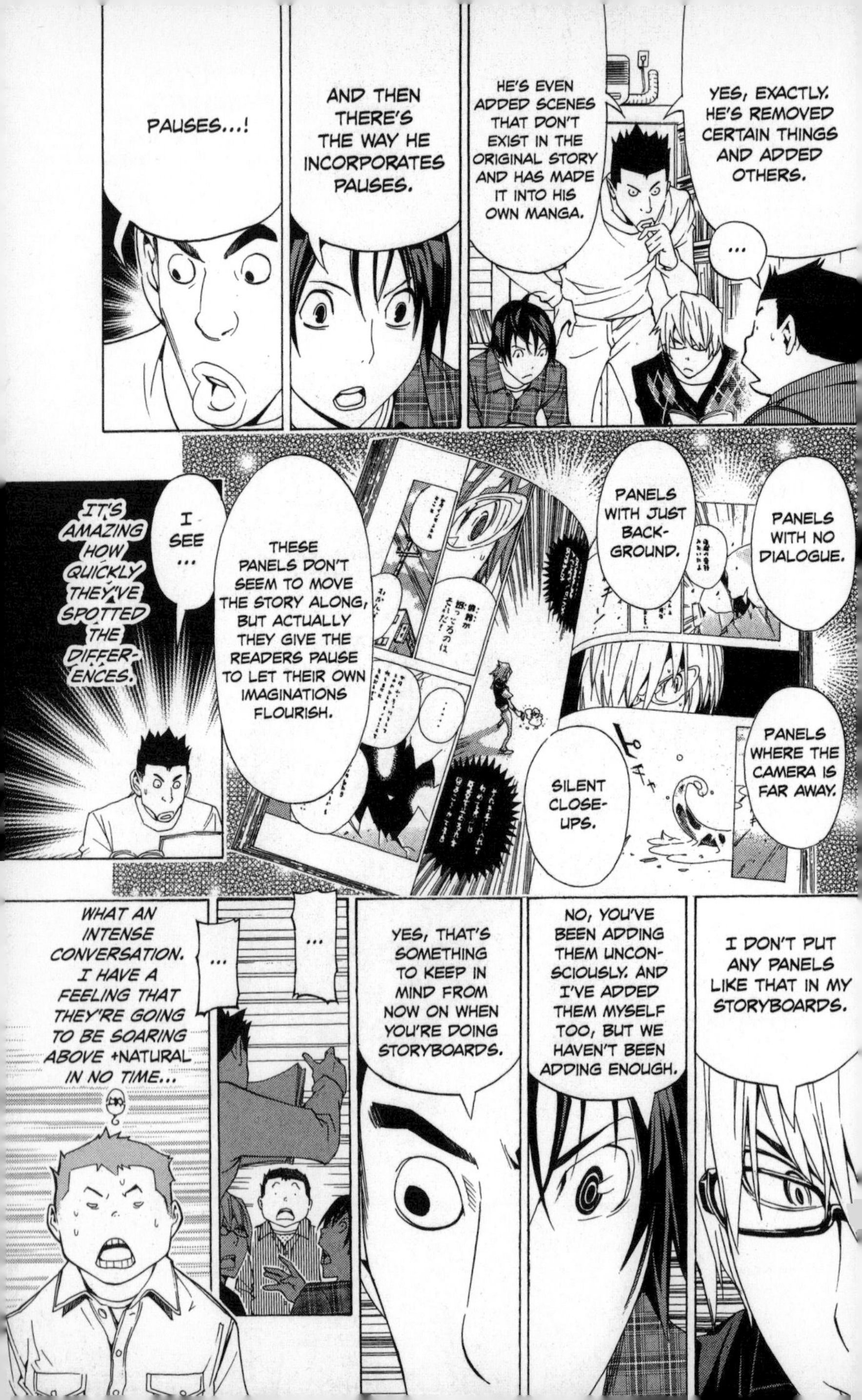
YES, EXACTLY. HE'S REMOVED CERTAIN THINGS AND ADDED OTHERS.
HE'S EVEN ADDED SCENES THAT DON'T EXIST IN THE ORIGINAL STORY AND HAS MADE IT INTO HIS OWN MANGA.
...
AND THEN THERE'S THE WAY HE INCORPORATES PAUSES.
PAUSES...!
PANELS WITH NO DIALOGUE.
PANELS WITH JUST BACK-GROUND.
PANELS WHERE THE CAMERA IS FAR AWAY.
SILENT CLOSE-UPS.
THESE PANELS DON'T SEEM TO MOVE THE STORY ALONG, BUT ACTUALLY THEY GIVE THE READERS PAUSE TO LET THEIR OWN IMAGINATIONS FLOURISH.
I SEE...
IT'S AMAZING HOW QUICKLY THEY'VE SPOTTED THE DIFFER-ENCES.
I DON'T PUT ANY PANELS LIKE THAT IN MY STORYBOARDS.
NO, YOU'VE BEEN ADDING THEM UNCON-SCIOUSLY. AND I'VE ADDED THEM MYSELF TOO, BUT WE HAVEN'T BEEN ADDING ENOUGH.
YES, THAT'S SOMETHING TO KEEP IN MIND FROM NOW ON WHEN YOU'RE DOING STORYBOARDS.
...
...
WHAT AN INTENSE CONVERSATION. I HAVE A FEELING THAT THEY'RE GOING TO BE SOARING ABOVE +NATURAL IN NO TIME...

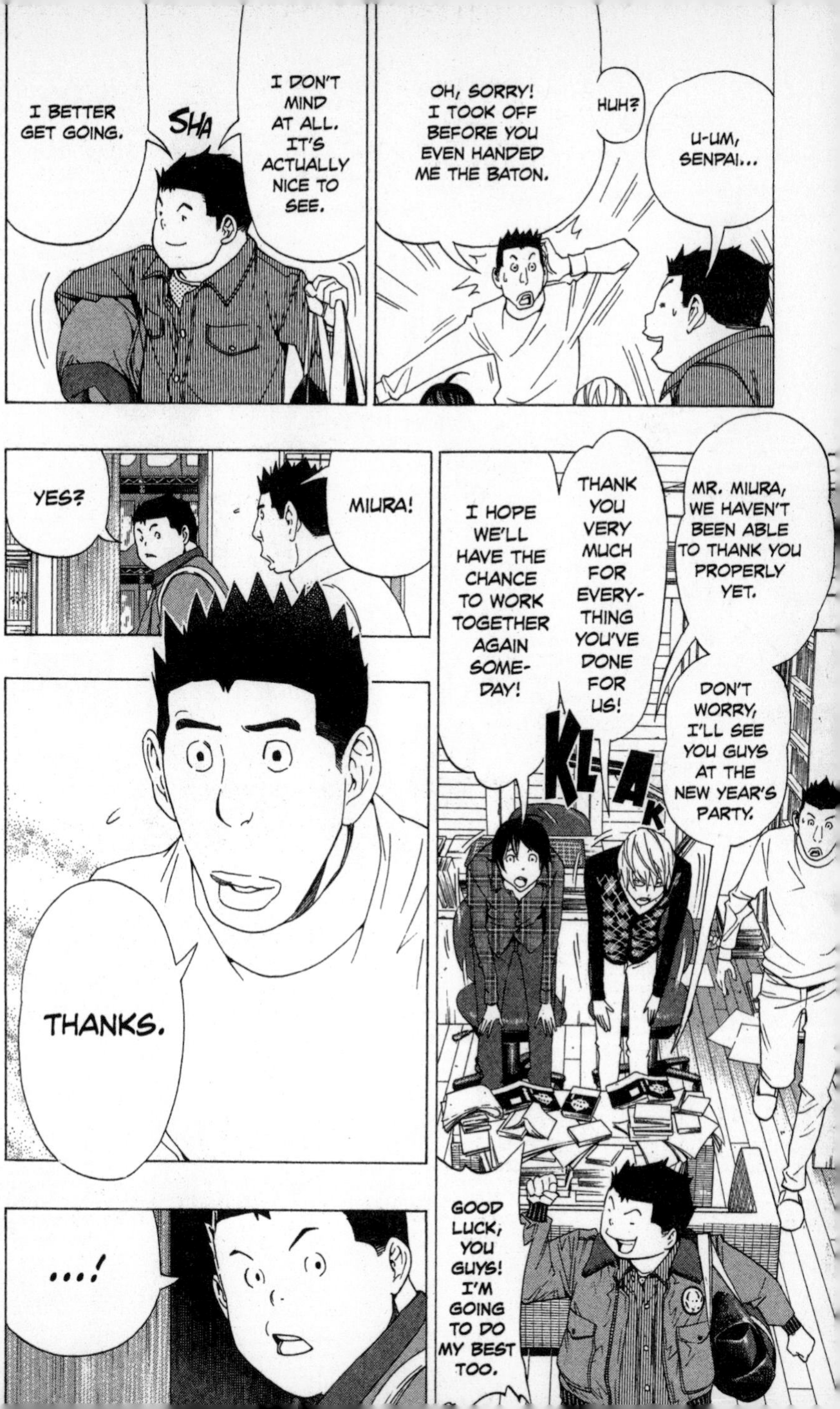
U-UM, SENPAI...
HUH?
OH, SORRY! I TOOK OFF BEFORE YOU EVEN HANDED ME THE BATON.
I DON'T MIND AT ALL. IT'S ACTUALLY NICE TO SEE.
SHA
I BETTER GET GOING.
MR. MIURA, WE HAVEN'T BEEN ABLE TO THANK YOU PROPERLY YET.
THANK YOU VERY MUCH FOR EVERY-THING YOU'VE DONE FOR US!
I HOPE WE'LL HAVE THE CHANCE TO WORK TOGETHER AGAIN SOME-DAY!
KLAK
DON'T WORRY, I'LL SEE YOU GUYS AT THE NEW YEAR'S PARTY.
GOOD LUCK, YOU GUYS! I'M GOING TO DO MY BEST TOO.
MIURA!
YES?
THANKS.
...!

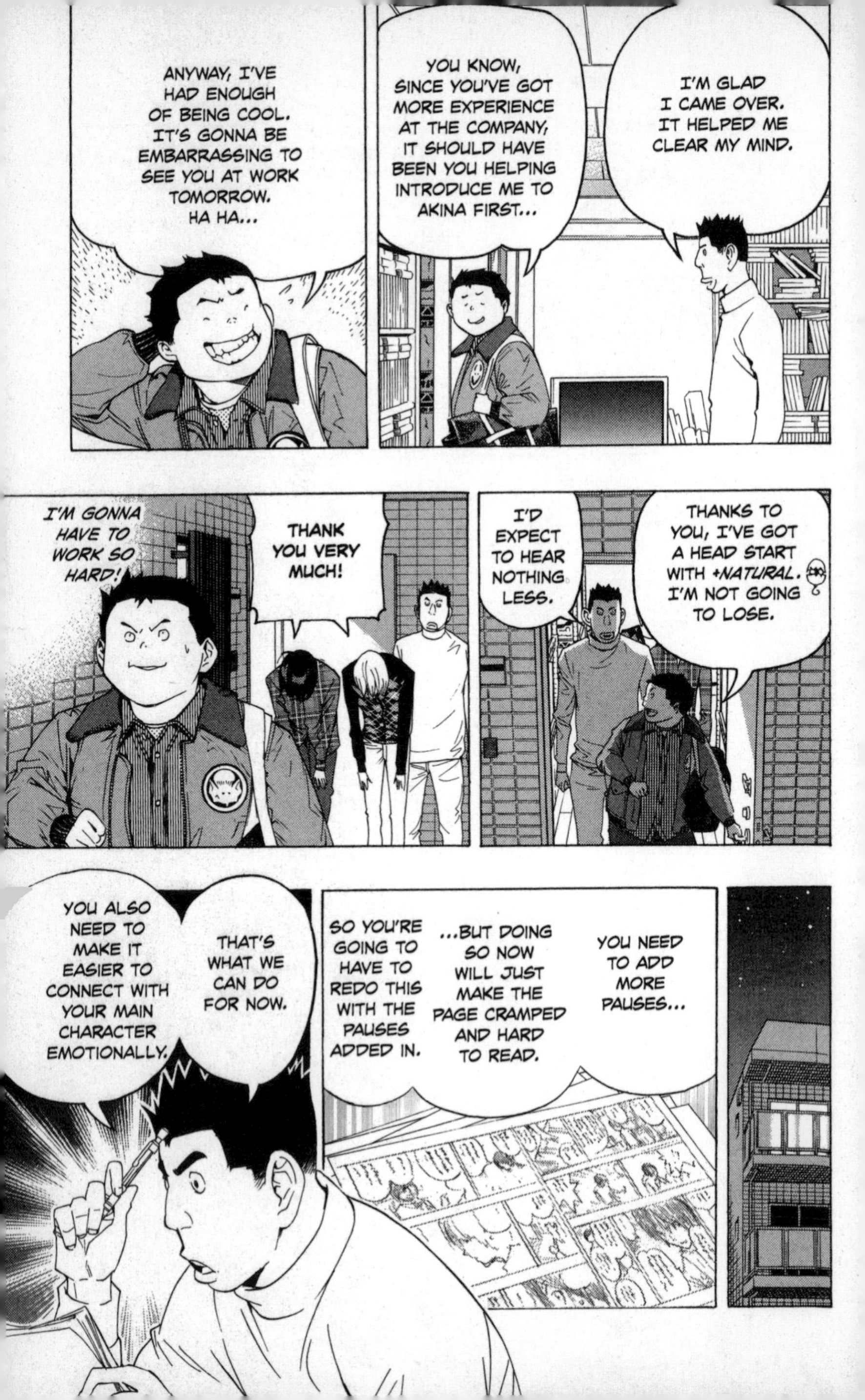
I'M GLAD I CAME OVER. IT HELPED ME CLEAR MY MIND.
YOU KNOW, SINCE YOU'VE GOT MORE EXPERIENCE AT THE COMPANY, IT SHOULD HAVE BEEN YOU HELPING INTRODUCE ME TO AKINA FIRST...
ANYWAY, I'VE HAD ENOUGH OF BEING COOL. IT'S GONNA BE EMBARRASSING TO SEE YOU AT WORK TOMORROW. HA HA...
THANKS TO YOU, I'VE GOT A HEAD START WITH +NATURAL. I'M NOT GOING TO LOSE.
I'D EXPECT TO HEAR NOTHING LESS.
THANK YOU VERY MUCH!
I'M GONNA HAVE TO WORK SO HARD!
YOU NEED TO ADD MORE PAUSES...
...BUT DOING SO NOW WILL JUST MAKE THE PAGE CRAMPED AND HARD TO READ.
SO YOU'RE GOING TO HAVE TO REDO THIS WITH THE PAUSES ADDED IN.
THAT'S WHAT WE CAN DO FOR NOW.
YOU ALSO NEED TO MAKE IT EASIER TO CONNECT WITH YOUR MAIN CHARACTER EMOTIONALLY.

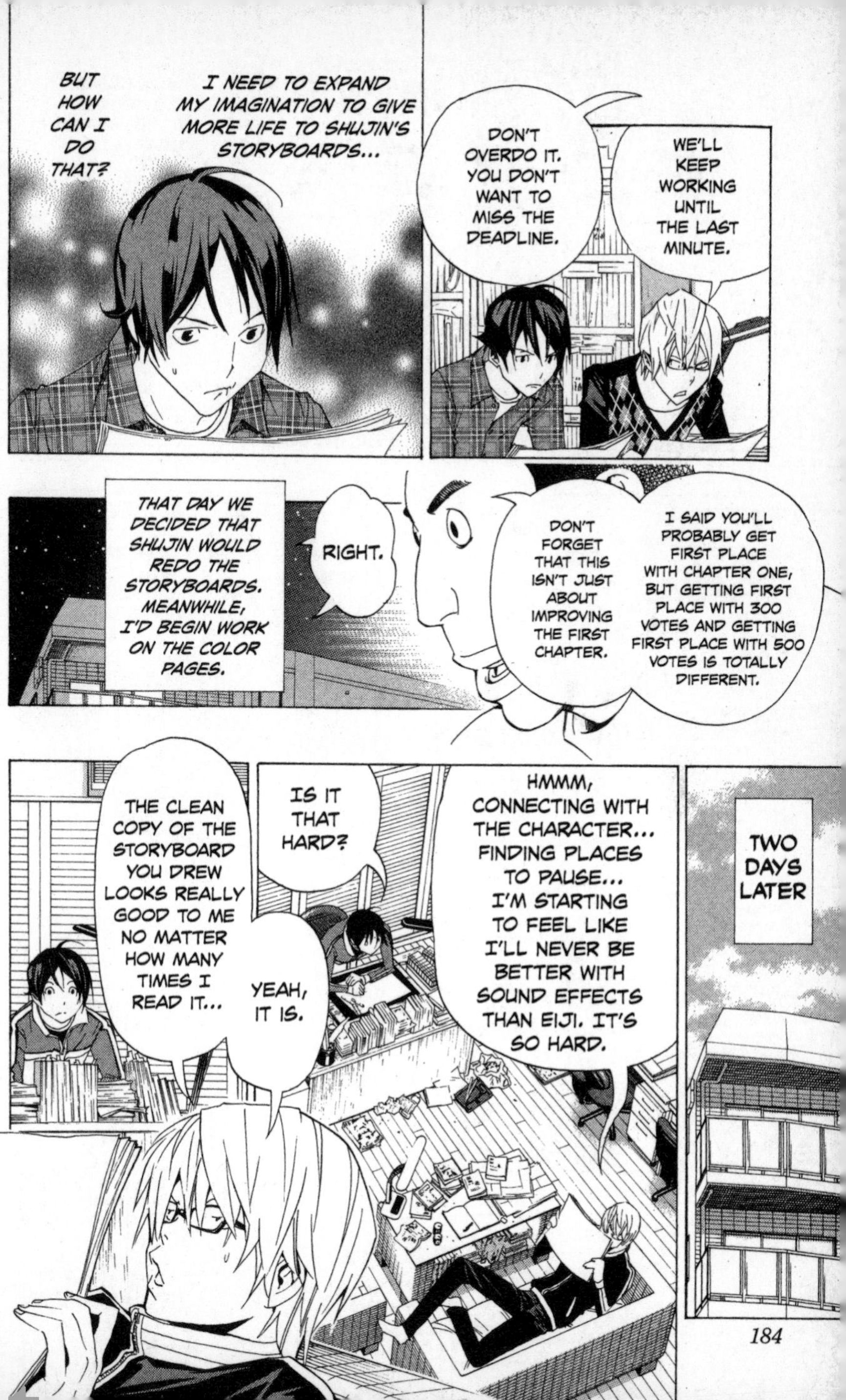
WE'LL KEEP WORKING UNTIL THE LAST MINUTE.
DON'T OVERDO IT. YOU DON'T WANT TO MISS THE DEADLINE.
I NEED TO EXPAND MY IMAGINATION TO GIVE MORE LIFE TO SHUJIN'S STORYBOARDS...
BUT HOW CAN I DO THAT?
I SAID YOU'LL PROBABLY GET FIRST PLACE WITH CHAPTER ONE, BUT GETTING FIRST PLACE WITH 300 VOTES AND GETTING FIRST PLACE WITH 500 VOTES IS TOTALLY DIFFERENT.
DON'T FORGET THAT THIS ISN'T JUST ABOUT IMPROVING THE FIRST CHAPTER.
RIGHT.
THAT DAY WE DECIDED THAT SHUJIN WOULD REDO THE STORYBOARDS. MEANWHILE, I'D BEGIN WORK ON THE COLOR PAGES.
TWO DAYS LATER
HMMM, CONNECTING WITH THE CHARACTER... FINDING PLACES TO PAUSE... I'M STARTING TO FEEL LIKE I'LL NEVER BE BETTER WITH SOUND EFFECTS THAN EIJI. IT'S SO HARD.
IS IT THAT HARD?
THE CLEAN COPY OF THE STORYBOARD YOU DREW LOOKS REALLY GOOD TO ME NO MATTER HOW MANY TIMES I READ IT...
YEAH, IT IS.

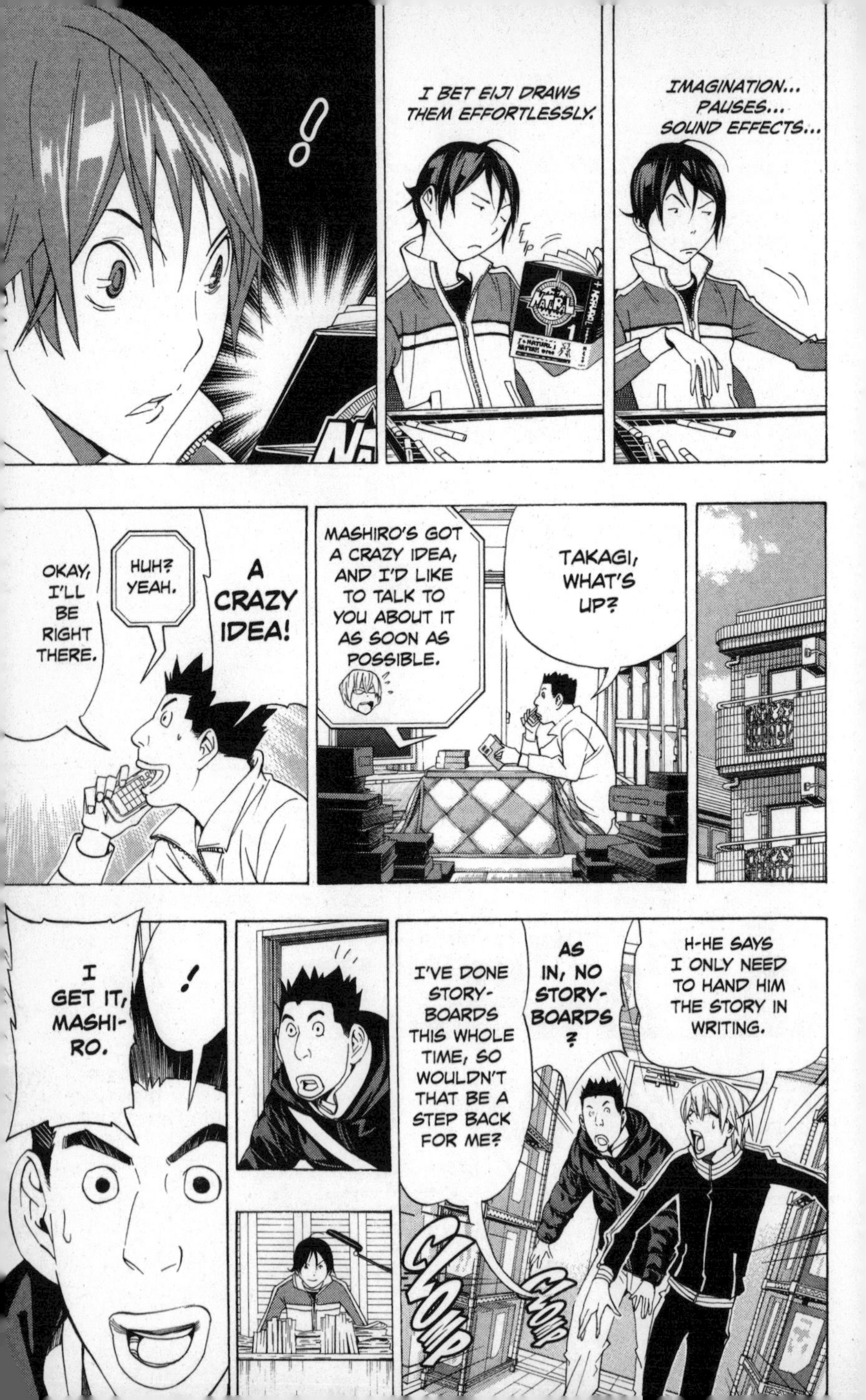
IMAGINATION... PAUSES... SOUND EFFECTS...
I BET EIJI DRAWS THEM EFFORTLESSLY.
!
TAKAGI, WHAT'S UP?
MASHIRO'S GOT A CRAZY IDEA, AND I'D LIKE TO TALK TO YOU ABOUT IT AS SOON AS POSSIBLE.
A CRAZY IDEA!
HUH? YEAH.
OKAY, I'LL BE RIGHT THERE.
H-HE SAYS I ONLY NEED TO HAND HIM THE STORY IN WRITING.
AS IN, NO STORYBOARDS?
I'VE DONE STORYBOARDS THIS WHOLE TIME, SO WOULDN'T THAT BE A STEP BACK FOR ME?
CHOMP
CHOMP
!
I GET IT, MASHIRO.

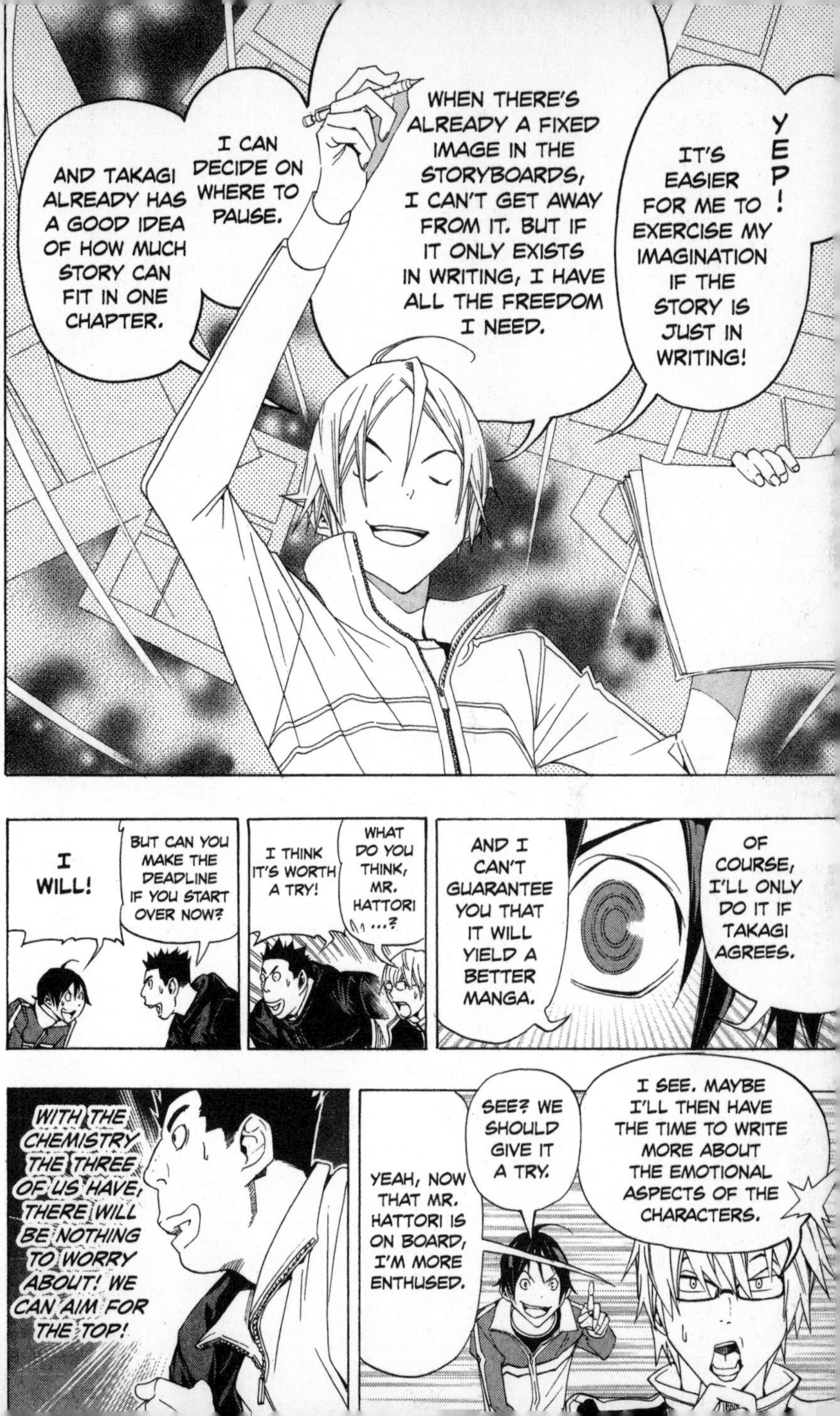
YEP!
IT'S EASIER FOR ME TO EXERCISE MY IMAGINATION IF THE STORY IS JUST IN WRITING!
WHEN THERE'S ALREADY A FIXED IMAGE IN THE STORYBOARDS, I CAN'T GET AWAY FROM IT. BUT IF IT ONLY EXISTS IN WRITING, I HAVE ALL THE FREEDOM I NEED.
I CAN DECIDE ON WHERE TO PAUSE.
AND TAKAGI ALREADY HAS A GOOD IDEA OF HOW MUCH STORY CAN FIT IN ONE CHAPTER.
OF COURSE, I'LL ONLY DO IT IF TAKAGI AGREES.
AND I CAN'T GUARANTEE YOU THAT IT WILL YIELD A BETTER MANGA.
WHAT DO YOU THINK, MR. HATTORI...?
I THINK IT'S WORTH A TRY!
BUT CAN YOU MAKE THE DEADLINE IF YOU START OVER NOW?
I WILL!
I SEE. MAYBE I'LL THEN HAVE THE TIME TO WRITE MORE ABOUT THE EMOTIONAL ASPECTS OF THE CHARACTERS.
SEE? WE SHOULD GIVE IT A TRY.
YEAH, NOW THAT MR. HATTORI IS ON BOARD, I'M MORE ENTHUSED.
WITH THE CHEMISTRY THE THREE OF US HAVE, THERE WILL BE NOTHING TO WORRY ABOUT! WE CAN AIM FOR THE TOP!

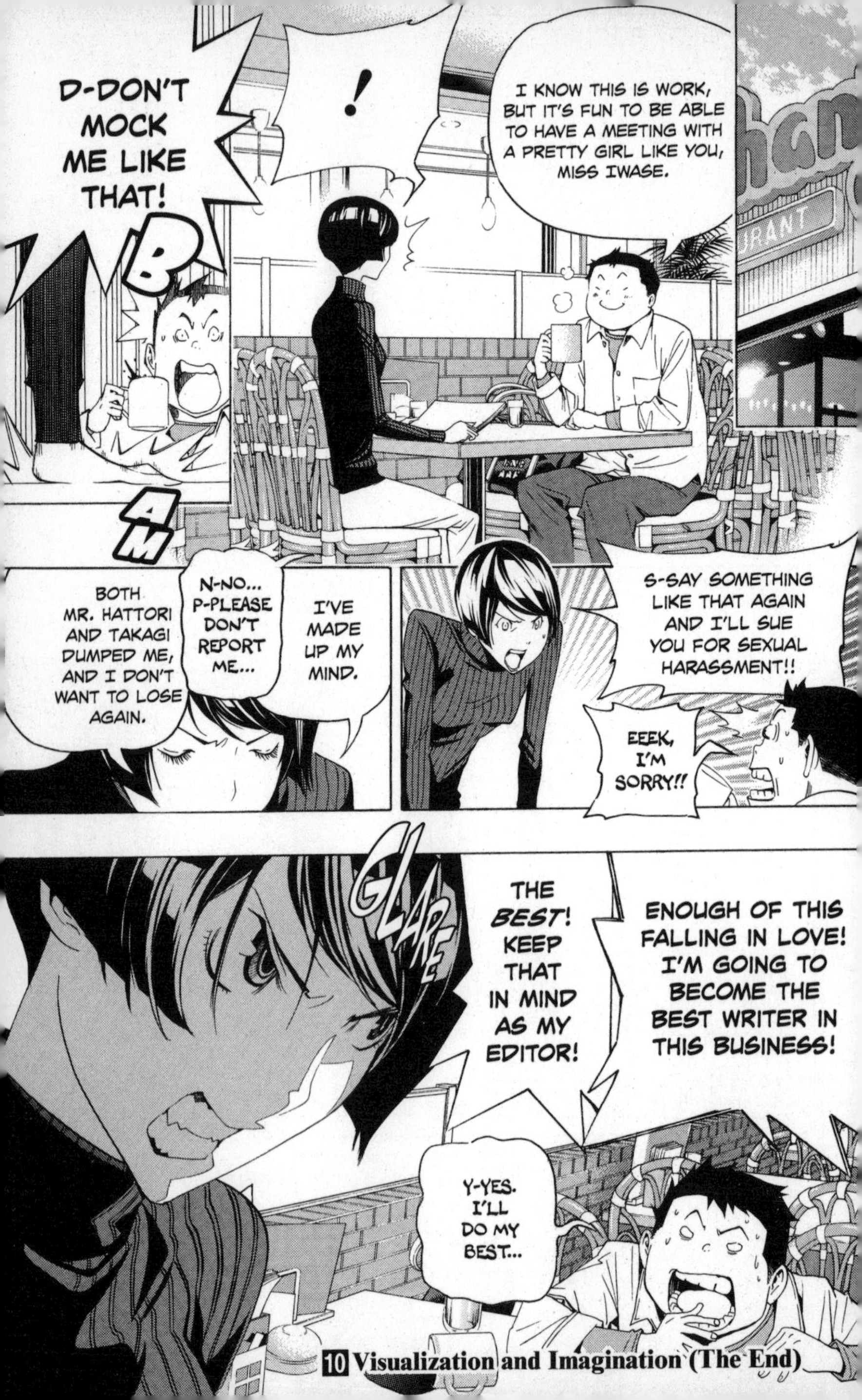
I KNOW THIS IS WORK, BUT IT'S FUN TO BE ABLE TO HAVE A MEETING WITH A PRETTY GIRL LIKE YOU, MISS IWASE.
!
D-DON'T MOCK ME LIKE THAT!
BAM
S-SAY SOMETHING LIKE THAT AGAIN AND I'LL SUE YOU FOR SEXUAL HARASSMENT!!
EEEK, I'M SORRY!!
I'VE MADE UP MY MIND.
N-NO... P-PLEASE DON'T REPORT ME...
BOTH MR. HATTORI AND TAKAGI DUMPED ME, AND I DON'T WANT TO LOSE AGAIN.
GLARE
ENOUGH OF THIS FALLING IN LOVE! I'M GOING TO BECOME THE BEST WRITER IN THIS BUSINESS!
THE *BEST*! KEEP THAT IN MIND AS MY EDITOR!
Y-YES. I'LL DO MY BEST...
10 Visualization and Imagination (The End)

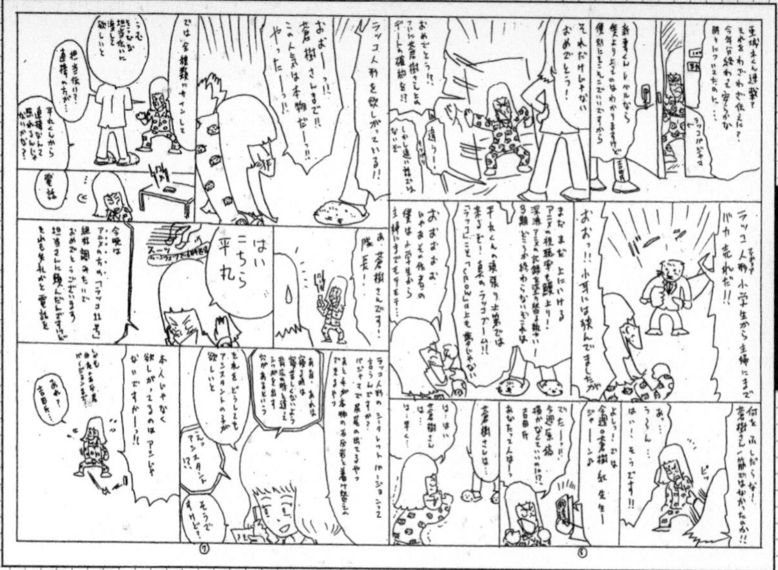

OHBA'S STORYBOARD

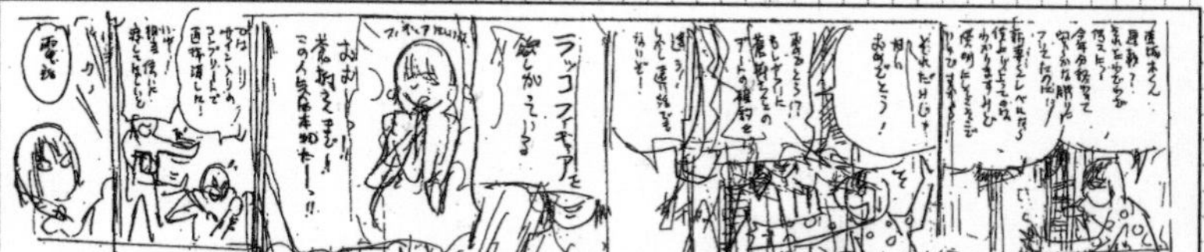

OBATA'S STORYBOARD

COMPLETE!

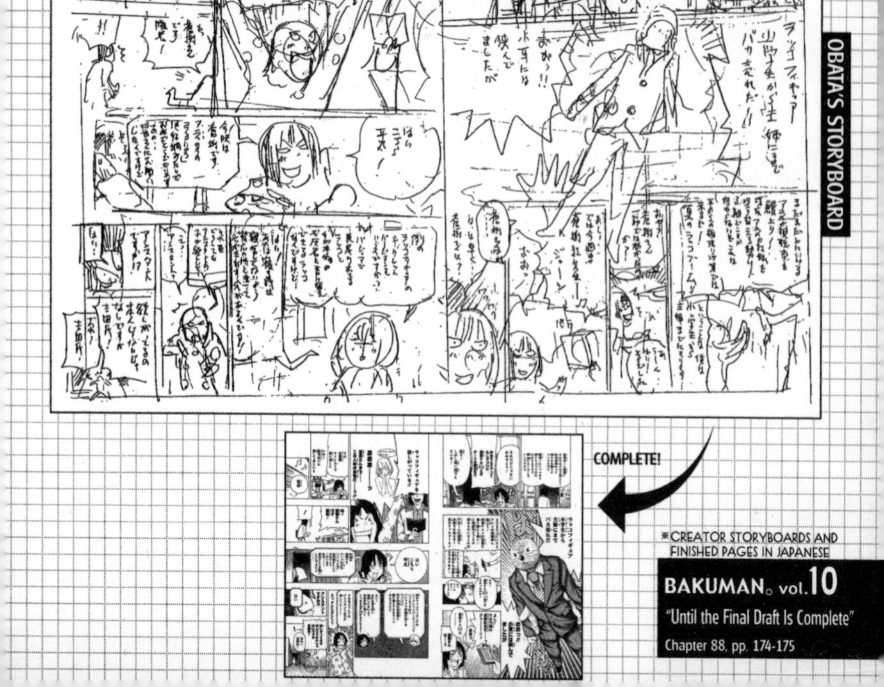

※CREATOR STORYBOARDS AND FINISHED PAGES IN JAPANESE

BAKUMAN。 vol.10

"Until the Final Draft Is Complete"

Chapter 88, pp. 174-175

BAKUMAN。

In the NEXT VOLUME

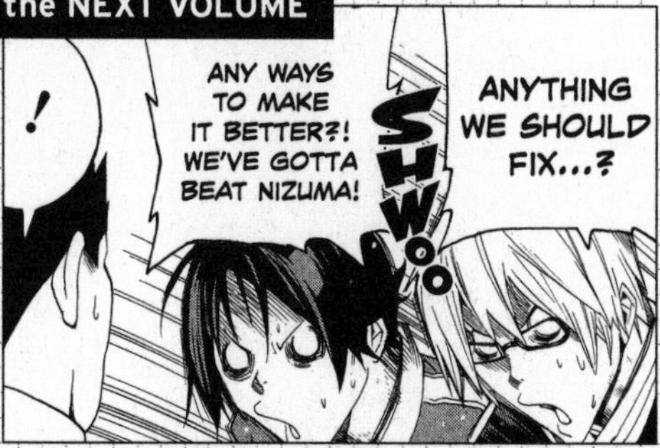
ANYTHING WE SHOULD FIX...?
SHWOO
ANY WAYS TO MAKE IT BETTER?! WE'VE GOTTA BEAT NIZUMA!
!

With the announcement of their new series in *Shonen Jump*, Moritaka and Akito are overjoyed! But when they find out just how close the voting actually was, their desire to keep improving their work goes into overdrive. Moritaka will need to refine the character designs while Akito thinks up the perfect series title!

Available June 2012

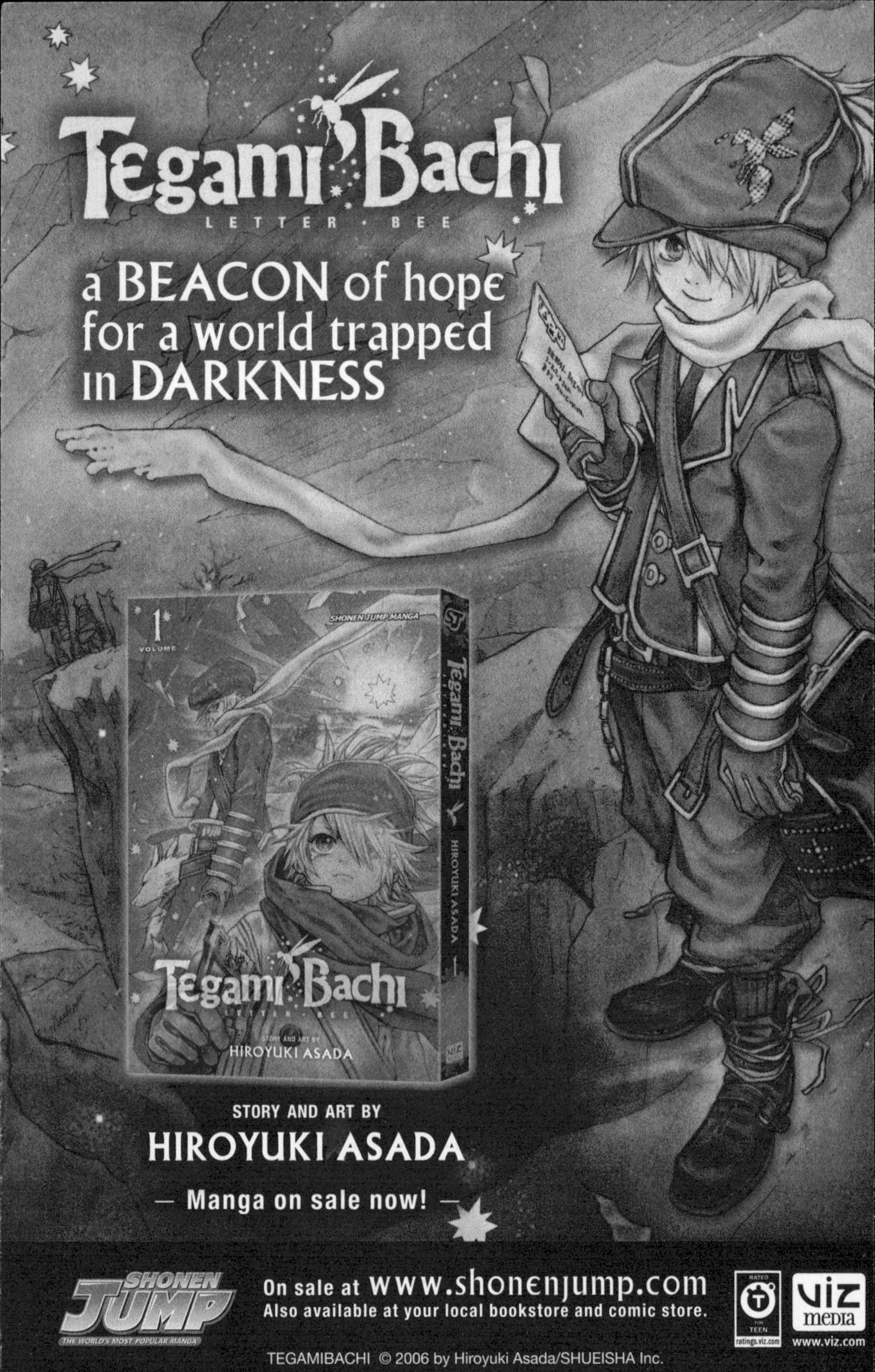

Tegami Bachi
LETTER • BEE
a BEACON of hope for a world trapped in DARKNESS
1 VOLUME
SHONEN JUMP MANGA
Tegami Bachi
LETTER • BEE
STORY AND ART BY
HIROYUKI ASADA
STORY AND ART BY
HIROYUKI ASADA
— Manga on sale now! —
SHONEN JUMP
THE WORLD'S MOST POPULAR MANGA
On sale at www.shonenjump.com
Also available at your local bookstore and comic store.
RATED T FOR TEEN
ratings.viz.com
VIZ media
www.viz.com
TEGAMIBACHI © 2006 by Hiroyuki Asada/SHUEISHA Inc.

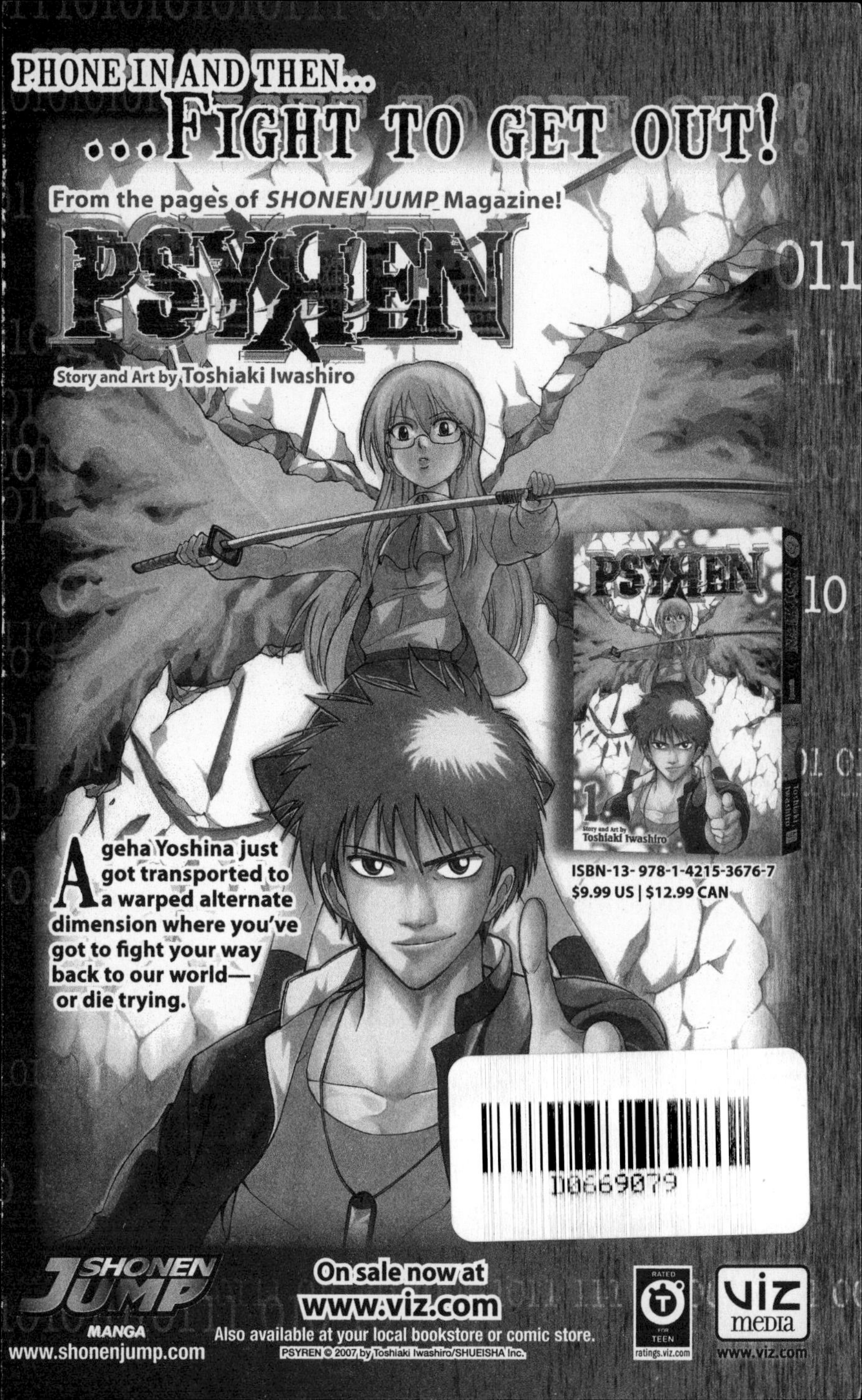
PHONE IN AND THEN...
...FIGHT TO GET OUT!
From the pages of SHONEN JUMP Magazine!
PSYREN
Story and Art by Toshiaki Iwashiro
Ageha Yoshina just got transported to a warped alternate dimension where you've got to fight your way back to our world—or die trying.
PSYREN
1
Story and Art by Toshiaki Iwashiro
ISBN-13- 978-1-4215-3676-7
$9.99 US | $12.99 CAN
SHONEN JUMP
MANGA
www.shonenjump.com
On sale now at
www.viz.com
Also available at your local bookstore or comic store.
PSYREN © 2007 by Toshiaki Iwashiro/SHUEISHA Inc.
RATED
T
FOR TEEN
ratings.viz.com
viz media
www.viz.com